GETTYSBURG'S
SOUTHERN FRONT

GETTYSBURG'S SOUTHERN FRONT

Opportunity and Failure at Richmond

Hampton Newsome

University Press of Kansas

Published by the University Press of Kansas (Lawrence, Kansas 66045), which was
organized by the Kansas Board of Regents and is operated and funded by Emporia
State University, Fort Hays State University, Kansas State University, Pittsburg State
University, the University of Kansas, and Wichita State University.

Library of Congress Cataloging-in-Publication Data

Names: Newsome, Hampton, author.
Title: Gettysburg's southern front : opportunity and failure at Richmond /
Hampton Newsome.
Other titles: Modern war studies.
Description: Lawrence, Kansas : University Press of Kansas, 2022. | Series:
Modern war studies | Includes bibliographical references and index.
Identifiers: LCCN 2021057707
ISBN 9780700633470 (cloth : alk. paper)
ISBN 9780700633487 (ebook)
Subjects: LCSH: Dix, John A. (John Adams), 1798–1879. | Gettysburg
Campaign, 1863. | Richmond (Va.)—History—Civil War, 1861–1865. |
United States—History—Civil War, 1861–1865—Campaigns.
Classification: LCC E475.51 .N49 2022 | DDC 973.7/349—dc23/eng/20211214
LC record available at https://lccn.loc.gov/2021057707.

British Library Cataloguing-in-Publication Data is available.

Printed in the United States of America

10 9 8 7 6 5 4 3 2 1

CONTENTS

Photo gallery appears following page 142.

LIST OF MAPS

Introduction

Every rash act of this war has been crowned with success and here is the most glorious opportunity ever afforded.

—Assistant Secretary Gustavus Vasa Fox, US Navy Department

ON A SUMMER MORNING IN LATE JUNE 1863, a line of Federal gunboats and transports plied northwest up the Pamunkey River into Confederate territory just east of Richmond. Peering into a light fog, the pilots guided the procession through a channel so narrow in places "there was hardly room for some of [the] steamers to turn around." The flotilla twisted through eight hairpin curves, one after the other, a path that transformed a dozen miles by land into a much longer journey.[1] Cavalryman George Cruikshank, an Iowan serving in the 11th Pennsylvania aboard one of the transports, found the waterway "one of the most winding rivers I ever saw."[2] As the boats churned around the final bend, White House Landing came into view on the south shore, the site of the Army of the Potomac's base of operations a year earlier during George B. McClellan's ill-fated Peninsula Campaign against Richmond. Just upstream from the landing in the distance, the piers of the Richmond and York River Railroad bridge spanned the channel. The flotilla steamed past a group of Black women and children on the bank waving a white flag and enthusiastically cheering. On the boats themselves, blue-clad cavalrymen prepared to disembark at the wharfs on the port side and proceed to the fields of the White House plantation beyond, 50 acres of grassy meadow brimming with clover mottled here and there with blackberry patches.

The Federal horse soldiers were not the only troops moving that day. One hundred and fifty miles to the north on the banks of the Potomac, Robert E. Lee urged his Army of Northern Virginia toward Pennsylvania as part of an expedition that would bring his troops to the town of Gettysburg less than a week later. While Lee's columns tramped north, the Federal boats at White House Landing unloaded a thousand cavalrymen and horses a mere 20 miles east of Richmond. Soon after, thousands of additional Federal troops would arrive. The date was Thursday, June 25, 1863, and another offensive against the rebel capital had begun.[3]

The ensuing campaign, sometimes called the "Blackberry Raid" or "Dix's Peninsula Campaign," would provide a clear window into Union military performance in the eastern theater during the war's first years. Over the course of the operation, a force of 20,000 US soldiers, a collection of mostly inexperienced units from the Fourth and Seventh Corps led by Major General John A. Dix, would launch a series of strikes against Richmond's defenses and its supply lines from its temporary base at White House on the Pamunkey. To meet the Federal threat, a threadbare rebel force struggled to guard the city's multiple approaches. Over the course of a few weeks, the Federal operations ignited several engagements in the fields east of Richmond and at the vital railroad bridges on the South Anna River to the north.

Dix's campaign against Richmond formed a small, oft-overlooked component of the massive operations taking place during the Gettysburg Campaign. Preparations for the offensive began with a short mid-June dispatch from General-in-Chief Henry Halleck ordering John Dix "to threaten Richmond, by seizing and destroying their railroad bridges over the South and North Anna Rivers, and do them all the damage possible."[4] In response, Dix, who had lived a life of considerable public service but possessed limited military experience, gathered his men and began a slow advance. In Washington, the effort drew the attention of President Abraham Lincoln and other administration officials during a hectic, dangerous time. To some, Dix's campaign presented a tremendous chance to strike hard at Richmond while Lee's army was away threatening Pennsylvania. To others, the offensive was an unnecessary lark that tied up forces more effectively deployed in protecting Washington or fending off Lee.

Indeed, many issues occupied officials in the US capital in June 1863. In the east, Lee's invasion threatened the region's rail lines and key cities, including the capital itself. In Tennessee, Federal commander William Rosecrans sought to gain ground and push Confederate commander Braxton Bragg's army from Tullahoma. Eyes and ears also trained farther west to the Mississippi for news from Vicksburg as Ulysses S. Grant continued his efforts to capture the rebel citadel there.

Word of Dix's arrival on the Pamunkey in late June spread alarm and panic in Richmond at a time when officials and citizens also focused on developments in Pennsylvania and Mississippi. Confederate leaders in the city, Daniel Harvey "D. H." Hill and Arnold Elzey as well as Secretary of War James A. Seddon and even President Jefferson Davis, scrambled to meet the US forces, cover the many approaches to the capital, and shield its supply lines. Their task was formidable. With limited troops, they could not protect everything at once.

In addition to Dix's move against Richmond, there were Federal efforts elsewhere. In fact, Dix's effort formed but one component of a loosely developed plan devised by Henry Halleck to threaten Robert E. Lee's communications as the Army of Northern Virginia streamed north. Knowing the Confederates had depleted their defensive strength to fuel the offensive into Pennsylvania, Halleck sought to gain advantage during Lee's absence from Virginia. After sending Dix to Richmond, he added to the program by ordering raids in North Carolina and southwestern Virginia to damage the rail lines feeding the Confederate capital. These three operations together formed a little-noticed Federal attempt to land a counterpunch on rebel supply lines as Lee advanced into Pennsylvania.

As these military developments unfolded, the Confederates also looked to advance their cause through diplomacy. Vice President Alexander Stephens traveled to Richmond in late June from his Georgia home to propose a mission to Washington. He hoped to meet with US officials and discuss prisoner exchange policies and perhaps an end to the conflict. President Davis and his cabinet embraced the mission, expecting that positive results from Lee's offensive would generate decisive leverage at the bargaining table. As the fighting began at Gettysburg and outside Richmond, Stephens would head for the Federal base at Fort Monroe seeking to confer with Lincoln administration officials.

Diplomatic issues aside, Dix's operation against Richmond had the potential to significantly affect Lee's fortunes in Pennsylvania, particularly his army's supply. In heading north in early June, Lee marched away from Virginia's key railroads and the logistical hub at Richmond, all the while leaving an increasingly attenuated supply line behind him. After he crossed the Potomac, the closest rail stations to his forces lay at Staunton in the Shenandoah Valley and Culpeper east of the Blue Ridge Mountains. For much of the Gettysburg Campaign, the Confederates would ship men and supplies from Richmond north along the Virginia Central Railroad over the South Anna and then west to Staunton. Accordingly, the Central Railroad, particularly its larger bridges, became crucial to the Army of Northern Virginia's safety during the Gettysburg Campaign. Halleck understood this, and his orders to Dix created the possibility for

US troops to inflict real damage on the Confederate cause, for a break in Lee's supply lines or the outright capture of Richmond had the potential to change the war's course.

In addition to their impacts on key logistical issues, the operations in central Virginia in the summer of 1863 reflected shifts in an evolving Union war policy. Like many of his fellow War Democrats, John Dix favored a cautious, deliberate approach to fighting the war. Although steadfastly loyal to the Union and a reliable supporter of the Lincoln administration, Dix advocated a moderate, conciliatory approach to the conflict, one that focused on coaxing equivocal white Southerners back into the fold and shielding civilians from the war's impacts. Again and again, Dix's orders to his subordinates revealed an overarching concern about avoiding damage to civilian property. He frequently admonished his troops to refrain from destroying anything not directly useful to the Confederate military. However, the events in June and July would demonstrate that not all of his officers and men shared his caution but instead were ready to embrace a more aggressive approach.

The campaign against Richmond in the summer of 1863 also highlighted the key role African Americans played in Federal efforts in Virginia, even before Black men formally joined the army ranks. From the war's first days, Black civilians had pursued their freedom and contributed to the fight against their former enslavers. During McClellan's Peninsula Campaign in 1862, African Americans in eastern Virginia, both free and enslaved, helped shape the US military effort by scouting, gathering intelligence, and applying their labor to the cause. The story of US operations outside Richmond during the Gettysburg Campaign is no different. Even though no Black regiments served in Dix's Department of Virginia at the time, Black civilians repeatedly stepped forward to aid his operations outside of Richmond. Throughout the offensive, the impact of African Americans was manifest, underscoring the fact that, even in the war's first years, Black men and women made substantial contributions.

Ultimately, Dix's operation presented a significant opportunity. Lee's march north laid bare the Army of Northern Virginia's communications, forcing Confederates to strip troops from other departments and opening possibilities for the Federal high command. The US soldiers who marched on the rebel capital as part of Dix's force recognized the possibilities in front of them and proceeded toward Richmond with the hope of accomplishing something decisive. Ultimately, though, it was not to be, and the resulting campaign quickly faded into obscurity, buried by its own ending and overshadowed by news from Gettysburg and Vicksburg. Nevertheless, this seemingly disconnected sideshow constitutes an important, overlooked southern front to the Gettysburg Campaign.

This study is not an account of large battles and grand victories. Instead, it is a story of might-have-beens, confusion, and failure. At the time, however, the events were not viewed as trivial by the decision makers. In fact, political and military leaders on both sides carefully weighed Dix's Richmond campaign and recognized its potential for far-reaching impacts. A closer look at this operation reveals the often unrealized value in examining the war's lesser-known military efforts. Indeed, despite its obscurity, this piece of the Gettysburg Campaign may rank as one of the Union war effort's more compelling lost opportunities in the East. Of course, whether and how Federal leaders could have achieved momentous success at Richmond must remain a matter of speculation. In any event, the offensive, remembered by many Union veterans as the Blackberry Raid for the plump fruit filling the shrubs along their march, could have changed the course of the War of the Rebellion.

PART ONE
An Opportunity in Virginia

In early June 1863, Robert E. Lee marched his Army of Northern Virginia away from its positions south of Fredericksburg into the Shenandoah Valley and north toward Maryland and Pennsylvania. The movement understandably alarmed officials in Washington, who directed Joseph Hooker, commander of the Army of the Potomac, to shadow Lee's army and shield Washington and other Northern cities. At Richmond, in Lee's wake, the city's garrison was left with a small force of local troops and a few veteran infantry brigades. Henry Halleck, coordinating operations in the US War Department, saw opportunity in the vacuum Lee had left in Virginia.

I

Lee Heads North

"SHOOTING AND CUTTING EACH OTHER IN DESPERATE FURY"

THE FIRST MAJOR CLASH OF THE GETTYSBURG CAMPAIGN occurred on June 9 at Brandy Station, a stop on the Orange and Alexandria Railroad near Culpeper, within sight of the Blue Ridge. The engagement, a sprawling duel between US and Confederate mounted forces, dwarfed the war's previous cavalry engagements. The image produced by thousands of riders thundering across the pastoral Virginia Piedmont would inspire artists and storytellers for years to come. It was a swirling mess of a fight. Throughout the battle, opposing lines launched a dizzying series of charges and countercharges. The mounted forays, with their pounding din, perilous speed, and sensational violence, dominated the scene. At times, the engagement devolved into vicious close-quarters combat, with cavalrymen fighting, according to one witness, "hand to hand, shooting and cutting each other in desperate fury, all mixed through one another, killing, wounding, and taking prisoners promiscuously."[1]

One of the Confederate officers on the field that day was Robert E. Lee's second son, William Henry Fitzhugh Lee, or "Rooney," as his family called him. At 6 feet, 2 inches, the twenty-six-year-old Lee possessed a calm, determined demeanor beyond his years. According to one comrade, he was as "steady, firm, and immovable as any soldier" but, off the field, always "considerate and kindly."[2] Early in the fight, Rooney Lee advanced his men to meet the US columns that had unexpectedly crossed the Rappahannock River that morning. As the fight opened, he positioned his brigade along a stone wall topping a knoll just south of the Hazel River and gathered with his staff near a hickory tree.[3]

During the fight, Rooney Lee experienced his full share of the fray. At one point, according to a postwar account, a Federal shell just missed him and hit the hickory branches above his head, producing a shower of broken limbs and scattered leaves. Late in the morning, with the enemy troopers still pushing against his front and more appearing to the south, he withdrew his regiments to pivot and address the new threat. The horsemen passed over Yew Ridge and continued to backpedal toward a long, low rise known as Fleetwood Hill. Later during the combat, Lee found himself within feet of General Wesley Merritt of the Union forces. When the Yankee officer boldly announced that Lee was his prisoner, Lee responded, "The hell I am!" and swung his saber at the Northerner's head. Merritt blocked the slash and the two quickly disengaged.[4]

As the Federals pressed forward, the Confederates turned on their pursuers and charged. On his part of the line, Lee initiated the counterpunch himself, shouting "Forward!" to his men. In the thick of the action, as a "shower of bullets" filled the air, one missile passed through Lee's thigh, narrowly missing his femur and femoral artery.[5] The brigadier calmly handed his sword to an orderly and directed a nearby soldier to alert the second-in-command. The fight soon ended. Rooney Lee's counterattack had proved crucial, helping to break the Federal advance and bring the long battle to an end.[6] Stymied, the blue riders withdrew over the Rappahannock. In the following days, the Confederates—tens of thousands of men in scores of regiments—would march north toward Pennsylvania with Federal columns trailing in pursuit. But Rooney Lee would stay behind in Virginia. Accompanied by his younger brother Robert, he traveled east to recuperate in safety at the Hickory Hill plantation, the home of his wife's aunt and uncle north of Richmond near Hanover Court House. For Rooney Lee, the Gettysburg Campaign was already over.

"THE RISK OF ACTION"

The battle at Brandy Station marked the beginning of a chess match between Lee and the Federal high command that would eventually end at Gettysburg. In crossing their cavalry over the Rappahannock on June 9, US commanders hoped not only to land a blow against the enemy but also to discover the location of Lee's forces and his plan for the ongoing operations. The Union Army of the Potomac's mounted arm advanced that morning with orders to "disperse and destroy the rebel force assembled" at Culpeper and threaten its "trains and supplies."[7] Although the Federals did not hold the field at the end of the day, they did manage to confirm that Lee's entire cavalry force was on the move. But, failing to penetrate the Confederate mounted units, they did not reveal the larger picture leaving many questions unanswered. Was this a large rebel cavalry raid? Did Lee intend to conduct a movement behind the Army of the Potomac with a portion of his force? Or was the Confederate cavalry presence the sign of something much larger?[8]

If the Federals had broken through the cavalry screen on June 9, they would have likely encountered rebel infantry, particularly elements of Lieutenant General Richard Ewell's Second Corps, heading northwest. In doing so, they would have discovered that Lee's Army of Northern Virginia was pulling away from its lines south of Fredericksburg and heading toward the Shenandoah Valley. As the Federals would eventually learn, Lee's force was marching toward the Potomac into Maryland and, eventually, deep into Union territory. Back on June 3, Lee had begun to withdraw from his defensive line along the Rappahannock and Rapidan Rivers and send his men marching west toward the Valley and away from the railroads forming his connection to Richmond. On June 9, it was no accident that Major General J. E. B. Stuart's cavalry corps was at Brandy Station. In fact, the horsemen had been positioned south of the Rappahannock to shield the army movement from prying eyes. Following the Brandy Station victory, the gray infantry columns continued their trek.

Planning for Lee's offensive had begun back in the winter. In February, Thomas "Stonewall" Jackson quietly directed his cartographer, Jedediah Hotchkiss, to draft a map of the Shenandoah Valley and the country extending north to Harrisburg and east to Philadelphia. In early April, in correspondence with Secretary of War James Seddon, Lee suggested that a move by his army into Maryland would provide the best means to relieve enemy pressure in Tennessee and South Carolina.[9] A week later, in communications with President Jefferson Davis, he proposed to assume "the aggressive" in Virginia for the same purpose. Further, in May, following the Battle of Chancellorsville and Jackson's death, Lee spoke with officials in Richmond about taking his army into Pennsylvania.[10]

Lee's desire to take the offensive was not surprising. Throughout his tenure in command, aggression and audacity served as his guiding principles. During 1862 and into 1863, he repeatedly sought to seize the initiative against a revolving cast of Federal commanders. Throughout, he managed to keep US forces away from Richmond with determined assaults and risky flanking maneuvers. When he assumed command of the Confederate forces protecting the city following Joseph Johnston's wounding at the Battle of Seven Pines in the summer of 1862, Lee took the offensive against George B. McClellan's army and pressed the Federals away from the Confederate capital during the Seven Days battles. Several weeks later, he pushed his men into northern Virginia, defeated John Pope's force at Second Manassas, and entered Maryland to fight more at

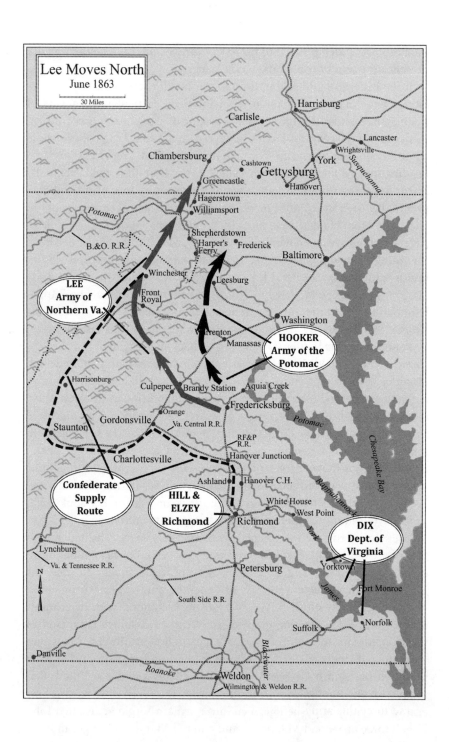

Lee Moves North
June 1863

30 Miles

Antietam. Beaten back into Virginia, he dug in behind the Rappahannock River, defeating Ambrose Burnside at Fredericksburg in December 1862 and then Joseph Hooker, Burnside's replacement, at Chancellorsville in early May 1863.

In June, instead of waiting for the next Federal offensive, Lee began his march north. His exact reasons for doing so remain somewhat murky. He never set out the precise goals or intentions for the movement in detail; neither did he readily share his full plans, even with superiors and close subordinates.[11] Although Lee may have been vague about his designs, several factors clearly motivated him to take his army into Pennsylvania. Supply was certainly a concern. The war had stripped central Virginia nearly clean, leaving his troops dependent on shipments from the south. Commissary and quartermaster officials struggled to transport food, equipment, and provisions over the Confederacy's fragile rail network to the Army of Northern Virginia's camps. By moving north, Lee could mitigate these problems by feeding his men from Yankee larders and relieving central Virginia from the conflict's ravages while bringing the war to the enemy's soil in the bargain.[12]

In essence, Lee viewed a prolonged defensive stand in Virginia as untenable. The Army of Northern Virginia could not remain static and continue to absorb endless Union attacks that would wear his men down and eventually bottle them into the Richmond defenses. Instead, he wanted to push north and pull the enemy away with him. By doing so, he could disrupt any Federal offensive designs and put his opponents on their heels.[13] Lee believed a move into Pennsylvania could create an opportunity to defeat the Army of the Potomac piece by piece—"one corps back and another," one of his officers recalled him saying—as the Federals stretched themselves out on the march north.[14] The day before the Brandy Station fight, when many of his troops were already in motion, Lee wrote the following to Secretary of War Seddon:

> As far as I can judge, there is nothing to be gained by this army remaining quietly on the defensive, which it must do unless it can be re-enforced. I am aware that there is difficulty and hazard in taking the aggressive with so large an army in its front, intrenched behind a river, where it cannot be advantageously attacked. Unless it can be drawn out in a position to be assailed, it will take its own time to prepare and strengthen itself to renew its advance upon Richmond, and force this army back within the intrenchments of that city.

In the same dispatch, Lee acknowledged a siege against Richmond might occur anyway. Nevertheless, he believed a move into enemy territory was "worth a trial to prevent 'catastrophe.'" However, should the administration prefer him to "guard as far as possible all the avenues of approach, and await the time of the enemy," he would follow such a directive and adopt a passive defense.[15]

Lee also understood the potential political benefits of battlefield victories on Northern soil. Confederate military success would erode Union morale and bolster conservative politicians seeking to negotiate the war's end. This was not lost on Lee. In a letter to his wife, he predicted military victories would bring "a great change in public opinion" in the North, destroy the Republicans, and deposit the "friends of peace" into office.[16] In the summer of 1863, he was surely aware of the growing unrest. In May, for instance, a Union military tribunal sentenced Ohio politician Clement Vallandigham to prison for speeches he had made against the war. President Lincoln commuted the sentence to exile in the Confederate states. Confederate officials, including Lee, followed such developments and recognized war opposition was growing in the North and any Confederate effort to encourage such resistance would only aid the rebel cause.[17]

In addition, Lee knew his plan could affect operations elsewhere, particularly the standoff in Middle Tennessee between Braxton Bragg and William Rosecrans as well as the siege operations at Vicksburg between Ulysses S. Grant and John Pemberton. Lee followed ongoing discussions within the Davis administration about transferring troops from Virginia to aid the Vicksburg garrison. But despite the threats in the West, Lee resisted proposals to dilute his own force to send troops there, painting the prospects of such a transfer as "unfavorable" given the distance and the uncertainty of conditions in Mississippi. Instead, he vigorously pressed for his proposed move north into Pennsylvania.[18]

Finally, Lee believed his upcoming campaign would keep US forces off balance. In 1862, he had managed to change the face of the contest in the East by moving northward during the Maryland Campaign. Consistent with those previous operations, he hoped to seize the strategic initiative or assume "the aggressive," as he put it to Seddon earlier that spring. "We must decide between the positive loss of inactivity and the risk of action," he explained to Seddon in early June.[19] Seddon concurred, noting that "aggressive movements" were "indispensable to our safety and independence." In any case, at the time of this exchange with the secretary of war, Lee had already decided to go on the offensive.[20]

Not everyone agreed with Lee. Some, after weighing the expedition's risks and tradeoffs, expressed concern. Davis and many in his cabinet worried about Vicksburg's impending fall and cast about for some way to turn the tide there. In addition, Braxton Bragg, the overall Confederate commander in the western theater, urged Richmond to send reinforcements. Furthermore, P. G. T. Beauregard, in charge of Charleston's harbor defenses, far preferred a force concentration in Mississippi to Lee's operations in the East. He would later complain, "Of what earthly use is that 'raid' of Lee's army into Maryland, in violation of all the principles of war?" Similarly, Edward Porter Alexander, an insightful, young artillery officer in the Army of Northern Virginia, would later question Lee's focus on conducting an offensive at Vicksburg's expense. He doubted Lee's force was large enough to generate success in Pennsylvania. Likewise, James Longstreet, Lee's best corps commander, initially recommended transferring troops west after Chancellorsville, but Lee eventually managed to sell the invasion plan to his "old war horse." Officials in Davis's cabinet and in the War Department at Richmond also considered the risks of leaving the capital open to attack and inviting the enemy to trade key objectives. Such concerns did not change the ultimate result, however. In the end, Lee managed to convince the most important decision maker, Jefferson Davis. Thus, in the first days of June, Lee slipped his men out of their lines at Fredericksburg and headed north.[21]

"AN OX JUMPED HALF OVER A FENCE"

From the first days of Lee's operation, Federal leaders knew something was afoot. Intelligence sources, coupled with vague rumors, suggested unusual activity in the rebel camps south of the Rappahannock. On June 2, Major General Erasmus D. Keyes reported from his Fourth Corps headquarters at Yorktown that "the idea prevails over the lines that an invasion of Maryland and Pennsylvania is soon to be made." At Fredericksburg two days later, George Sharpe, colonel of the newly formed Bureau of Military Information, informed Joseph Hooker that the Confederate camps in front of the Army of the Potomac were "disappearing at some points." Reports even appeared in Northern newspapers that Lee was gearing up for another invasion. Whispers also found their way into the Richmond papers, but most Southern editors dutifully reported in their papers that Lee's army remained at Fredericksburg along the Rappahannock.[22]

Nevertheless, it soon became clear to everyone that Lee's troops were

in motion—for what purpose, though, was not known. Learning of
the Confederate withdrawal from his front, Hooker saw an opportunity. Rather than cautiously track the departing forces, he proposed to
press forward and "pitch into" Lee's rear. This plan, presented directly to
Lincoln, revealed an aggressiveness not often seen from previous Union
commanders in the East. To initiate this gambit, Hooker established a
small bridgehead on the south bank of the Rappahannock below Fredericksburg. However, Lincoln rejected the proposal, fearing such a venture
would straddle the Army of the Potomac on the river like "an ox jumped
half over a fence."[23] Resuming a conservative posture, Hooker sought
to divine Lee's intentions. Over the next several days, more information
pointed to a substantial Confederate movement. The newspapers even
speculated about a Confederate invasion into Maryland and Pennsylvania. Hooker, however, was still thinking about taking the offensive. On
June 10, the day after the cavalry fight at Brandy Station, he floated an
even more audacious scheme to go straight at Richmond and ignore the
rebel columns streaming northwest from his front. But Lincoln again dismissed the idea.[24]

While the president may have appreciated Hooker's initiative, his views
on operational priorities, particularly with regard to Richmond and Lee's
army, had evolved over the previous months. After Antietam in October
1862, he urged army commander George McClellan to consider advancing on Richmond to operate against Lee's communications, a move not
unlike the one proposed by Hooker.[25] However, by the beginning of 1863,
Lincoln began to shift his thinking. Instead of the Confederate capital, he
identified Lee's army as the enemy's center of gravity in the East. In January, he explained to McClellan's successor, Ambrose Burnside, that "in
all our interviews I have urged that our first object was, not Richmond,
but the defeat or scattering of Lee's army."[26]

In managing Hooker's operations in early June, Lincoln repeated this
refrain. He doubted a lunge at Richmond would force Lee to retire south
and cover his army's communications. He also questioned whether the
Army of the Potomac would achieve a quick victory against the Confederate capital's strong fortifications. "If you had Richmond invested
to-day you would not be able to take it in twenty days, meanwhile, your
communications, and with them your army, would be ruined," he warned
Hooker. At the same time, Lincoln expected a move to the south would
jeopardize Hooker's own connections and, with it, the Army of the Potomac. The president, it seems, had concluded that swapping queens—
Washington for Richmond—would leave the Federals on the short end of

the bargain. Echoing his January guidance to Burnside, Lincoln emphasized to Hooker that Lee's army, and not the rebel capital, was the "true
objective point."[27] Others shared the president's concern about a drive
on Richmond. With Lee in motion, anxiety about Washington's safety
increased. In the previous weeks, Secretary of War Edwin Stanton had
worried about the adequacy of the city's defenses and fretted over rumors
of Confederate cavalry raids, including one fantastic story that an entire
blue-clad rebel brigade was advancing to kidnap Lincoln and other senior
officials. Now with Lee headed north, concerns about the city's safety
only increased.[28]

Under the circumstances, Hooker's suggestion was not entirely out
of line. Richmond was a grand prize—a key logistical center and the rebellion's political core. Its capture would land a severe and perhaps even
mortal blow to the Confederacy. Indeed, some saw potential in Hooker's
program. After the war, Porter Alexander, the perceptive Confederate
artillerist, wrote that "by all means, [Hooker] should have marched to
Richmond . . . which would have been sure & easy with his immense
force." But Lincoln certainly weighed these possibilities and, in all likelihood, simply doubted Hooker's troops could capture Richmond quickly
enough to warrant the attempt. He also worried such a move would
expose Hooker's communications, giving Lee the chance for a sweeping
victory in the North long before the Army of the Potomac could break
into Richmond.[29]

Following the rebuff, Hooker's relationship with Lincoln and administration officials soured. A Republican much admired by the Radicals
in Congress, Hooker had stepped into command with much promise.
During the winter, he instituted enlightened organizational changes for
the army. In April, he devised an aggressive plan to bring the fight to Lee
in what became the Chancellorsville Campaign. However, he lost that
fight, and his army was herded back across the Rapidan. In early June,
with his own plan twice rejected and with no direct orders, Hooker faced
uncertainty and, most likely, a degree of confusion. By June 13, as part of
his efforts to shadow Lee's movements in northern Virginia, he began ob-
taining supplies via the Orange and Alexandria Railroad and abandoned
the waterborne connection at the Aquia Creek depot on the Potomac.[30]

While Hooker sought to gain traction with Lincoln, Union officials
watched with alarm as Lee's army continued its drive north. On June 14,
the rebel vanguard, Richard Ewell's Second Corps, overran the US garrison at Winchester in the Shenandoah Valley, scooping up thousands of
prisoners in the process. Soon, Lee's lead units reached within a few miles

of the Potomac River even as some of his troops had barely begun their departure from the Fredericksburg front. As the details of Lee's movement became clearer, Hooker's forces shifted north and the awkward communication with Washington continued. On the 14th, Lincoln suggested that, if the head of Lee's army was in the Valley and the tail still at Fredericksburg, "the animal must be very slim somewhere." Yet the president issued no affirmative orders to attack. Over the next few days, while Hooker continued to track the Confederates and drive his men north, he kept Lincoln informed, floated proposals, sought concrete directives from Washington, and generally exhibited a reluctance to make his own decisions given the constraints placed on him by the War Department.[31]

Behind the scenes, General-in-Chief Henry Halleck supported Lincoln's directives to Hooker and often followed up with his own dispatches echoing the sentiments of the chief executive. Halleck, who had a poor opinion of Hooker dating back to acrimonious, prewar business dealings in California, sensed the tide was turning against the army commander. For months, Hooker had communicated directly with Lincoln on many matters, an arrangement that largely sidelined Halleck, who later observed that the president "ran the machine himself." Now, in dealing directly again with Hooker in June, Halleck may not have had that other general's best interests in mind.[32]

"CUT OFF OUR COMMUNICATION WITH THE SOUTH"

The departure of Lee and Hooker from the Rappahannock front did not empty Virginia of troops. There was more to the war there than the struggle between the Army of the Potomac and the Army of Northern Virginia. Beyond these principal forces, several Confederate and Union army departments, vital supply lines, and key strategic locations added to the calculus of the conflict in the Old Dominion. In marching toward Pennsylvania in June 1863, Lee's men moved away from Richmond, striding west beyond Gordonsville and through the Blue Ridge gaps into the Shenandoah Valley. With this movement, Lee's force uncoupled itself from the Confederate rail network, the lifeline that had fed and supplied the army over the previous year.

The railroads were essential to military operations in Virginia for both sides. The Confederate-controlled rails supplied Richmond and rebel troops in the field with food and war materiel from the south, and the

Federal lines supported US forces at nearly every point, with the exception of those posts easily reached by water. Beginning in the war's first days, rebel control of the Virginia rail network gradually shrunk. By the end of 1862, Union forces controlled about 15 percent of the state's rail mileage, including a large portion of the Orange and Alexandria line in northern Virginia and routes in the southeast around Norfolk.[33] The Confederates, however, still controlled the two lines that had supplied the Army of Northern Virginia at Fredericksburg: the Virginia Central and the Richmond, Fredericksburg, and Potomac (the RF&P). Both of these roads ran north from Richmond roughly parallel for about 25 miles and then crossed each other at Hanover Junction, where the Confederate government had constructed a supply depot in 1861.[34] Beyond the junction, the RF&P continued north to Fredericksburg while the Virginia Central stretched off west to Gordonsville, then Charlottesville, and into the Valley through Staunton.[35]

The Virginia railroads had proved an imperfect tool for the Confederate war effort. By the first months of 1863, overuse and inadequate maintenance had led to worn-out lines. Locomotives, cars, and tracks all began to sag under the war's strain. Railroad officials struggled to manage the constant tug and pull as the Confederates sought to haul men and materiel to the front. On the Virginia Central, conflict and chaos wreaked havoc on efforts to maintain orderly operations. The problems mounted. The need for troop transport reduced the cars available for provisions and forage. In addition, a limited number of locomotives and cars remained on hand, and available equipment had not held up well. Furthermore, a shortage of iron plagued maintenance efforts to replace worn-out track, a problem throughout the Confederate rail network.[36]

The RF&P had problems as well. The line had become notoriously slow and ineffective in supplying troops during 1862 and into 1863. Its poor performance may have stemmed in part from the covert efforts of its superintendent, Samuel Ruth. Secretly loyal to the United States, Ruth did his best to impede operations on the RF&P and would later directly aid the Union spy network in central Virginia.[37] However, Ruth's sabotage was not the only problem for the Confederates. A few miles south of Hanover Junction, both routes crossed the South Anna River over trestle bridges vulnerable to Yankee raiders. North of the junction, the RF&P also passed over the North Anna River. In 1862, the Federals had targeted these lines—successfully burning bridges, temporarily occupying segments of track, and destroying railroad buildings as well as equipment. After the destruction of the 590-foot long RF&P bridge over the South Anna in May of that year, Confederate officials and railroad personnel spent five months completing repairs, an extraordinarily protracted period perhaps lengthened by Ruth's machinations.[38] During the Chancellorsville Campaign the next year, Union cavalry under George Stoneman reached these lines, dismantling track and destroying property at Hungary Station, Hanover Junction, and Ashland. But Stoneman's raid failed to inflict substantial damage, and in a matter of days the traffic resumed unhindered.[39] Concerned about further incursions, Confederate officials took measures to strengthen fortifications at the bridge crossings on the North Anna and South Anna, impressing slaves from their owners to provide some of the labor.[40]

The more Lee pushed north in June 1863, the farther he marched away from his supply lines and the more attenuated his connection to Richmond became. Once in the Valley, his army's closest rail connections were at Culpeper and Staunton. On June 15, Lee asked Richmond officials to route all communications and troops to him via either of these two stations.[41] Although some latecomers detrained at Culpeper and marched through the Blue Ridge gaps, Lee's force mostly relied on Staunton as the primary railhead for shuttling men and supplies from Richmond during the latter half of June. The frequency and quantity of the shipments during the days and weeks before the fighting at Gettysburg are unclear given the lack of surviving records. However, on June 15, Lee directed James Longstreet to send all convalescents rejoining the army through Staunton, which may have been the preferred location because the roads along the Valley were less exposed to Federal troops.[42] In addition, ordnance and equipment shipments would reach Winchester from Richmond via Staunton.[43] The traffic went both ways. On June 18, for instance, members of the 54th North Carolina escorted 2,000 prisoners captured by Ewell at Winchester through Staunton and aboard Virginia Central cars back to Richmond. The Tar Heels immediately returned to Staunton and marched back to Winchester in the first days of July to guard an ordnance train.[44] However, while men and ammunition moved along the route, it is unlikely there were many rations sent north along the rails. Indeed, during the campaign, Lee's men largely subsisted on food gathered from local farms in Maryland and Pennsylvania, obviating the need for large ration shipments from Richmond.[45]

Lee's foray not only stretched his army's connections to Richmond; it also left the city and its links to the other Confederate states vulnerable. In 1863, these lifelines to the south were few. Federal forces controlled the coast in Virginia and North Carolina, preventing any Confederate naval transport. In addition, the long overland distances made supply by wagon impracticable. Accordingly, Confederates in Virginia relied on the feeble southern railroad system for supplies from the other states. The network of tracks, a collection of mostly short lines owned and operated by different companies, did not serve the Confederacy well. As in Virginia, inconsistent gauges, iron shortages, and limited spare parts plagued rail operations throughout the South; poor management, constant demands from Confederate officials, and Union raiders added to the dysfunction.[46]

Confederate leaders remained ever-mindful of Richmond's limited connections. In Virginia, only two lines linked the state to the balance of the Confederacy. One ran south from Petersburg and connected to the Wilmington and Weldon Railroad near the North Carolina border. In the summer of 1863, this connection furnished Richmond with a critical tie to the two uncaptured ports on the Atlantic Coast, Wilmington and Charleston. Virginia's link through Weldon also provided access to depots throughout South Carolina, Georgia, and beyond. Accordingly, all freight traffic traveling from the Old North State to Virginia rolled along the Petersburg Railroad from Weldon, which had a capacity of 225 tons in early 1863, with two freight trains running on the typical day.[47] In 1862, Lee had explained that the loss of this line would "cut off our communication with the South" and lead to a "hopeless disaster."[48]

Virginia's other link, the Virginia and Tennessee Railroad, stretched southwest from Lynchburg through the Blue Ridge and into the Volunteer State. It passed through the Blue Ridge at Big Lick (modern-day Roanoke), then Wytheville, and connected at Bristol to a series of lines joining Virginia to Chattanooga and the Deep South. The line also carried supplies from southwestern Virginia, including salt, a rare commodity in the Confederacy.[49] Future president James Garfield, who served with US troops in the region, described the Virginia and Tennessee as the "grand lever on which the rebellion hangs."[50] In 1861, the line had more locomotives and rolling stock than any other railroad in Virginia. In the war's first years, it ferried large quantities of meat for Lee's army from Tennessee and Georgia. In the spring of 1863, it had a capacity of 240 tons, with two trains running daily each way.[51]

"DEPARTMENT"

More than railroads occupied the landscape in and around Virginia during the war. Federal units and enclaves were nearly everywhere. Adding to the Washington, DC, garrison and the nearly constant presence of the Army of the Potomac, no less than three Federal departments loomed on the edges of central Virginia. First, the Department of Virginia, whose headquarters at Fort Monroe lay only about 70 miles east of Richmond, encompassed large portions of the York–James Peninsula and the cities of Norfolk and Suffolk to the southeast. In the summer of 1863, Major General John Dix commanded this sector from his headquarters at Fort Monroe. Second, to the south, the Department of North Carolina contained about 20,000 men under Major General John G. Foster at coastal strongpoints there. Finally, in the rugged mountains of western Virginia, a diffuse collection of units there made up a force that would soon form the newly created "Department of West Virginia."[52]

Beginning early in the war, US troops in western Virginia protected the Baltimore and Ohio Railroad, an important east–west rail trunk, while threatening the Confederate-controlled Virginia and Tennessee line to the south. For most of 1863, the Federal troops in the west formed part of the Middle Department headquartered in Baltimore. However, in June, several days after the new state of West Virginia formally entered the Union, the War Department designated the region as a separate military command: the Department of West Virginia, led by Brigadier General B. F. Kelley.[53] In this region, the Federals manned a screen of posts stringing southwest from the Baltimore and Ohio between Charleston and Grafton and maintained smaller outposts in the mountains.[54] Facing the Federal forces in West Virginia, Major General Samuel Jones managed the affairs of the Confederate Department of Western Virginia from his headquarters at Dublin, about 100 miles west of Lynchburg.[55] In addition, farther north in the Shenandoah Valley, Brigadier General John Imboden commanded a cavalry brigade near Staunton, keeping watch over Federal operations to the northwest.[56] In these western mountains, the opposing forces clashed frequently, often during raids designed to damage the other's rail lines but which usually caused little long-term harm.[57]

Union troops stationed in North Carolina also affected Confederate fortunes in central Virginia. In the spring of 1862, forces under Ambrose Burnside captured key positions on the coast during one of the war's first major successful US offensives. Afterward, Federal troops ensconced in their base at New Bern posed a constant threat to the Wilmington and Weldon Railroad as well as the port at Wilmington itself. However, Union commanders did not prioritize efforts in the Old North State, and with the exception of a few damaging raids, the region saw few major operations while enduring a nearly constant stream of low-intensity combat.

By the end of May 1863, Foster's department contained about 19,000 troops spread over four posts, at Beaufort, Washington, Plymouth, and his main base in New Bern.[58] As the fighting continued, Confederate leaders in North Carolina wrestled with growing political opposition to the war. D. H. Hill, in charge of Confederate operations there, recognized the danger to the Confederacy and predicted the Federals would turn their attention away from Charleston and toward North Carolina.[59]

2

John Dix and the Department of Virginia

"IF ANY ONE ATTEMPTS TO HAUL DOWN THE AMERICAN FLAG, SHOOT HIM ON THE SPOT"

ALTHOUGH SEVERAL UNION POSTS beset Richmond in 1863, the Department of Virginia east of the city posed the most acute threat. From the war's first days, the troops in this region manning Fort Monroe at the tip of the James–York Peninsula furnished an anchor for Federal operations in southeastern Virginia. In the summer of 1862, Union forces used that foothold to capture Norfolk and then support McClellan's Peninsula Campaign against Richmond. Following that unsuccessful effort, the Federals kept troops stationed at Fort Monroe, Norfolk, and other nearby positions. In June 1863, the department's forces included the Fourth and Seventh Corps and totaled about 30,000 men.[1]

At that time, Major General John Adams Dix commanded the department. Born in New Hampshire in 1798, Dix had enjoyed a long and distinguished life of public service. A junior officer during the War of 1812, he remained in the army until 1828, when he left military service to practice law in Albany, New York. Over the years, he forged a distinguished record in a string of private and public positions. He served as a railroad president, edited a newspaper, and worked for a spell as a postmaster. For much of his career, he remained active in Democratic Party politics and won election to the New York statehouse as a representative and later made it to Washington as a US senator. He also held a position in the Treasury Department during President Franklin Pierce's administration.[2]

Attractive yet unimposing, Dix was of medium height, with blue eyes, light brown hair, a "friendly countenance," and a "gentle, understated humor." His photographs from the 1860s reveal an older man with a slender face, ample eyebrows, full, unkempt gray hair, and, in some portraits, a bushy, white neck beard, which tufted out from his collar. Although he was generally liked and respected, some apparently found him pompous in "demanding the respect and prerogatives due him" and perhaps preoccupied with his rank.[3]

During the secession crisis, Dix understood what was at stake and planted himself in the middle of the chaos. Appointed secretary of the Treasury in January 1861 at the tail end of President James Buchanan's term, he focused on protecting US offices and property from the rebels. While Buchanan equivocated, Dix urged resolve and advocated a hard line against the insurrectionists. To Robert Anderson, the officer in charge of Fort Sumter, Dix wrote: "I need not say—maintain your ground to the last—because I know you will do it at all hazards."[4] A week later, Dix faced challenges of his own as the secessionists sought to seize Treasury Department installations and property throughout the South. When the Southerners threatened revenue cutters in New Orleans, Dix sent the following instruction to a Treasury official there: "If anyone attempts to haul down the American flag, shoot him on the spot."[5] The directive became a rallying cry for the Union effort and appeared in newspapers everywhere as well as on patriotic envelopes and widely produced metal coins known as "Dix tokens." During the first months of 1861, Dix also helped organize and lead the Union New York Defense Committee and aided in the formation of seventeen regiments.[6]

Throughout the conflict, Dix elevated the Union's preservation above all else. He faithfully executed his duty to the country and actively supported Lincoln's presidency, despite personal disagreements with many of the administration's policies. He loathed the slave power and bridled at the outsized influence Southerners had exercised on the national stage. Decades before the war, he surmised that the Southerners had gained advantage through "their better political organization . . . and in their strict Union by the single interest of Slavery." At the same time, Dix was no abolitionist. At best, he advocated only a vague, gradual end to the institution of slavery.[7] Before the war, he would occasionally speak against slavery while, in the same breath, urging the Federal government to leave it to the Southern states to decide when to eliminate the institution. In addition, like many of his contemporaries, he favored foreign colonization for enslaved people.[8]

Dix also expressed skepticism about Lincoln's pursuit of emancipation as a war policy. Early in the conflict, he worried that freed people would "long run wild and destroy all within their reach."[9] Fearing the abolitionists would push Lincoln to overplay his hand, Dix also expected that a focus on abolition would detract from the war effort and "divide the North and consolidate the South."[10] In 1861, he wrote that if "madmen"

in Congress adopt the "miserable scheme of emancipation" or the "di-
abolical project of arming slaves against their masters," "all hope of a
pacification will be at an end" and states such as Kentucky would join the
Confederacy.[11] Likewise, he was not enthusiastic about enlisting Black
men in the Union army, viewing them as inferior and doubting their desire to serve.[12] Although he was careful and measured in his language, in
essence he saw only a limited role for African Americans to play in the
contest.[13]

Dix also supported a cautious approach to prosecuting the war. His
views aligned with those who promoted moderation in dealing with the
secessionists. Concerned about preventing excesses against the white civilian population in his Department of Virginia, Dix declared his intention to "conduct the war on principles of humanity."[14] He fretted about
the "revolting" actions of undisciplined soldiers in the field and feared
that the "shameful pillage of unprotected families" would disgrace his
command. He also predicted aggressive measures against Confederate
infrastructure (i.e., "hard war" policies) would drive white Southerners
further away from the Union. He and like-minded officers, fellow War
Democrats such as McClellan, advocated restraint, moderation, and con-
ciliation and focused on countering and blunting enemy efforts. These
men hoped many Southern leaders would eventually abandon the war
and the rebellion under the right conditions. In their view, ruthless, aggressive policies would eliminate any chance of such a shift.[15]

However, two years into the conflict, that view was losing traction
as it became clear most prominent Southerners had no such inclinations
and remained firmly attached to the Confederate project.[16] Nevertheless,
in the summer of 1863, Dix continued to instruct his troops to avoid
destroying civilian property except where it directly aided the enemy. It
is unclear whether Dix clung to hopes for reconciliation or simply disap-
proved of aggressive war measures, though it was probably the latter.[17] In
a letter to his wife, Catherine Morgan Dix, he confided there "is nothing
to me so revolting in this war as the lawlessness of some of our men.
Notwithstanding all my efforts to prevent it, they rob & plunder without
the slightest regard to what I say." If the guilty parties could be found in
such cases, Dix vowed to have them shot.[18]

Whatever differences he might have with other officials, Dix continued
to back President Lincoln. He became the consummate War Democrat,
vigorously backing the war effort and maintaining support for the administration, though he would often disagree with Lincoln's policies. For
example, when the president announced the preliminary Emancipation

Proclamation, Dix did not shy from sharing his concerns. "I certainly should not have advised it," he remarked. However, in writing to a group of Wisconsin Democrats in 1863, he urged continued support for the fight and warned that anyone who embarrassed the government "in the prosecution of the war" was an "auxiliary of the public enemy." He never wavered in this view. In 1864, he would enthusiastically champion Lincoln's reelection and reject both the "Chicago platform," adopted by the members of his own party, as well as George McClellan's candidacy. He cautioned that a negotiated peace or any "cessation of hostilities" would result in independence for the rebellious states. Instead, he pushed for the war's "steady persistent and unremitting prosecution."[19]

On the battlefield, no one looked for Dix to win brilliant victories. His only experience leading soldiers in the field occurred during the fighting at Crysler's Farm during the War of 1812, where fifteen-year-old Ensign Dix briefly led a detachment of twenty men to the front only to be ordered rearward to guard prisoners.[20] In 1861, he was better known for his organizational acumen than any martial prowess. A few months into the conflict, he received an appointment to Major General of the Volunteers, making him the most senior officer holding that rank. For a few months he commanded the Department of Maryland, where he sought to stamp out "secession sentiment" in Baltimore. He then moved to the Department of Pennsylvania, even farther from the front lines. However, in the summer of 1862, he was transferred to Fort Monroe to command the Department of Virginia, where not much occurred after McClellan's failed Peninsula Campaign in that same summer.[21]

Trade, not combat, proved to be Dix's primary challenge in eastern Virginia. Questions about Norfolk's blockade status tested Dix's administrative abilities as controversy over the issue dragged on for months. Eventually, Dix gained permission to increase trade through Norfolk, a move that reduced the suffering of local inhabitants but also may have helped feed Confederate forces in Virginia.[22] Beyond the trade headaches, Dix managed the troops stationed in his department. By the spring of 1863, his force equaled nearly 30,000 men spread across the Virginia Tidewater at Fort Monroe, Norfolk, Suffolk, and Yorktown. His outposts were remarkably close to Richmond. The position at Yorktown, for instance, lay only 45 miles away from the rebel capital. But things were mostly quiet. His units occupied themselves with garrison duty interrupted occasionally by modest operations, usually in the form of small raids against enemy positions.[23] For the most part, the region remained quiet as Dix gave little thought to a move against Richmond. Instead, he maintained a defensive posture and focused on protecting Norfolk and Fort Monroe, which he viewed as the "two points of great importance" in the department—the "former as a military position, commanding the Chesapeake Bay and the rivers that enter into it," he explained, "and the latter as a naval station for the repair of our gunboats and transports."[24]

During his tenure at Fort Monroe, Dix received periodic requests from Washington to support the efforts of the Army of the Potomac. In late 1862, officials asked him to distract the Confederates from Union offensives elsewhere. At the beginning of the Fredericksburg Campaign in December, for instance, Henry Halleck queried Dix whether he "could make a diversion by a demonstration on Richmond?"[25] Dix did not exactly jump at the opportunity. "I am doing all my means will allow to make a diversion," he responded. This apparently amounted to a small operation in Gloucester County north of the York River and little else.[26]

In the spring of 1863, activity in the department increased somewhat. With his army in winter camp on the Rappahannock, Lee sent Lieutenant General James Longstreet's corps to capture Suffolk and gather supplies from the surrounding countryside. One of Dix's subordinates, Major General John Peck, ably defended the post in a confrontation that lasted nearly a month. During the campaign, Confederate commissary agents were able to gather provisions from southeastern Virginia while Longstreet penned the Federals into the Suffolk defenses.[27] But in late April, when Joseph Hooker moved against Lee at Chancellorsville, Longstreet halted his Suffolk operations and headed back north.[28] Dix, in turn, abandoned the town completely and consolidated his troops there closer to Norfolk.[29]

"FOREVER FREE"

In April, as Hooker planned his Chancellorsville offensive, Halleck once again reached out to Dix about a possible diversion east of Richmond.[30] The general-in-chief suggested Dix occupy West Point, a town located in King William County where the Pamunkey and Mattaponi Rivers join to form the York. Originally the site of the Mattaponi Tribe settlement named Cinquoteck, West Point also served as the eastern terminus of the York River Railroad, which ran directly to Richmond and thus provided a convenient base for attacking forces. In addition, upstream from the town, the Pamunkey connected to the South Anna River, where the Virginia Central and RF&P railroads crossed. In response to Halleck's request, Dix took action, though not with any remarkable speed.[31] He assigned the mission to Brigadier General George H. Gordon, a division commander in Erasmus Keyes's Fourth Corps.[32]

On May 7, gunboats and transports carrying 5,000 men, two batteries, and 100 cavalrymen approached the "charred timbers" of the wharf at West Point, relics from McClellan's operations the year before. Using beams and planks from a deserted house, the Federals soon rebuilt the pier, and within hours Gordon's men were busy "piling sleepers from the railroad, throwing up earth for parapets, and cutting down trees for abatis." By evening, a strong line cordoned the town and, within days, heavy 20-pounder Parrott rifles poked out from embrasures in the works, which ran astride the railroad and covered the landing, making a "complete circle of fire."[33]

Immediately upon Gordon's arrival at West Point, a small detachment of cavalrymen from the 6th New York and 5th Pennsylvania ventured west along the railroad toward White House Landing, about 15 miles upstream. The probe soon encountered rebel forces. In the ensuing scuffle with videttes from the 15th Virginia Cavalry, Lieutenant Robert Crozier of the 6th New York died when his horse, wounded in the neck by a rebel ball, threw him on his head and then crashed down on his body. The patrol returned to West Point having established the camp's outer boundaries.[34]

The forty-two-year-old Gordon and his command remained at West Point during May. A week after their arrival, Gordon sent out a raid to destroy local grain stores in nearby King and Queen County following a tip from freed people who had entered his camp. The gunboat *Morse* transported a small detachment from the 142nd New York across the mouth of the Mattaponi to the north bank of the York.[35] During the operation, the New Yorkers did more than burn grain. They "seized horses, mules, bacon, &c., and great numbers of negroes," according to the unit's official record of events.[36] Indeed, King and Queen County, as well as adjacent King William County, had remained mostly untouched by the 1862 Peninsula Campaign. As well-known secessionist and local slave owner Edmund Ruffin explained, King William remained a "rich & tempting prize to the foraging & plundering expeditions of the Yankees."[37]

The soldiers in Gordon's command found their new post a pleasant one. One New Yorker and his comrades set up their tents on raised platforms under a beautiful grove of pine trees and regularly swam in the Pamunkey. Many joked that they "would like to spend the balance of their years at this beautiful camp."[38] They also foraged freely in the

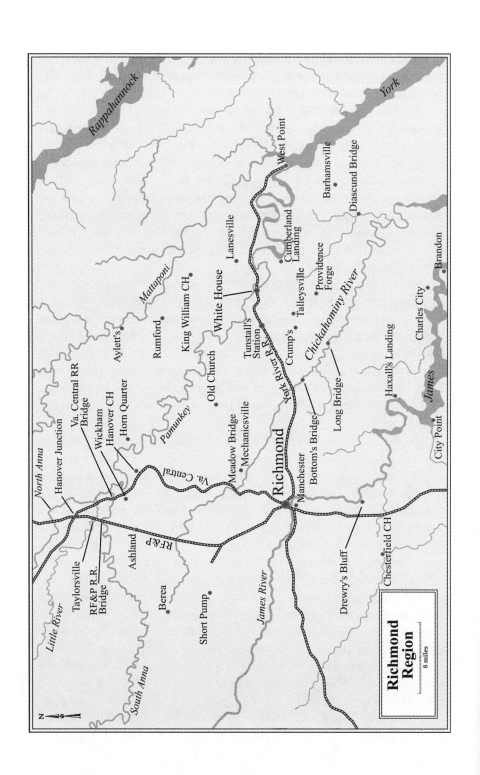

Richmond Region

8 miles

N

Rappahannock

York

West Point

Barhamsville

Cumberland Landing

Diascund Bridge

Lanesville

Brandon

Mattaponi

King William CH

White House

Providence Forge

Chickahominy River

Talleysville

Rumford

Tunstall's Station

Crump's

Charles City

Aylett's

Old Church

James

Va. Central RR Bridge

Horn Quarter

Pamunkey

Haxall's Landing

Wickham

Hanover CH

Meadow Bridge

York River R.R.

Long Bridge

North Anna

Mechanicsville

Bottom's Bridge

City Point

Hanover Junction

Va. Central

Richmond

Manchester

Taylorsville

Ashland

RF&P

Chesterfield CH

RF&P R.R. Bridge

Berea

James River

Drewry's Bluff

Little River

Short Pump

South Anna

surrounding woods and plantations, shooting game and livestock, much to the chagrin of the local landowners. According to Gordon's memoir, hogs ran free through the woods, making Virginia seem one "vast pigpen." The men also gathered wood wherever they could find it, an endeavor that led Gordon to wryly note his soldiers' "unreasonable opposition" to fences, for wherever they "march . . . rails become traditions of the past." The general, however, frowned on his men's efforts to loot local farms. On one occasion, he stopped a group of his soldiers from shooting a cow "purchased" by a private for 25 cents.[39]

While white civilians may have viewed Gordon's West Point outpost as a menace, the enslaved people in the surrounding area took a decidedly different view. Once word of the new Federal position made its way into the countryside, African American civilians began streaming into Gordon's camp from local plantations, fitting a pattern seen elsewhere whenever US troops marched or took positions near enslaved populations. As the refugees continued to arrive day after day, an astounded Gordon figured "the whole surrounding country must be stripped of slaves." Officers with McClellan during the previous year's Peninsula Campaign may have asked the same question given the influx of refugees into Union camps at the time. Nevertheless, six months after the Emancipation Proclamation in 1863, thousands of enslaved people remained on plantations in eastern Virginia not far from Federal outposts. A firm abolitionist from Framingham, Massachusetts, General Gordon encouraged these escapes. "Far and wide did I send for them to come in," he recalled. Some freedmen would arrive and then return to their plantations the next day to rescue their wives and children. Back in Gordon's camp, they shared intelligence about rebel plans to attack the West Point post as well as information about enemy stores in the area.[40]

Gordon knew the value these freed people offered to the war effort and later recalled understanding "the absolute necessity, as a measure of military precaution and success, of using these slaves for our good." During Gordon's stay at West Point, self-emancipated individuals brought in more and more intelligence on enemy strength and positions. Gordon's faith in these scouts "was over and over again confirmed by deeds of daring," he noted later. One man conducted a night reconnaissance of nearby enemy picket posts, creeping through the woods close enough to count the exact number of guards at each location. Gordon also employed the former slaves in more conventional roles, assigning men to the quartermaster's department and women to work on the camp's washing and cooking.[41]

The exodus of newly emancipated people from the region's plantations predictably alarmed the local slave owners, who, according to Gordon, resorted "to every expedient to put off the final hour when they would have to depend solely on their own resources, or starve." While the new arrivals recounted stories of their former owners' cruelties, including beatings and murders, unabashed slaveholders petitioned Gordon for the return of these people. One such plea from a King William County plantation owner claimed the departures had left wives without husbands and children without parents.[42] In response, Gordon explained the men and women in his lines were "forever free" and he had no right to return them to slavery, even if he wished to. He was correct. Congress had clearly resolved such matters the year before by prohibiting officers from returning formerly enslaved refugees to their disloyal former owners.[43] Gordon added that this slaveowner's attachment to these people did "not seem to be mutual" and that the slaveowner's "affection is unrequited." Then, broadening his lens, Gordon informed the slaveowner:

> Sympathizing with you in your distress as every human being should, you will be consoled by the knowledge thus brought home to you that the accursed institution of slavery is almost swept from your hearthstone; that the day is dawning when neither mother nor child will have to outrage Nature's laws to breathe the air of liberty; and it will gladden your heart to know that wherever our star-spangled banner waves, freedom follows. While praying for pardon for the sins of your people in causing this atrocious rebellion against a just Government, you will yet have the proud consciousness of knowing that you have been an agent in freeing the oppressed in our land; and thus it may happen that that sin, which is as scarlet, may be washed whiter than snow.[44]

Gordon's candid response reflected the deep abolitionist strain running through some officers in the Department of Virginia. Not everyone shared Gordon's views, though. Often, Union officers and soldiers exhibited ambivalence and even hostility toward African Americans who had escaped their bondage and gained refuge in Federal camps. His commander, John Dix, for instance, had taken pains to avoid aggravating local slaveowners by packing orders to his officers with admonitions to spare private property and the like. Although Gordon did not aggressively pursue "hard war" practices while his command was at West Point, he clearly had little patience for the slave-owning class. Following the exchange, more enslaved people arrived at Gordon's camp. During an inspection of his outer lines one day, he met a large group of refugees. "When I encountered this motley crowd," he recalled, they were "shouting with joy at their deliverance. No manifestations of regret did they utter, no solicitude did they express; but with a perfect trust, mothers and children laid down their weary loads, and waited to begin the new life of freedom." Gordon remembered that "one mother had four children with her, another two, and so on; whitish children with light hair and blue eyes, and children black as night." After these refugees arrived at the West Point camp, the Federals transported many to safety at Fort Monroe.[45]

"I DO NOT KNOW HOW FAR I CAN GO IN THAT DIRECTION"

The Confederates took more than a casual interest in Gordon's presence at West Point. Robert E. Lee and Richmond officials viewed the lodgment there as a serious threat. They monitored his force closely and sought to determine whether the Federals would use the outpost to move against Richmond's communications.[46] The uncertainty continued throughout May, as rebel officials shuffled troops around Richmond. In addition, to guard against the threat from West Point, Lee stationed George Pickett's division southeast of Fredericksburg and posted Brigadier General J. Johnston Pettigrew's brigade at Hanover Junction. Pettigrew speculated that Gordon's presence on the York "was intended as a refuge for stealing parties, runaway slaves, &c, but I fear they will give us more trouble than that." He also worried Gordon would march on the RF&P railroad at the North Anna River or attack the lines farther south near Hanover Court House, using White House on the Pamunkey as a base.[47] Jefferson Davis did not know what to make of the threat; hedging his bets, the Confederate president sought reinforcements from North Carolina to further protect Richmond.[48]

But the occupation of West Point by US forces was temporary. Near the end of May, Major General Edward Ord received overall command of the force there and concluded that the position, while strong, was "too much exposed." He feared the rebels would erect heavy batteries on the south bank of the York or attack by land from the west. Absent the addition of 4,000 men, more than two dozen guns, and a bridge across the Pamunkey, Ord concluded West Point should be abandoned. Heeding that recommendation, Dix informed Hooker at the end of May of plans to leave the post.[49]

The Federal withdrawal from West Point eliminated an immediate threat to Richmond and may have affected the timing of Robert E. Lee's march north.[50] On June 3, the day after news of the withdrawal reached Lee, he began to march some of his first troops out of the Fredericksburg lines. Several days later, he explained to Davis that uncertainty about threats "along the coast of North Carolina and between the Rappahannock and James River . . . has caused delay in the movements of this army."[51] Although it is not clear that the abandonment of the Federal position at West Point specifically triggered Lee's campaign into Pennsylvania, it certainly removed the threat to Lee's flank and freed him to proceed with his plan to move north.[52]

On the York–James Peninsula in early June, John Dix also developed plans of his own to occupy the Confederates in his front and prevent them from funneling more men to Lee's army. First, he planned to send troops west beyond Suffolk toward the Blackwater River and Petersburg, now that Longstreet's force had left the region. Second, he hoped to conduct a demonstration from Williamsburg along the Peninsula toward White House, the location of the depot on the Pamunkey River the previous year and the railhead for the York River Railroad. Despite these plans for offensive operations, he worried about reports of increased enemy strength on the Peninsula. Perhaps seeking to buffer expectations, he informed Hooker that "I do not know how far I can go in that direction." However, before launching these efforts, Dix's officers had a different operation in mind.[53]

3

The Union Raid on Aylett's Foundry

"NOT USEFUL TO TROOPS IN THE FIELD"

IN 1853, WASHINGTON CARROLL TEVIS, a young Philadelphian born to Unitarian parents, changed his name to Charles and joined the Catholic Church. He was living in Paris at the time. The next year, he traveled east, enlisted in the Turkish army, embraced the moniker "Nessim Bey," and fought in the Crimean War, earning a medal for his performance at the Battle of Kars. A year later, he returned to Paris, where he attended lavish balls in his Turkish uniform, wrote a book about guerrilla warfare, and patented a revolver. During his time in the City of Light, Tevis's reckless, mercenary ways earned him a reputation. Some labeled him a bad lot, a "mauvais sujet," according to the diary of one US official living in London. The disrepute stuck, and when Tevis tried to enlist in the Persian army in 1858, officials at the border turned him back, brandishing a written order that tagged him "a blackguard, a dangerous character" and directed the guards "not to let [him] even get into the country." Tevis eventually returned to the United States, where he joined the army to stamp out the slaveholder rebellion. In the first days of June 1863, Tevis, a lieutenant colonel in the 4th Delaware at Yorktown, received orders to load a group of infantrymen onto transports and conduct a raid up the Mattaponi River.[1]

Following the withdrawal from West Point, John Dix and his generals did not altogether cease operations along the York River. On the morning of June 3, only a few days after Gordon's departure, Fourth Corps commander Erasmus Keyes approved a strike against a rebel foundry on the Mattaponi at Aylett's (or "Aylett"), a sleepy village George Washington's troops had passed through on their way to Yorktown.[2] The next day, Keyes circulated orders for the operation, a combined expedition of naval and land forces led by Tevis (for the army) and Lieutenant Commander James H. Gillis (for the navy). The mission called for 400 men to be transported by four vessels—two navy gunboats (the *Commodore Jones* and *Commodore Morris*), an armor-plated army gunboat *Smith Briggs*, and the transport *Winnissimet*. For the bulk of the force, four infantry regiments—the 4th Delaware, 168th New York, and the 169th and 179th Pennsylvania—contributed a hundred volunteers each.[3]

Keyes ordered Tevis and Gillis to destroy the Aylett's foundry, capture or destroy "all collections of supplies for the rebel army," and seize horses and livestock if possible. He also counseled restraint and explicitly ordered the men not "to take anything, or to destroy anything, not useful to troops in the field," an admonition consistent with John Dix's conservative, "conciliatory course" for those people "not under arms."[4] At Yorktown on the evening of June 4, three of the companies gathered on the wharf and filed aboard the vessels carrying nothing but their overcoats, canteens, and cartridge boxes filled with fifty rounds. The flotilla stopped at Gloucester Point to bring on more soldiers and, by early evening, glided past an empty West Point. In the early morning hours, the task force churned up the Mattaponi led by the *Commodore Jones*, an armed side-wheel ferry purchased only weeks before in New York.[5]

According to the log of the *Commodore Jones*, a "colored pilot" guided the vessel up the river. This was not unusual. Union forces frequently relied on local pilots to navigate the waters of eastern Virginia. For instance, Terrill Bradby, a member of the Pamunkey Indian Tribe, piloted the *Smith Briggs* throughout operations in June and had served on other vessels at other locations, including South Carolina and Baltimore. His home stood on Pamunkey Island, just across the river from White House Landing. The Pamunkey Tribe, loyal Unionists to a person, contributed significantly to the Federal war effort. After the war, Bradby's testimony before the Southern Claims Commission revealed that as many as fourteen members of the tribe served as river pilots for the US forces.[6] In addition, records show that at least two tribe members, Archie Miles and Bradby, served as pilots for the Union navy on the Pamunkey, York, and the Mattaponi Rivers. In fact, Union records confirm that Lieutenant Commander Gillis had frequently employed Bradby as a scout and that Bradby had aided Dix's forces during operations that June.[7]

The vessels in Tevis's expedition steamed north for 25 miles up the Mattaponi toward Walkerton, threading through many narrow bends and passing forests, fields, and, in some places, imposing bluffs that frowned down on the river in the darkness. Around 3 a.m. on June 5, the boats arrived at Walkerton in King William County at a spot where the river narrowed considerably. The soldiers disembarked onto enemy territory and began the march to their target, the hamlet of Aylett's, 10 miles away. Pockets of Confederate troops threatened the Federals on nearly all sides.

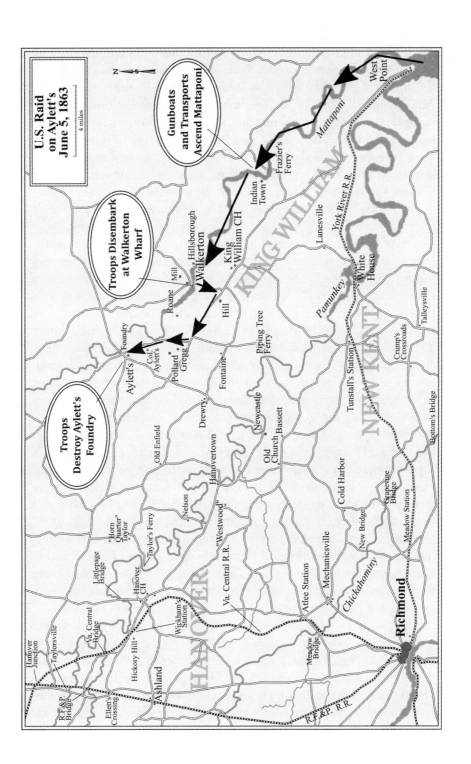

U.S. Raid
on Aylett's
June 5, 1863

4 miles

N

Gunboats
and Transports
Ascend Mattaponi

Troops Disembark
at Walkerton
Wharf

Troops
Destroy Aylett's
Foundry

West
Point

Mattaponi

Frazier's
Ferry

Indian
Town

Lanesville

York River R.R.

White
House

Pamunkey

Talleysville

Hillsborough

Walkerton

Roane's
Mill

KING WILLIAM

King
William CH

Hill

Piping Tree
Ferry

Foundry

Aylett's

Col.
Aylett's

Pollard

Gregg

Fontaine

Drewry

Newcastle

Old
Church Bassett

Crump's
Crossroads

NEW KENT

Tunstall's Station

Bottom's Bridge

Old Enfield

Hanovertown

Cold Harbor

Grapevine
Bridge

Meadow Station

"Nelson

"Horn
Quarter"
Taylor

Taylor's Ferry

Hanover
CH

Va. Central R.R.

"Westwood"

Mechanicsville

New Bridge

Chickahominy

Meadow
Bridge

Richmond

Littlepage
Bridge

Wickham's
Station

Atlee Station

Hanover
Junction

Taylorsville

Va. Central
Bridge

Hickory Hill

Ashland

HANOVER

R.F.&P.
Bridge

Ellett's
Crossing

R.F.&P. R.R.

Ten miles to the southwest lay the rebel outpost at White House, and, to the west and north, the right flank of the Army of Northern Virginia held by George Pickett's division occupied ground near Newtown and Tappahannock. Unperturbed by these dangers, Charles Tevis unloaded his men near Walkerton and marched about a mile along the main county road, turned right, and headed northwest for Aylett's. To screen his tiny force, he posted small detachments of New Yorkers and Pennsylvanians at intersections along the road, including the route leading off to the King William Court House, about 2 miles to the southeast.[8]

Tevis's main force proceeded northwest with Delaware skirmishers under Captain M. B. Gist at the front and the 179th Pennsylvania under Major William Yerkes protecting the rear. After a three-hour march, the column arrived at Aylett's around 8 a.m. and found the rumored foundry there. Pickets fanned out to watch the surrounding roads as the rest of the men located "molds for cannon and projectiles, and a number of shell and solid shot lying on the ground." The facility itself, owned by J. T. Caldwell, consisted of "a large machine-shop, a lumber-yard, a store-house filled with agricultural implements, tobacco, cotton, turpentine, and other articles, and five Government houses, containing several thousand bushels of corn." Tevis's men put all of this to the torch.[9] According to local reports, the Federals also destroyed Caldwell's personal residence and all the outer dwellings, causing $100,000 in damage in all.[10]

News of the raid reached local rebel detachments. On the shore at West Point, lookouts had noted the passage of the four vessels early in the morning. Soon, the home guard had formed at King William Court House, but the militia soon dispersed after hearing rumors of a large attacking force. However, one member, an older man named Mortimer Cobb, lingered on the county road and fell asleep beside a fence corner. After some time, the stamp of the raiding column startled him awake. Impulsively, Cobb rushed into the middle of the road, raised his "old single-barreled squirrel gun," and shouted shrilly, "Halt Halt thar, every damned one of you!" The effort stopped the entire column, but only temporarily, and Cobb soon joined the expedition, as a prisoner.[11]

There were other Confederates in the area in addition to Mortimer Cobb and the understandably skittish members of the home guard. Not far away at White House, Brigadier General Henry A. Wise received reports of the raid at 5 a.m. and sent out Major John R. Bagby to Lanesville across the Pamunkey, about 9 miles south of Walkerton, with two infantry companies, two cannons, and about sixty cavalrymen. Bagby rode with his improvised command toward the courthouse to search for the raiders and placed a few pieces of artillery on the bluffs at Frazier's Ferry, overlooking the Mattaponi.[12]

But confusion soon crippled the Confederate response. In his initial dispatch to Major General Arnold Elzey in Richmond, Wise warned that the Yankee raid appeared to be headed for Piping Tree Ferry on the Pamunkey and possibly toward Hanover Junction and the railroads. However, as Wise dispatched men toward the Mattaponi to repel the Union column, orders arrived from Elzey halting the efforts.[13] Instead of pursuing the Yankees in King William, Elzey wanted the forces to shield the rail lines west of the Pamunkey.[14] Wise fired back, complaining that his men could not check the raid in King William if forced to march toward Hanover. A confusing, time-consuming exchange followed. Jefferson Davis entered the fray, asking Elzey to seek aid from George Pickett and his division to the north and declaring that the raiding force must be "captured or destroyed." With his division near Tappahannock about 17 miles from Aylett's, Pickett had a chance to crush Tevis's tiny expedition. But Elzey's request ran through Johnston Pettigrew at Hanover Junction, and hours were consumed getting word to Pickett, a delay that effectively kept him and his division out of the fight.[15]

While Charles Tevis and his men headed to Aylett's, Captain John C. Lee, who commanded the army gunboat *Smith Briggs* back at Walkerton, led fifteen men in a cutter to the Mattaponi's east bank and pushed inland, driving back a few rebel videttes. During the excursion, the captain and his men came upon a nearby sawmill, removed the machinery, and destroyed what was left inside. While this work went on, the rebels returned and formed in the woods across a pond near the mill. A short firefight followed, and one of the Southerners was killed. Not wishing to wait for more of the enemy, Captain Lee gathered his men and returned to the river. Once there, an African American man reported that more Confederates were forming on the shore 6 miles downstream to prevent a safe return. With Tevis's force still at Aylett's, Lee relayed the alarming news to Lieutenant Commander Gillis, who then ordered the *Smith Briggs* to move downriver and clear the way.[16]

Back to the northwest, Tevis turned his raiders south after destroying the Aylett's foundry, assigning Lieutenant Hezekiah Cullen of the 4th Delaware to guard the formation's rear. After marching about 2 miles, the Federals passed a mill owned by Colonel W. R. Aylett and wrecked or burned nearly everything they could find, including several millstones, as well as many barrels of flour and bushels of wheat. The destruction continued as Tevis and his men made their way back to Walkerton. The command visited nearly every plantation along their return route. Detachments broke off the main road to probe up side paths and driveways leading to the area's larger estates. At the Pollard plantation about 2 miles southeast of Aylett's Mill, Tevis's men put the Pollard women under guard and, according to one witness, rifled the house of "every thing that excited their cupidity, including knives, forks, silver, parlor ornaments, &c." A Union surgeon was heard to express how much he regretted "the damned rebel house wasn't burnt."[17]

The Federals also found the nearby Roane plantation near the banks of the Mattaponi halfway between Aylett's and Walkerton. According to a story recorded by diarist Judith Brockenbrough McGuire in Ashland, Tevis himself appeared at the Roane farm and announced he had heard the property contained the "finest horses" in the county. A member of the Roane family stepped forward and replied, "They are not yours, and you can't get them." Displeased by such defiance, Tevis threatened to burn down the entire complex. When the owner did not bend, the lieutenant colonel "handed a box of matches to a subordinate," and soon men in blue scurried about setting most everything afire. McGuire heard that fourteen buildings burned, including storehouses and slave quarters. "Scarcely any thing was saved, not even the family clothes," she wrote.[18]

The conflagration did not go unnoticed. From the Marlbourne plantation, 10 miles to the west near Mechanicsville, Edmund Ruffin, the aged fire-eater, and his family could see smoke rising from three large fires in King William County as Tevis torched the plantations along the Mattaponi.[19] Over in King and Queen County to the east, a captain in the 24th Virginia also saw "smoke ascending from three or four different points."[20]

The Federal column continued its trek back toward the gunboats. Before turning off the county road toward the river and Walkerton, some of Tevis's men called on Doctor R. G. Hill's farm and took all the medicine and papers they could find and burned the office.[21] Other plantations that received similar visits included those owned by Doctor D. H. Gregg, A. H. Perkins, Warner Edwards, the Hills, and the Kings. During the raid, many enslaved persons (about a hundred according to Union reports) joined the column and gained their freedom. Later, Tevis estimated his men destroyed twenty barns, 20,000 wheat bushels, 2,000 pounds of bacon, as well as large quantities of tobacco, cotton, and whiskey. The men also seized eighty head of cattle and more than a hundred horses and mules along with two Confederate soldiers, one of whom had been taken before and had violated his parole.[22]

During the Federal withdrawal, Confederates nipped at the rear of the column. A detachment of gray cavalry from the Holcombe Legion joined Major John R. Bagby at Lanesville. Some of the riders headed east to the bluffs downriver from Aylett's while others, under Captain Washington Williams, proceeded to King William Court House and beyond to ambush the raiding column as it returned to its boats at Walkerton. From the courthouse, Captain Williams hoped to strike through the woods and take a position between the returning column and the river. To accomplish this task, he sent out two officers with more than 200 men to lay in wait, while keeping a force in reserve. But as Tevis's troops approached the improvised ambuscade, it became clear the Federal force was too large and the woods too compact to permit an effective attack. The rebels remained hidden until the rear of the column passed, at which point the small force pounced. The advance produced a lively exchange with members of the 168th New York, but, given the disparity in numbers, the Confederates withdrew.[23] During the fighting, one New Yorker was killed and two were wounded. In addition, a bugler, William H. Dickerson, received a minié ball in his left arm when his own weapon discharged while he rode his horse. Finally, one unfortunate corporal straggled from the column and failed to board the gunboats, becoming a prisoner.[24]

"TO GET FREE!"

Tevis's column returned to Walkerton about 5:30 p.m. At the wharf, officers prepared to load the gunboats and transports and shove off. The men spent the next half-hour clambering onto the vessels. A sense of urgency prevailed, caused in part by reports that Pickett's division was not far away. While waiting to board, Calvin Hutchinson, the paymaster of the *Commodore Morris*, met a boy dressed in rags who had gained his freedom only hours before. The youngster wished to come aboard the gunboat "to get free!" His former owner, John Toliver, had recently beaten him for failing to catch soft shell crabs in the river. Once on the vessel, Hutchinson found that many freed people had joined the Union soldiers on the cramped deck.[25] According to official reports, the limited space forced the Federals to leave some of the captured livestock on shore. The three boats shoved off at 6 p.m. to join the *Smith Briggs* downstream. In the procession, the *Commodore Jones* led in front with the *Commodore Morris* 500 yards behind, towing the *Winnissimet*.[26]

One account painted a somewhat different picture of the departure.

J. W. Nelson of the 169th Pennsylvania recalled decades later that, while the abandoned horses and livestock were put to fright, many "poor contrabands, that had caught the first breath of freedom, gathering up all the finery they could 'tote,' were lining up on shore crying, praying, and shouting" to be allowed on the vessels, but no room was available. Nelson surmised that he was spared the "revolting scene that followed" when the Confederate soldiers later arrived to "wreak their vengeance on the innocent and helpless negroes."[27] Neither official Union reports nor Confederate accounts mention that refugees had been left behind.[28]

As the boats steamed away, their occupants braced for a difficult journey. With much of the day to prepare, pockets of Confederates lined the banks downstream from Walkerton waiting for the Federal flotilla to steam by. The *Smith Briggs*, the armor-plated tug that preceded the main force, had departed Walkerton several hours before. Taking no chances, the boat's gunners threw "her huge shells far out" onto the banks, peppering "the woods on both sides" with its large Parrott rifle. On a bluff 3 miles downriver, Captain Lee spied about a hundred Confederates and sent a shell that scattered the gathering. The *Smith Briggs* continued a couple more miles, finding small groups of the enemy here and there along both banks. Captain Lee exchanged fire with these forces, apparently shouldering a rifle himself, managed to hit at least one of the Confederates. Finally, reaching a 70-foot-high bluff 6 miles from Walkerton at Indian Town, he encountered another large group of the enemy but brushed them off with more fire; he remained there to await the three other boats.[29]

The rest of the vessels took similar measures during their journey to brush back any enemy troops lurking on the banks. With the boats keeping up a steady fire, some curious onlookers flocking to the river got more than they expected. A local doctor from over in King and Queen County, who made his way with several other civilians to the Mattaponi near the Hillsborough plantation, arrived just in time to witness a Union shell land near his party and explode. The physician glimpsed three boats raining more rounds on the opposite shore, the King William County side of the river. The doctor recalled that "[s]hells were thrown at citizens at various points, one at Mrs. R. Douglass, sitting in the porch at Frazier's Ferry with a child in her arms," and at another property the Federals fired "a volley of small arms" at one man (a "Mr. H.") and his children standing in a yard.[30]

The *Commodore Jones*, leading the balance of the flotilla, continued to fire rounds at cavalrymen clustered along the banks and atop the bluffs. The way ahead looked precarious. "The whole country through which we passed had been aroused," reported Gillis, "the banks being lined with those who would have been delighted in taking the lives of the 'invaders of their soil.'"[31] For several hours, the gunners maintained their fire. According to the log from the *Commodore Jones*, the crews dropped "shells into many deserted houses and completely scoured the banks, and sweeping all the points on the river," keeping up a "constant discharge of shrapnel, doing much execution and destroying all the houses at which signal lights were shown." However, the log also indicated that the boats avoided firing on those houses "flying a white flag."[32] Eventually, the flotilla managed to run the gauntlet and reunite with the *Smith Briggs* downstream from the high bluff below Indian Town.[33]

Later, the Federals reached the relative safety of the York River. During the harrowing journey along the Mattaponi, the *Commodore Jones* had fired off nearly a hundred shells, including thirty from its 9-inch gun. The crew members were green. Many had joined the boat's compliment only weeks before, and the Aylett's raid was the first time they had fired the boat's gun after its commissioning in early May. The task force returned to Yorktown at 2 a.m. on June 6, roughly twenty-four hours after its departure. It had been a successful operation. With few casualties, Tevis and Gillis had destroyed their primary objective, the Aylett's foundry, and in the bargain managed to seize property and emancipate many slaves.[34]

"THESE RAIDS . . . ARE GRADUALLY CONVERTING MY MEN INTO SOLDIERS"

Like many efforts conducted by troops in the Department of Virginia in 1863, the Aylett's raid grabbed few headlines. That winter and spring, the 4th Delaware had conducted similar, though less successful, expeditions from their camps at Gloucester Point to Hickory Fork, Gloucester Court House, and, only two weeks before, Matthews County. Many of these operations resulted in small, intimate deadly actions that kept the rebel forces and citizenry on edge.[35] Union commanders continued to see benefits to these raids in the region but also worried about sending small parties into enemy territory so frequently. But Fourth Corps commander Erasmus Keyes was convinced of their efficacy. "These raids, being all successful thus far, are gradually converting my men into soldiers," he told Dix. "As yet however, I have not sufficient confidence . . . to meet superior numbers of the enemy & to guarantee success."[36]

As was often the case with Union operations in Virginia, information provided by freed or enslaved people helped US forces in their efforts.[37] As Tevis and Gillis prepared to return from Walkerton, one Black man had warned of the rebels gathering downstream to block the flotilla. Such assistance was common. In fact, the Confederates certainly understood that slaves were aiding the Union cause. Back in December, for instance, Brigadier General Henry Wise acknowledged to a fellow officer that "I have no doubt the negroes are in constant contact and regular communications with the enemy . . . whenever [the Federals] desire to disappoint your movements or make their own."[38]

The raid on Aylett's also carried with it more than a whiff of hard war. Aggressive Union operations against Confederate civilian property, agricultural assets, and manufacturing equipment had been slow in coming in the Old Dominion, with some notable exceptions such as the spasm of aggression associated with John Pope's tenure commanding the short-lived Army of Virginia in 1862. John Dix, in running the Department of Virginia, had generally opposed the destruction of civilian property, hoping his path of moderation would bring throngs of reluctant Southern Unionists back into the fold.[39] But by June 1863, no hidden well of Unionism had emerged in the Commonwealth, and the administration's policies, including the Emancipation Proclamation, had erased any hope of turning the majority of white Southerners against the Confederacy. The Aylett's operation, along with other recent raids in Matthews and King and Queen Counties, suggested there might be a sharper edge to further efforts in the department. Nevertheless, Dix and his lieutenants continued to carefully tailor their orders. For the Aylett's raid, Keyes had instructed Tevis to capture or destroy all supplies for the Confederate army and take horses while excluding anything not of use to the Confederate military.[40]

It was not always an easy task. Such instructions required commanders in the field to judge for themselves what property qualified as legitimate targets and what was purely civilian in nature with no connection to the war effort. Official reports from the spring revealed the difficulty involved with such decisions. In his April account of a raid conducted into King and Queen County, Charles Tevis explained that he destroyed a mill because Confederate pickets were using the grain there to feed their horses and because the owner had "confessed to correspondence with" Confederate leaders. During the same operation, Tevis burned another mill that had ground large amounts of grain "for the use of the Richmond army."[41] Similarly, in May, George Gordon sent men from the 142nd New York on a small expedition to seize grain at the Robinson plantation in King and Queen County after an African American guide informed the Federals that the plantation owner had been "in the habit of shipping grain to Richmond."[42]

During the Aylett's raid, Tevis was pushing boundaries. He identified a wide range of civilian property that, in his opinion, was potentially useful to Confederate troops. In his view, millstones, wheat, flour, bacon, tobacco, cotton, and whiskey—not to mention the barns and buildings—all appeared to qualify as legitimate targets for seizure or ruination. But Tevis's actions during the raid, with its destruction and indiscriminate shelling, may have ruffled feathers. Dix apparently raised concerns about the operation in a telegram to Keyes. In response, Keyes generally expressed support for such missions, arguing that they "have a wonderful effect by producing discontent among the people against the Confederate Government." Keyes predicted that, with continued operations, "the old and sick will call home their sons and brothers to protect their homesteads, and in that way the rebel army will be melted away." In arguing so, he articulated one of the rationales behind the growing shift in Federal strategy toward a harder war.[43]

Despite Dix's concerns, there is no indication Tevis was officially reprimanded for the raid. In fact, Keyes complimented the lieutenant colonel for his "splendid daring."[44] But Tevis would make missteps later in the war, one related to election interference in the fall of 1863 and another involving horse-race betting by his men in New Orleans the next year. He was eventually discharged for the latter infraction in the summer of 1864 but maneuvered successfully several years later to remove the dismissal's stain and even managed to obtain a retrospective promotion to brevet brigadier general, a result engineered by powerful friends.[45]

After the war, Tevis resumed his mercenary lifestyle. In 1866, he became an adjutant general of the Fenian Brotherhood and participated in that organization's failed invasion of Canada. He then worked as a spy for the British minister to the United States, was an officer in Pope Pius IX's army, served as French brigade commander in the Franco-Prussian War, and finally went back to the Egyptian and Turkish armies, eventually sheathing his sword in 1877 to pursue work in diplomacy, journalism, and espionage. In 1900, at the age of seventy-two, he died in Paris and was buried in Montparnasse Cemetery. As historian William Kurtz has suggested, Tevis, despite his relative obscurity, may deserve the rank of "greatest American condottiere of the nineteenth century." Ultimately, the raid on Aylett's may rank as Tevis's largest accomplishment in the Civil War.[46]

"INFERNAL WORK"

The Confederates understood what the Aylett's raid portended. Secretary of War James Seddon was livid. In a letter to Robert E. Lee, he complained that the Yankees "destroy or drive out the whole faithful population, including women, children, and the men, helpless, aged, and infirm." This "atrocious system of warfare," he continued, "has never been practiced by any people professing civilization and Christianity, and must awaken the abhorrence of Christendom, as it has aroused among our people glowing indignation and thirst for vengeance."[47] In addition, General Henry Wise, who had been Virginia's governor several years before but now commanded the collection of units east of Richmond, dwelled on the slaves that the Federals "took off," putting the number at 131.[48]

The Richmond newspapers broadcast the results with their usual flair. According to the *Examiner*, the expedition laid "waste the county of King William with fire and sword—burning the barns, destroying the growing crops, and breaking up the agricultural implements."[49] A story in the *Enquirer* called the raid "infernal work" aimed at preventing civilians from raising food. The editors complained that the Yankees "have brought starvation at once upon helpless women and children." "[T]hey warred, with the torch, against helpless old men, women, and children, and non-combatants. Soldiers of the Confederacy, remember these facts in your next battle."[50] The press predicted additional enemy operations and urged the public to prepare. A correspondent to the *Sentinel* no doubt captured the view of many Confederate loyalists when he concluded: "I hope, soon, the old country will be able to meet them, as her old men and boys are awakened and preparing for a death struggle."[51]

As the Confederates digested accounts of the Aylett's raid, they prepared for more. From the outpost at White House on the Pamunkey, General Wise rode out in the days following the attack to examine the bluffs and ferry crossings along the Mattaponi. He also checked in with Arnold Elzey in Richmond, complaining that neither Pickett nor Pettigrew had made an effort to mobilize and repulse the Yankees at Aylett's.[52] Wise also sought more troops to protect the upper ferries on the Mattaponi and planned to station more cavalry at White House instead of Richmond's defenses. In Richmond, clerks and other employees of various government departments readied to mobilize and fill the fortifications ringing the city.[53]

The raid also caught the attention of the Confederate chief executive. On June 6, President Davis wrote Robert E. Lee about the attack. For his part, Lee, then gathering his forces for the march north, pointed at Pickett, blaming his fellow Virginian for encouraging such enemy operations by failing to respond aggressively to earlier incursions. He admonished Pickett to "drive them back" should the Federals attempt a similar venture. Lee understood his reprimand would serve little immediate purpose, because most of his army, including Pickett's division, would soon form up into the long, winding column headed for the Potomac and beyond.[54]

Federal commanders prepared for more as well. John Dix remained in contact with Hooker and monitored rumors about Lee's northward movement. From Williamsburg on June 9, Dix warned he could not do much with his limited command but nevertheless continued to execute his plans for the two small operations to pressure Richmond, one on the Peninsula and another south on the Blackwater River. "I shall move up the Peninsula from Williamsburg and on the Blackwater from Suffolk on Thursday [June 11]," wrote Dix. "My forces are not large, and on the Peninsula the enemy has appeared in some strength, within two days, so that I do not know how far I can go in that direction." Dix's dispatch did not radiate aggression or energy, and neither did it promise much. Over the next several days, the complexion of matters in Virginia would change as it became clear that Lee was indeed headed for Northern soil. With the bulk of Confederate strength vacating the lines at Fredericksburg, Dix's force would remain on the Peninsula east of Richmond. But soon there would be new instructions for the commander of the Department of Virginia.[55]

4

Halleck's Plans to Counter Lee's Invasion

"GENERAL-IN-CHIEF"

As LEE's FORCE MARCHED AWAY FROM CENTRAL VIRGINIA, Henry Halleck knew the supply lines behind the Army of Northern Virginia would be vulnerable and that Richmond would be, in all likelihood, lightly defended. He sensed an opportunity and began to consider possible operations against the railroads in Virginia and North Carolina, as well as against Richmond itself. He understood that a large-scale offensive was out of the question. With Hooker moving north and the administration prioritizing Washington's safety, there were limited troops available. Nevertheless, Halleck concluded that a modest advance against Richmond, or at least Lee's supply lines, might yield benefits.

By 1863, Henry Wager Halleck had become a central figure in the war effort, a prominent cog in the US military machine. In the antebellum years, he gained professional success as a businessman and lawyer while earning a reputation as a prominent military thinker, in part due to his published translation of works by the influential French theorist Antoine-Henri Jomini. As for Halleck's appearance, one observer wrote, "he was short and stout; his head was large, his eye bright, his expression sharp and searching; his manners gruff and harsh."[1] Like many generals in the army, Halleck was a Democrat. In 1862, he oversaw military operations out West, often managing matters from afar while subordinates such as Ulysses S. Grant gained victories at battles such as Fort Henry, Fort Donelson, and Shiloh. But Halleck made a direct impact, too, by managing successful operations against Corinth. During his tenure in the West, he earned accolades in the press as well as the trust of President Lincoln and Secretary of War Edwin Stanton. In the summer of 1862, Halleck received a promotion and traveled east to serve in Washington as "general-in-chief" in command of all Federal land forces."[2]

Halleck's new role charged him with managing and coordinating

operations across the entire map and facilitating communications between the generals and the War Department. An intelligent, able admin-
istrator who excelled at dealing with logistical issues, he proved adept at
navigating the internal politics of the Lincoln administration. But despite
his many talents, troubling patterns in his performance emerged that may
have diminished his contributions. For some, his initial luster as a military
leader gradually dulled as he began to demonstrate a corrosive tendency
toward indecision. Too often, he failed to make the hard choices that
came with his position, and too often he failed to provide clear, unequivocal directives, instead leaving officers in the field with vague generalities
or recycled Jominian maxims. He also refused to overrule the decisions of
subordinate generals, even when President Lincoln directed such action.
However, where some may have seen a refusal to exercise command,
others have credited Halleck for providing much needed strategic insight
and communication within the administration while giving commanders
on the ground the flexibility to make decisions.[3] Although there were,
and continue to be, differing opinions about Halleck's performance, it is
clear that his vacillation sometimes irritated the president and others in
the administration. For instance, when Halleck refused to provide direction to Ambrose Burnside after the Fredericksburg defeat in late 1862,
an exasperated Lincoln wrote: "Your military skill is useless to me if you
will not do this."[4] Others took an even dimmer view. Secretary of the
Navy Gideon Welles concluded that Halleck "in short, is a moral coward, worth but little except as a critic and director of operations, though
intelligent and educated." Welles later labeled Halleck "heavy-handed;
wants sagacity, readiness, courage, and heart."[5]

Despite these concerns, Lincoln held on to his general-in-chief. Although Halleck may not have performed with the vision and assertive-
ness hoped for by officials such as Welles, he was not lazy. He worked
tirelessly and with conviction. He kept in constant contact with various
departments, sending an endless stream of correspondence to commanders in Virginia (first Burnside, then Hooker), Tennessee (Rosecrans), and
the West (Grant and Nathaniel Banks). In overseeing the various theaters
of operation, he often did little more than offer general directives and
occasional suggestions, believing he was in no position to second-guess
leaders on the ground. He summed up this approach when he wrote: "I
hold that a General in command of any army in the field is the best judge
of existing conditions."[6]

After several months in Washington, the pressures of the position
began to take a toll on Halleck's health. He suffered from insomnia,

exhaustion, and hemorrhoids, which he treated with opioids unwisely supplemented at times with large doses of alcohol. His effectiveness diminished. George Templeton Strong, who visited him as part of a Philadelphia delegation in the fall of 1862, found Halleck "weak, shallow, commonplace, vulgar . . . his silly talk . . . conclusive as to his incapacity."[7] Despite these health challenges, Halleck continued to bear the responsibility for coordinating the Union effort on a grand scale, wrestling with the gaggle of personalities fighting the war, including McClellan, Burnside, Rosecrans, John McClernand, Banks, and Grant. The summer of 1863 brought more difficulties. Rosecrans remained mostly stationary in Tennessee, and Grant struggled to land a lethal blow at Vicksburg. But the immediate crisis appeared in the East in mid-June when Robert E. Lee launched his Northern offensive.

"THREATEN RICHMOND"

By the second week of June, Halleck determined that Lee's departure from central Virginia had created an opening for the Federals. He began to develop a general plan to threaten Richmond. On June 14, he initiated that effort with a note to Dix. At noon that day, a telegram from Halleck in cipher arrived at Dix's headquarters at Fort Monroe: "Lee's army is in motion toward the Shenandoah Valley. All your available force should be concentrated to threaten Richmond, by seizing and destroying their railroad bridges over the South and North Anna Rivers, and do them all the damage possible. If you cannot accomplish this, you can at least find occupation for a large force of the enemy."[8] As the orders indicated, Halleck believed Lee's movement had created vulnerabilities for the Confederates. In addition to Richmond, Halleck had his eyes on other locations as well. Just a few days earlier, he informed John Foster in North Carolina that the Confederates had sent many reinforcements north to bolster Lee's army. He saw an opening in the Old North State. "It is suggested," he told Foster, "that your army corps could resume offensive operations, destroy railroads, &c."[9]

In Virginia, Halleck's directive formed the blueprint for what would become Dix's own Peninsula Campaign: another Federal move against Richmond. Later, questions would arise about Halleck's intent and Dix's interpretation of the general-in-chief's instructions. But those issues lay in the future, and on June 14 Dix understood he needed to gather his department's forces and move on the rebel capital.[10] Dix responded to

Halleck's June 14 orders immediately but could not commit to a move right away because, as he explained, his command suffered from a shortage of transports. In fact, shortly before Halleck's dispatch arrived at Fort Monroe, Secretary of War Stanton had ordered Dix to send all available transports north to Aquia on the Potomac to ferry military stores and sick men from Hooker's army to Alexandria.[11] Dix, whose forces were spread throughout his department, had already begun to comply with Stanton's directive, leaving him with limited means of bringing the troops from Suffolk to the Peninsula.[12] Stanton's request for transports, only minutes before Halleck's orders arrived, suggested little coordination in the national capital. This state of affairs pointed to one conclusion. Dix would not be moving against the Confederate capital anytime soon. Nevertheless, he assured Halleck that he would concentrate all his force and move toward Richmond once the transports returned.[13] Halleck's effort to threaten Lee's communications was not off to a promising start.

In Washington, Lee's offensive had pulled the focus away from Richmond. On the evening of June 14, naval secretary Welles visited the War Department's telegraph office to find President Lincoln, a regular in that room, accompanied by Stanton and a cigar-puffing Halleck. The group discussed rumors about the fall of Winchester, Virginia, and the destruction of the Union garrison under Major General Robert H. Milroy's command there, as well as questions about whether the Confederates would advance to Pennsylvania. Welles was struck by how little information Lincoln appeared to possess of ongoing operations. During the impromptu gathering, Welles also confirmed his decidedly negative view of the general-in-chief. "Halleck does not grow upon me as a military man of power and strength; has little aptitude, skill, or active energy," he wrote later that evening. "In this state of things, the able Rebel general is moving a powerful army, and has no one to confront him on whose ability and power the country relies." Welles also sensed the president and his advisers had lost all confidence in Joseph Hooker, whose reputation for intemperance was working against him.[14]

"TO PREVENT THE ENEMY FROM SENDING RE-ENFORCEMENTS"

When Halleck's orders arrived at Fort Monroe on June 14, Dix was in the middle of his two-pronged, slow-motion operation in southeastern Virginia designed "to prevent the enemy from sending re-enforcements to General Lee from this department." In charge of the first prong, Erasmus Keyes, the Fourth Corps commander, had left Yorktown several days earlier and proceeded up the Peninsula toward the Chickahominy in the direction of Richmond. The operation had not progressed much.[15] Second, John Peck, leading troops from the Seventh Corps, had marched west from Suffolk to threaten Confederate outposts on the Blackwater River but failed to pierce the Confederate screen shielding the railroad bridges.[16]

After receiving Halleck's June 14 orders to go after Richmond, Dix began to reel back his men from the failed Blackwater expedition and Keyes continued to plod up the Peninsula. With the navy's cooperation, Keyes conducted a minor raid at the mouth of the Chickahominy near the James and, in the process, managed to capture a "few horses and cows" but mostly rankled his navy counterparts with his "irregular and objectionable" requests. But otherwise, he accomplished little.[17] By June 16, units from General George Gordon's division in Keyes's Fourth Corps had reached New Kent County.[18] Along the way, the soldiers grappled frequently with bushwhackers. Gordon, back with the Fourth Corps after his West Point occupation, later complained that the irregulars "fired on and murdered my patrols, and there were no houses near to burn in retaliation." One Michigan soldier reported home that twenty men in his unit had been shot by rebel ambushes.[19]

Keyes's tentative advance earned some mention in the Richmond newspapers. Rumors circulated that the Yankees were "laying waste" to the country east of the city. Reports also appeared about Confederate scouts tangling with Union pickets on the roads around Diascund Bridge west of Barhamsville, a spot marking the divide between opposing forces over the previous months. On June 12, John Beauchamp Jones, a prolific, well-sourced clerk and diarist in the Confederate War Department, noted a "street rumor" that the Federals had appeared on the Chickahominy and the James, although no one could tell whether it was an attempt to "embarrass Lee" or a "determined and desperate assault on" the city.[20]

Although the advance caused "considerable excitement" at first, the Confederate press soon labeled the new Federal presence on the Peninsula "a foraging expedition." The *Daily Richmond Examiner* predicted the Union forces would "eat out the substance of the neighborhood, and then proceed to fresh fields and pastures" and would "have their way on the Peninsula and there is none to make them afraid."[21] Writing in his diary from his Marlbourne plantation on June 19, an unhappy Edmund Ruffin blamed Confederate officials for failing to drive off the "robbers &

devastators," who were stealing provisions, taking away enslaved laborers, and hampering crop production. He also noted that many plantation owners in the area had moved away, taking their slaves with them as the Union troops pressed westward.[22]

"NO TIME SHOULD BE LOST"

As Dix's offensive continued to inch along, Halleck, occupied with Lee's movements, wrote on June 18 that "no time should be lost in carrying out the movements proposed for your troops."[23] But time was in fact lost and six days had passed before any of Dix's men had done much of anything. What happened during this time is unclear. When Halleck's June 18 note arrived, Dix had regained some of the transports and had begun shuttling men to the Peninsula. From Suffolk, Brigadier General Isaac Wistar's brigade boarded vessels from Norfolk, and Colonel Samuel P. Spear's cavalry regiment, the 11th Pennsylvania, prepared to do the same. West of Williamsburg, Keyes's force continued to creep along toward Richmond as George Gordon's division pushed across Diascund Bridge.[24] But none of these movements were particularly remarkable, and the Confederates had enjoyed ample opportunity to gather their available forces.

As Dix tried to nudge his command ahead, he considered the best approach for staging his operations against Richmond. The direct route passed overland along the roads running across the narrow York–James Peninsula through New Kent County.[25] But it was the York and the James Rivers, not the roads, that perhaps offered the most promise. To the south, Dix, with the navy's help, could transport his forces up the James and disembark on that river's left bank for an advance through Henrico County southeast of the city. Acting Rear Admiral Stephen Phillips Lee saw potential benefits in such an approach, noting that the navy could contribute two powerful ironclads then stationed in the James. However, this route would first require the time-consuming reduction of Fort Powhatan, a strong rebel work on the right bank of the James due south of Charles City. In addition, and perhaps most important, the James River approach would make it difficult for Dix to reach the bridges north of Richmond, one of Halleck's core goals for the operation.[26]

A better approach perhaps lay with the York River and its tributary, the Pamunkey, which provided an avenue to transport troops directly to White House Landing, McClellan's main base in 1862. A lodgment at White House, which lay only about 20 miles east of Richmond, offered several benefits. It featured a direct water connection to the bases at York-town and Fort Monroe and put Dix's men within striking distance of both the capital and the two key rail lines north of the city. It also sat on the York River Railroad, which ran straight toward Richmond. Dix chose this approach.

He also considered how many men he needed to commit to the advance. He commanded 30,000 troops in his entire department. The Seventh Corps, led directly by Dix in June, and its two divisions under Michael Corcoran and George W. Getty, contained the bulk of this strength. The rest of the troops came mostly from Keyes's Fourth Corps, which included Gordon's division, Rufus King's division, and several detached brigades.[27] Dix decided to bring about two-thirds of his command to White House Landing and leave about 10,000 men behind to guard key locations at Fort Monroe, Norfolk, Yorktown, and other posts. However, still wanting for transports, he could float only so many men up the river.[28]

In advancing on Richmond, Dix would rely on both the roads and waterways. Erasmus Keyes and the Fourth Corps would reach White House overland, pushing up the roads that wound through the countryside between the Chickahominy and the Pamunkey. In addition, the Seventh Corps, as well as cavalry under Samuel Spear, would cram into the available transports and reach White House on the York and Pamunkey Rivers.

As Dix cobbled together the offensive, officers in his command digested reports of Lee's movements northward and weighed the prospects for their own operation.[29] Keyes believed the expedition against Richmond had potential. "If I had 25,000 men and the command of the gunboats. I should without hesitation push on for Richmond at once," he explained to Dix. "If Lee's army is moving up the Shenandoah, I would take the rebel capital or destroy the railroads in its vicinity."[30] Dix himself would express similar thoughts to Admiral Lee several days later, musing that, with 10,000 additional men, he could "go into Richmond without any difficulty."[31]

In Washington, officials saw promise in Dix's project as well. The potential advantage was hard to ignore. During a cabinet meeting on June 16 held amid the drama playing out between Hooker, Lincoln, and Halleck, Secretary of the Treasury Salmon P. Chase suggested that operations against Richmond might disturb Lee's offensive and asked whether Union forces could, at the least, demonstrate against the rebel capital. According to Navy Secretary Welles's notes, Lincoln gave the suggestion "no countenance." For his part, Halleck apparently chose not to weigh in on the Richmond question but, according to Welles, simply sat there smoking, swearing, and scratching his arms, an odd posture given his orders to Dix only two days before. Perhaps, Welles's diary failed to capture the entire discussion. In any case, Halleck's behavior at the meeting certainly reinforced Welles's negative impression; he wrote afterward that the general-in-chief "exhibits little military capacity or intelligence; is obfuscated, muddy, uncertain, stupid, as to what is doing or to be done."[32]

Some in the Northern press agreed with Chase and supported an offensive against Richmond. On June 17, a suspiciously well informed story in the *New York Daily Herald* succinctly laid out the case for an advance on the city while also taking a swipe at Halleck. "It behooves us to look to the rear of the enemy, and not only endeavor to cut off a retreat, but capture the rebel capital, with its immense fortifications," which, in the writer's estimation, was "for the present almost without a garrison." According to the column, success would "be the greatest achievement of the war." The author encouraged action. "Let the Seventh Army Corps be at once ordered to advance on Richmond."[33] Several days later, an editorial in the *Herald* raised the issue again, arguing that additional troops were available for the assault and predicting that Dix, with 20,000 men, could take the city "now almost destitute of troops . . . without difficulty." In the editors' view, the effort would either capture Richmond outright or force Lee to return to defend it, allowing Hooker to gobble up his forces in detail. Edmund Ruffin, who continued to observe events from his plantation, agreed that such an approach might be a "good notion" for the Yankees, but he predicted Dix would not have adequate strength to threaten Richmond, though he might do immense harm by "marauding & damaging raids."[34]

Nearly ten days after Halleck's initial orders, Dix finally got things properly moving. On June 23, he issued a directive for Spear's cavalry to board transports and steam from Yorktown up the York River and then the Pamunkey to White House.[35] In addition, units from Keyes's Fourth Corps received instructions to pack five days of rations, load three wagons for every regiment, and march from their camps then at Williamsburg and Barhamsville.[36] Furthermore, men from the Seventh Corps continued to board boats at Suffolk headed for the Peninsula. As one Connecticut soldier recalled, "while enjoying the oysters, crabs, peaches, and sweet potatoes to be had in abundance, the regiment was ordered up the Peninsula." Richmond lay ahead.[37]

5

Richmond's Defenders

"NEGLECT NO HONORABLE MEANS OF DIVIDING AND WEAKENING OUR ENEMIES"

ROBERT E. LEE, RIDING NORTH WITH HIS MEN toward Pennsylvania in June, grappled with more than the details of the coming military campaign. Political matters occupied his mind. In his letters to Richmond at the time, he revealed a clear appreciation that battlefield victories alone would not win the war. He understood the Confederates had limited time to achieve their independence and that the Federal advantage in materiel and men, girded by Northern political support, would eventually doom the rebel war effort. "We have no right to look for exemptions from the military consequence of a vigorous use of these advantages," Lee counseled. He also knew the Confederacy's resources were diminishing while the enemy's were "steadily augmenting." In correspondence with Jefferson Davis, he discussed the impact of recent victories in shaping Northern opinion and fueling the rebellion's prospects. His letters to the Confederate president suggest the issue had become a matter of great concern. In three separate dispatches during June, Lee discussed Northern dissatisfaction with the war and the need to stoke opposition against Lincoln among the electorate. He also remained attuned to the acrimony generated by the Copperheads, including the recent row involving Clement Vallandigham. In essence, Lee hoped efforts to encourage dissatisfied elements in the North would help bring about a negotiated peace before the brutal computation of men and supply produced an inevitable Confederate defeat.[1]

In a June 10 letter from Culpeper, Lee urged President Davis to drive the wedge deeper. "We should neglect no honorable means of dividing and weakening our enemies," he wrote, adding that Confederate leaders should give "all the encouragement we can" to the "rising peace party of the North." Lee asked Davis to make common cause with anyone seeking a cessation to the hostilities. In doing so, he recommended Davis ignore "nice distinctions" between those pushing for peace at any price, including letting the Confederacy go its own way, and those seeking to restore the Union. Lee firmly viewed an independent Confederacy as the prize, and in his view, any negotiations, no matter how half-hearted, would help that cause.[2] He emphasized the point again in a letter written near the Potomac River on June 25, in which he explained that everything designed to "repress the war feeling in the Federal States will inure to our benefit." In short, Lee believed it was a good time for the politicians to talk, and Davis, who generally welcomed Lee's advice, heartily concurred.[3]

"WEAK AND FRAIL FROM MY CRADLE"

Far to the south in central Georgia, Vice President Alexander Stephens also sensed opportunity in June following Lee's recent victories in Virginia. From Liberty Hall, his plantation in Crawfordville, the vice president cultivated thoughts of diplomacy and a proposal to bring US officials to the bargaining table. Stephens was a conspicuous, enigmatic figure on the Confederate landscape. Two years before, the nascent Confederate Congress had handed the vice presidency to this former Whig and Unionist, expecting that the Georgian's presence in the government would shore up support for the rebellion in the Upper South. Once appointed, Stephens firmly embraced the Confederate cause. His so-called Cornerstone Speech, delivered in March 1861 at the Savannah Athenaeum, laid bare the true goal of secessionist leaders and would make a lie to any later claim that something other than slavery lay at the core of the Confederacy's heart. During his iconic speech, Stephens proclaimed the new Confederate government's "foundations are laid, its cornerstone rests, upon the great truth that the negro is not equal to the white man; that slavery, subordination to the superior race, is his natural and normal condition."[4] Stephens's words would echo in the state secession ordinances as well as in the speeches of Southern secession commissioners who crisscrossed the South marketing disunion.[5] By the summer of 1863, Stephens believed the time was ripe to broach the notion of peace with his enemies in the North.

Neither magnetic nor imposing, Stephens was, instead, a sickly wisp of a man. In his youth, his 5-foot, 7-inch frame carried only 94 pounds. In his wartime photographs, the middle-aged Stephens had the look of a tired, ailing, unkempt schoolboy. To be sure, he suffered a variety of illnesses throughout his life, including neuralgia and rheumatism. "Weak and frail from my cradle," he once wrote, "my whole life has been one of constant physical pain. Health I have never known." He never married. His closest companion and confidant was his younger half-brother, Linton Stephens, a Georgia lawmaker who lived in Sparta about 20 miles south of Liberty Hall. The two corresponded constantly on topics ranging from Confederate politics to the management of their respective plantations. In his personal relations with friends and family, Stephens was thoughtful and warm, particularly with those close to him. However, in official dealings, he could be aggressive, arrogant, and close-minded. He held himself out as a self-proclaimed "champion of human rights"— although not for Black people, of course—and often focused rigidly on "constitutional principles" to the detriment of other considerations.[6]

In the years prior to the Civil War, the vice presidency had been a post of little consequence in the government of the United States. Through 1863, that role in the Confederacy had been no different. The Cornerstone Speech aside, Stephens's tangible contributions to the rebellion had been minimal. He visited Richmond infrequently and chose to spend most of the war at his Georgia plantation. During his Confederate career, he often played the role of political commentator, lobbing his personal observations at Richmond, a practice the helped earn his later sobriquet "the Sage of Liberty Hall."[7]

In the first years of the war, Stephens occasionally advised legislators and gave speeches, but he mostly produced heaps of letters stuffed with opinions. Although he generally avoided broadcasting his views publicly, his private correspondence over the course of the war took aim at several Confederate policies implemented by President Davis, including conscription, the suspension of habeas corpus, and impressment. Still, his letters sometimes found their way into the newspapers and attracted attention, a public airing not always welcome by his fellow Confederate leaders. Predictably, as the vice president sounded off far away from Richmond, he did not forge a particularly firm bond with Davis, though, at least according to Stephens, their relationship remained cordial in 1863.[8]

In April, Stephens made one of his infrequent visits to Richmond and met with Davis for a few hours. At the War Department, he popped into clerk John Beauchamp Jones's office for a minute with, according to Jones, the look of one "afflicted with all manner of diseases" who seemed destined for "speedy dissolution." However, Jones, who knew Stephens had borne this appearance for decades and was not alarmed, saw a spark in the diminutive Georgian's eyes and judged the vice president's mind was "in the meridian of intellectual vigor."[9]

After returning home to Georgia, Stephens drew encouragement from the victory at Chancellorsville and continued to hope for progress on the political front. The win in Virginia and Grant's slow going at Vicksburg spurred the vice president to consider, as he later put it ever vaguely, "a freer discussion of these momentous questions." He also watched, with earnest hope, as Copperheads stirred up the Northern populace. On June 12, two days after Lee's letter from Culpeper urging Davis to explore diplomatic measures, Stephens wrote the president about opening discussions with Northern officials, offering his own services for the task.[10] Stephens recommended approaching the Federals specifically on the issue of the failing prisoner exchange system. The cartel had traveled a rough road. By June, it was clear the arrangement forged by D. H. Hill and John Dix the year before had begun to unravel. In late 1862, Davis blocked the parole of Union officers in retaliation for the execution of a New Orleans citizen ordered by Major General Benjamin Butler. Shortly afterward, matters degraded further when Confederate officials refused to exchange captured Black soldiers who had joined the Federal ranks following the Emancipation Proclamation.[11] Weighted down by these various issues, the prisoner exchange had mostly ceased altogether by May.

Suspension of the cartel generated stress on both sides. The excess of prisoners strained transportation networks, burdened military prisons, and generally raised the stakes for men captured in combat. With parole and exchange no longer likely, prisoners now facing prolonged confinement looked for ways to escape by any means necessary. A particularly dramatic event in the waters off Fort Monroe in early June clearly illustrated the shift. About a hundred Confederate prisoners aboard the steamer *Maple Leaf* in Hampton Roads turned on their guards and commandeered the vessel after learning that a Northern prison, instead of a quick exchange, lay in their future. After a "sudden and violent" assault, they piloted the boat south, disembarking in Princess Anne County, evading enemy cavalry patrols, and eventually reaching Richmond. The *Maple Leaf* incident represented only the beginning. The cartel's breakdown would generate more dramatic escape attempts in the years to come.[12]

In addition to monitoring developments with the overall cartel, Stephens paid particular attention to the issue of Black US prisoners. In April, he became alarmed by a letter to President Davis from Major General David Hunter, then in command of Union troops at Port Royal, South Carolina. Asserting that the "United States flag must protect all its defenders, white, black, and yellow," Hunter complained that several African Americans soldiers, captured by Confederates, had been "cruelly murdered" and others sold into slavery. Hunter threatened to retaliate by executing "the Rebel of highest rank in my possession; man for man," for every Black US soldier murdered or sold into slavery. Hunter concluded his letter to the Confederate president with this pointed broadside:

> You say you are fighting for liberty. Yes, you are fighting for liberty—liberty to keep 4,000,000 of your fellow-beings in ignorance and degradation; liberty to separate parents and children, husband and wife, brother and sister; liberty to steal the products of their labor, exacted with many a cruel lash and bitter tear; liberty to seduce their wives and daughters, and to sell your own children into bondage; liberty to kill these children with impunity, when the murder cannot be proven by one of pure white blood. This is the kind of liberty—the liberty to do wrong—which Satan, chief of the fallen angels, was contending for when he was cast into hell.[13]

Hunter's unbridled appraisal outraged Stephens, who later described the dispatch as having a "character not much short of savage." But the vice president also believed the letter had furnished a potential angle for Confederate negotiations. Indeed, on top of his genuine concern with the cartel, it seems Stephens viewed the exchange policy as a hook for broader negotiations with Union officials. He hoped Hunter's provocation might lead to further "conferences" between Confederate leaders and Washington officials, talks that might reach beyond the narrow matter of prisoner exchange. In his June 12 letter to Davis, he explained:

> I think possibly I might be able to do some good—not only on the immediate subject in hand; but were I in conference with the authorities at Washington on any point in relation to the conduct of the war, I am not without hopes, that indirectly, I could now turn attention to a general adjustment, upon such basis as might ultimately be acceptable to both parties, and stop the further effusion of blood in a contest so irrational, unchristian, and so inconsistent with all recognized American principles.[14]

In this typically convoluted sentence, Stephens proposed to use the prisoner exchange issue as a means to discuss more fundamental issues. He hoped to talk with US officials about a "general adjustment" to "stop the further effusion of blood." In essence, it appears that Stephens wanted to broach a negotiated end to the war and achieve a settlement that recognized "the Sovereignty of the States, and the right of each in its Sovereign capacity to determine its own destiny." Not knowing that Lee was already on the march northward, Stephens believed it was time to reach out to Union officials during a period of relative tranquility when the armies in the East were not actively engaged in combat and, as he would explain later, "disaffection was springing throughout the North."[15]

An air of mystery hangs around the specifics of Stephens's proposal. He cloaked his June 12 letter to Davis in vague phrases and generalities. In later years, he would claim he had not proposed a "peace mission at all."[16] But the June 12 letter belies that assertion. Although his general intent was clear, his particular goal or angle remains hidden in the tangled words of his proposal. Nevertheless, it seems Stephens hoped to use the failing prisoner exchange to propose a broader, negotiated peace. In addition, his preoccupation with Hunter's proclamation suggests a special interest in a specific aspect of the prisoner exchange issue, namely the free and formerly enslaved Black men fighting for the United States. Stephens may have had other issues on his mind as well, such as foreign involvement or the need to generate sympathy in public opinion in the North and South by forcing Lincoln to reject a Confederate peace offer.

Whatever Stephens's precise intentions, Davis embraced the general plan. From Richmond, he wired the vice president: "Yours of the 12th. Inst. Just received. Please come here at your earliest convenience."[17] As Stephens packed his bags for Richmond, he did not share the details of his upcoming trip with Linton but merely referred vaguely to recent correspondence with Davis. "Be careful and do not speak of me being called to Richmond," he pled on July 22.[18] With that, he boarded a train for Virginia.[19]

"A THOUSAND CONJECTURES"

On a Sunday morning in the spring of 1861, days after Virginia state troops seized key US installations, Richmond's church bells began to ring unexpectedly. As services abruptly ended and apprehensive worshipers emptied into the cobblestone streets, the reason behind the clamor soon became clear. The Union gunboat *Pawnee* was reportedly steaming up the James River to bombard the city. Confusion and panic followed. "The streets were alive with men and boys rallying from all points with every description of weapons," wrote an onlooker.[20] A cry echoed through the streets: "The Pawnee, with thousands aboard, is approaching the city!" Sallie Brock, a nurse, later recalled: "Hasty embraces, sudden wrenchings of the hand, tearful glances of affection, and our men rushed to their armories to prepare they knew not for what."[21]

To meet the threat, members of the 1st Virginia Infantry regiment marched out of the city as a band played the popular ballad "Ever of Thee I'm Fondly Dreaming." Old men and young boys, many armed with double-barreled shotguns crammed with buckshot, answered the call as well and lined up in the ranks at Rocketts Landing, prepared to repel the invaders. Artillery teams pulled caissons, limbers, and guns southeast through Henrico County toward Fort Powhatan on the James. In the suburbs, some defenders stood in the ranks for nearly four hours waiting for the attack. But the *Pawnee*, which never made it past Newport News, did not appear; and Richmond's anxiety decreased, at least for a time. The incident soon became known as "Pawnee Sunday," a phrase often repeated during subsequent emergencies later in the war and even afterward when people looked back at the conflict. The very name became a feared specter, "a raw head and bloody bones, to men, women, and children," recalled one resident.[22]

By the summer of 1863, Richmond had endured a string of Pawnee Sundays. Throughout the Peninsula Campaign the previous year, the citizenry had remained on edge during a series of brutal, large-scale engagements only a few miles east of downtown. During the Chancellorsville Campaign in the spring, George Stoneman's raid had rattled nerves as Yankee riders tore through Hanover County north of the city. There were other Federal threats. In fact, by the summer, the editors of Richmond's *Daily Dispatch* counted eight "On to Richmond" efforts by US forces up to that point in the war.[23] In June, with the Army of Northern Virginia far to the north, Richmonders listened for news of Lee's progress as fresh reports about the threat of John Dix's troops to the east appeared in the papers. "Everybody is awaiting with impatience for the news beyond the border, and as accounts come in slow and not altogether reliable, the anxiety increases rather than diminishes," wrote a North Carolina soldier in John R. Cooke's brigade, stationed below Richmond.[24]

Word from Lee's army to the north was spotty. During the third week of June, stories of Lieutenant General Richard S. Ewell's Winchester victory appeared in the newspapers. Days later, when hundreds of Union prisoners from that battle arrived in Richmond, residents rushed to see these "very dirty" men; and locals stepped forward to exchange bread with the Northerners for much-coveted Yankee greenbacks. But beyond scattered rumors about Lee's offensive, little was known about what was happening. "There are a thousand conjectures as to General Lee's present destination," wrote the *Examiner*. "Pittsburgh, Chambersburg, Harrisburg, Philadelphia, and Washington are all mentioned as the point at which he is aiming. But, on this subject, as little is known here as at the North, though there is not quite the same degree of anxiety."[25]

Soon, more stories about the invasion appeared as Lee's vanguard neared the Potomac. On June 20, the *Sentinel* reported that the Confederates had captured Harpers Ferry, and two days later the *Examiner* put Major General Robert Rodes's division from Ewell's Second Corps at Hagerstown, Longstreet's First Corps at Harpers Ferry, and General Lee himself at Winchester. Word also arrived that the Confederates had destroyed sections of the valuable Baltimore and Ohio Railroad. The papers also covered the news from Vicksburg. For months, the safety of that Confederate citadel had preoccupied citizens and officials alike as Ulysses S. Grant looked for a way to invest the city and starve the Confederates there into submission. In June, Richmonders hoped for a miracle on the Mississippi, and rumors circulated about large Confederate reinforcements headed for beleaguered Vicksburg.[26]

But while Lee's and Grant's efforts captured the attention of many, Confederate officials also worried about Richmond's safety in light of reports that John Dix's column was ascending the Peninsula. They knew what the city's fall would yield. Over the previous two years, Richmond had become not only the Confederacy's political heart but also a busy economic and military center. Its loss would not only threaten Lee's connections south but also possibly deliver a lethal punch to the rebellion.

From the war's first days, thousands of newcomers arrived to work in the city's armories and ironworks and to staff the various departments of a growing bureaucracy. In addition, enslaved people, many hired out by their rural owners, filled Richmond. In the spring of 1863, more than battles and raids drew the attention of old residents and new arrivals. In March, a horrific explosion had devastated the Confederate Laboratory on Brown's Island, killing more than thirty workers, many of them young women employed at the facility.[27] The next month, more than a thousand women conducted a protest in the city's center and demanded that Governor John Letcher address the scarcity of food. The Richmond "bread riot," which followed several other similar events in the South but was by far the largest and best organized, underscored increasing dissent in the Confederacy fueled by declining economic conditions.[28]

Other issues occupied the minds of the city's residents. During 1863, the threat of Union espionage had become a growing concern for the Confederate citizenry. Many Richmonders remained loyal to the Union throughout the war, and some served their country as spies against the Confederacy. Notable among these Richmond operatives was Elizabeth Van Lew, a wealthy Church Hill resident who helped steer a loosely organized but effective consort that gathered military information for US generals and helped captive Federals escape the city's military prisons. Stories appeared in the newspapers about various Confederate investigations to combat these efforts. For instance, that summer, the papers buzzed with accounts of the arrest and interrogation of Theodore Woodall, a Confederate detective accused of providing information to the Federals.[29] In addition, officials arrested Mary Caroline Allan, wife of the prominent Virginian Patterson Allan, in July for sending sensitive information north to General John Dix's father.[30]

Confederate officials also looked to the city's physical defenses. From the war's first weeks, they had dispatched soldiers and slaves into the suburbs to improve the fortifications. Progress was slow as the work moved forward in starts and stops. In January 1863, the chief Confederate engineer, Jeremy Gilmer, sought more than 500 men from slave owners in the city to dig works. Two months later, he expanded his request to impress enslaved persons from twenty-nine surrounding counties. He also directed officials to force several thousand free and enslaved Black men to toil on the fortifications during the spring, while fending off complaints from unhappy slave owners irked about losing their bondsmen.[31]

As the spring of 1863 arrived, a three-ring defensive network began to take shape.[32] In the first layer, which lay about two miles from the Capitol, more than a dozen large, detached, star-shaped forts formed the interior line. The second ring contained a nearly continuous curtain of earthworks and battery positions, punctuated every few hundred yards by lunettes and redans. This second "intermediate" line stretched from Westham Iron Works west of town on the banks of the James, then wrapped north and east, and then south around the city linking back to the river. Finally, a third "outer" line contained a less-cohesive collection of detached batteries, rifle pits, and trench segments well north and east of the city, tracing the Chickahominy and its tributary Brook Run.

Gilmer and his officers also attended to the safety of the two railroads connecting Richmond to points north, the Virginia Central and RF&P. In the middle of May, Brigadier General Johnston Pettigrew, in charge of forces at Hanover Junction, worried that Gordon's Federals at West Point would not only conduct minor raids and harbor "runaway slaves" but also "march up in force, threaten the railroad north of North Anna, perhaps attack it, or cross suddenly at Hanover Court-House."

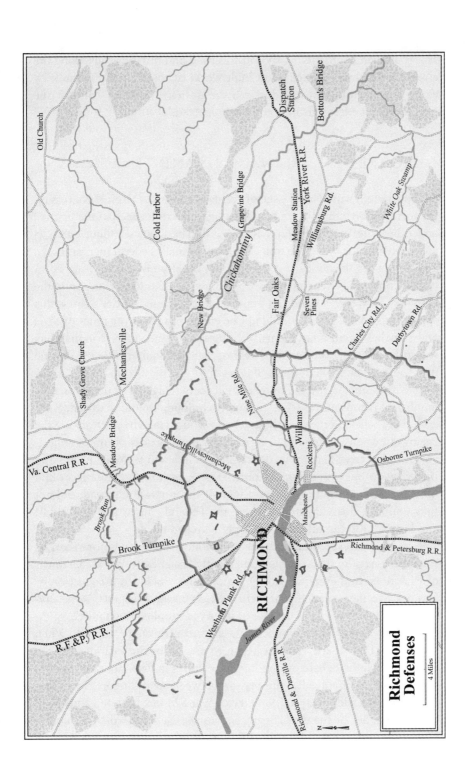

Old Church

Cold Harbor

Grapevine Bridge

Chickahominy

New Bridge

Shady Grove Church

Mechanicsville

Meadow Bridge

Va. Central R.R.

Brook Run

Brook Turnpike

R.F.&P. R.R.

Dispatch Station

Bottom's Bridge

Meadow Station
York River R.R.

Williamsburg Rd.

White Oak Swamp

Fair Oaks

Seven
Pines

Charles City Rd.

Darbytown Rd.

Nine Mile Rd.

Mechanicsville Turnpike

Williams

Rocketts

Osborne Turnpike

Manchester

Richmond & Petersburg R.R.

Westham Plank Rd.

RICHMOND

James River

Richmond & Danville R.R.

**Richmond
Defenses**

4 Miles

N

He recommended fortifying the various road and rail crossings along the rivers. In turn, the Confederates built works at the South Anna and, by early June, an officer there declared the position "strong," though the lines were not extensive and remained untested.[33]

"AGGRESSIVE, PUGNACIOUS AND TENACIOUS"

Troop strength was also an issue of constant concern. Despite progress on the fortifications, there were rarely enough men to protect all the bridges and other vital points around Richmond. The city's standing garrison and part-time local defense units could repel small Federal incursions. In addition, a few heavy battery companies, cavalry units, and other commands constantly occupied a few positions at various locations within the network. However, should Dix bring a large force to the city's gates, this sprinkling of local forces would not be enough to cover the miles of forts and trenches against large enemy columns. Instead, rebel commanders would have to rely on a mobile defense, which required them to shuttle men to the right spots in times of crisis.[34]

In early summer 1863, Confederate leaders struggled to determine the number of troops necessary to defend Richmond. Opinions varied. Robert E. Lee, believing the city's best defense would come from attacking the enemy elsewhere, wanted to bring as many units as possible into Pennsylvania. In his view, Federal leaders were less likely to threaten Richmond if they were busy repelling a Confederate invasion. Other officers and officials, particularly those responsible for defending Richmond, did not fully embrace this view and worried the Federals might call Lee's bluff and lunge at the capital while his army marched north.

No one, however, doubted that Richmond would need more than its standing garrison. The troops permanently assigned to the Department of Richmond and commanded by Arnold Elzey included a collection of about 5,000 men, made up of Henry Wise's infantry brigade, some cavalry, and the various local defense units. As Lee looked to go north, questions arose about which units would stay to protect the capital. When the Army of Northern Virginia began to uncoil for the long march into Pennsylvania, the debate over troop dispositions in Richmond heated up. The discussion involved a tug-of-war between many actors, including Lee, Elzey, President Davis, Secretary of War Seddon, and, most notably, the commander of the department encompassing southern Virginia and North Carolina, Daniel Harvey Hill.[35]

D. H. Hill was difficult to ignore. He possessed a bright mind, an aggressive confidence, deeply held religious beliefs, and a sarcastic wit—a mix of qualities that, for better or worse, set him apart from many of his colleagues. Earlier in his career, he distinguished himself in fighting during the Mexican–American War and then joined the faculty at Washington College in Lexington, Virginia, where he taught mathematics and published books about calculus and Christianity. He then moved to North Carolina in 1854 to teach at Davidson College. At the outbreak of the Civil War, he served as the colonel of the 1st North Carolina Infantry, leading the regiment at Big Bethel. He rose rapidly in command, receiving promotion to brigadier general and then major general. During the campaign outside Richmond in 1862, he commanded a division at Seven Pines and demonstrated an acumen for independent decision-making. At South Mountain during the Maryland Campaign, he played a key role in delaying Union forces, which helped Lee to consolidate his dangerously dispersed units. During the fighting at Antietam, Hill led his division at the Sunken Road, and at the moment of great crisis, pulled together enough men to hold that key position.[36]

In addition to his capacity for command, Hill demonstrated unusual resolve and fearlessness in combat. At Seven Pines, with many of his men under heavy fire for the first time, he mounted his horse, shoved a cigar in his mouth, and rode slowly along the battle line in full view of his men and the enemy. This was no isolated example. Hill was a consistent, conspicuous presence to his men in the heat of battle. A South Carolina veteran recalled that Hill "seemed to go from choice into the most dangerous place he could find on the field." A Virginia gunner recalled that Hill was "as aggressive, pugnacious and tenacious as a bull-dog, or as any soldier in the service, and he had a sort of monomania on the subject of personal courage."[37]

Hill was also a master of the quip. He occasionally adorned his correspondence with clever turns of phrase, witticisms, and unusual statements. In rejecting a brigade band's request for furlough, he wrote "shooters before tooters." In a battle report in 1862, he observed how his men's fire at the enemy "was followed by the most rapid running I ever saw." He also concluded a dispatch to the secretary of war saying, "I hope that you have had the patience to read this long letter."[38]

But Hill's willingness to stray from convention had its downsides. In dealing with fellow officers and men in the ranks, he too often exhibited a remarkable lack of tact and unwisely shared his judgment of others' combat performance. In the midst of the fighting at Seven Pines, for instance, he openly criticized Brigadier General William Mahone's Virginians, earning an immediate rebuke from Mahone, who denounced the "mendacious slander" told by an "infamous liar and coward." The Virginia veterans never forgot the exchange or ceased to express their disgust with Hill's statements. At Malvern Hill, Hill openly chastised Brigadier General Robert Toombs for dereliction, reportedly shouting into the middle of the fight: "[Y]ou are the man who pretends to have been spoiling for a fight. For shame! Rally your troops! Where were you when I was riding up and down your line rallying our troops?" Following the battle, the Georgian demanded "satisfaction," but Hill rejected the challenge out of hand on principle and agreed to apologize—but only if Toombs could demonstrate that the criticism had been unfounded. Though Hill won the exchange, he made an enemy of the frustrated and angry Toombs, who labeled Hill a "poltroon."[39]

Hill did not limit his indiscretions to the heat of the battlefield. He filled his official and not-so-official dispatches with biting, often sarcastic observations and criticisms. He openly shared his opinions with apparently little concern for the consequences, going out of his way to comment on matters well beyond his immediate responsibility. He seemed unable to restrain himself or, perhaps, naively believed his superiors would welcome unsolicited criticisms from a division commander. Often long and overly detailed, his reports and letters brimmed with observations, criticisms, and recommendations. He did not hesitate to call out his subordinates where he saw fault and routinely commented on the actions and plans of those above him, even the army commander. In opining on orders issued by Lee during the Seven Days battles, Hill noted that the "result, as might have been anticipated, was a disastrous and bloody repulse." After Malvern Hill, he asserted the battle would have been a success "had not our artillery and infantry been fought in detail." Following the Maryland Campaign, he took aim at Lee's decision to separate his division from Longstreet's. Had Lee kept the two formations together, the "Yankees would have been disastrously repulsed," carped Hill. It got worse. He went on to gripe about the rations his men received and then detailed the "three causes" behind the Confederate army's failure to attain a "glorious victory" in Maryland: lack of concentration, poor artillery management, and straggling—all matters largely outside Hill's responsibility.[40]

Predictably, over the course of the 1862 campaigns, Robert E. Lee developed a decidedly negative view of Hill. After the Seven Days, Lee stated in correspondence with the president. "I fear General Hill is not entirely equal to his present position. An excellent executive officer, he does not appear to have much administrative ability. Left to himself he seems embarrassed and backward to act." During the Maryland Campaign, Hill became implicated in the infamous "Lost Order" episode, when Union soldiers recovered a copy of Lee's operational orders destined for Hill's headquarters. Though responsibility for that fumble did not ultimately stick to Hill, the incident surely did not help his reputation.[41]

Beyond his tactlessness, Hill's personal health perhaps stood out as his main liability. Throughout 1862, he suffered from severe back pain. In fact, at the beginning of 1863, he announced his intention to resign from the army because of his illness. However, after much cajoling from his friends, he remained and soon found himself responsible for operations in North Carolina and southeastern Virginia. In the spring of 1863, he conducted limited operations against New Bern and Little Washington and coordinated matters with James Longstreet during the siege of Suffolk.[42] From his headquarters at Petersburg, Hill oversaw the defense of a long front stretching from the James River south to Wilmington, an area that included Suffolk, Weldon, Rocky Mount, Goldsboro, and Kinston as well as the Wilmington and Weldon Railroad. To protect this vast area in the summer of 1863, he needed men. His department contained about 22,000, mostly concentrated in seven brigades. But three of those units, Matt Ransom's and John R. Cooke's North Carolina brigades along with Micah Jenkins's South Carolina brigade, belonged to Lee's army and might be called north at any time.[43]

In May, Hill's desire for troops to cover his department triggered an awkward tug-of-war with Lee himself, who was looking to bring every unit he could find with him to Pennsylvania. Seeking some sort of arrangement in a letter to Secretary Seddon, Hill proposed to hand over several of his own full-strength brigades in exchange for depleted, veteran ones in Lee's army.[44] When Seddon forwarded Hill's dispatch to Lee, the army commander rejected the proposition, arguing that the exchange would reduce the Army of Northern Virginia's "real strength" and would leave him with "more to feed but less to depend on." Exchange or no, Lee urged Hill to send as many units as he could spare based "upon the strength of the enemy in your front."[45] Finally, he asked Hill to return Ransom's and Cooke's veteran brigades back to where they belonged: in the Army of Northern Virginia. In his response to Lee's overtures, Hill did not strike a cooperative chord. Instead, he refused to detach any troops from his department without "positive orders."[46]

Lee obliged. On May 25, he directly ordered Hill to send Ransom's brigade up from North Carolina and Micah Jenkins's brigade, then on the Blackwater River, to rejoin Pickett's division near Hanover Junction. To cushion the loss, Lee allowed Hill to hold on to Cooke "for the present" and offered Brigadier General Beverly Robertson as well.[47] But the matter did not end there. Hill wrote Davis directly to complain about the arrangements. The president, in turn, asked Lee whether removal of Ransom, Cooke, and Jenkins from Hill's command would "abandon the country to the enemy."[48]

Hill's stubbornness exasperated Lee. When given discretionary instructions, Hill had refused to make a decision. When given positive orders, he balked and complained. Lee threw up his hands and vented his frustration to Davis. "I am unable to operate under these circumstances, and request to be relieved from any control of the department from the James to the Cape Fear River." Lee also identified the various units that had been (or would be) swapped and transferred between his army and Hill's department.[49] But Lee was done with the frustrating exchange and suspended his orders, directing Hill to wait for further instructions from Richmond.[50] The same day, the War Department, no doubt at the president's behest, asked Hill to identify the units he could spare for General Lee. Davis also sent a conciliatory note to Lee, which rejected the Virginian's request to be relieved of responsibilities for North Carolina and, instead, suggested Lee take command of all operations along "the Atlantic slope." Lee did not embrace the suggestion.[51]

In pressing the manpower issue, D. H. Hill had riled Lee and surely further damaged his reputation with Confederate officials. He sincerely believed the troop transfers would leave the Wilmington railroad vulnerable, a serious threat to the Confederacy as a whole. He also worried about Lee's plans for an offensive. In fact, he later privately questioned the wisdom of Lee's movement north. To his wife, he wrote: "Genl. Lee is venturing upon a very hazardous movement and one that must be fruitless, if not disastrous."[52] Hill, however, was playing a losing game. If President Davis was going to pick sides in such a dispute, he would not choose Hill. Indeed, in a long letter to Lee, a contrite Davis expressed his "regret that I did not earlier know all that you had communicated to others" and his desire to meet Lee's need, confiding "as I always do, as well in your judgment as in your information."[53]

The War Department finally resolved the matter by ordering Jenkins's and Ransom's brigades to remain with Hill and sending Joseph Davis's brigade, a mix of green and tested regiments, and Cooke's Tar Heel veterans north to join Lee, though the latter would be delayed at Richmond.[54] The final arrangement also clarified the number of troops available to protect Richmond and points south. Hill's department contained five brigades—under commanders Clingman, Colquitt, Martin, Jenkins, and Ransom—to cover eastern North Carolina and southeastern Virginia, as well as the miles of rail line connecting Wilmington to Richmond. Each of the five units contained roughly 2,000 men, with Ransom's being the largest with an effective strength of 2,897 at the end of May.[55]

"ANY APPREHENSION OF AN ATTACK UPON RICHMOND"

In contrast to Hill, Robert E. Lee continued to show little concern about the number of troops covering the capital and rails to the south and instead hoped to protect Richmond by threatening Washington. Even while on the road to Pennsylvania, he considered new ways to throw the Federals off balance. In a June 23 letter to Davis written from his field headquarters, Lee suggested an unorthodox plan. He recommended that Davis strip troops from the Carolinas and bring them to Culpeper under P. G. T. Beauregard's command. "It would not only effect a diversion most favorable for this army," he asserted, "but would, I think, relieve us of any apprehension of an attack upon Richmond during our absence."[56] Lee believed Beauregard's presence would enhance "even a small demonstration, and tend greatly to perplex and confound the enemy." Lee raised the suggestion again in a letter two days later from Williamsport, Maryland, on the Potomac. Fueled by rumors that his foray north had already drawn Union troops from all points, he expected Beauregard's army at Culpeper, "even in effigy," would afford significant relief elsewhere. It was an audacious suggestion typical of Lee. He was reading the enemy. Two years of campaigning had convinced him Federal commanders and officials would look to Washington's safety above all else and give little thought to a counterstroke should an opening appear. Lee now hoped an additional Confederate threat in the form of Beauregard's shadow army at Culpeper would inoculate Richmond from any serious hazard.[57]

President Davis, however, focused on the immediate threat to Richmond. As Dix slowly shifted his forces toward White House on the Pamunkey, the alarm sounded in the rebel capital. On June 20, signal officers learned US troops in Suffolk had gathered at Yorktown and "that a demonstration upon Richmond [was] expected with not less than 20,000 men." The next day, Davis passed this information on to Arnold Elzey, still commanding the forces in the capital, and warned that the enemy was moving with the "avowed purpose of advancing upon" the city.[58]

To bolster Richmond's defense force, Secretary Seddon called on D. H. Hill to send units north. With Cooke's brigade already in Richmond, Hill brought Ransom's brigade from Petersburg north to Drewry's Bluff and ordered Jenkins's command to abandon the Blackwater line.[59] North of the city, George Pickett, whose division had joined Lee's army on the march north, had left not only Jenkins's brigade south of Richmond but also one of his Virginia brigades, Montgomery Corse's, at Hanover Junction.[60] With matters heating up at Richmond, Hill still worried about North Carolina's vulnerability. On June 21, he warned Seddon that the North Carolina "front of 300 miles, containing an infinite number of approaches, is feebly guarded by three regiments of cavalry. We are obliged to meet with disaster at some point, if the Yankees show any enterprise."[61]

To augment these regular army units, city officials also relied on forces within the Richmond Department, including Henry Wise's brigade along with local defense troops. These latter commands included the "Public Guard," a small unit that predated the war. In addition, other units had formed since the first months of the war, including a command compiled in 1861 from workers at the Tredegar Iron Works and another known as the "City Battalion" established by Wyatt M. Elliot. Confederate officials also looked to organize thousands of the city's factory workers and clerks not already assigned to existing units.[62] In early June, John Beauchamp Jones petitioned Secretary Seddon urging the "voluntary organization of non-conscripts" for local defense armed with "every superfluous musket" on hand. Seddon agreed and the process began to add these men to the Richmond defenders.[63] The effort bogged down when Davis stepped in to micromanage aspects of the effort and irritated state officials. Jones saw danger in this squabbling. "A jealousy I fear . . . is growing up between Confederate and State authority. This when the common enemy is thundering at our gates!"[64] Further problems arose when a rumor emerged that General Elzey, no fan of the bureaucrats within the War Department, threatened to keep the clerks on militia duty indefinitely "so others must be appointed in their places." Nevertheless, the recruitment effort continued, and by June 19 the clerks had each been issued forty cartridges.[65]

"WE ARE LIVING IN FEAR OF A YANKEE RAID"

Reports of Dix's advance continued to circulate in the Richmond news-papers. Civilians in town and the surrounding area had been on edge since the US troops first occupied West Point in May. "We are living in fear of a Yankee raid," observed Judith McGuire in Ashland. "They have a large force on York River, and are continually sending parties up the Pamunk[e]y and Mattaponi Rivers, to devastate the country and annoy the inhabitants."[66] The *Daily Dispatch*, referring to the recent skirmish-ing in New Kent County, warned that the "Yankees are clearing out the country below there. They burned the house of Mr. Pinckney Walker last week, and are carrying off all the negroes they can lay their hands on." But despite such stories, no concrete information arrived to confirm the presence of US forces in large numbers. As the *Daily Examiner* noted, "[W]e began to congratulate ourselves that the city has missed its 'star-tling' rumor—as people sometimes, even in the most malarious districts, miss a chill."[67]

But on Tuesday, June 23, stories of enemy troops landing "at some point" on the York appeared in the *Daily Dispatch*.[68] Then, late the next day, half a dozen policemen emerged from Richmond's City Hall, rushing past the building's four huge columns and clattering down broad steps, with each man carrying stacks of freshly printed handbills under their arms. The notices, which bore Governor Letcher's name, heralded danger. "Troops are being landed by the enemy both at Brandon, on the James River, and at the White House, on the York River, and it is their purpose doubtless to make an attack upon the city of Richmond, as diversion, to compel the withdrawal of troops from Lee's army." The proclamation ordered all men "liable to duty" for local defense to gather at Capitol Square at 7 p.m. to organize into a body and prepare to repel the enemy.[69] "There is another 'big scare' in town tonight," wrote William Walker Cleary, a clerk in the Treasury Department.[70]

That evening, the citizenry headed for the Capitol grounds, and by the appointed time upward of 15,000 had gathered under cool, cloudy skies. Letcher soon emerged from the governor's mansion and walked to the Capitol's steps. During his talk, he called the crowd to arms with a series of rhetorical flourishes. The enemy had overrun the state, insulted its women, destroyed "property," and "disregarded the teachings of hu-manity and of the civilization of the age." The Richmond mayor, Joseph Mayo, followed with a warning that the city "would never be safe until all its citizens slept on their arms" and then vowed the Confederate capital would never be "subjugated."[71] The speakers estimated 7,000 Federals at White House on the Pamunkey and 14,000 at Brandon on the James. According to Cleary, who witnessed the event, it did not appear that many men "were volunteering," though he predicted that would change "if there is really occasion."[72]

Word of the Brandon landing turned out to be a "groundless rumor" generated by confusing reports from signal officers downstream on the James.[73] But the accounts about a movement up the York and Pamunkey Rivers would eventually prove to be true, though the Federals would not actually reach White House Landing until June 25. Just as William Cleary predicted, the new volunteers gathered at Capitol Square to receive their arms on Thursday morning. During their drill, a shower passed over and, according to a witness, "the whole concern, rank and file, hoisted their umbrellas" while the drillmaster dodged the puddles and continued to shout out the instructions.[74] The *Sentinel* later quipped that, while the umbrella deployment "was somewhat unsoldierlike," it was "nevertheless a comfortable way of playing soldier." The editors hoped the militiamen, after some practice, would "be prepared to encounter the storms of bullets with less trepidation than they stood up to the rain."[75]

On Thursday, June 25, Secretary of War Seddon informed D. H. Hill in Petersburg about enemy vessels on the Pamunkey and troops marching up the Peninsula and ordered him to send Jenkins's brigade to Richmond. Hill did not respond with a simple "yes" but instead explained that, given the presence of Ransom's brigade at Drewry's Bluff just south of Richmond, he was reluctant to send Jenkins's entire brigade until the enemy movement was "more fully developed." But Hill did not shrink from the danger emerging toward the east. He was eager to meet the enemy. "Should there be an advance upon the north side," he wrote Seddon, "I would respectfully ask that I may not be kept back at this place." In the ranks outside Richmond, however, the defenders sensed no danger. "Little apprehension is felt here . . . such a movement by [the Federals] will only end in failure no one doubts," declared a member of Cooke's brigade. But, as they would soon find out, the threat was real and the Yankees would soon arrive.[76]

PART TWO
Spear's Strike Against the Virginia Central

ON JUNE 25, 1863, troops from General John Dix's command finally reached White House Landing on the Pamunkey River. That morning, hundreds of cavalrymen under Colonel Samuel P. Spear disembarked from their transports and stepped onto the soil of New Kent County. Downriver, more boats carrying infantry from the Seventh Corps were not far behind. To the east, additional foot soldiers from Erasmus Keyes's Fourth Corps made their way overland along the roads of the Peninsula. Within hours of their landing at White House, Spear's riders were on the road headed northwest toward the rail bridges spanning the South Anna River in Hanover County to conduct what would become the first operation of Dix's own Richmond campaign.

6

Dix Begins His Peninsula Campaign

"LEE'S ARMY HAD GOTTEN SO FAR NORTH"

WITH CONFEDERATE OFFICIALS IN RICHMOND looking out for the Federals to the east, Robert E. Lee's men continued their steady advance toward Pennsylvania, passing through the Shenandoah Valley, across the Potomac River, and into the wide Cumberland Valley. On June 22, a division from Richard Ewell's Second Corps filed into Greencastle, Pennsylvania, becoming the first large Confederate force to enter the Keystone State during the campaign. Over the next several days, Lee's other two corps, the First Corps under Longstreet and the Third Corps led by A. P. Hill, splashed across the Potomac at Shepherdstown and Williamsport. At the same time, cavalry commander J. E. B. Stuart began his ride between the Army of the Potomac and Washington, DC, drifting far away from Lee and the infantry corps. In addition, John Imboden's cavalry, operating on Lee's left flank, destroyed tracks and bridges along the Baltimore and Ohio Railroad and cut the canal bearing the same name.

In Richmond, as Dix's Federals approached White House Landing, Generals D. H. Hill and Arnold Elzey readied their mixed force of regular brigades—under Cooke, Ransom, Jenkins, Wise, and Corse—along with the existing city defense units as well as additional men mobilized by Governor John Letcher. As the defenders prepared, Richmond residents devoured any news they could find about Lee's invasion as well as Vicksburg's status. Lee's goals, his army's location, and Pemberton's real chances for survival on the Mississippi remained unknown; any accurate picture was clouded by speculation and rumor.[1] On June 24, Richmond's *Daily Dispatch*, for instance, claimed Confederate forces had cut Grant's supply connections, forcing him to hurl "a desperate assault" against the well-defended works. The next day, passengers from Staunton stepping off the Virginia Central train in Richmond reported that "Lee's army had gotten so far north that it was a difficult matter to hear from it."[2]

The Federals also struggled to divine Lee's intentions and prepare. In Washington, Secretary of War Stanton and General-in-Chief Halleck sought to mobilize every available man to repel the invasion. Emergency orders, proclamations, and other measures followed. In the midst of this activity, Joseph Hooker's fortunes as commander of the Army of the Potomac went from bad to worse. On June 25, days after Confederate troops swept into Pennsylvania, the forward element of Hooker's force lingered south of the Potomac. Rebuffed in his earlier proposals to ignore Lee and attack Richmond, Hooker had followed the directives from President Lincoln and Halleck and positioned his men between the Army of Northern Virginia and the US capital. On June 15, Halleck stepped in and informed Hooker that "your army is entirely free to operate as you desire against Lee's army, so long as you keep his main army [away] from Washington."[3] The next day, Lincoln distanced himself from Hooker, telling him that Halleck would directly oversee operations. "I will direct him to give you orders and you to obey them," the president wrote.[4] Halleck then added: "You are in command of the Army of the Potomac, and will make the particular dispositions as you deem proper. I shall only indicate the objects to be aimed at."[5] Halleck's reappearance in the chain of command did not bode well for Hooker's prospects as head of the army.[6]

Hooker sought to catch up with Lee while maintaining his covering screen of Washington. As he tried to gather all available forces to confront Lee's army, the flexibility promised by Halleck proved illusory. Soon, disagreement and confusion emerged about Hooker's authority over troops in the Washington defenses and along the Potomac. Questions also arose about Hooker's command of Harpers Ferry, a key Federal position directly in Lee's path. Hooker wanted to abandon the post and transfer the troops from there to his force. Halleck, however, refused to hand over control of the garrison and ordered the commander on site to ignore Hooker. The decision seemed to cast aside the hard-earned lessons of the Maryland Campaign, during which the rebels captured the troops at Harpers Ferry en masse. The discord reached a boiling point, and on June 27, in the middle of the campaign, Hooker asked to be relieved of command. His request was accepted without hesitation. In his place, Pennsylvanian George G. Meade was tapped to take over and immediately began to steer the Army of the Potomac into his home state in pursuit of Lee's columns.[7]

"SEND THE TROOPS HE CAN SPARE"

As the command issues unfolded, Halleck continued to consider ways to counter Lee's invasion. He still had hopes for Dix's effort to threaten

Richmond and the railroads. However, with the exception of a note or two to Dix, he had not devoted much energy to the project.[8] Despite the promise of operations against Richmond, Halleck, along with other officials in Washington, mainly focused on gathering units, managing the Federal pursuit and concentrating troops to meet Lee. This was a prudent, conventional response to Lee's advance, a defensive-minded strategy emblematic of the Federals' approach to the war up to that point. Halleck, despite his June 14 orders to Dix, did not seem interested in devoting much attention or resources to attacking lightly defended Richmond with a large force.

Beyond Dix's Richmond offensive, Halleck still had other operations in mind to damage Lee's communications, particularly in North Carolina and western Virginia. On June 20, after reading papers full of news about Lee's offensive, John Foster in North Carolina had offered Halleck his full support, particularly in the form of troops.[9] The North Carolina Department contained about 20,000 men spread throughout the eastern part of the state, primarily at New Bern, Beaufort, Plymouth, and Washington.[10] Foster's offer was an unusual one. Department commanders rarely raised their hand to volunteer their own troops. However, Foster, an intelligent, enterprising commander, understood what was at stake with Lee's offensive. Foster and Halleck also recognized that Lee's threat created opportunities for the Federals in North Carolina. The Wilmington and Weldon Railroad, the primary logistical lifeline for Richmond and Lee's army, still ran largely untouched north through the state's piedmont to Virginia.[11]

Halleck considered his options in the Tar Heel State. He could extract troops from Foster's department to reinforce operations in the north, or he could order Foster to threaten Confederate positions in North Carolina, or he could do a little of both. He chose the third option. First, he gladly accepted the offer for men, sending a note on June 22 ordering Foster to "send the troops he can spare to Fort Monroe."[12] Over the next several days, ten regiments, as well as Foster himself and Generals Henry Prince and Francis Spinola, boarded transports at New Bern for the ocean voyage to Fort Monroe, on the Chesapeake Bay.[13] Ultimately, however, the utility of these particular units turned out to be limited, as many had long sick lists and all were soon scheduled to muster out of service.[14] They would provide little help in the upcoming efforts in Virginia. Second, Halleck urged Foster to conduct active operations in North Carolina, including a strike on the Wilmington and Weldon line to threaten rebel communications with Virginia. Foster began to plan such an operation immediately and, during the last days of June, kept Halleck apprised of his efforts to conduct a raid within the state.[15]

In addition to North Carolina, Halleck eyed opportunities in western Virginia, where the Virginia and Tennessee Railroad transported supplies to Richmond from the west. As long as Braxton Bragg fended off William Rosecrans in Middle Tennessee, this rail line would remain open to provide food and materiel and a connection to key locations such as Chattanooga, Atlanta, Montgomery, and Mobile. With Lee vulnerable to the north, Halleck believed a raid against this line was in order. On June 25, he asked Brigadier General Benjamin F. Kelley, the commander of the newly formed West Virginia Department, "to organize a small mounted force, to ascend the Great Kanawha, cross the mountains, and cut the Virginia & Tennessee Railroad."[16] To conduct this task, Halleck recommended Brigadier General Eliakim Scammon, a West Point graduate and mathematics professor.[17] Concerned about whether the strength of Scammon's cavalry was adequate for such an operation, Kelley answered that "I am not prepared to answer advisedly,"[18] a response that did not suggest aggressive action.

Kelley's discouraging reply aside, Halleck had identified three operations to threaten Confederate supply lines as the rebel army marched into Pennsylvania: Dix would attack the Confederate center at Richmond, Foster would seek to damage the lifeline in North Carolina, and Kelley would sever Virginia's important rail connection to Tennessee. Although the trio of strikes did not really add up to a large, coordinated offensive, it demonstrated that Halleck was willing to consider indirect approaches to threaten the Confederate advance into Pennsylvania. At the same time, he showed no signs of treating these operations as a serious priority. He did little to oversee the three officers tasked with these expeditions and did not dispatch additional troops in support other than the sickly, homebound regiments sent north by Foster. With the Army of Northern Virginia spilling into Pennsylvania, Halleck's energy was focused elsewhere; Dix, Kelley, and Foster were largely left to themselves to achieve results. Dix's offensive would be the first out of the gate.

"IF WE WERE IN THE RIGHT CHURCH, WE WERE IN THE WRONG PEW"

John Dix's buildup on the Peninsula had been slow. However, finally, on June 24, the first wave of his offensive, about a thousand cavalrymen under Colonel Samuel Spear, headed up the York River in nine transports led by three gunboats in the procession that would trigger alarms in Richmond. During the voyage, the men of Company G from the 11th Pennsylvania Cavalry found themselves crammed onto the 178-foot armed transport *Western World* in a spot on the deck not far from the vessel's large Parrott rifles. Their proximity to the ordnance made some of the cavalrymen uneasy. "We thought in case of a fight," one remarked, "that, if we were in the right church, we were in the wrong pew."[19] Aboard other transports, the cavalrymen spread oats across the deck to feed their horses. On the boats carrying the Pennsylvanians in Company C of the 11th Cavalry, one of the animals slipped overboard while reaching for the feed near the gangway. The vessel turned around and lowered a rescue boat, but the horse was too heavy and the crew gave up and resumed its course. The poor beast continued to struggle toward the boat but, weighted down by its saddle and blanket, struck out for shore and eventually reached the sandy bank, to the relief of all watching. After the incident, other problems arose. The members of Company A learned there was no fresh water on board their vessel. "Eating hard tack without coffee was dry work," recalled one.[20] During the afternoon, the gunboat *Smith Briggs*, so instrumental in the Aylett's raid three weeks earlier, led the procession to West Point at the mouth of the Pamunkey and seized a rebel scow in the process.[21] By evening, most of the boats had anchored there, and the 9th Vermont infantry disembarked to occupy the post.[22]

Back at his Fort Monroe headquarters, apprehension nagged at John Dix. He remained uncertain about the overall prospects of his enterprise. Chatter in the press had raised expectations about the offensive. There was talk of Richmond's outright capture. Dix, however, worried his force was simply too small to accomplish such a feat. Subtracting the troops left behind to guard Fort Monroe and Norfolk, he planned to bring about 20,000 men on the expedition, a sizable total but by no means a massive strike force.[23] Earlier, he had confided to Admiral Phillips Lee that, with an additional 10,000, "he could go into Richmond without any difficulty."[24] He expanded on this line in a June 25 letter to his wife:

[S]o much has been said about my going to Richmond. The papers go there immediately, and increase the preparations and precautions of the enemy. For such an enterprise, my force is entirely inadequate. However, I can make a disturbance and probably call off some of Lee's dogs from Pennsylvania. The papers say Richmond is entirely unguarded. This is a . . . mistake. There are troops there, and within

reach by the various railroads some ten thousand men. Behind entrenchments this is a strong force. You may rely on my doing all that
can be done.[25]

Plagued by these concerns and suffering from an acute bout of diarrhea, Dix sought to manage expectations. On June 25, he informed
Halleck of the potential problems ahead. Reports suggested George Pickett's 8,000-man division remained at Hanover Junction only a few miles
from the South Anna bridges. Dix feared those spans were so "strongly
guarded" that his men would not be able to "get at them." In truth, Pickett's men had been marching north with Lee's army for weeks, and only
the brigades of Brigadier Generals Montgomery Corse and Micah Jenkins
were left behind. But Dix did not know this. His ignorance suggests much
about the weakness of US intelligence-gathering in the region.[26] In any
case, the major general leaned into the task ahead. With the transport
shortage continuing to impair his operation, he expected the bulk of his
force would not reach White House Landing until June 26. He could then
weigh whether to launch an assault directly on Richmond's defenses. But
first, Colonel Spear's 11th Pennsylvania Cavalry would strike out alone
to the South Anna. The preparations were coming to an end, and Dix's
force prepared for action.

"SUCH AN ENTERPRISE"

Early Thursday morning, June 25, the flotilla carrying Spear's cavalry left
West Point, entered the Pamunkey, and steamed up the dizzying series
of sharp curves creating the river's winding course. Approaching White
House Landing, the boats passed some African Americans on the bank
cheering the arriving Federals. When the vessels rounded the last of many
turns, the Richmond and York River Railroad bridge came into view as
well as the landing and the ruins of the White House manor. The US cavalrymen crammed aboard the transports churning up the Pamunkey and
prepared for the work ahead.

Spear's force contained about 1,000 riders drawn from several units,
including the 800 or so members of the 11th Pennsylvania who had
boarded the vessels at Yorktown after leaving Suffolk on June 22 along
with a force of 250 troopers from Gloucester Point led by Lieutenant Colonel Hasbrouck Davis. This group included a battalion of the 2nd Massachusetts (Companies A, B, and K) under Major Caspar Crowninshield,

some members of the 2nd New York Cavalry, and a detachment of the 12th Illinois. It was an interesting mix of units. For example, most members of Company A of the 2nd Massachusetts hailed from California and were known as the "California Hundred." Similarly, some companies of the 11th Pennsylvania were not, in fact, from the Keystone State. Most members of Company A were Iowans, and many in Company I hailed from New Jersey just across the Delaware River from Philadelphia.[27]

Colonel Spear was a good choice to lead the operation. In a department short on enterprising, combat-tested officers, Spear stood out. He was experienced and aggressive, "a very brave man, but a reckless adventurer," by one assessment. He had served in Florida and Arkansas in the 1840s, fought in the Mexican–American War, and remained with the army in the West during the 1850s. In commenting on a planned operation weeks before, a fellow officer remarked that "Spear is the soul of such an enterprise." Another veteran recalled that Spear was "as brave as a lion" and "always led . . . in person" whenever a charge was ordered.[28] However, despite the respect he gained among his peers as an effective officer, it seems his men had mixed feelings. One soldier later described him as "a strict disciplinarian—a complete martinet" who nevertheless exhibited "undaunted bravery and fine fighting qualities."[29]

Early Thursday morning, as the boats rounded the last turn in the Pamunkey River, the Federals spied Confederate cavalry scrambling onto their mounts and racing away "as fast as they could go" through the haze. A shell burst ahead of the flotilla (whether from the shore or one of the Federal boats is unclear). A reporter aboard the *Western World* recalled that "the gunners flew around buckled on their short swords and stood manfully to the guns," which soon opened up and filled the air with "a blazing fire."[30] The boats glided on, landed unopposed at White House, and began unloading men and horses onto the soil of New Kent County using a canal boat as a makeshift wharf. It was about 7:30 a.m.[31]

Near the landing, the Federals discovered that the rebel pickets had abandoned not only their positions but also their breakfasts. Several of the bluecoats sat down and enjoyed the captured ham, eggs, and "slapjacks" set out before them. The Northerners also seized two tons of hay and a single prisoner, an old sutler who provided little useful information. However, several Black civilians came forward to report that the defending force had consisted of about fifty men, a mix of cavalry and infantry, which had been there to guard the York River Railroad bridge.[32] According to an account in the *Richmond Enquirer*, the Confederate detachment at White House had included four scouts from Company C of the 15th

Virginia Cavalry, along with a dozen riders led by Captain Edward W. Capps and Lieutenant Milton P. Seneca, who considered challenging the Yankees but "deemed it prudent to retire" after grasping the size of the landing force.

Spear immediately sent a detachment to pursue the Confederates. As the rebels dashed away, Union cavalrymen unleashed a volley, hitting a horse, and then took up the chase. The pursuit continued at a gallop for several miles and nearly ended poorly for Captain Capps, who just managed to escape after he tumbled from his horse while leaping a ditch, suffering an ankle sprain and many bruises. The Federals did, however, manage to capture two rebel privates. The prisoners informed Spear that General Wise had 5,000 men within 7 miles of the White House plantation, made up of a cavalry regiment, 3,000 infantrymen, and pivot guns mounted on rail cars. A rumor also circulated that the Confederates would soon return aboard a train pulling a railroad battery.[33]

At White House itself, the Federals found more than slapjacks. The sutler's store on the riverbank housed some whiskey and tobacco. Spear ordered the men to pour the former in the river and to divide the latter among themselves. The troopers also made a more menacing find. Near the intact railroad bridge, the Federals discovered a nearly completed revolving railroad battery built on a turnstile. "The whole work displayed skill and ingenuity," noted a *New York Daily Herald* reporter with Spear at the time, "and I am very glad, indeed, it was not finished before our arrival."[34] Spear ordered his men to destroy the contraption. He shared the reporter's relief at having arrived before the battery had become operational. "Every thing was prepared by [the enemy] to sweep us as we came up the river, but our hour was a little too early."[35]

Some of the cavalrymen and infantrymen took a little time to explore the area beyond the landing. The White House plantation belonged to Rooney Lee, Robert E. Lee's son who had been wounded at Brandy Station sixteen days before. The younger Lee had become the owner of the property in 1857 following the death of his mother's father, George Washington Parke Custis. A century before, George Washington had courted Martha Custis there. In fact, Rooney's mother, Mary Anna Custis Lee, was Martha Custis's great-granddaughter. During the Federal occupation at White House, a Connecticut quartermaster met an elderly freedman who said he was 102 years old and remembered meeting George Washington.[36] The census of 1860 listed the land's value at $70,000 and the "value of personal estate," including the enslaved people there, at $90,000.[37] When McClellan's forces arrived at the property during the

Peninsula Campaign in 1862, a member of the Lee family had attached the following notice to the front door: "Northern soldiers who profess to reverence Washington, forbear to desecrate the home of his first married life." However, the Federals did not heed this plea. A year later, Spear's men had trouble finding much of anything of value left on the grounds. The main house, put to the torch the year before, now consisted of a few lonely chimneys and scattered piles of brick. Unknown to Spear and his men, Rooney Lee himself was not far away. In fact, as the cavalrymen stepped ashore, he was recuperating from his Brandy Station wound at Hickory Hill, the Wickham family plantation 25 miles to the northwest near Hanover Court House.[38]

Spear immediately prepared to leave for the South Anna. While surplus baggage was loaded on the transports for return to Yorktown, the cavalrymen packed a two-day supply of forage for their mounts and three days' rations for themselves. Gun crews also hitched two howitzers to their limbers.[39] The men guided their horses into column and formed up for the march.

"RAIDS HAVE A WONDERFUL EFFECT"

By the summer of 1863, raids had become a common feature of the war. It was dangerous business, usually involving cavalry, sometimes infantry, always operating in hostile country far away from support, and often close to enemy militia and regulars. Raids typically targeted military-related infrastructure such as railroads and bridges and supply depots. Railroads were a favorite target because they served as the lifeline for armies and were vastly superior to roads for moving troops, ammunition, subsistence, and forage. Raids could also generate results reaching far beyond their immediate military or logistical impacts. As Fourth Corps commander Erasmus Keyes had noted to Dix on June 16: "[R]aids have a wonderful effect by producing discontent among the people of the Confederate Government."[40]

Whatever their goals, successful raids required both exceptional planning and canny improvisation. To avoid failure or worse, raiding columns often approached and returned from their objective using different routes and altered their course as conditions demanded. In addition, raiding forces remained on the move most of the time, limiting rests to avoid ambushes. Success required bold and aggressive commanders and cavalrymen with the requisite fortitude, endurance, and bravery.

As historian Edward Longacre has noted, fruitful raids generally shared a few common characteristics. First, a successful effort often contributed to the goals of a larger operation or campaign by, for example, cutting key supply arteries to an enemy force or destroying vital materiel at the right time. Second, the raiding force had to be the appropriate size: small enough to travel rapidly through enemy country, but large enough to complete its appointed tasks against enemy resistance. Third, when cavalry made up the raiding force, the horse soldiers had to be adept at fighting dismounted and otherwise conducting business under harsh, varied conditions. They often operated as "dragoons or mounted infantry" instead of traditional "saddle-bound" cavalry, the typical approach during the first part of the war. However, things had begun to change in 1863. Finally, familiarity with the local geography was vital to a successful operation. Union raiders in the southern countryside necessarily relied on knowledgeable scouts and sympathetic local civilians, including African Americans and white Unionists.[41]

Yet even where raiding forces managed to destroy mission targets, they did not always yield significant results. Throughout the war, brief forays against enemy railroads made for good storytelling and newspaper copy but rarely inflicted meaningful long-term damage. Without a permanent lodgment by the raiding force, railroad officials often repaired bridges and tracks in little time. However, when delivered at the vital moment, hit-and-run cavalry raids had the potential to cause a real impact by denying troops and supplies to an enemy in need. Accordingly, timing was crucial. After a large Confederate raid against the B&O line in the spring of 1863, for instance, railroad officials and workers acted with speed and efficiency to restore the line to full operation within weeks, despite the destruction of several large iron trestles.

However, in other instances, destroying bridges could prove very effective. In fact, the Federals had hit the central Virginia railroads earlier in the war. In 1862, they burned several bridges on the Virginia Central and RF&P lines. Repairs on the latter crossing did not occur for months, forcing railroad officials to halt trains and carry supplies and passengers over rivers by wagon bridge or ford. The slow repairs hampered rebel efforts to transport Stonewall Jackson's troops from the Shenandoah Valley during the Peninsula Campaign. But other raids north of Richmond were not as successful. George Stoneman's effort in May during the Chancellorsville Campaign had left little lasting damage. In fact, officials managed to get the trains running on the Virginia Central and RF&P only days after Stoneman's men departed from the area. Given these previous experiences, the impact of John Dix's efforts against the railroads, even if successful, were difficult to predict.[42]

"TO MAINTAIN MY COMMUNICATIONS"

As Spear's men formed up on the banks of the Pamunkey, they prepared to head for the rail bridges on the South Anna. They understood a break there would hamper Confederate quartermaster efforts to transport supplies to the Army of Northern Virginia as that force flooded into Maryland and Pennsylvania. The Confederates also knew the importance of the connections, an appreciation only strengthened by recent operations. Following earlier warnings from Confederate officers, new batteries and earthworks appeared along the South Anna by early June, though the scope and strength of those fortifications at that time has never been clearly established. In March, Lee had asked Secretary of War Seddon to impress slaves to work on the Virginia Central. "I am convinced that a portion of the levy of negroes called for to work on the fortifications can be much more beneficially employed on this road, to prevent it from failing us at a time when we shall most need it," he wrote. Throughout much of the war, Virginia Central officials used slave labor to help maintain the line. The company's surviving records contain dozens of preprinted forms used to record its obligations to slave owners. Officials generally paid $400 per quarter for the labor of a single enslaved person, who, according to the forms, was to be returned to his owner "well clothed in the usual way, and with a Hat and Blanket."[43]

In addition to slave impressment, Confederate officials juggled other issues. Seddon agreed with Lee's own assessment of the crisis, explaining that "our railroads are daily growing less efficient and serviceable." Seddon pledged to convene a conference of the railroad presidents and to urge Congress to facilitate the adoption of "more regular schedules" and dedicate more trains to carry freight.[44] The Virginia Central officials concurred. Railroad president Peter V. Daniel would later observe that the "severe and constant use" of the company's machinery was degrading the effectiveness of operations.[45]

The very day Spear's men prepared for their march on the South Anna rail bridge, Robert E. Lee pondered his supply situation from the banks of the Potomac. His army had traveled well beyond Virginia's rail network. From Williamsport, where he paused on June 25, the nearest stations to his army lay over 100 miles away—at Staunton (near the western terminus of the Virginia Central in the Valley) and at Culpeper (on the Orange and Alexandria line east of the Blue Ridge). As his men tramped north throughout June, Lee directed officials in Richmond to send troops and supplies on trains to either Staunton or Culpeper, from where they would reach the army by foot or wagon.[46] However, at the Potomac, Lee began to doubt whether he could continue to use these supply lines at all. "I have not sufficient troops to maintain my communications, and, therefore have to abandon them," he explained to Davis. Indeed, Lee's units were far away from a reliable supply source, and his lead elements, under Richard Ewell, were marching deep into Pennsylvania and foraging widely. Ewell's men fanned out into the countryside, not only gathering food but also seizing free Black civilians to send South into slavery.[47]

At first glance, Lee's June 25 letter seems to suggest the Army of Northern Virginia was completely untethered and not dependent on the rail bridges north of Richmond. With Lee's army living off the land in Pennsylvania, a burned bridge or the destruction of track north of Richmond would have little immediate effect on his army's prospects.[48] However, as his aide Charles Marshall would later acknowledge, Lee was more dependent on his connections to the south than his June 25 statement implied. Shipments of troops and ordnance continued to move between Richmond and Staunton during June.[49] Furthermore, the loss of the Virginia Central would substantially delay reinforcements and new ammunition shipments, which would be needed should the foray into Pennsylvania produce extended fighting. Indeed, should combat empty Confederate limber chests and cartridge boxes, a broken rail connection back to Richmond would have the potential to trigger disaster for Lee's campaign and for his cause.

7

Spear's Raid to the South Anna

"SLIPPERY CLAY HILLS AND STUMP OBSTRUCTED RAVINES"

BY NOON ON THURSDAY, JUNE 25, most of Colonel Samuel Spear's cavalrymen were mounted and ready to head out. It was a cool, cloudy day with temperatures hovering around 70 degrees.[1] John Dix's instructions for the mission were short and simple: "Special Order A. No. 1" directed the cavalry to proceed from White House along the west bank of the Pamunkey and "destroy or burn the railroad bridges over the North Anna and South Anna rivers, tearing up the track of the railroad." Should rebel forces block his return, Spear was to proceed to West Point along the Pamunkey's opposite bank. With the Aylett's raid fresh in his mind, Dix forbade "pillaging or destruction of private property," clearly seeking to distance himself from any suggestion of hard war. Finally, the orders admonished Spear to waste no time heating and twisting rails at the bridges but rather to simply heave them into the river.[2]

In launching this first effort of his campaign against Richmond, Dix tracked Halleck's orders and focused on damaging Lee's communications, not threatening the city itself. Nevertheless, a direct attack against Richmond was still on the table. Despite his concerns about the city's strength, Dix continued to entertain thoughts of doing something more than a raid, but just what he planned is not entirely clear. The 19,000 infantry and artillerymen of the Fourth and Seventh Corps arriving at White House would help keep his options open. In the days ahead, he would begin to weigh the possibility of a direct attack on the rebel capital. But Spear's effort would come first.[3]

Early in the afternoon, the cavalry began riding west along the rail line with the troopers from Major Caspar Crowninshield's battalion in front. Once in motion, the string of horses stretched back a mile.[4] A few troopers remained behind briefly at White House to finish gathering supplies for the expedition. George L. Cruikshank, a sergeant in Company A of the 11th Pennsylvania, delayed his departure to gather rations for the mission ahead. Working with several other comrades, he dumped hardtack out of boxes and into empty oat sacks, which were then slung from their saddles. Cruikshank also strapped bags of tea and coffee to his horse. He and his comrades soon set off, seeking to catch up with the column, but after a few minutes the hardtack inside the bags began to break into pieces, shaken by the ride. Soon, pulverized crackers sifted through the sacks, covering the riders with a dust that made them "look like millers," according to Cruikshank. Thus adorned, the men rode on to catch up with the tail of the column.[5]

A typical cavalry column moving over flat, dry roads could travel about 3 miles per hour, taking ten-minute breaks every fifty minutes. Spear's men, however, did not face such ideal conditions on Thursday afternoon. Ground soaked by rain impeded progress as the horses clopped over "slippery clay hills and stump obstructed ravines." In some low areas, the animals sank "nearly to their knees" and the riders became mud spattered. In Cruikshank's little band, the man carrying the meat rations toppled to the ground when his horse stumbled into a muddy hole and scampered off into the woods, forcing the caked rider to advance on foot until he procured a mule. After covering 4 miles, the horsemen approached Tunstall's Station at about 5 p.m. Officers silently passed along orders to pause, and Lieutenant Colonel Hasbrouck Davis rode along the column "informing the men of the duty expected of them and enjoining steadiness and unity of action."[6]

Driving ahead to Tunstall's Station, Spear's men encountered about a dozen rebel pickets. All but one managed to escape west toward Richmond. The Federals galloped through the station, pausing there to snip the telegraph wires and torch a sutler's store and other buildings. A Richmond newspaper later reported the store, owned by a Mr. Dabney, contained a full, recently purchased stock of goods, which the Federals destroyed on the pretext that the business served as a Confederate post office. According to the paper, the raiders "did not rob the money drawer of the store, something most remarkable for a Yankee." Finished with Tunstall's Station, the column turned north and west on Old Church Road, moving with the Pamunkey's course off to their right flank.[7]

After a march of about 12 miles, the riders bivouacked in a large field, most likely on the Bassett farm about two miles east of Old Church, although accounts are vague. The men tied their horses to nearby fence posts and lay down for a "short rest" under a heavy downpour.[8] George Cruikshank and his comrades made their beds at a fence corner, where they formed makeshift pallets with fence rails. They drew rubber blankets over their heads, leaving their feet "to stick out in the rain," and tried to catch a few hours of sleep.[9]

"MY DIVISION WILL BE, I THINK, DECIDEDLY THE WEAKEST"

As Spear prepared to drive north into Hanover County the next day, he remained largely ignorant of what enemy forces lay ahead. He also had no idea that a recent shuffle of Confederate troops in the region would make a substantial difference in the raid's results. For the previous few weeks, Montgomery Corse's entire Virginia brigade, one of Pickett's units left behind by Lee, had guarded the lines and bridges in the vicinity of Hanover Junction.[10] But Pickett was not happy about Corse's continued presence there, having been also forced to leave Micah Jenkins's South Carolinians behind at Richmond as a result of the horse-trading between Lee and D. H. Hill. On June 21, Pickett pleaded with Lee's adjutant for Corse's release or at least for the addition of another unit "merely as an act of justice to my division and myself." He worried that "my division will be, I think, decidedly the weakest" during the upcoming operations.[11]

Lee, seeking to have every unit possible with him on Northern soil, agreed with Pickett. From his headquarters at Shepherdstown on June 23, he had sought to spring Corse's brigade loose, asking Richmond officials to send the unit northwest to Winchester via Culpeper and Chester Gap in the Blue Ridge. Shortly after, Corse received orders from the War Department to leave Hanover Junction and head west. Within hours, his regiments were on their way, boarding cars on the Virginia Central for Gordonsville. Although the exact date of Corse's departure is not clear, it is certain that, as Colonel Spear's blue-clad horsemen rode toward the South Anna on June 25, Corse's brigade had traveled more than 50 miles away to the northwest. In Corse's place, a regiment detached from Johnston Pettigrew's brigade, the 44th North Carolina led by Colonel Thomas C. Singeltary, took defensive positions around Hanover Junction. Singeltary split up his Tar Heels, deploying the individual companies and small detachments at key bridges and fords in the area—seventeen in all by his count—stretching from Milford down toward Hanover Court House.[12]

With Singeltary's small command stationed at the bridges, news of Spear's movement began to reach Confederate officials. Throughout the day on June 25, Confederate scouts had sent a stream of reports to Richmond. In the city that afternoon, word reached Major General Arnold

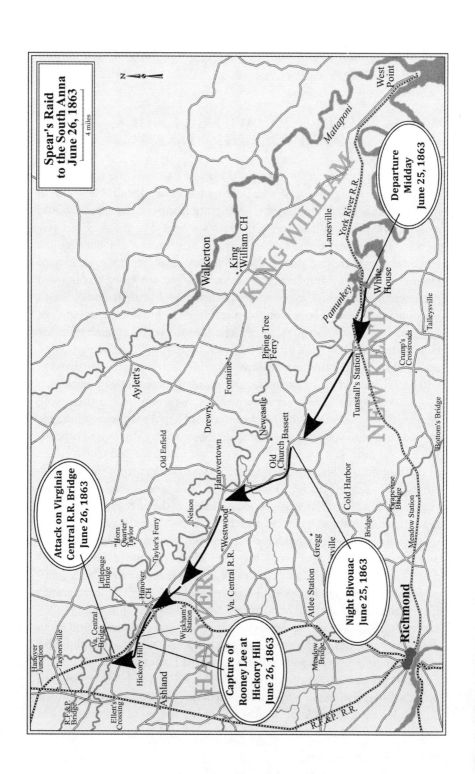

Spear's Raid
to the South Anna
June 26, 1863

4 miles

West
Point

Departure
Midday
June 25, 1863

Mattaponi

KING WILLIAM

Lanesville

York River R.R.

Walkerton

King
William CH

Pamunkey

White
House

Tunstall's Station

Crump's
Crossroads

Talleysville

NEW KENT

Piping Tree
Ferry

Fontaine

Newcastle

Old
Church

Bassett

Cold Harbor

Bottom's Bridge

Aylett's

Drewry

Hanovertown

Grapevine
Bridge

Bridge

Meadow Station

Old Enfield

Nelson

"Westwood"

Attack on Virginia
Central R.R. Bridge
June 26, 1863

Taylor's Ferry

Va. Central R.R.

Atlee Station

Gregg
ville

Night Bivouac
June 25, 1863

"Horn
Quarter"
Taylor

Littlepage
Bridge

Hanover
CH

Wickham's
Station

HANOVER

Va. Central
Bridge

Hickory Hill

Meadow
Bridge

Richmond

Hanover
Junction

Taylorsville

Capture of
Rooney Lee at
Hickory Hill
June 26, 1863

Ashland

R.F.&P.
Bridge

R.F.&P. R.R.

Ellett's
Crossing

Elzey about Federal cavalry on the York River Railroad and at Tunstall's Station. In addition, Colonel William P. Shingler's pickets at Cumberland sighted more than a dozen Union steamers on the Pamunkey headed upstream to White House. According to the *Richmond Dispatch*, some farmers in King William, New Kent, and Charles City Counties took measures to send their cattle and horses toward Richmond's fortifications as soon as they got wind of the raid. It was becoming clear the Yankee activity east of the capital was more than a reconnaissance.[13]

"AS HARD AS OUR HORSES WOULD RUN"

Early Friday morning, Samuel Spear's men washed down hardtack with their coffee, mounted their horses, and rode out of New Kent County and into Hanover. At about 6 a.m., they passed through the hamlet of Old Church, where they captured several rebels—a captain, a surgeon, and five privates—along with six large boxes of tobacco, which they "quickly divided among" themselves. The column continued north and passed by Edmund Ruffin's plantation Marlbourne about a mile beyond Old Church. Ruffin, at one of his other plantations south of the James at the time, would fill his diary in the coming days with news of both the raid and his family's efforts to shuttle their enslaved workers westward away from the Federal troops. Later, he would fret about getting his crops harvested following, as he described it, the "loss of labor from the negroes removed" and by the "indolence of those remaining."[14]

The cavalry reached the small village of Hanovertown on the Pamunkey around 8 a.m. Along the march, detachments of horsemen fanned out across the countryside and seemed to pop up nearly everywhere, at least according to the newspapers. The *Staunton Spectator* reported that Circuit Court Judge John A. Meredith observed three horsemen in the distance as he rode a ferry across the river to Hanovertown. Although a boy on the bank assured him no Yankees were in the vicinity, the judge suspected trouble and asked the ferry pilot to head back across the river. The horsemen raced to the bank reportedly firing shots at Meredith, who managed to escape unharmed.[15]

The blue riders showed up elsewhere. West of Hanovertown, they rode onto Doctor William Brockenbrough's Westwood plantation, where they seized horses and freed some of the slaves there. Afterward, Confederate newspapers greeted the reports of such encounters with their usual skepticism. The *Richmond Sentinel*, for instance, asserted that only death threats from the Union soldiers brandishing arms spurred the exodus.[16] Judith Brockenbrough McGuire, the doctor's sister, recorded from Ashland that the Yankees "came up the river, destroying crops, carriages, etc., stealing horses and cattle, and carrying off the servants from every plantation." According to McGuire, some of the enslaved at Westwood, who had "resisted all Yankee entreaties" on two previous raids, "were forced off." This story, however, does not seem credible. Nothing in Union orders or reports mention emancipation as a goal of the raid, and it seems unlikely the horse soldiers would take affirmative steps, at gunpoint no less, to burden their mounted column with pedestrians. McGuire also heard that the Union soldiers attempted to torch the wheat, but the rain the night before "made it too wet to burn," certainly a more believable account given the results of the recent Aylett's raid.[17]

About 2 miles beyond Westwood, Spear passed Nelson's Bridge, which crossed one of the many bends of the Pamunkey into King William County. The colonel identified this span as a potential lifeline for his return. He recognized that, should the rebels block roads in New Kent and Hanover, his men could make their way back to White House by crossing at Nelson's and traveling through King William. With this contingency in mind, he detached men from Companies B and K of the 2nd Massachusetts to hold the bridge.[18]

Nearing Hanover Court House (often referred to simply as "Hanover"), a Black man informed the riders of a rebel cavalry force ahead. This individual, who may have risked much to inform the soldiers, was most likely enslaved. Before the war, Hanover County, with more than half of its population African American, contained about 9,000 enslaved persons and only 300 free Black residents.[19] In addition to information provided by this unnamed person, reports provided to Spear by Confederate foragers captured along the route indicated that "Longstreet's" quartermaster train had camped near Hanover.[20]

Spear's men pushed forward. The riders in the van sighted a large wagon train halted atop a hill about a mile south of Hanover Tavern, the haunt of young Patrick Henry before the American Revolution and later the home of several slaves who helped plan Gabriel's Rebellion, the unsuccessful uprising in central Virginia in 1800. The lead riders waited for the rest of the column to close up. The men formed for a charge and "started as hard as our horses would run." William Shirley, a Pennsylvanian from Company G, tumbled out of his saddle when his horse tripped over some logs.[21] But the rest of the cavalrymen swarmed around the wagons. It was not much of a contest. The mules, which had been unhitched from the wagons, were milling about feeding as the cavalrymen swarmed around them. The teamsters present, most likely enslaved workers, offered little or no resistance. Spear's men had not found Longstreet's wagons per se but nevertheless captured "a large quartermaster's depot," including a "train of 35 wagons, 6 mules to each team, covers, bows, &c., complete, and ready for the road" plus a hundred mules.[22] Major Samuel Wetherill, with a squadron of Pennsylvanians, gathered fifty wagons and a couple hundred mules, along with some commissary stores, and turned south to take the captured material back to White House via Nelson's Bridge.[23]

Advancing into town, the cavalry prepared for more than teamsters and wagons. Troopers from the 2nd Massachusetts and Company A of the 11th Pennsylvania, all led by Lieutenant George S. Ringland, drew their sabers and trotted forward, leaving the captured supplies behind for Wetherill to handle. Within 500 yards of the courthouse, the "charge" order rang out again. The men spurred their mounts to a gallop and thundered forward expecting a terrible clash in the streets. Instead, they encountered maybe half a dozen Confederate soldiers, all of whom were captured after a short struggle.[24] The attacking force then split up. Some cavalrymen went off to cut telegraph wires while others headed to a train then idling on the tracks of the Virginia Central. However, the locomotive, pointed south toward Richmond, managed to get under way just as they approached firing scattered shots. After the train's departure, a rumor made the rounds that the cars contained 500 Union soldiers captured at Winchester about a week before; but this story was never verified.[25]

Spear's arrival spread panic among Hanover's residents. Margaret Wight, at Hanover Tavern with her family, recalled that the "whole household were in commotion hiding all the silver and valuables." But after learning the Federals were not there to destroy private property, Wight "began to breathe rather more freely." The cavalrymen circulated throughout the town, taking and burning "government stores" and tearing up some rails on the Virginia Central.[26] They also managed to destroy three thousand bushels of wheat and capture several Confederate wagons "used for hauling grains for the subsistence department of Richmond."[27] According to William Shirley, Spear's men also seized about twenty Confederates and then freed several African Americans confined in the jail.[28] Afterward, the raiders departed, riding northwest toward their main target: the rail bridge over the South Anna River. "Now the fun was ahead," recalled a Pennsylvanian sergeant.[29]

"AN EVER LENGTHENING LINE OF
COMMUNICATION"

In reaching Hanover Court House on June 26, Spear's force had managed to sift through the screen of Confederate units in the region with little opposition. Most of the rebel sentinels in the area had been off to the east in the wrong place. The previous day, Captain L. W. Allen's company of local men from Caroline and King and Queen Counties scouted the roads east of the Pamunkey in King William County, where they found no sign of any Federals. But Spear had taken the inside track west of the Pamunkey, and no Confederate force of any size had picketed the roads in New Kent and Hanover despite Spear's appearance at Tunstall's Station the previous afternoon. The Confederates had, in fact, managed to detect the overall movement to White House, providing officials in Richmond with fairly accurate news of Keyes's movement up the Peninsula. But these reports missed the fact that a thousand Yankee riders were headed north toward the South Anna rail bridges.[30]

Definitive warnings of Spear's foray eventually arrived in Richmond. At 10 a.m. on Friday morning, General Elzey telegraphed Colonel D. J. Godwin at Hanover Junction that an enemy force was headed his way. With Corse's brigade already off in Gordonsville, Godwin would have to face Spear with his handful of cavalry companies along with Colonel Singeltary's lone North Carolina infantry regiment.[31] From the junction, Godwin immediately sent Captain Allen's cavalry company to the Virginia Central and dispatched two companies under Captain R. R. Hord and Captain John K. Littleton to watch the RF& P bridge.[32] But, with Spear's column only miles from its target, Singeltary's regiment would have to provide the backbone of the defense.

Singeltary's 44th North Carolina had not seen much fighting during the war. Formed near Raleigh in March 1862, the regiment began its service with guard duty at Greenville in the eastern part of the state. After receiving their first taste of combat at Tranter's Creek in June 1862, the men participated in operations designed to blunt John Foster's raid on the Wilmington and Weldon Railroad in December. The regiment remained in North Carolina until June 1863, when it traveled to Virginia and joined Johnston Pettigrew's brigade. But when Pettigrew marched toward Pennsylvania with Lee, the regiment was left behind to guard the rail lines north of Richmond. On June 26, however, many of the Tar Heels would see plenty of action in the coming hours.[33]

Singeltary's infantry companies were spread all over the area. Several, under Major Charles M. Stedman, protected the RF&P rail line to Fredericksburg at the North Anna. Six more commanded by Lieutenant Colonel Tazewell Hargrove took up positions south at Hanover Junction itself as well as at several rail bridges over the South Anna and Little Rivers.[34] Hargrove chose to join the fifty or so men of Company A, known as the "Granville Regulators," at the Virginia Central crossing of the South Anna. These men, armed with older Model 1841 "Mississippi" rifles, were led by Captain Robert L. Rice.[35]

The Carolinians under Hargrove knew the crossings over the South Anna formed part of the most direct supply line to Lee's army and prepared to hold them at all hazards, understanding that a break here by Union raiders could impact Lee's operations by preventing efforts to transport troops and supplies north into the Shenandoah Valley. "If [Spear's raid] succeeded," recalled one of Hargrove's men, "Lee's army would have been crippled for the want of supplies and direct communication with the Confederate capital."[36] After the war, former soldiers, reflecting on the events of June 26, would emphasize the essential nature of the South Anna Bridge. Another veteran wrote that "there extended in [Lee's] rear an ever lengthening line of communication where food and ammunition and supplies must constantly pass from . . . Richmond. It was necessary to guard this line of communication."[37] The defenders also looked to protect Hanover Junction and the supply depot there, which included at the time "thirty thousand stands of arms, with ammunition," at least according to one veteran's recollection.[38] But the Virginia Central bridge over the South Anna, which sat only a few miles from Hanover Court House and served as a vital link to Gordonsville, Staunton, and Lee's army, certainly ranked as the most inviting target for the Yankees.

Lieutenant Colonel Hargrove did not hesitate to place himself at the point of greatest danger. This decision was not surprising. The tall, dark-haired, thirty-three-year-old native of Granville County had a reputation for courage. He had attended school in Virginia at Randolph-Macon College and practiced law in Oxford in the 1850s. He also became a leading voice among Carolina secessionists as a member of the state House of Representatives and as a delegate to the Secession Convention. At the beginning of the conflict, he joined the 44th as a captain in Company A and later rose to major and then lieutenant colonel. One of his comrades recalled that he was "one of the bravest of the brave and knew no such word as fear."[39]

"MY ORDERS ARE TO BURN THE BRIDGE"

Four miles southeast of the bridge defenders, Spear's force departed from Hanover Court House late in the morning and headed for the South Anna on the road running parallel to the Virginia Central.[40] Along the route, the cavalrymen received word that a Confederate train was headed toward them from Hanover Junction. They prepared to greet it, piling timber on the track near Wickham's Station. The locomotive arrived at the ambuscade and promptly plowed into the makeshift blockade but managed to remain on the rails as the Federals raised their carbines and unleashed a volley that pinged off the engine. The engineer reversed the locomotive, and the train squeaked backward toward the South Anna and Hanover Junction, no doubt spreading news about the Union force.[41]

Back at the South Anna, Hargrove had sought details about the approaching riders. To accomplish this task, Lieutenant William McKnight, an injured member of the 17th Virginia left behind by Corse's brigade, volunteered to hike south with some of his comrades. Just as McKnight's scouting party crested a small hill northwest of Wickham's Station, it stumbled into the lead elements of Spear's column. The Federals snagged McKnight and his cohort and sent them back to the courthouse under a guard led by George Crosby. The captured rebels were defiant. "They were quite saucy," a Pennsylvanian remembered later, "and told us that we would not go far before we would meet our match."[42]

About 2 miles beyond Wickham's Station, Spear reached an intersection and turned north onto a narrow, tree-covered road leading to the South Anna railroad crossing. About midday, the column emerged from the woods. The road stretched north and east, angling slightly toward the railroad off to the right and framing an open field south of the river bordered by trees on both sides. Spear's first objective of the raid appeared beyond the open ground and slightly off to the right—a 150-foot rail trestle spanning the river. To the left, the wagon road also crossed the water, though the bridge itself had been destroyed. Out in his immediate front, Spear spotted rebel earthworks, probably not much more than rifle pits, as well as a small camp in a grove of trees. A low bluff lined the opposite bank where a small railroad hut, described as a "block-house" or a watchman's hut in some accounts, stood just to the left of the tracks surrounded by bushes and trees and festooned with a Confederate banner. As Spear and his men would soon learn, another section of breastworks lay just east of the rail line, about 300 yards beyond the river facing

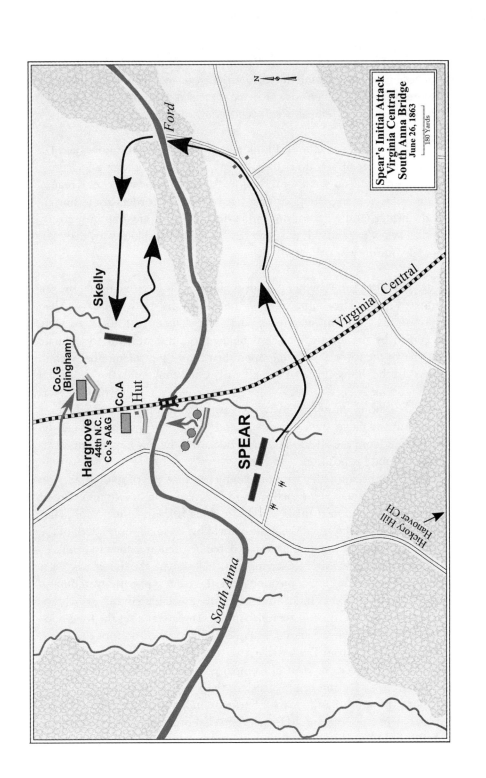

Spear's Initial Attack
Virginia Central
South Anna Bridge
June 26, 1863

180 Yards

N

Ford

Virginia Central

Skelly

Co.G
(Bingham)

Co.A
Hut

Hargrove
44th N.C.
Co.'s A&G

SPEAR

South Anna

Hickory Hill
Hanover CH

southeast. Surveying the ground ahead through his field glasses, Spear remarked: "They certainly have no artillery, or they would fire on us."[43] Before ordering his men forward, Spear paused to address them and, by one veterans' likely embellished recollection years later, said:

> Soldiers of my command, I look for no more from you now then I have often seen you do before, that is, obey your officers and fight your enemy. You see the railroad bridge, it is in General Lee's rear, and he is now marching for your native state. My orders are to burn the bridge, and we must do it if it cost the life of one man or it cost the lives of me and half the command. Soldiers! You know my orders and your duty as soldiers.[44]

The arrival of Union cavalry did not escape the Tar Heels guarding the rail bridge. "A blue streak appeared on the hills to the south of us," recalled one Confederate, and in a few minutes the "slopes just above us were occupied by the enemy."[45] The defenders found it difficult to estimate the size of the force descending upon them, some put the number well in excess of the thousand or so actually in Spear's command. But the actual odds—about twenty-to-one—were daunting enough. Nevertheless, Hargrove had no intention of giving up easily. He planned to use whatever means available to stave off defeat and looked for any advantages he could find from the river, the steep banks, and the few earthworks scattered around his position.

The fight began with a cautious Union advance. A group of about 300 Federal skirmishers crept forward and "succeeded in drawing the fire of the enemy, posted near the bridge." Watching from the north bank, Hargrove quickly determined the position held by his small force south of the river was "entirely untenable" and ordered his men over the rail bridge to the opposite bank. After "exchanging a few shots," the Tar Heels "skedaddled" across taking a position near the tracks and the watchman's hut. They crouched behind "trees and any available cover," which apparently included some loose railroad ties. Understanding the long odds before him, Hargrove sent a courier north, who raced on foot to call for reinforcements. From Taylorsville, two and a half miles to the northwest on the Little River, the men of Company G of the 44th North Carolina received the order and began a rush to the South Anna Bridge.[46]

With the south bank cleared, Spear did not wait long. He ordered a detachment from the 2nd Massachusetts, led by Major Caspar Crowninshield, including the Californians in Company A, to head directly toward the bridge. At the front, about half of the West Coasters dismounted and pushed forward on foot, carbines in hand, through a cornfield along the tracks. On the opposite side of the river, the Confederates remained concealed along the north bank. When the Federals drew within rifle range, the rebels opened up. "They commenced popping at us," wrote a Californian, "the bullets flying in rather too close to our heads." The Confederates took their shots crouched behind trees and bushes near the bridge.[47]

The Federals returned the compliments whenever they could make out the gray-clad soldiers through the branches and leaves. Within a hundred yards of the bridge, the Californians reached an empty breastwork or line of pits running parallel to the south bank and tucked themselves behind it, "loading and firing as opportunity offered" and toppling "over more than one of" the bridge defenders by their reckoning. Spear also ordered his two howitzers to the front. The crews rolled the pieces into position behind the Californians and began to throw "shot and shell" at the enemy position. However, the fire was inaccurate and had little effect. According to some accounts, several Union cavalrymen also ventured forward to the bridge but fell back in the face of fire from Confederate riflemen, including sixteen-year-old Private Joseph H. Cash, who reportedly knocked two of the Yankees off the span. According to a Californian, "we exchanged lead with them quite familiarly for about three quarters of an hour" while every "man was ready with his carbine, and woe to the unlucky man who exposed himself in his hiding place."[48]

"TO SLIDE DOWN THE BANK INTO THE RIVER"

While the Californians probed in front, Spear looked for a better way to pry the small band of Confederates from their position. When the column had approached the field earlier, several local African Americans had informed him of a ford about 700 yards downriver from the railroad bridge. To explore that approach, Spear sent two companies from the 11th Pennsylvania east along the river under the command of Major Franklin A. Stratton. The force soon located the ford and urged their mounts into the water. It was not an easy crossing. "The horses had to slide down the bank into the river and scramble out the farther side," recalled George Cruikshank. Once on the other side, Stratton's group slogged through several dozen yards of swampy ground before reaching firm soil with about twenty men from Company A, the Iowans in the 11th Pennsylvania, in front. The Hawkeyes, led by Captain James A. Skelly, rode out onto a wheat field that stretched back west over rolling ground. Near the railroad about 800 yards away, Skelly's men could see Confederates scrambling into earthworks on his side of the tracks.[49]

These gray-clad men were the reinforcements from Taylorsville. As Stratton's force crossed the river, about forty members of Captain Robert Bingham's command, Company G of the 44th North Carolina, had arrived to support Hargrove. Made up mostly of men from Orange County, this group had marched double-time from their post at Little River Bridge. With Hargrove and Company A still crouching in the trees and bushes near the watchman's hut, members of Bingham's company took their places in a breastwork a few hundred yards north of the bridge and just east of the railroad. Spaced about 2 feet apart, the men received orders "to take deliberate aim, but not to fire till ordered."[50] A Private Cates of Company "G" climbed on top of the trench to look out for any Union advance while Bingham, as he recalled, stood "at the other end of the work, for a like purpose."[51]

From his spot downriver in the wheat field, Captain Skelly could see the entire Confederate position to the west laid bare before him. There was not much there by his estimation, and he immediately ordered a small group to advance. The men urged their horses forward, keeping to the right of the wheat field and steering for what they thought was the weak Confederate left flank. Then the attack began. To Bingham and his Tar Heels in the works, the approaching blue-clad riders "seemed to be half a world full of cavalry." Hooves pounded the ground, and scabbards, canteens, and cartridge boxes clumped and clanked with the rhythm of the charge. Robert P. McRae, a Pennsylvania sergeant, remembered later that some of the Iowans, expecting a hail of lead, hung along their horses "like Indians."[52]

The Carolinians, many of whom "could knock a squirrel out of the highest tree," according to Bingham, readied their rifles and picked their targets. With the cavalrymen gaining speed in their front, the defenders cracked off their first volley. Private Edward Kendall from Company A in the 11th Pennsylvania caught a bullet that shattered a bone in his leg. Another missile grazed the scalp of Corporal Carver Smith. Many other rounds zipped past the riders. Skelly's group soon broke. Realizing his force was too small for the task, the captain ordered a retreat back downriver near the ford where Stratton and the rest of the detachment waited.[53]

After Bingham's company repulsed Skelly's charge, Hargrove tightened the Confederate perimeter. Men withdrew from the bushes lining the river and shifted farther back near the watchman's hut. The opening created an opportunity for members of the 2nd Massachusetts under Caspar Crowninshield on the south bank. Captain J. Sewall Reed, one of the original organizers of the California contingent, ordered forward Company A and about fifty Massachusetts men from Company C.[54] The California Hundred, in combat for the first time, crossed the river "on a foot log, about one hundred yards above the bridge," led by Lieutenant John L. Roper of the 11th Pennsylvania. Although the felled tree allowed for passage of only one soldier at a time, the force somehow managed to cross without alerting the rebels. The attackers concealed themselves in the bushes and undergrowth on the north bank and waited for the attack signal.[55]

"BLOODY WORK GOING ON"

Spear had reached the South Anna, deployed his men, and probed the rebel position. But with the afternoon hours burning away and the RF&P bridge still untouched to the west, it was time to end his dance with the bridge defenders. He came up with a simple plan. Stratton's mounted force near the ford would advance again, this time with more men than Skelly had led in the first charge. However, the force would conduct only a feint to draw the defenders' attention while at the bridge itself Crowninshield's dismounted men would rush in for the main attack.[56]

With a plan solidified, the attack began. Stratton's force, men from Companies A and G of the 11th Pennsylvania once again led by Skelly, thundered through the wheat field toward the Confederate left flank. The horsemen reached a wide depression about 300 yards from Bingham's earthwork, crossed a small ditch, and reformed on the other side. According to Sergeant George Cruikshank, the depression mostly shielded the men so that only their "heads were visible from the rebs' works." The North Carolinians began to crack off shots at these challenging targets. With the balls whizzing past them, the Federals ducked and dodged "their heads as if bumble bees were about." Skelly, understanding he had no time to spare, ordered his men to charge and "away they went," drawing the attention of all the defenders. Bingham's men as well as Hargrove's at the watchman's hut emptied their rifles at the cavalcade. But Skelly drove ahead, and the feint became a full assault. The riders got closer and closer. The defenders continued to fire until the feet of the Federal horses "struck the works." Bingham's men threw down their rifles and raised their hands. Their fight was done. Skelly's men had captured nearly half of the bridge's defenders in their intrepid rush. But closer to the crossing, Hargrove's detachment at the watchman's hut was still very much in the fight.[57]

The Federals at the bridge took advantage of the commotion created by Skelly's charge. "The cavalry in the rear, attracted the attention of the men in the [forward] earthwork, and received a volley in their midst," wrote a New Yorker right after the fight. "The enemy were completely dumb-founded." The charge on the flank gave Crowninshield's dismounted men the opening they needed. "At a given signal, we gave a short dash from the bushes in a body, and following our commander, rushed upon them," wrote one of the men.[58] Captain Reed reportedly cried, "Boys, remember California!" As the dismounted Union cavalrymen poured over the river, the combatants soon clashed at the hut and pressed together into a single mass of blue and gray. Alexander Peace, a soldier in Hargrove's com-mand, led a group of seven near the bridge. The small squad fired into "the faces" of the attacking Federals and "attempted to club them," but the advancing Yankees soon swept over Peace and his comrades. "Those in front, being pressed forward by those in their rear," Peace later wrote, "gathered our seven men in the human mass," which drifted up the rail line and over to and "around the watchman's cabin, and we were all together in one general melee." Lieutenant Colonel Hargrove did not give up despite the tremendous odds. In fact, he and his men—probably only about a few dozen by this point in the engagement—fought with an unusual determination despite the hopelessness of their stand.[59]

Popular accounts, sketches, and paintings of the Civil War teem with stories and images of ferocious close-quarters fighting, depicting men clubbing each other with rifle butts and slashing their opponents with bayonets. In reality though, such hand-to-hand fighting was rare outside of mounted cavalry scrums. Indeed, infantry combat during the conflict usually involved lines of combatants exchanging rifle fire at long range. However, the small fight at the South Anna on June 26, 1863, would prove one of those rare instances of close-quarters combat and would turn out to be as brutal as any exchange. In his letter home immediately after the fight, Caspar Crowninshield briefly conveyed the nature of the struggle: "The fighting was mostly hand to hand and our men ran the rebels through with their sabres."[60]

It was indeed an unusual engagement that generated multiple, often inconsistent accounts that are difficult to disentangle.[61] The South Anna Bridge defenders would later recall many aspects of the attack but would pay particular attention to the close combat around the watchman's hut. A compact mass of violence dominated the scene. The jumble of combatants made it impossible for others looking on to fire their weapons without endangering their own men. "Men in ranks and out of ranks, mounted and on foot, armed and disarmed, were on all sides, while horses without riders ran wild in every direction through the fields," wrote Alexander Peace, who drafted a short letter to his family immediately after the battle and prepared a lengthy account years later. Peering in from outside the fray, many of the Union cavalrymen could only stand there and "wait for something to turn up . . . while on the inside there was bloody work going on." Peace himself received a pistol wound above his hip bone from a discharge so close it ignited his clothes and burned him "severely across my bowels," a wound that later caused more pain than the gunshot itself. The captured Robert Bingham, who witnessed the melee from back at the earthworks, recalled the fight would have been bloodier had the Federals not been in "each other's way."[62]

Lieutenant Colonel Hargrove remained at the center of the fight and became a focal point of the contest. "Some of our men seized the Lt Col in command of the rebels to pull him out of the house," recalled the Iowan Cruikshank. "The rebels behind got hold of him and pulled him [back] in."[63] During the brawl, Hargrove, slashed by sabers and pierced by bayonets, fought back while emptying his pistol at the attackers and then hurling the empty revolver at one cavalryman's face, knocking him down and smashing several teeth. Alexander Peace remembered that Hargrove received a saber cut from a Federal who was then immediately "felled across him." Another Northerner stood on the tracks over the lieutenant colonel with his saber raised but was "clubbed in the mouth" and then shot through the chest by Sergeant William H. Strum. The Federals continued to close in on him but were so tightly packed they were unable "to sabre or pistol him."[64]

Hargrove continued to urge his men on, and his Tar Heels persisted. Private Joe Cash, the sixteen-year-old who had dispatched some of the attackers at the bridge earlier, "ran a sabre bayonet through a Yankee, the bayonet sticking half a foot behind his back." However, when Cash pulled his weapon out for another jab, two Federals shot the teenager in the head.[65] According to a different account, Cash encountered Colonel Spear himself during the melee, who called on him to give up. The young Tar Heel reportedly replied "Not until my colonel commands me" and then lunged forward leading with his bayonet. But before he could stab Spear, two rounds to his head brought him down.[66] According to one

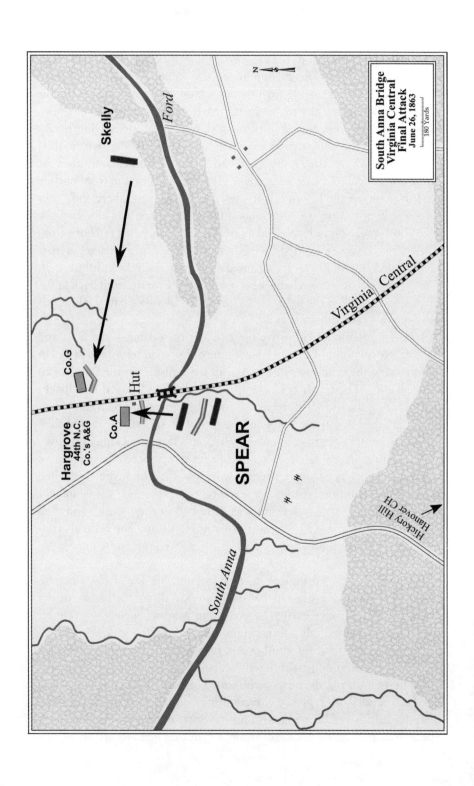

South Anna Bridge
Virginia Central
Final Attack
June 26, 1863

180 Yards

N

Skelly

Ford

Virginia Central

Co.G

Hut

Hargrove
44th N.C.
Co.'s A&G

Co.A

SPEAR

South Anna

Hickory Hill
Hanover CH

story, Spear stood near Cash's body after the fight and said, "Poor boy, I am sorry; but if I had not shot him as soon as I did, he would have killed me."[67] There were more brutal encounters. In recalling the fight years later, Peace, in what is surely a loose compilation of different recollections from fellow veterans, described what befell several of his comrades:

> Private [Michael] Satterwhite receives a blow on the back of his head, knocking him to his all fours, his gun flying from his hands. He crawls to where a sabre is lying, seizes it and before he has fully straightened himself up, strikes down the man before him. Corporal [Steven G.] Knot capturing two men and taking their arms from them to the rear, where he finds a solid column of Pennsylvanians ready to receive them. Sergeant [James G.] Hayes, a man of most powerful muscle, runs amuck through the crowd, knocking from one to two men down at a stroke with the butt of his gun, but is felled to the ground by a blow across his nose by a carbine. Sergeant [John R.] Buchanan, just up the railroad outside the ring, breaking the monotony of a constant fire from his rifle, is shot through the lungs and is captured after a struggle with half a dozen Federals. Another confederate soldier with clothes on fire is furiously attacking, with the butt of his gun, the inner column of the enemy's ranks.[68]

Finally, Hargrove, engulfed by enemy troopers, relented and shouted out "I surrender!" The brawl quickly ended when the Union cavalrymen "went in and parted the combatants, pushing their comrades back, and placed a guard" around the prisoners. Some of the Confederates sought to escape below the bridge but soon gave up, "ran the muzzles of their guns into the ground, [and] threw up their hands."[69] But the violence did not stop completely. According to the Pennsylvanians' regimental historian, one of the Confederate prisoners lunged forward and killed Richard McFarlan, the first sergeant of Company B, with a bayonet thrust to the heart. McFarlan's comrades immediately shot the rebel, and some even fired into the other prisoners, "it being supposed that hostilities had resumed," recalled a Pennsylvanian. However, this flareup soon ceased and the fight ended.[70]

"NOTHING IS LEFT"

In the end, the vicious melee had lasted perhaps no more than fifteen minutes, but the overall encounter, beginning with Spear's arrival at the bridge, had consumed several hours.[71] For Hargrove and his men, it was an achievement. The small force of fifty or so Tar Heels, later augmented by Bingham's company of forty or so, had held off more than a thousand Federal horsemen for a large portion of the afternoon and, most important, provided Confederate officers time to reinforce other locations. Nevertheless, after the fighting subsided, Spear's men, armed with torches and pitch, soon fired the Virginia Central bridge. An anonymous Californian, lifting a quote from the poet Matthew Prior, wrote that the blaze was "'growing small by degrees and beautifully less,' very fast when I last saw it."[72] A less varnished line appeared in Spear's report: "I completely destroyed the bridge and burned it till it fell into the river. It was fired above and below, and nothing is left."[73]

Near the bridge, both sides gathered their wounded and counted their dead. Though small in absolute numbers, the engagement's losses were high in relation to the men involved, at least on the Confederate side. As was often the case, casualty estimates varied. Spear reported nine Confederates killed and many seriously wounded. From his own command, he counted three killed and eight wounded.[74] Colonel Singeltary, Hargrove's superior, listed in his report seven killed and thirteen wounded.[75] A story in a California newspaper put the number of rebel prisoners at 111, though Colonel Godwin estimated about fifty.[76]

At the watchman's hut, one of the New Yorkers surveyed the scene after gathering up the scattered muskets, cartridge boxes, and ammunition. "And it was here that the full horrors of war first presented themselves," he recounted. "Men in gray uniforms lay stretched upon the ground dead. A young boy not more than fourteen years of age, was the first face I ventured to look upon. It made me shudder. Blood was upon his face and head, and his clothing was dyed with precious drops." The cavalryman wondered who this boy was—"his name, home, and history." The body was no doubt that of Joseph Cash. The Federals conveyed the rebel wounded south across the bridge and laid them out in a slave hut. Later, Colonel Singeltary reported the wounded had been "cut with sabers, and some burned with powder from pistols," telltale signs of close combat.[77] After the Federals withdrew, a "Mrs. Winston," most likely Sarah Terrell Winston from the nearby South Wales Farm, and others entered the dwellings to tend to the suffering men, who were soon transported to Ashland and placed on the train for Richmond the next day.[78]

Following the fight, men from both sides discussed the engagement.[79] For the Californians in Crowninshield's battalion, the day had brought their first exposure to battle and, most likely, their first look at the enemy in the field. One of the Westerners asked a captured rebel what he was fighting for. The Southerner gave no answer and went on to explain that he was poor, uneducated, and had been forced into the army. One Union guard asked Robert Bingham whether he was the man "standing at the other end of the work, with sword and pistol." When Bingham answered yes, the cavalryman replied, "[W]ell you are hard to hit, I took four deliberate cracks at you at hardly 150 yards, but I am glad I missed you." There were more compliments. Colonel Spear reportedly offered kind words to Hargrove and his men. While sharing his whiskey flask, Spear asked Hargrove why he had fought "so hard without hope." "For time," was the straightforward response. Years later, Robert Bingham recalled Spear saying: "Colonel Hargrove, you have ruined my reputation. I came here to destroy all four of the bridges and the Junction, and I must retreat after burning only one bridge, and capturing only a handful of men. Your resistance is the most stubborn known to me during the whole war."[80]

Whether or not Bingham recalled Spear's quote accurately, the statement's substance rings true.[81] Indeed, Spear failed to reach the RF&P rail bridge, which stood intact only a few miles to the west. Confederate Colonel D. J. Godwin, in his official report, painted a dramatic picture of Spear's "desperate effort to get in the rear of our forces at" the Fredericksburg rail bridge, an attempt supposedly repulsed by Captain L. W. Allen's cavalry company. Godwin claimed the Federals sought to advance to the RF&P span along the south bank of the river. "Seeing this move," wrote Godwin, "I immediately crossed Aylett's [Ellett's] Bridge [the road span just west of the rail bridge] above with all the cavalry force I had, and charged the enemy on his flank. This move saved that bridge, for, after a few minutes' fighting, he retired in the direction of Hanover Court-House, with my cavalry in pursuit."[82]

Godwin's assertions seem questionable. Although some of Spear's men may have probed in that direction, the colonel's own report contains no hint of the drama detailed in Godwin's dispatch. According to Spear, the Federals, after the fight, learned Confederate reinforcements were headed to the RF&P bridge. That information convinced Spear that any attempt to carry the bridge "with prudence or safety" would be impossible, especially given his exhausted command and low ammunition.[83] A story in the Confederate press appears to bear out Spear's account. According to the *Richmond Dispatch*, a civilian detained by the Federals warned that "two brigades" guarded the RF&P bridge as well as Hanover Junction. This report, which was false, may have deceived Spear into ending the raid. In reality, as Confederate dispatches would later reveal, only a handful of companies guarded the nearby bridges.[84]

By destroying the Virginia Central bridge on June 26, Spear had achieved the first success of Dix's operation. He had cut the main rail connection to Lee's army, currently marching into Pennsylvania. But, with the RF&P railroad still intact, Confederates could continue to carry supplies on that line and then transfer them to the Virginia Central at Hanover Junction. Thus, it was unclear whether the destruction of the South Anna Bridge alone would inflict a critical blow or merely hamper Confederate logistical efforts.

Spear's appearance and subsequent attack in Hanover County triggered a chain of Confederate alarms.[85] Officials in Richmond responded. Disturbed by the threat to the Virginia Central road, they sent a "large number of well equipped and thoroughly organized troops." At 6 p.m., a train left the Virginia Central depot on Broad Street carrying Colonel John A. Gilmer's 27th North Carolina from Cooke's brigade. After reaching Hanover Court House, Gilmer reported that the South Anna Bridge had burned after a "gallant defense" by the Tar Heels there. Concerned the Federals would isolate his own regiment, and "deeming it useless to pursue" the Yankee raiders, Gilmer returned south to take up a position in the defenses north of Richmond. Other reports indicate Colonel Edward D. Hall's regiment, the 46th North Carolina, also from Cooke's brigade, left the city for the South Anna three hours after the attack. Another stated that a train departed Richmond at 7 p.m. with two pieces of artillery, but when no gunners were available to service the ordnance, the flatcar carrying the guns was detached. Later, according to the report, "our reinforcements came quietly back to town." The Confederates regrouped and prepared for the next Federal move.[86]

8

Rooney Lee's Capture

"THE YANKEES ARE IN THE LANE"

BY THE TIME SAMUEL SPEAR'S CAVALRYMEN appeared in Hanover County, Rooney Lee had been recuperating from his Brandy Station wounds for nearly two weeks at Hickory Hill, the plantation owned by his wife's aunt and uncle, Anne Butler Carter Wickham and William Fanning Wickham. Aided by his younger brother Rob and his enslaved servant Scott, Rooney had traveled after the fight to the Wickham estate, located less than 2 miles south of the Virginia Central Bridge and only a few hundred yards from Wickham's Station. Greeted by his wife, Charlotte Georgiana Wickham Lee, he settled into what he hoped would be an uneventful convalescence.

The Wickhams enjoyed a prominent spot in the extensive web of Virginia's wealthy slaveholding clans. Anne Butler Carter Wickham, whose family owned both the Shirley plantation and Hickory Hill, also happened to be a niece of Robert E. Lee's mother. Anne Wickham's son, Williams Carter Wickham, commanded a brigade in J. E. B. Stuart's cavalry and had fought at Brandy Station. Her husband, William Wickham, was the son of prominent Richmond lawyer John Wickham, who defended Aaron Burr in his treason trial.[1] William and Anne moved to Hickory Hill after their marriage in the 1820s. A wooden frame house formed the estate's centerpiece; a sizable three-story brick addition, constructed shortly before the war, clung to the rear. An impressive formal garden, which included a boxwood maze, occupied ground off the house's southwest corner. Beyond the immediate grounds, sprawling tracts with names such as "The Lane" and the "Old Quarters Lot," amounting to more than 3,000 acres, stretched out into the Hanover County countryside. Wheat ranked as the plantation's principal crop, but the Wickhams also grew oats, corn, fruits, and vegetables. Tobacco took up some of the acreage as well but did not serve as a primary source of income. Of course, slave labor produced nearly everything at Hickory Hill, and by 1860 the Wickhams kept a population of about 275 people in bondage there, making the estate one of the largest slaveholding plantations in the Commonwealth.[2] The plantation's enslaved people lived in huts dotting a tree-bordered, 8-acre field west across a small creek from the main house. The slave community, marked as "Quarters" on a map of the estate prepared by the Wickham family, also included a cemetery for enslaved persons north of the dwellings, which contained many burials sites.[3]

Rooney Lee's convalescence at Hickory Hill had gone well. By the last days of June, the wound in his leg began to "heal finely" in the comfortable, familiar surroundings.[4] The patient bunked in a two-room, one-story wooden outbuilding (referred to by the family as the "Office") a few dozen yards from the main house's east wing. Rob, Rooney's younger brother, bunked in the adjacent room. Thirteen-year-old Henry Wickham, grandson of William and Anne, later shared his recollections of Rooney Lee's stay at Hickory Hill. In a speech given before the Virginia General Assembly in 1940, the aged Henry recalled that time passed quickly during those weeks, as he "was made generally useful running errands, and bringing hot water from the kitchen." For his reward, he was allowed to spend time in the Office. When Lee's wound was dressed, Henry recalled seeing "a large hole where the bullet went in, but there were two holes some inches apart where parts of the bullet came out." He also remembered much discussion about the nature of the wound. Family members speculated that the Yankees had begun using Spencer carbines at Brandy Station and had fired "a soft-nosed bullet with a zinc cap on the back" that would detach and remain in the wound to cause "gangrene, blood poisoning and death." They presumed that Rooney Lee had avoided such a fate when the round that hit him passed completely through his thigh.[5]

During June, Rooney Lee's mother and sister occasionally visited from Richmond to check in. In addition, his father sent letters during the march north. On June 10, the army commander wrote his wounded son from his traveling headquarters: "Take care of yourself, and make haste and get well and return." To Rooney's wife, who struggled with bouts of rheumatism, Robert E. Lee expressed relief that her spouse's wound was not life-threatening. "With his youth and strength to aid him, and your tender care to nurse him, I trust he will soon be well again." The general also was thankful the injury had given Rooney to her "for a time" but instructed that "I shall look to you to cure him soon and send him back to me."[6]

Late Friday morning, June 26, with breakfast finished at Hickory Hill, Rob Lee and Anne Wickham stepped out onto the front porch of the main house. Anne Wickham recalled shortly afterward: "We had no fear or thought of danger, when the alarm was given by a breathless boy 'The Yankees are in [The] Lane.'" Young Rob Lee was advised "to save himself," and Moses Napper, a man enslaved at the plantation, was ordered to save Rooney Lee's horses, according to Wickham. "In ten minutes the barbarians were galloping across the lawn," she wrote.[7] By Rob Lee's later recollections, which differ somewhat from Anne Wickham's contemporaneous account, several shots rang out in the distance beyond the plantation's outer gate near a large hickory grove, sounds he attributed to squirrel hunters. As Rob recalled, Anne Wickham dispatched him to quiet the racquet. "I got my hat, and at once started off to do her bidding," he wrote. "I had not gone over a hundred yards toward the grove, when I saw, coming up at a gallop to the gate I was making for, five or six Federal cavalrymen."[8] Whatever the details of the Yankees' approach, the family knew trouble had arrived.[9]

The bedridden Rooney Lee directed his brother to leave immediately and save himself as well as their horses, then pastured at the North Wales farm across the Pamunkey. Heeding Rooney's appeal, Rob fled and ducked into a nearby hedge just as the cavalrymen reached the house. He gained the nearby woods and hid in a spot that afforded a view of smoke rising from Hanover Court House. After a decent interval, he returned to the grounds via the "luxuriant shrubbery" of the formal gardens. When he reached the last boxwood, he observed "quite a number of blue coats" in the yard "standing, sitting and walking about." He withdrew a few yards into the garden and pressed himself flat on the ground near a fir, covered by its low-hanging branches. From his hiding place, Rob Lee looked over toward the Office and witnessed three or four of the enemy cavalrymen conveying his brother away atop a mattress.[10]

A bitter Anne Wickham recorded the scene the next day. "That Lieutenant & that Surgeon—wicked monsters so elated at the prize they had in their power—the son of Gen. R. E. Lee—nothing could soften or turn them from their savage purpose & three or four of them tore him from his bed to the carriage." However, she also claimed many of the Federal cavalrymen admitted that Lee should not have been taken from his sickbed into captivity. Lee himself reportedly had words for the soldiers, telling them: "Well I can do nothing else, but if I had my brigade here, there would be more fun in taking me. Please use me easy, as I am not over my wound."[11] Lee's wife, Charlotte, went about "collecting & packing up such things as he required, looking deathly pale," according to her aunt.[12] The cavalrymen deposited Rooney Lee and his bedding into the

Wickham's carriage, which was pulled either by the Wickham's team, as Rob Lee later recalled, or Federal cavalry horses, according to one Union veteran.[13] When the Federals took Rooney away, Charlotte "gave way in a burst of feeling that must have softened the hearts even of [the] two dreadful officers had they witnessed it."[14] The Federals finally departed Hickory Hill around 5 p.m.[15]

The path to Rooney Lee's capture remains somewhat murky. The corrosion of memory, differing perspectives, and the general unreliability of witness recollections have produced a stew of conflicting stories. However, when pieced together, the various reports and accounts suggest one of Rooney Lee's own slaves or another man enslaved at Hickory Hill may have tipped off Spear's men to the presence of the wounded general.[16] According to the regimental history of the 11th Pennsylvania, Colonel Spear, while managing the bridge fight, learned from a member of Company D that "an old colored man" had informed his command "that Brigadier General Wm. F. H. Lee, a son of Robert E. Lee, was at the residence of General Wickham . . . not far away." The unit history states that Spear ordered a detachment from Company F under Lieutenant David O. Tears to the plantation.[17] Another version, written in 1884 by William J. Shirley of Company G, states that an advance guard encountered a Black man on the road north who exclaimed, "God bless you all; General Lee is [just] ahead." Confused, the troopers explained that General Lee was then marching north with the Confederate army. The man clarified that he was referring to the General's son, "William Fitzhugh Lee." "His colored man is driving his coach with two bob-tailed horses. A fast team," the man explained.[18]

Although Rooney Lee was not in the carriage, other accounts confirm that one of his enslaved servants, perhaps the young man named "Scott," was, in fact, exercising the horses that morning. Rob Lee, in discussing the mounts following the Union raid, wrote that the "one lost, my brother's favourite and best horse, was ridden straight into the [Union] column by Scott, a negro servant, who had him out for exercise. Before he knew our enemies, he and the horse were prisoners."[19] Additional information later provides further substantiation. An account published in the *Richmond Dispatch* in the late 1890s revealed that "it is possible a negro betrayed [Lee's] whereabouts."[20]

Other accounts suggest Colonel Spear and his officers learned about Lee's location through different means. For instance, Captain Stephen Tripp, a Pennsylvanian from Company K, asserted in 1896 in a letter to the *National Tribune* that a bugler from his regiment, "who was on a foraging expedition of his own, in some way learned that Lee was at Gen. Wickham's." As recounted by Tripp, the young man rode back to the South Anna and informed Spear of the report, who then ordered a detachment to capture Lee "if he was able to ride."[21] Still, another story suggested Spear learned about the wounded Lee from a Richmond newspaper picked up at Hanover Court House.[22]

Understandably, Rooney Lee's capture profoundly affected his family. Hickory Hill's matriarch, Anne Wickham, called the seizure a "cruel act" and confessed that she lived "in constant fear of [Federal] visitations" following the incident. "Fitzhugh [Rooney] behaved with great calmness & dignity & dear Charlotte bore up wonderfully till it was over," and "then her grief was heartrending," Wickham reported in a letter several weeks later.[23] William Fanning Wickham wrote Robert E. Lee two days after the incident, calling it a "great outrage" and assuring that Rooney, who bore the arrest with "great composure," would not suffer "serious inconvenience." Wickham then added that "he was not treated with the least incivility, with exception of one or two words to my wife, by which rough men meant nothing, [and] we have no reason to complain of the Yankees, further than their taking your son prisoner & their carrying off my horses & negroes of which I lost a good number."[24] The entire incident surprised William Wickham, who admitted that he had not realized the Federals had advanced so far into Hanover County at the time.[25]

Not surprisingly, Rooney Lee was displeased as well. According to a postwar account from Pennsylvanian Stephen Tripp, Lee asked Spear to parole him soon after his removal from Hickory Hill. Lee argued that he had "captured thousands of Union soldiers, and would probably capture thousands more, and that he had always paroled his wounded prisoners" where they were taken. Spear, as Tripp recalled, simply informed Lee he would have to go to Fortress Monroe and the discussion ended there.[26] A story in the *New York Daily Herald* claimed Colonel Spear refused to parole Lee on the spot because of the "dastardly tone the rebel leaders have taken toward our own officers captured in the actual conflict, and their refusal to surrender certain ones on account of this, and account of that." However, the precise reasons behind Spear's decision remain unclear.[27]

Rooney Lee was correct in asserting that victors during the war frequently paroled wounded prisoners on the battlefield, just as Spear did that day at the South Anna Bridge. But this common practice probably reflected considerations of simple convenience in most cases. Military law at the time did not specifically forbid taking the wounded Lee from Hickory Hill. General Orders 100, the "Lieber Code," issued by the War

Department only months earlier, contained no specific prohibition on capturing wounded enemy soldiers; neither did it require their parole.[28] Spear's decision was also consistent with the Dix–Hill cartel governing the exchange of prisoners, which generally delayed parole until an exchange was arranged. However, as illustrated by the *Maple Leaf* incident only weeks before, the cartel was rapidly eroding and heading toward a swift demise. This did not bode well for Rooney Lee. Ultimately, Spear appears to have believed his duty lay in transporting his prisoner back to Dix's headquarters at White House—Rooney Lee's own plantation—an irony surely not lost on anyone involved.

Adding to the Confederate outrage, the incident at Hickory Hill generated rumors that the Federals had conducted the raid specifically to capture Rooney Lee. In discussing the matter with British officer Arthur Lyon Fremantle a week and half after the incident, Robert E. Lee claimed the Federals had conducted the raid "for the express purpose of arresting his badly wounded son . . . who was lying in the house of a relation in Virginia."[29] After the war, the rumor expanded to include the suggestion that the Federals targeted Rooney Lee to use him later as a bargaining chip in the ongoing prisoner exchange disputes. Indeed, he would play a role in such disagreements over the coming months during a saga that would generate threats of execution and weigh heavily on his family. However, there is no evidence Spear targeted Lee for capture or hoped to use him for any larger purpose. Instead, it appears the Federals had no knowledge of Lee's convalescence at Hickory Hill until the day of the South Anna Bridge raid.[30]

Lee's capture also produced conflicting stories about the role of enslaved persons in the incident. For Rob Lee, the day reinforced his appreciation for the loyalty of the servants enslaved by the Wickham and Lee families. In his recollections published in 1904, he remembered that "all the horses but one had been saved by the faithfulness of our servants." He also recalled that "Scott," one of Rooney Lee's slaves, was captured by the Federals while exercising his brother's favorite horse but "watched his opportunity, and, not being guarded, soon got away" by "crawling through a culvert" and along a "deep ditch in the adjoining field" to reach the horses and hide them in the woods. Rob Lee's story, emphasizing the well-worn Lost Cause notion of the "loyal slave" and widely disseminated through his book of recollections about his father, has found purchase as the standard account of the event.[31] In addition, Henry Wickham would recall in 1940 that Moses Napper and Scott Davis, two enslaved men who had been given to Charlotte Wickham Lee by her grandfather as a wedding present, "came back to the house and said that in the confusion they had slipped away, crossed the River" with the horses, and took them into the woods there.[32]

However, in attempting to recall that day's events many years later, the younger Lee may have conflated matters somewhat. A letter written by Anne Wickham immediately after the raid suggests something different. In writing to Robert E. Lee's brother on June 27, she noted that when the cavalrymen arrived "Robbie was ordered to save himself & Moses to save the Gens horses."[33] Accordingly, in this telling, "Moses," most likely the Moses Napper mentioned by Wickham, may have been the enslaved individual who saved the horses as recalled by Rob Lee. Whereas a different individual named "Scott" (most likely Lee's slave "Scot[t] Davis" as identified later by Henry Wickham) may have been exercising Rooney Lee's personal horse that morning and encountered the Federals out on the road, perhaps losing Lee's horse and alerting the soldiers to Rooney Lee's presence.

In all likelihood, the precise course of events may never be known. It is fairly clear, however, that many of the enslaved persons at Hickory Hill walked off the plantation that day. From their numerous quarters across a small stream and through a strip of woods west of the main house, many persons held in bondage at the plantation took the opportunity to join Spear's column. William Fanning Wickham, who had taken the 8 a.m. train into Richmond that morning, returned to Hickory Hill the next afternoon to find that, in addition to capturing Rooney Lee, the Federal raiders had "carried away with them 18 of my negroes. Almost all young men & boys & five horses." He worried whether his remaining laborers would be able to harvest the wheat crop.[34] Later, in a July 30 letter, Anne Wickham informed a relative that "between 30 & 40" slaves had left Hickory Hill, "mostly young men without families," and forty escaped from the farm at North Wales.[35] A report in a Richmond newspaper indicated that, in addition to freeing some enslaved people at Hickory Hill and North Wales, Spear's men "drove off with" seven from South Wales, the home of the Winstons, and several from neighboring plantations.[36]

"GRASP THE HAND OF THE HORSEMAN, SWING UP BEHIND AND GO AWAY"

Late in the afternoon, Spear's column rode back from South Anna River. During the earlier fighting, Henry Wickham and his cousin Frank Nelson had wandered up from Hickory Hill to the bridge in search of revolvers from the "bodies of fallen Yankees." But the pair did not get far. "We had approached within about 400 yards of the bridge when a bugle sounded and instantly, we heard the zip! zip! zoo! Of Minie bullets," recalled Wickham in a speech nearly eighty years later. "That sound is unmistakable, and once heard is never forgotten." The boys did not find any revolvers and "retreated in great disorder dodging behind the shocks of wheat" until they made it back to the main road, where many slaves sat waiting for the Federals to return from the bridge fight. Eventually, Spear's column appeared, and Wickham watched from the side of the road as mounted Federals passed by, some horses with dead men "on the pummel of the saddle, head hanging down on one side and feet on the other." Wagons, taken from local farms including South Wales, followed with their cargos of wounded cavalrymen. Finally, at the end of the line, the limbers pulling Spear's two guns passed followed by a "strong rear guard." As the final horsemen rode by, the young Wickham saw "a number" of enslaved onlookers, both men and women, get up and run alongside the riders so as to "grasp the hand of the horseman, swing up behind and go away."[37]

At Hanover Court House, Margaret Wight witnessed the raiders' return and noted that the cavalrymen brought "their prisoners, killed and wounded and some of ours as well as Negroes, wagons, &c in abundance."[38] In the town, Spear found that Major Wetherill, who had remained there during the fight, had burned forty wagons under repair, 300 harness sets, a blacksmith shop, a wheelwright, stables, and 1,000 bushels of corn.[39] Spear's men then gathered whatever captured wagons and materiel remained and headed southeast along the same route they had used earlier that day. Along the way, Rooney Lee spoke with some of his captors. Caspar Crowninshield of the 2nd Massachusetts, whose cousin had roomed with Lee at Harvard, told a relative several days later that "I went up & spoke to him, he remembered me well. I offered to and did all I could for him. I had a long talk with him he asked all about his old friends."[40] Lee did not speak with everyone, though. According to Captain Stephen Tripp, the prisoner was "very reticent," refusing, for instance, to talk to a sergeant from California who had served with him in the army before the war.[41]

In the early evening after leaving Hanover Court House, Colonel Spear altered his return route. Near Nelson's Bridge, he learned that General Wise had organized a force to intercept his path along the west and south side of the Pamunkey. To avoid another fight, Spear crossed his column over the river. The move was not free of some drama, though. During the afternoon, Corporal George Crosby and a handful of men had guarded the rebels captured that morning near Wickham's Station—Lieutenant William McKnight and the other wounded members of the 17th Virginia left behind by Corse. Crosby escorted his exhausted, footsore prisoners during the afternoon, lending out his horses to spell the rebels from time to time. At Nelson's Bridge, Crosby's group paused under some roadside trees while Private George Olcott ventured ahead to fill canteens at a nearby house, leaving only two men to watch the Virginians. As Olcott went off on his errand, a squadron of Confederate horsemen appeared across the fields galloping toward the weary group. The mounted rebels, led by Colonel William Shingler of the Holcombe Legion, bore down, threatening not only to spring the prisoners but also to scoop up Crosby and his men in the bargain. Shingler's horsemen freed Lieutenant McKnight and his band, but Crosby managed to escape, turning just for a moment to yell back: "Good-bye Lieutenant!" Private Olcott, though, returned with his full canteens at the wrong time and was soon on his way to prison in Richmond.[42]

Shingler's rebels soon departed, leaving the road open. Later, Spear's main column arrived and crossed the river unmolested over Nelson's Bridge and into King William County, removing the planks behind them after the last man was over. Spear's horsemen bivouacked for the night just north of the river at Wyoming, the Nelson plantation, which consisted of "a large, wooden, tumble-down house with a considerable garden and some fine beech trees nearby." The cavalrymen slept on the plantation's grounds while the officers bunked in the house.[43]

That evening at Wyoming, according to a story that made its way into a North Carolina newspaper, Colonel Spear spoke about the bridge fight with a few civilians detained that day near Hanover Court House. He conceded that, "if all the Confederate men fight as these fifty men have done, this war will last much longer than I have ever expected." He also marveled at the desperation and ferocity of the engagement, including its hand-to-hand combat. "Why, sir," he continued, "some of them used their bayonets and stabbed several of my men severely" even after they were completely surrounded. Spear also supposedly revealed that his effort was only a preliminary raid and vowed that he "would certainly return again."[44]

Wyoming's proprietor, Henrietta Nelson, often referred to as "the Widow Nelson," expressed her unhappiness with the Yankees crowding into her home. However, when she learned Rooney Lee was to be a guest for the night, she changed her demeanor and offered the best the household could gather for supper and granted the prisoner the finest bedroom in the house.[45] Colonel Spear did not interfere and, with "good humor," indulged Nelson's hostility.[46] That evening, Captain Stephen Tripp drew guard duty for the notable prisoner and posted a sentry outside the room in the hall, choosing to provide Lee some privacy. Late in the evening, Lee requested to speak with a captured Confederate surgeon who was on the grounds attending to the wounded. The surgeon remained in Lee's room the entire night, leaving the others uncared for until the Union doctors had finished with their own. In the morning, Lee took his time getting ready for the march ahead. Annoyed at the delay, Colonel Spear "fretted and fumed" and, fearing the rebels would attempt a rescue, finally insisted that Lee move. Eventually, Lee obeyed but complained about the "discourteous treatment."[47]

On Saturday morning, June 27, Spear's force left the Wyoming estate and resumed its return to White House Landing. The column traveled through King William County, passing through Newcastle and King William Court House along the way. On the march, the men skirmished occasionally with "bushwhackers" but eventually reached White House after their long, eventful journey. During the return, they captured a Confederate agent bringing payment from Richmond for stores purchased from local sellers and seized $15,000 in rebel bonds. They arrived at White House Landing on that evening, bringing "some baggage of no mean order." There they found Dix's command—nearly 20,000 infantry and artillerymen—waiting for them. Pennsylvanian William Shirley recalled: "When we got to White House we found a fleet of transports, lots of artillery, engines and everything from sutlers to newsboys." The infantrymen at White House gave "cheer after cheer," which, admitted Shirley, "made us feel as if we had done our duty." The raiders brought with them dozens of prisoners from the South Anna, 500 mules, 200 horses, thirty-five army wagons, the captured bonds, many freed people, and Rooney Lee. The cavalrymen camped north of the River on Pamunkey Island. No one at the moment seemed to focus on the fact that the RF&P bridge was still standing.[48]

"DETERMINED AND DESPERATE GALLANTRY"

News of the raid girded Confederate resolve. Officers returning from Hanover on the train reported the Yankees had destroyed the trestlework near the courthouse and pulled up sections of track. In addition, Hargrove's performance at the South Anna soon became known. Editors at the *Richmond Dispatch* declared that perhaps no one yet in the war had exhibited "more determined and desperate gallantry" than the bridge defenders.[49] Stories of the Tar Heels' fight and particulars of their capture rapidly circulated. So did other details. Writing home to a Greensboro newspaper, a member of Cooke's brigade reported that Spear's men compelled the prisoners "to pile up their knap-sacks and blankets and set fire to them with their own hands" and "even threatened hanging." In addition, Hargrove's jacket was retrieved near the bridge after the fight, shredded by eight saber cuts.[50]

For the captured men, the engagement initiated a long journey through Federal installations and prisons, a saga prolonged by the breakdown of the Dix–Hill exchange cartel. After the fight, Hargrove headed to the prison at Johnson's Island in Lake Erie, then to Fort Delaware, and then to Point Lookout in April of the next year. He did not take the oath of allegiance until July 1865.[51] After the war, he served in public office as a Republican, an unusual affiliation for a Confederate veteran, and was elected North Carolina's attorney general in the 1870s, speaking out against the Ku Klux Klan during his campaign.[52] He died December 16, 1889, and was buried in Townesville, North Carolina.[53]

Reports of the fight also produced tension between Virginia and North Carolina troops, triggered by a *Richmond Enquirer* story incorrectly identifying Colonel Godwin's Virginia cavalrymen as the bridge defenders. A chaplain in the 44th North Carolina wrote to correct the mistake but, in doing so, accused Godwin's Virginians of cowardice during the fight. This precipitated an angry exchange that dragged on for a few weeks in the papers.[54] Although acrimony between the two states predated the war, dislike and distrust had grown in the first years of the conflict. The squabbling would increase following the disastrous charge on the third day at Gettysburg as Virginians and North Carolinians argued over their respective roles in the Confederate debacle there. The South Anna Bridge fight produced similar friction on a smaller scale.

News of Rooney Lee's capture rankled Confederate officials and their supporters. The *Fayetteville Observer* described Spear's act as "quite cruel and brutal enough to be perpetuated by yankees."[55] Southeast of Richmond, Edmund Ruffin paused from his ceaseless scribbling about crops and slaves to cry foul. "This barbarity was a superfluous trouble," he complained to his diary, "as the wounded general could have been paroled & left, & thereby equally secured as a prisoner." On top of Clement Vallandigham's arrest, Ruffin viewed the incident at Hickory Hill as further evidence of Lincoln's policy of "illegal force" and, overall, an "admission of weakness & fear."[56]

But no amount of rebel grumbling would spring Rooney Lee. The Federals took him to Fort Monroe and deposited him close by at Hampton. A *New York Daily Herald* correspondent, who witnessed the procession of prisoners, believed that Lee looked "feeble." The Federals carried him to Doctor Eli McClellan's hospital at Camp Hamilton. Once there, Lee again requested an exchange and a parole, but with the cartel's disintegration his chances for such an outcome diminished by the day. The Federals were blunt with Lee on the subject. When the Virginian expressed concern about an exchange, Dix's aide-de-camp, Lieutenant Colonel William H. Ludlow, "informed him that the matter rested altogether in the hands of the rebels, who at present refuse to exchange our officers." Despite his disappointment, Lee made a positive impression on many of his captors. "He has all the bearing of a refined and courteous gentleman," wrote the *Herald* correspondent. "He is firm looking, and calculated to produce the most favorable opinions of his abilities as a leader" and has "made no small number of friends by his manners."[57]

"MEN, WOMEN, AND CHILDREN"

The raid's impacts stretched beyond Rooney Lee's capture and the destruction of the South Anna Bridge. For hundreds of people enslaved on plantations northeast of Richmond, the operation proved to be a door to freedom. In addition, for Federal soldiers, it demonstrated the tangible contributions enslaved persons made to the Union cause. Spear and his men liberated many people along the route or, at least, created the conditions that allowed them to free themselves. According to a North Carolina newspaper, the raiders carried away more than "three hundred valuable negroes . . . worth more than a half million of dollars."[58] The Confederates filled their newspapers and diaries with accounts of African Americans walking off their plantations to join Spear's column. Many insisted they had not left voluntarily. But neither Spear nor any of his men mentioned slave liberation as a goal of the enterprise; given the stated aim of the mission (the destruction of the bridges), they had other matters to attend to. In his report, Dix confirmed that a "large number of slaves (men, women, and children) followed Colonel Spear's train." One Federal soldier, in listing the results of the raid in his diary, finished by noting the column had brought "lots of negroes" back to White House. Not surprisingly, the refugees sought to remain with the Union forces. Accordingly, Dix decided to put the men to work at his temporary base and send the women and children east to Fort Monroe.[59]

Although the Federals may not have focused on aiding the enslaved people in the region, many of those held in bondage in the area clearly contributed to Spear's success. While not detailed in any Union reports, it is clear that, from the first minutes of the effort, Black civilians had stepped forward to help the raiders repeatedly. First, at White House Landing on Thursday morning, June 25, several civilians reported the strength of Confederate forces in the area. Then, outside Hanover Court House the next day, a Black man alerted the troopers to the presence of a rebel cavalry force nearby. At the South Anna Bridge, enslaved people pointed the Federals to the ford downstream from the bridge, information pivotal to Spear's attack, which allowed the cavalrymen to outflank the rebel position there. Finally, it appears one or more slaves at Hickory Hill may have informed Spear's men of Rooney Lee's presence at the plantation, information that possibly led to his capture.

This consistent pattern of aid underscores the commitment Black people in the region held for the Union cause. The actions also highlight their willingness to take significant risks to damage the Confederacy. The examples of assistance to Spear's mission also matched a pattern noted by others examining similar operations and campaigns. For example, in his study of the 1862 Peninsula Campaign, historian Glenn Brasher demonstrated that enslaved people not only provided essential labor to US operations but also furnished vital intelligence that informed Federal tactics and strategy.[60] The same pattern appeared in North Carolina, where thousands of self-emancipated people arrived at Federal bases and served the army by digging fortifications, gathering intelligence deep in enemy country, and eventually enlisting in newly formed regiments. All these contributions helped the Federal war effort and convinced many civilians in the North that emancipation was a military necessity.[61]

"GALLANT AND JUDICIOUS"

John Dix had nothing but praise for the raid. "Colonel Spear's conduct has been gallant and judicious," and "I am satisfied that [he] has accomplished all that could be done," he wrote Halleck. "He is one of the best cavalry officers in the service. I commend him . . . to the consideration of the Government." Dix's dispatch to Washington emphasized that Spear had "completely destroyed the Virginia Central railroad over the South Anna, captured Gen. W. F. Lee," took other officers, soldiers, wagons, horses, mules, and brought back $15,000 in Confederate bonds. The press also took note of the expedition. A column in the *New York Times* called Spear's effort an "important and successful expedition"; a correspondent for the *New York Daily Herald* described it as the "most successful raid yet made from this point," and another labeled it "a most signal and successful victory."[62]

However, in the opinion of some men who actually conducted the raid, the credit was not doled out evenly. Cavalrymen from California, Massachusetts, and New York believed reporters had showered far too much praise on the Pennsylvanians in Spear's command. One New Yorker, writing home to Saratoga Springs, complained that "the 11th Pa.[] appear to receive from the press the entire credit for this successful expedition through the enemy's country, and the 2nd Mass. cavalry are scarcely mentioned." His fellow New Yorkers had also been "prominently engaged" as well as ready for emergencies, yet "the selfish nature of our Pennsylvania comrades has become so notorious[] that we prefer to yield them our portion, rather than share it with them." Caspar Crowninshield, from the 2nd Massachusetts, fingered Colonel Spear for failing to spread the accolades evenly and complained that the commander "gives almost all the credit of the affair to his own regt." Noting the general anger shared by officers and men alike, Crowninshield expressed his particular disappointment that the New York papers failed to "even mention that we were there."[63]

But no matter where the credit fell, it could only stretch so far. Spear's operation could not qualify as anything but a partial success because the RF&P bridge over the South Anna remained untouched. In addition, although orders from both Halleck and Dix mentioned the North Anna bridges, including the Virginia Central span there, Spear did not seem to give those targets much thought, a reasonable posture given that the immediate impact of cutting the rail line to Fredericksburg would be minimal. Nonetheless, the connection to Lee's railheads at Culpeper and in the Shenandoah Valley at Staunton remained unbroken. For certain, the destruction of the Virginia Central bridge would cause disruption. Indeed, one of the last trains to travel on that railroad contained, among other things, 100 pounds of blasting powder to Richmond. Another train, carrying a large number of Union prisoners captured at Winchester, reportedly managed to stop just before reaching the South Anna that afternoon, thus avoiding Spear's men.[64]

Spear's raid did not land a fatal blow to Confederate logistics in Virginia. However, the destruction of the South Anna Bridge likely caused delays and a change in operations by forcing all traffic between Richmond and Hanover Junction onto the RF&P line. Once at the junction, workers could shift northwestern-bound cargo from the RF&P cars onto the Virginia Central trains.[65] As long as that bridge stood, the Confederates could rely on this cumbersome arrangement. They had Tazewell Hargrove and his Tar Heels to thank for the bridge's preservation. The stubborn defense helped ensure that Spear and his Yankees had neither the time nor energy to reach the other span several miles upstream. But the threat remained. As the *Richmond Enquirer* explained a few days after the raid, the destruction of the RF&P would "result in serious interruption in our communication."[66]

The raid also shed some light on Federal war policy in Virginia—or at least on how the conservative John Dix wanted his troops to fight. In his report for Spear's operation, the general emphasized that "no private property has been touched," echoing his firm orders for Spear to protect civilian structures and possessions.[67] It also further revealed Dix's belief that hard-war policies would not serve the Union war effort. In all likelihood, Dix knew of the complaints circulating in Confederate newspapers of recent behavior by his command in eastern Virginia. With his cautionary instructions to Spear, he may have sought to avoid the complaints that had plagued earlier expeditions, particularly Colonel Tevis's raid at Aylett's only weeks before. Spear managed to conduct the mission to the South Anna with little damage to civilian property, although the Richmond press did not fail to hurl accusations of damage at Tunstall's Station and the Brockenbrough plantation.

Despite its limited results, Spear's expedition made good headlines in the North. But Dix had more to accomplish if he was going to fulfill Halleck's orders for operations against Richmond. His initial plan before Spear's arrival has never been clear. Perhaps he hoped Spear would destroy both bridges and free the main force, the Fourth and Seventh Corps, for operations directly against Richmond. But Spear's failure to burn the RF&P bridge left one of the key objectives of the campaign unaccomplished. The raid had also tipped Dix's hand, alerting the Confederates that the rail bridges were important goals of the operation. If Dix wanted to finish the task at the South Anna, he would have to send another column there, an expedition that would most likely face greater numbers of Confederate defenders.

With thousands of infantrymen from the Fourth and Seventh Corps gathered on the Pamunkey, Dix began to plan his next steps. The RF&P bridge over the South Anna still beckoned, but so did a larger prize: the Confederate capital itself. As Robert E. Lee's columns spread across Pennsylvania, Dix would have to decide whether he could land a mortal blow in central Virginia. His instructions from Halleck on the matter were ambiguous at best. Back on June 14, Halleck had ordered: "All your available force should be concentrated to threaten Richmond, by seizing and destroying their railroad bridges over the South and North Anna Rivers, and do them all the damage possible."[68] Since then, the general-in-chief had not augmented those orders, leaving questions about whether Halleck wanted Dix to attack Richmond directly or limit his operations to the railroads. Without further input from Washington, Dix would have to make decisions on his own using his best judgment as he prepared for the next stage of the operation against Richmond.

9

Rebel Diplomacy

"AS YOU THINK THE CIRCUMSTANCES JUSTIFY"

THE DAY AFTER SAMUEL SPEAR'S WEARY TROOPERS returned to White House, Major General George Meade assumed command of the Army of the Potomac in the wake of Joseph Hooker's sour request to be relieved from command. Meade immediately sought to divine not only the location of the Army of Northern Virginia but also the disposition of some of his own forces. As it turned out, the Army of the Potomac's seven designated corps had made it across the Potomac River and were converging on Frederick, Maryland. From Washington, Henry Halleck commenced a vigorous exchange with his new army commander, affording Meade an operational flexibility he had denied Hooker, particularly with respect to the troops at Harpers Ferry. In fact, one of Halleck's first dispatches to Meade on the afternoon of June 28 read: "The garrison at Harper's Ferry is under your orders. You can diminish or increase it as you think the circumstances justify."[1] It was quite a slap to the previous army commander. But no one, save perhaps Hooker, likely focused on such things at the time. In the East, the entire Union high command waited for news of enemy movements.

The Confederates seemed to be everywhere. Lee had spread his forces across a good portion of southern Pennsylvania. The tip of the spear, Ewell's Second Corps, had led the way nearly a week earlier, plundering the villages and farms on its way into the heart of the state. By June 27, his lead units had stretched east beyond Carlisle and headed for the banks of the Susquehanna River near Harrisburg and south near Wrightsville. The balance of Lee's army—the better part of Longstreet and Hill's corps—concentrated near Chambersburg west of South Mountain. From his headquarters there, Lee waited for reports of the Federals and planned his next move. But with calvary commander J. E. B. Stuart well to the southeast near Washington and his only other cavalry units guarding the Blue Ridge gaps south of the Potomac, the Confederate commander remained largely ignorant of his enemy's location.

To this point in the campaign, Lee's army had operated for the most part unmolested, enjoying several days of relative tranquility in the Keystone State. The Southerners busied themselves filling commissary and quartermaster wagons with all manner of provisions and supplies. They also continued to round up free Black civilians from the surrounding towns and farms and ship them southward into slavery. Much to the dismay of the loyal citizens of the state, it appeared the rebels were settling down for a long stay. "We are here and the Yankees can't run us away," crowed a Georgia surgeon in a letter home.[2] By Sunday, June 28, Ewell's advance units reached the outskirts of the state capital at Harrisburg on the Susquehanna. Ewell was poised to capture the city and land a huge blow against the Federals, putting Lee in a position to move against Baltimore and even Philadelphia.[3]

But any plans for Harrisburg evaporated Sunday night when a spy hired by James Longstreet arrived at Lee's headquarters in Chambersburg with news that the Army of the Potomac was heading rapidly for Pennsylvania. The information forced Lee to put an end to Ewell's far-flung operations and his army's extensive foraging efforts and order his units to concentrate near Cashtown, east of Chambersburg across South Mountain and just a few miles away from the crossroads town of Gettysburg. Later, according to Lee's after-action report, he chose to draw in these forces to deter the enemy "from advancing farther west, and intercepting our communication with Virginia." He also now had an opportunity to engage the Federals.[4]

With these new scouting reports, the rail lines running north from Richmond—the targets of Dix's operations outside the Confederate capital—regained importance. After Lee learned the various Union corps were already across the Potomac and only miles away from his dispersed army, he had a new problem. His aide Charles Marshall, echoing statements in Lee's own report, later recalled that the general expected the Federals would "enter the Cumberland Valley south of our army, and obstruct our communications through Hagerstown with Virginia." Such concern over the rail connections is noteworthy. Only three days earlier, Lee had informed Davis that, without sufficient men to guard his communications back to Virginia, he had abandoned those links. However, the army commander clearly had not cast aside his concern over his supply lines altogether. He still needed a tether to the South, and as the enemy Army of the Potomac drew closer, he took action to protect his escape route home. Indeed, by Marshall's recollection, Lee never viewed his connection to Richmond as completely severed. "While he did not consider that he had complete communication with Virginia," Marshall remembered Lee saying, "he had all the communication that he needed, as long as the enemy had no considerable force in the Cumberland Valley."[5]

Marshall later explained that, given Ewell's foraging efforts, Lee's "principal need for communication with Virginia was to procure ammunition," and Lee believed such supplies could reach him through the Shenandoah and Cumberland Valleys under an escort. However, a significant enemy presence in the Cumberland Valley would render such a lifeline "impossible." Therefore, as Marshall recalled, the news from Longstreet's scout shifted Lee's focus to keeping the Army of the Potomac east of the mountains and away from his communications through the Cumberland and Shenandoah Valleys. He also looked to implement his longstanding plan to engage the Army of the Potomac as it arrived in pieces tired after hard marching.[6] Events during the upcoming week—namely, the tremendous clash at Gettysburg—would reveal whether Lee would need intact rail lines in Virginia to ferry additional supplies and troops.[7]

"LOOKING TO A CESSATION OF HOSTILITIES"

On Friday, June 26, as Lee's troops swept through central Pennsylvania and Colonel Spear's cavalry burned the South Anna Bridge, a travel-weary Alexander Stephens stepped off the train in Richmond ready for his upcoming diplomatic mission. That evening, the Confederate vice president reached his personal residence, Baskerville House, at the corner of 8th and Franklin a block from the capitol building. At 8 p.m., he sat down to write a note to his brother Linton back in Georgia. "Just got here [and] have not seen the President yet. The city is in quite excitement. . . . The enemy is making another demonstration on this place." Other issues occupied his mind as well. Days before, back in Georgia, he had dwelled on the proclamation of General David Hunter of the Union about executing rebel higher-ups in retaliation for Black prisoners so treated. Newly arrived in Richmond, he took the time to write Linton that Federal officers in North Carolina were "concocting to have a general insurrection among the slaves on the 1st day of August" (or so he had heard during his journey).[8]

On Saturday, Stephens met with President Davis to discuss the nature of his mission and its relation to Lee's operations in Pennsylvania. Like nearly everything associated with Stephens's diplomatic effort, the details of this exchange are unclear. Sometime before his arrival in Richmond, he had learned, to his surprise, that Lee had launched an offensive into the North. At the capital, he found "an entire change in the military aspect of affairs." In his June 12 letter, he made his suggestion with the understanding that Lee was "resting quietly on the Rappahannock." Now with Lee in the field, Stephens did not believe a diplomatic overture was appropriate. In his view, the new rebel offensive "would greatly excite the war spirit and strengthen the War Party" and lead Lincoln to reject any proposed discussion. Stephens recommended that Davis abandon the plan altogether.[9]

Davis disagreed. He understood the vice president's reservations but nevertheless believed "Mr. Lincoln would more likely receive such Commissioner if General Lee's army was actually threatening Washington City, than if he was lying quietly south of the Rappahannock." Davis and Stephens vetted the issue at a cabinet meeting held the same day, during which Stephens conveyed his doubts about the timing of the diplomatic mission given the military developments. The cabinet members sided with the president on the matter, believing Lee's operations "rendered the occasion most opportune for making the effort for the conference suggested."[10] Stephens apparently did not press the issue. In his private correspondence with Linton, he did not bother to mention his disagreements with Davis. After his initial meeting on Saturday, he simply reported: "To-day I had an interview with the President. I may go further before my return." He did, however, convey some other war news—touching on Dix's threat to the city, the latest Confederate commerce raiding, and the news from Vicksburg. He also wrote of Lee's offensive: "No news from Lee. Nobody here knows where he is."[11]

On Sunday, June 28, Stephens, battling a pounding headache, continued to monitor the apprehension building in the capital as reports arrived about a large Federal force gathering at White House on the Pamunkey. "The excitement in the city continues, all citizens under arms, but nothing definitely known," he relayed. All the while, he did his homework for the upcoming diplomatic mission, combing through every document he could find related to the prisoner exchange cartel. He had concluded that the "state of controversy" between the Federals and Confederates on the matter was "in a very unsatisfactory condition" and expected the emergence of "the bloodiest and most barbarous system of retaliation." Again, he focused on the issue of Black Union soldiers. He fixated on the Federal refusal to exchange rebel prisoners in retribution for the Confederacy's stated policy to execute officers in charge of United States Colored Troops units. Stephens doubted he could defuse the controversy but was "willing to do all I can, but am not hopeful."[12]

By Tuesday, June 30, with his headache gone, Stephens had plowed "partly well through" the stacks of papers and correspondence he had collected on the prisoner exchange. Still, he felt ill-at-ease. His days in Richmond were hectic, being crammed with visitors and other distractions, a far cry from the quiet of his Georgia plantation. "I have to write by snatches," he complained to Linton. "Being so frequently interrupted by calls. I cannot provide myself ten minutes of leisure to write." While Davis moved forward with plans for a diplomatic mission, Stephens projected pessimism in his letters back south. "From what I can see of the state of the questions, I have but little hope of being able to effect anything." However, in his scribblings to Linton, he confided that Davis wished "to have the effort made and the overture rejected before resort to retaliation, which is now apparently the next step before us." He did not clarify what this "retaliation" was or who would carry it out. As he continued to prepare on Tuesday, Stephens also monitored Dix's threat to Richmond, informing Linton that the citizens were "all out under arms this evening."[13]

On Wednesday, July 1, he met with Davis again. The president was, in Stephens's words, "quite sick with dysentery, and . . . suffering greatly." Chief of Ordnance Josiah Gorgas noted in his diary that week that Davis's physician was "seriously alarmed." With the Federals threatening from the banks of the Pamunkey, Gorgas worried it was "the most serious calamity that could befall us" should the president succumb. But on Wednesday, Stephens reported that Davis was fit enough to talk "very freely, unreservedly, and most confidingly on all matters." Members of the cabinet—"all in authority here"—likewise seemed equally open with Stephens about their hopes for his mission. Davis proposed a grand scheme for the diplomatic effort. He asked Stephens to head north and join Lee's army and, under a flag of truce, pass through the Union lines and head to Washington as a military commissioner bearing a communication from Davis for Lincoln. The vice president was skeptical and doubted he would be allowed to pass through the Federal lines. He also believed Lee's threatening posture all but eliminated any chance the Federals would agree to meet at the bargaining table.[14]

But Davis continued to press the opposite view, expecting the threat of Union military disaster would only increase the enemy's willingness to talk. When the cabinet considered the issue again on July 1, Stephens once again found himself alone in his views.[15] Years later, in his memoir,

Stephens would explain that Davis and the cabinet believed Lee's operations provided the leverage needed to obtain results in negotiations. He also recalled that Secretary of War James Seddon "was particularly anxious" for Stephens to embark on his mission to repair the broken prisoner cartel before Vicksburg's thousands of defenders fell into Federal custody.[16]

On Wednesday evening, Stephens again wrote Linton and confirmed it was "pretty well settled at this time that I will go further." As he prepared his letter, he expected the secretary of war to visit at any moment with the final word. In his dispatch to Linton, he again hinted that his mission might involve more than the terms and protocols of prisoner exchange. "Would that my powers . . . were equal to what they desire me to accomplish!" Stephens remained doubtful about the task ahead under the "present condition" but nevertheless chose to yield his "judgment to theirs." Seddon soon arrived with news that Stephens would depart for Washington on Friday. The vice president completed his letter to his brother, once again discussing his ongoing concerns about whether Union officers were seeking to foment slave insurrection.[17]

In the documents prepared for the mission, Davis and Stephens carefully avoided specifics. The president's instructions emphasized that "your mission is simply one of humanity and has no political aspect." He directed Stephens to focus on the prisoner cartel and then listed difficulties that had plagued past exchanges.[18] Davis also raised a few separate issues for Stephens to discuss with Union officials. In his memorandum, he complained about the reported execution of captured Confederates and railed against Union officers who violated "all the rules of war by carrying on hostilities . . . against noncombatants, aged men, women and children." He also pointed to enemy troops who had destroyed "all private property within their reach." For Davis, this was a personal issue. Weeks earlier, he had received reports of an enemy visit to his brother's plantation, where Federals had rifled through "every trunk and box" and taken silver and jewelry. Only days before, the president had received word from family in Louisiana that Union soldiers had captured civilians, freed slaves, and threatened to burn the nearby town. In commenting on these stories, Davis remarked that "we have to deal with savages possessing the power of civilized people but will spare no effort to comply with the wishes of the families of the oppressed citizens."[19]

By raising issues of prisoner and civilian treatment, Davis focused on the increasing violence associated with the conflict—the "hard war" that had begun to emerge. His concern echoed the issues troubling John Dix, who had consistently urged his officers to shield civilians and their property during Federal operations. But there was plenty of destruction to go around. In fact, those in open rebellion against the United States were busy conducting their own share of theft, destruction, and kidnapping. While Davis objected to Federal transgressions, Robert E. Lee's men had completed several days of plunder in Pennsylvania, seizing property of all kinds, shelling towns, and enslaving free Black people. As Davis attempted to claim the high ground in his letter to Lincoln, he simultaneously threatened vague retaliation for the wrongs he perceived. "These usages justify and indeed require redress by retaliation as the proper means of repressing such cruelties as are not permitted in warfare between Christian peoples," he warned.[20]

Stephens's personal correspondence at the time sheds little light on the details of his upcoming mission. His personal letters, which betrayed a preoccupation with US policy toward Black soldiers and slaves, left few details in this regard. After the war, Stephens would deny there was more to the scheme than concern over prisoner issues, claiming in his memoir that the effort did not involve the issue of peace at all. In a postwar interview, he spoke of the cartel's failure and the misery its demise promised to visit upon captured soldiers languishing in prisons. He expressed no doubt about where the blame lay. "The men at the head of affairs at Washington were solely responsible for all these sufferings."[21] He did not speak of any other motive behind his diplomatic mission.

But it seems there may have been more to Stephens's effort than prisoners and protests. Contemporary evidence suggests that Stephens—as well as Davis, for that matter—hoped for more in approaching Washington officials. In his convoluted June 12 letter, the vice president had proposed to use the prisoner exchange matter as a means to discuss more fundamental issues with Federal officials—a "general adjustment" to "stop the further effusion of blood," as he put it.[22] Other information also hinted that there was more behind the mission. Postmaster General John H. Reagan, a witness to the deliberations in Richmond, recalled that Stephens "seemed to think something could be done to arrest the carnage of war by negotiations." Although Postmaster Reagan acknowledged that Stephens and Davis had focused on the cartel's renewal, he also wrote that the vice president "hoped to offer suggestions looking to a cessation of hostilities."[23] Whatever the mission's scope, Stephens surely planned to arrive at the table with a full quiver of tools, including concessions, threats, and mutually beneficial proposals.[24] But just what measures he had in mind is unclear. Whatever the aims, in the first days of July—as the fighting began at Gettysburg and as Dix initiated the next steps in his own Peninsula Campaign against Richmond—Stephens packed his bags for the journey to Washington.

10

Richmond Prepares

"THE SPIRIT OF RESISTANCE IS INCREASING"

As STEPHENS PREPARED FOR HIS TRIP, the Confederate high command sought to maintain contact with Robert E. Lee. Before crossing the Potomac in late June, Lee had floated his unconventional plan for P. G. T. Beauregard to bring troops north from South Carolina, form up at Culpeper, and threaten Washington. He believed such a force, even if created only "in effigy," would divert enemy strength away from his front, eliminate any threat of an attack on Richmond, and generally confound the Federals.[1] When this proposal arrived in Richmond on June 28, Davis immediately doused it as impracticable. In the president's view, there were simply no troops available for such a gambit and the other challenges dotting the map were just too numerous. In South Carolina, Beauregard strained to hold back Union army and naval forces. In the Mississippi Valley, Joseph Johnston frequently called for more troops to support Vicksburg's defense. In Tennessee, Braxton Bragg tangled with William Rosecrans around Tullahoma, and in Virginia D. H. Hill had nearly emptied North Carolina of defenders in bringing men north to Richmond.[2]

The president's June 28 response to Lee was also full of additional details about the ongoing threat to Richmond. He reported that Dix's large force was at White House and there were "indications of an advance on Richmond." Home defense companies were organizing and "the spirit of resistance [was] increasing" in the capital. Davis gave much detail about the "very small" force around Richmond and in North Carolina, listing the brigades by name. He also revealed that the untimely shift of Montgomery Corse's brigade to Gordonsville resulted in the destruction of the South Anna Bridge by Spear's raid, exposing the "want of cavalry" in Richmond exacerbated by Lee's offensive. Although Davis did not believe Dix's command was as formidable as some reports suggested, he suspected the Federals had enough men to "render it necessary to keep some troops within reach, and some at Petersburg." Faced with all these challenges, Davis firmly rejected Lee's proposal to hurl a second column at Washington from Culpeper, explaining that there were simply not enough men available. In so many words, the president concluded that Confederate authorities had given enough to the commander of the Army of Northern Virginia and were concerned about protecting Richmond against Dix's offensive.[3]

The day after Davis penned his reply, Samuel Cooper, adjutant and inspector general, also wrote Lee. Cooper bluntly explained that the Culpeper proposal had no possibility of being "carried into effect" and had in fact "embarrassed" the president. He also emphasized the threat posed to Richmond by the enemy gathering on the Peninsula, a force he characterized as sufficient "in cavalry, artillery, and infantry to do much harm" to Richmond or break Lee's communications and devastate the country. Cooper also mentioned the recent destruction of the Virginia Central bridge and, much like Davis, dwelled on the unfortunate departure of Corse's brigade shortly before Spear's attack. Then, Cooper turned the tables and recommended Lee look to his own problems. "I would suggest . . . you might not be able to spare a portion of your force to protect your line of communication," he rejoined.[4]

These letters from Davis and Cooper betrayed a sense of fatigue and even annoyance with Lee's Culpeper proposal, his persistent requests for more men, and even perhaps with his overall offensive into Pennsylvania. The letters emphasized the inconvenience and potential harm generated by Lee's movement. With the Army of the Potomac bearing down on his command at the end of June, Lee certainly would not welcome such news and advice. However, in an interesting twist, the dispatches from Richmond never reached Lee at all because Union scouts captured the courier bearing them northward. The intercepted letters soon arrived at George Meade's headquarters, where Daniel Butterfield, the army chief of staff, devoured their contents and promptly forwarded them to General-in-Chief Halleck in Washington.[5]

Union officials seized on the captured intelligence—an exceptional cache of information on Confederate dispositions and intentions in Virginia and elsewhere. From this intercepted correspondence, they learned that Richmond officials had rejected Lee's urgent appeal for reinforcements. They knew Beauregard and Bragg had sent men to the Mississippi Valley and that, as Union secretary of war Edwin Stanton put it, the available Confederate forces were "too small to defend Richmond and protect Lee's communications." Most important, perhaps, Stanton observed that the letters, which provided "the best view" yet of rebel forces, revealed that Davis "could not spare a man" and that Lee must "fight his way through alone, if he can."[6] An elated Adjutant General Lorenzo Thomas announced that the Confederate cause was desperate and "we will now crush out the rebellion."[7] Within days, mention of the captured letters made their way into the newspapers, and eventually full transcripts appeared for everyone to read.[8] However, the letters would have no immediate effect for the events at either Richmond or Gettysburg; matters were fast coming to a head at both locations.

"UNCOMFORTABLE TIMES"

On June 27, Herbert A. Claiborne, an official with the Confederate Commissary Department, recorded in his diary: "Much excitement in the city—citizens under arms. Cavalry who burnt South Anna Bridge passed back last night by way of Newcastle. Rumors of a large force at Brandon. Uncomfortable times."[9] The initial panic that had spread throughout Richmond earlier in the week began to well up again. When Spear hit the South Anna, reports arrived from rebel scouts about the size of Dix's forces gathering at White House. War Department officials scrambled to cover the key roads and bridge crossings into the city as local defense units readied to meet the enemy.[10]

The tools available to drive off an enemy attack were limited but perhaps not as small as some reports had suggested. The forces permanently assigned to Richmond totaled about 6,000 and included the 2,500 men of Henry Wise's brigade (about 800 of whom were posted at Chaffin's and Drewry's Bluffs south of the city), roughly 1,500 gunners in heavy artillery units, and the approximately 2,000 part-time soldiers of Brigadier General Custis Lee's local defense forces, which had been recently augmented by Governor John Letcher's call to arms. Their commander—Robert E. Lee's eldest son—had spent most of the war in Richmond as an aide to President Jefferson Davis, a position that kept him away from the battlefield. In addition to these city defenders, more troops were available nearby. The War Department had ordered three brigades from D. H. Hill's command north to Richmond or at least near to the city—Cooke's (2,198), Ransom's (2,840), and Jenkins's (2,143)—bringing the total number of defenders to approximately 13,000. In addition, Thomas Singeltary's 44th North Carolina from Pettigrew's brigade remained at Hanover Junction, and Montgomery Corse's Virginia brigade, from George Pickett's division, was still in supporting distance at Gordonsville.[11]

During June, the capital's safety lay in the hands of commanders such as Arnold Elzey, Henry Wise, and Custis Lee, men who had not and would not rise to vital positions in the Confederate command structure. But D. H. Hill, close by at Petersburg, was a different sort and would stand out in the coming days, exhibiting a level of tenacity, confidence, and decisiveness apart from the others. As the Army of Northern Virginia moved north, Hill had continued to oversee matters in his command from Petersburg. On June 24, he conducted a review of Micah Jenkins's brigade there before a large crowd of "perfectly delighted" spectators. For the finale, Hill delivered "a very stirring and eloquent address" and, according to a member of the Palmetto Sharpshooters, complimented the South Carolinians and their commander, so much so that Jenkins "could hardly sit in his saddle." At the same time, Hill took the opportunity to denounce some of the civilians in the crowd, explaining "the citizen's dress worn by a stout and able-bodied citizen was a badge of infamy."[12] After the event, Jenkins expected his brigade would be doing more than parade-ground duty in the coming weeks. Two days before the review, he reported home that "it is supposed [the Federals] intend an attempt on Richmond, in which event we will have an active time."[13]

Throughout June, Hill had focused on his department, seeking to improve Petersburg's fortifications and asking for more enslaved workers from Confederate officials to dig the defensive lines, a request that was refused.[14] Hill focused on the threat posed by the New Bern garrison as well as Dix's earlier forays into southeastern Virginia. But with Dix ascending the Peninsula, Hill fully understood how the real danger lay at Richmond.[15] So did members of the Davis administration, and in the days ahead Secretary of War James Seddon and even President Davis himself would deign to manage details of the capital's defense.

In the last week of June, Seddon churned out frequent dispatches to Hill's Petersburg headquarters. On June 25, he confirmed that Union troops had left North Carolina to either attack Richmond or join the Army of the Potomac in confronting Lee. He guessed the latter but suspected a cavalry raid near Richmond was also in the offing. Should the Federals "really move on us," he hoped to bring Hill to the city's aid in its defense.[16] Later that day, when word of Spear's arrival at White House was confirmed, an alarmed Seddon warned Hill that "you better move [Jenkins's] brigade, and such other force as you can spare" from Petersburg into a supporting distance at Bermuda Hundred or into Richmond itself.[17]

Hill, as was his tendency, suggested a different course. Worried that Jenkins's departure would leave Petersburg largely unprotected, he chose to send only half of the South Carolinians to Drewry's Bluff.[18] But as the unease in Richmond continued to increase, he soon directed Matt Ransom's North Carolina brigade to man the defenses east of the city. That afternoon, Ransom's men received orders to cook three days' rations and prepare to march at a "moment's notice." By 6 p.m., the North Carolina regiments headed for Richmond and crossed the James to Rocketts Landing. Under a miserable rain that evening, the Tar Heels tramped out on the Charles City Road and reached the outer works around midnight.[19]

"A REAL ADVANCE"

Reports continued to arrive about the Federals east of Richmond. At Newport News, a loose-lipped commissary worker informed a rebel scout that Dix had emptied Suffolk and was leading a force of 25,000 up the Peninsula. The scout also heard a rumor that "negroes are being enrolled as fast as caught," an unlikely story given General Dix's disregard for recruiting Blacks.[20] From the War Department, Seddon relayed news of Dix's operation to Hill as intelligence trickled in, including word that the Federals had landed 6,000 at White House along with "two locomotives and [a] full train of cars." To Seddon, the train's presence was ominous, a "singular feature in this matter" suggesting "a real advance."[21]

D. H. Hill's blood was up. "The movement seems to be real. I hope so," he informed Seddon on June 26, the day Spear's cavalrymen rode through Hanover County toward the South Anna.[22] Hill and Seddon considered drawing more troops from North Carolina to balance Richmond's protection with the need to guard the "immensely important" railroad link to Wilmington. From Kinston, Alfred Colquitt stood ready to order his Georgia brigade north, assuring Hill that, should Dix move on Richmond, "we expect to be with you in welcoming them 'with bloody hands to hospitable graves.'"[23] Hill knew Richmond was the priority. Should the Union forces press an attack, he hoped to bring Corse south from Gordonsville and order Colquitt's 1,600 men north. With characteristic disdain for the enemy, he recommended to Seddon "an attack made upon the thieves"; in a caustic reference to the prisoner exchange system he had forged with Dix, he quipped: "We can, for an emergency, bring together enough troops to make Dix the subject of the cartel which he helped frame."[24]

On Saturday, June 27, Confederate leaders continued to shift troops here and there. Seddon, believing that 30,000 Federals had gathered at

White House and being convinced an enemy advance was imminent, ordered Jenkins's brigade to come north. However, he asked Hill to make
his own judgment about Colquitt's brigade, still in North Carolina. The
secretary of war also wrote Montgomery Corse at Gordonsville, suggesting the Virginian gather enough rail cars to allow a quick return to Hanover Junction should his brigade be needed there. But, as Seddon drew
troops toward Richmond, other Confederate leaders asked for men. Lee
and his staff continued to pester Richmond for Corse's return to the Army
of Northern Virginia.[25] And, from the south in the days ahead, Governor
Zebulon Vance of North Carolina pleaded to keep Colquitt's brigade
on the railroad in his state. Without troop strength there, the governor
warned, the railroads "will be at the mercy of the enemy cavalry."[26]

The troops from Petersburg soon arrived. Brigadier General Micah
Jenkins, "ever ready to show off the drill and efficiency of his brigade,"
put on a demonstration in the capital, forming his men and marching
through the streets in column of companies to the "stirring strains of
music." According to one of Jenkins's men, the procession woke the "old
city from its deep and sound rever[ie]" as people emerged to witness the
"steady and unwavering columns." Despite their pomp, the South Carolinians found that the response from Richmond civilians did not match
the enthusiasm they had encountered in Petersburg.[27]

As these reinforcements paraded, rumors piled up. Various reports
suggested that a strong Union force remained at White House, that Ransom's brigade had taken a blocking position east of the city, and that
General Elzey, who suffered from a head wound received at Gaines Mill
the year before, had fumbled the response to Spear's raid. There was
indeed unhappiness with Elzey. "Everybody abuses Gen. Elzey," wrote a
correspondent to the *Charleston Mercury*, "and the President is blamed
for retaining him in command." According to the writer, Elzey had dismissed reports of Spear's movement, saying simply that "I don't believe
a word of it." He had then allegedly rejected a suggested plan to thwart
the raiders, characterizing the enemy force as merely an advance guard of
the Federals at White House.[28]

On Sunday, June 28, Jenkins's brigade settled into camp on the Charles
City Road, while Ransom's Tar Heels bivouacked near the Seven Pines
battlefield after their march the night before.[29] The men found their new
surroundings less than comfortable. "I tell you things is torne here,"
wrote J. W. Calton of the 56th North Carolina. "The bones of the ded is
lying all over the land." Another, Murdoch John McSween of the 35th

North Carolina, did not enjoy the "low, swampy, and springy" country "thinly settled with indifferent society" and "very few fine farms." A lieutenant in the Palmetto Sharpshooters agreed, finding the land along the Chickahominy "awfully trodden" with "a terrible ghastly look." He expected "it will be an age before it is restored to a state of civilization again."[30]

But the soldiers found some comfort in their new camps. According to McSween, the commissary handed each man "half a pound of bacon, full rations of meal or flour, rice and peas, with some sugar." In addition, he found the "huckleberry gathering is a great thing now" in the nearby meadows brimming with fruit as June turned to July. This abundance was welcome in part because the surrounding farms had nothing in the way of food—no vegetables, buttermilk, or fruit. When McSween inquired at a local farm, an elderly women complained that the Confederate soldiers had taken nearly everything, including her chickens, hogs, potatoes, peas, raspberries, cherries, and cabbage. "I don't know what under heaven we are to do or how we are to live," she exclaimed.[31]

Following their exhausting march from Petersburg the previous day, some members of Ransom's brigade visited the Seven Pines battlefield on June 27. Captain William Burgwyn "could only see some bones of Yankees who were buried so shallow that they had been dug up by dogs."[32] Murdoch McSween and his friends encountered these unpleasant sights. His comrades found many graves, both Confederate and Federal, left from the fighting the summer before. Some of the Union headboards had the words "Fair Oaks" etched into them, the name the Northern soldiers had assigned to the previous summer's engagement. The deceased had not been buried well. "Several of these have been opened and it is found that the bodies are not entirely decomposed," reported an observer. One soldier dug up a corpse and found two and half dollars on the body, a discovery that triggered a wave of grave robbery. One North Carolinian noted that "the stench where the graves have been opened is said to be very offensive."[33]

On Sunday, June 28, Seddon called on D. H. Hill to come to Richmond with whatever troops he had at Petersburg. Hill warned that stripping the Cockade City would be "very dangerous" but nevertheless prepared to leave for the capital at 11 a.m. that day.[34] Once in the city, Hill requested command of the forces there. Seddon acquiesced. With three of Hill's brigades in or near Richmond, the secretary chose to hand him the reins, making the decision official in orders three days later. Richmond's current commander, the embattled Elzey, stepped aside with little complaint apparently, officially applying the next day to Samuel Cooper to be "relieved of the Department of Richmond by Maj. Gen. D. H. Hill."[35]

Upon his arrival, Hill found conditions to be less than ideal. Henry Wise, whose brigade was permanently assigned to the city's defense, informed the new commander of problems in the heavy artillery batteries. Magazines were damp and "tubes imperfect." Hill was also concerned about the city's picket lines and planned to send an inspector to look over everything.[36] Portions of Ransom's brigade marched out to the Williamsburg Road (also called the Richmond–Williamsburg Stage Road) under cloudy skies, pressing out for the enemy.[37]

As Hill's regulars took their positions outside the city, Richmond's local defense forces geared up to shield the capital. In June alone, several ad hoc battalions had formed, drawn from employees in the Armory, Clothing Department, Post Office, Treasury Department, and other offices within the city. The *Richmond Dispatch* praised the "promise, coolness, and . . . imperturbable stolidity" of the part-time citizen–soldiers and concluded they were "ready to enter the breach . . . and hurl back the ruthless invaders from their walls." The *Dispatch* also noted that the women of the city served as commissaries for the men, preparing the "inevitable rolls with legs of fine chicken inserted, and the sliced ham, with which the married men are particularly well supplied."[38] Many expected they would do more than eat chicken. The *Examiner* guessed, quite accurately, that Dix and Keyes had received orders from Washington to "do something, no matter what, to distract the attention of the Government from the scene of Lee's operations."[39]

Formerly enslaved people at Cumberland Landing in New Kent County, about 4 miles southeast of White House Landing on the Pamunkey River. Photograph taken by James F. Gibson in 1862. (Library of Congress)

White House Landing on the Pamunkey. (*Frank Leslie's Famous Leaders and Battle Scenes of the Civil War*)

The "Office" at Hickory Hill (the Wickham
Plantation), where Rooney Lee was captured on June
26, 1863. (Photo by author)

A destroyed bridge on the Richmond, Fredericksburg,
and Potomac (RF&P) Railroad. This one, photo-
graphed in 1864, spanned the North Anna River
about 5 miles north of the South Anna bridges
attacked by John Dix's forces in 1863. (Library of
Congress)

Wartime Richmond, looking east toward downtown. (Library of Congress)

Major General John A. Dix. (Library of Congress)

Major General Henry W. Halleck. (Library of Congress)

Lieutenant Colonel Charles C. Tevis. (Library of Congress)

Major General
Erasmus D. Keyes.
(Library of Congress)

Brigadier General
George Washington
Getty. (Library of
Congress)

Major General
Daniel Harvey
Hill. (South
Caroliniana
Library, University
of South Carolina)

Brigadier
General W. H. F.
"Rooney" Lee.
(Library of
Congress)

Lieutenant Colonel
Tazewell Hargrove, 44th
North Carolina Infantry.
(Clark, *Histories of the
Several Regiments and
Battalions from North
Carolina*, vol. 3)

Vice President
Alexander H. Stephens,
Confederate States of
America (Library of
Congress)

PART THREE
The Blackberry Raid

WITH SAMUEL SPEAR AND HIS CAVALRY BACK from their South Anna raid, commander John Dix weighed his options and decided to conduct a two-pronged advance against Richmond in early July. First, the Fourth Corps, led by Erasmus Keyes, would march west toward Richmond and conduct a feint at Bottom's Bridge across the Chickahominy River. Second, the Seventh Corps, under George Washington Getty, would take a larger force north into Hanover County to finish the job at the RF&P bridges along the South Anna. As the Federals advanced, the Confederates strained to protect the capital and its rail connections. Although Dix's entire campaign would become generally known as the "Blackberry Raid," many of the foot soldiers in his command attached that label specifically to the infantry expeditions led by Keyes and Getty. Indeed, it was during these operations in the sweltering first days of July that many weary men paused along the march to savor the ripe fruit lining the roads outside Richmond.

11

Dix Prepares the Second Wave

"AS A SOLDIER, I OBEY IT"

IN THE LAST DAYS OF JUNE 1863, newly minted commander George Meade steered the Army of the Potomac north in pursuit of Robert E. Lee and his Army of Northern Virginia. The Pennsylvanian, a competent, thoughtful, if somewhat testy officer, had provided solid service at division and corps command during the Army's uneven performances over the previous year. After receiving news of his promotion, he wrote: "As a soldier, I obey it, and to the utmost of my ability will execute it." However, dropped into the middle of an ongoing campaign, doubts hounded him. In correspondence with General-in-Chief Henry Halleck, Meade admitted knowing little about the enemy positions or, for that matter, his own army's condition. The army's assigned corps—seven in total—remained spread throughout Maryland. Nevertheless, Meade planned to continue pushing his troops toward the Susquehanna River while "keeping Washington and Baltimore well covered."[1]

Halleck, who had second-guessed ousted commander Joseph Hooker's every move only days before, struck a different chord with Meade. "I fully concur in your general views as to the movements of your army. All available assistance will be given to you," he wrote, responding to the new commander's first dispatch.[2] In the last days of June, Halleck would remain in nearly constant contact with Meade, exchanging more than a dozen messages on June 28 alone. From Washington, he focused on countering the threat from Lee's army, protecting the Federal-controlled rail lines, and shielding the cities lying in the Confederate army's path. He had little time to think about John Dix and his troops east of Richmond.[3]

On Tuesday, June 30, Meade provided an update to Halleck from Taneytown, Maryland, less than 5 miles south of the Pennsylvania border. He had placed "[t]wo corps between Emmitsburg and Gettysburg, one at Littlestown, one at Manchester, one at Union Mills, one between here and Emmitsburg, one at Frizellburg."[4] Meade's columns, marching hard for days, had managed to stay between Lee's troops and Washington,

Baltimore, and other key objectives to the east. Should Lee stride ahead to the Susquehanna, Meade hoped to pounce on the Confederates and pin them to the river's west bank. Halleck approved of Meade's scheme, and in the last days of June elements of the Army of the Potomac began to cross over the border into Pennsylvania.

Blinded by a lack of intelligence about the enemy's recent movements, Robert E. Lee had played a guessing game about the location of the Army of the Potomac. However, the uncertainty ended when news arrived that the Federals were closer than supposed and uncomfortably near his communications through the Cumberland Valley, so he ordered the concentration of his three corps at Cashtown. By June 30, Ewell's divisions were tracking back from the Susquehanna, Longstreet was marching east from Chambersburg, and A.P. Hill's corps had nearly reached Cashtown. Henry Heth's division of Hill's corps was poised to march into Gettysburg the next day, July 1.

"BY A RAPID MOVEMENT WE CAN ENTER"

During the last days of June outside Richmond, John Dix had been gathering his infantry units at White House. Troops from the Seventh Corps arrived by boat while Erasmus Keyes and his Fourth Corps units marched up the Peninsula, halting for a rest at Cumberland Landing, where the year before during the Peninsula Campaign photographer James Gibson had captured a compelling image of formerly enslaved people.[5] On June 26, Dix boarded a steamer downriver to meet the troops at Cumberland Landing. There he met with Brigadier General George H. Gordon, who found Dix full of optimism about the upcoming operations against Richmond. "There is no force to oppose us; and by a rapid movement we can enter," Gordon remembered Dix saying. Major General Keyes and Brigadier General Henry Terry soon joined the impromptu meeting and listened to their commander discuss his expectations for moving on Richmond. According to Gordon, Dix's plans "were not received with favor" by anyone. Gordon later remembered that he could think only of the obstacles ahead and the many unknowns as Dix raised the possibility of an attack on the capital.[6]

Whether Dix actually made such a proposal as recalled by Gordon on June 26 is unclear. In fact, he had doubts about the feasibility of a full attack against Richmond. In a letter to his wife only the day before, Dix expressed concern that his force was "entirely inadequate" for such an attack and expected only to make a demonstration and draw Lee back to Virginia.[7] Whether he planned to move on Richmond or not, Dix certainly felt pressure to do so. Others noticed such expectations as well. As General Gordon recalled, the desire for such a movement "was echoed in streets and in houses, in private and in public; it was accepted as a fact, and regarded as a duty."[8]

As Dix mulled over his next move, the rest of his troops arrived at White House. Keyes's men marched onto the fields there on Saturday, June 27, bringing about 6,000 men, mostly from Gordon's division.[9] A growing armed camp greeted the arriving troops. During the previous year's campaign, transports and supply vessels had crammed the river at White House, bringing men, provisions, and munitions to keep the Army of the Potomac in operation. Now, a year later, Dix's force replicated the scene on a smaller scale.

A few veterans of the 1862 Peninsula Campaign were overheard shouting "How are you White House?" as they stepped off their transports.[10] George Gordon recalled the scene at the landing. Along the wharfs, transports and gunboats lay at anchor and the "national flag and national airs saluted sight and hearing." Off to the north just upstream, the York River Railroad bridge remained intact and had been "planked over to render it passable for horse and foot."[11] At the landing itself, there was little left of Rooney Lee's plantation. James Howard, a member of Getty's headquarters staff, gazed on the lonely ruins of the mansion in the field beyond the wharfs.[12] "All that remains of the White House is the chimney and base with a few out buildings beside a number of negro huts," observed another soldier.[13] The plain off to the west occupied a low plateau rising about 30 feet above the river. The open space housed a sea of tents for 13,000 or so men from the Seventh Corps that "stretched far away in the distance." The arriving regiments set up their camps all over the expanse, much of it lush with clover. A New York reporter noted the tents, likely a vast collection of pup and conical-shaped Sibley models plus occasional wall tents for officers, stretched out across the fields as far as the "human range of vision extends."[14] As the men milled about, boats passed back and forth along the narrow channel not 50 feet from the bank. A correspondent with the *New York World* described the "very agreeably pretty" scene from the riverbank:

Thirty feet below, the Pamunkey glides along its torturous way, smooth, but not as clear as smooth, and the hills that rise at some distance from its banks are green and verdurous. The plain, with its clover covered expanse, is dotted with camps, from which rise the smoke of many little fires. All along the river banks are thick swamps and rat vines, fragrant with the perfume of many wild roses and trumpet flowers, while vines of various character climb the rough tree trunks and hang down low long clusters of leafy branches. A hundred varieties of birds make field and break musical. It seems a fitter place for summer pic-nics than for war.[15]

When Spear's cavalrymen returned from their South Anna mission, they camped north of the river on Pamunkey Island, home of the Pamunkey Tribe. In need of wood for their tent floors and cooking fires, the troopers along with infantry posted on the island demolished many of the houses in the community. In doing so, the vandals destroyed the home of river pilot and Pamunkey member William Terrill Bradby, who had served the Union navy in North Carolina and Virginia and had piloted vessels along the York and the Pamunkey during Dix's operations. According to a claim filed by Bradby after the war, the Union troops "tore down his house, kitchen & barn & used them to build quarters for themselves & the rest not so used they took for fuel." Bradby, who had been piloting the gunboat *Smith Briggs* during the campaign, arrived at White House to learn that his comrades had damaged his home. After gaining permission to leave his boat, Bradby raced to the island and found that his wife, alarmed by the soldiers, had locked up the house and departed to stay with Bradby's brothers. He recalled that the troops had taken everything—tearing off the weatherboarding, ripping up the floors, removing everything from the kitchen, and tearing down the barn. Later, Bradby observed that "it was very hard to have my property taken so where I was doing all I could for the United States government." At the time, the soldiers nearby assured him he would receive payment. But Bradby, who later could recall only that the men had been from General Getty's command, had to wait until 1871 to receive reimbursement and then only after filing lengthy forms and providing extensive testimony with the Southern Claims Commission.[16] How such destruction of private property occurred within yards of Dix's headquarters, given the general's distaste of such practices, is a mystery.

Those newly arrived soldiers who were not destroying local homes took note of their surroundings. The men found the farms of the region attractive but, as one commented, lacking in "what Northern people would call thrift." Still, such impressions did not prevent the Yankees from procuring provisions in the area. Some found the goods expensive, others not as much. One New Yorker pronounced the "country produce cheap up in these parts" and was able to buy milk butter and onions at reasonable prices.[17]

The fields around White House offered their own abundance. According to one member of Henry Terry's brigade, a 50-acre lot nearby teemed with blackberries, mulberries, and raspberries. The soldier expected the men would "not starve while we can get at them." Other flora drew attention in the ranks. In some places the ground was blue with flowers, a kind of passionflower in one soldier's estimation. A New Hampshire regiment bivouacked next to a magnolia swamp in full bloom. The trees produced a sweet pungency that made some soldiers queasy and forced the officers to shift the camp to a less fragrant location.[18]

One reporter detected a buoyant feeling in the ranks. "The scene around the whole plain bordering the river is one of life and excitement," wrote a New York correspondent. He detected high morale and "a healthful glow" suggesting the men were "sanguine of success." But others were not so optimistic. Martin Culver, a soldier in the 16th Connecticut, took in the surroundings at White House and concluded: "I don't like this place at all. I think we are going to have a hard time of it for a while."[19]

"IS IT WISE . . . TO TAKE CHANCES?"

At 3 p.m. on Saturday, June 27, Dix convened a more formal council of war at White House Landing, this time with Erasmus Keyes, Henry Terry, George Getty, and George Gordon—all the general officers in his command. To start things off, Dix repeated Halleck's general directive to "menace" the Confederate capital. The officers discussed the options before them, including the most promising approaches to Richmond, including a drive straight at the city across the Chickahominy River at Bottom's Bridge. The river, which formed a wide swamp stretching southeasterly across Richmond's entire eastern front, had played a crucial role in the 1862 campaign by dividing forces, stranding units, and impeding communications. According to Gordon's recollection, Dix believed Bottom's Bridge was "too serious an obstacle" to enable a "dash into Richmond." The other potential avenue led northeast in the direction of Old Church, Cold Harbor, and Mechanicsville, then into Richmond's northern suburbs. Dix seemed to favor this option but sought the officers' opinions.[20]

By his recollection, General Gordon expressed grave concerns about a strike directly against Richmond. He knew the city was "well protected with fortifications" and that a "repulse would invite the enemy to follow up and seriously threaten our line of communications." In his view, the need to protect the flanks would render any attacking column too small. Instead, he recommended something entirely different: cutting loose from the base at White House and marching to the rail lines north of Richmond. After destroying the roads and bridges there, he suggested the expedition continue on north to Aquia Creek near Fredericksburg to eventually join the Army of the Potomac in its fight against Robert E. Lee.[21]

Gordon also recalled that the discussion stretched beyond these tactical considerations to address the wisdom of a direct attack against the capital. "What do we want of Richmond?" he remembered asking. "Is it wise to dash our heads against its solid battlements; to take the chances, even of its capture, when with this force we could increase Hooker's army and destroy Lee, who is now rioting in Maryland?" Gordon did not expect Lee would "be fool enough" to abandon his operations for a mere demonstration against Richmond. To him, a fully committed effort to destroy the communications north of the city followed by a rapid movement to join the forces in Pennsylvania would contribute most to Lee's destruction. Should the Federals defeat the Army of Northern Virginia, Richmond would easily fall. No one other than Gordon described the conference's details; he provided his own recollection years later. In any case, the meeting ended with no resolution. If Dix had harbored any expectations for an assault on Richmond, they certainly were beginning to fade.[22]

On Sunday, June 28, under dark clouds, White House Landing presented "a busy spectacle" as more than a dozen transports crowded the wharf. In addition to the nearly constant delivery of troops, food, equipment, and ammunition, the boats ferried a light locomotive and six platform cars from Norfolk. Within twenty-four hours, the train began to operate on the York River Railroad, though much of the track from the line to West Point was missing, removed by the Confederates for use elsewhere. Throughout that Sunday, more Federal troops arrived, including another ill-equipped, short-term regiment from New Bern. More men also landed from Suffolk, which was now largely empty of units following Dix's instructions to completely demolish the forts and entrenchments there. True to form, he also forbade the destruction of any private property, emphasizing "I shall hold you responsible for any violation of this order."[23]

Sometime on that day, Dix and his staff made the rounds on horseback to inspect the new base at White House. A New Yorker from Getty's division serving on picket duty caught a glimpse of the general, describing him as "an old gray headed man & a noble looking Genl."[24] That evening, a band played in the camp. In addition, the 117th New York from Samuel Alford's brigade formed a parade square to hear a sermon from its chaplain, who admonished the soldiers to show themselves "as men and not cowards" in the coming days.[25]

On Monday, June 29, preparations in the camps at White House halted momentarily when a large number of emancipated people arrived in boats and homemade rafts across the river from King William County. They passed through the camp "in a large crowd; men, women, and children all together, each with a bundle." Word passed through the ranks that this group had "mutinied" after Confederate officials had planned to send a large number of them to Richmond. "They made a bold dash for freedom, and secured it," marveled Millett Thompson of the 13th New Hampshire.[26]

That morning in a small cabin, Dix held another planning session with his aides and general officers, including Erasmus Keyes, John Peck, George Gordon, Henry Terry, George Getty, Edward Harland, and Robert Foster.[27] With Samuel Spear's cavalry recovering, his force concentrated at White House, and Lee's men spreading through Pennsylvania, Dix had decisions to make. His orders from Halleck were somewhat open-ended, directing him to concentrate all his available forces "to threaten Richmond" by destroying the railroad bridges north of the city and "doing them all the damage possible" or at least occupying a large force of the enemy."[28] The operation had been partially successful so far. Spear had managed to destroy the Virginia Central bridge across the South Anna, and Dix had gathered nearly 20,000 men at White House, only 20 miles from Richmond. He knew that he needed to complete the job on the South Anna by destroying the RF&P rail bridge. But now, he continued to consider the possibility of doing something much larger. At the meeting that morning, he again asked his subordinates whether "it would be advisable, with the force I have, to make an attack on Richmond."[29]

It was a reasonable supposition. Although the exact size of the Confederate force protecting the city was unknown, Dix had reason to believe it was not unbeatable. At the South Anna during his raid, Spear had found only one infantry regiment guarding the Virginia Central bridge. For certain, Lee had taken as many men as he could on his march north.

But Dix and his officers simply did not know exactly what was in front of them. Nevertheless, an attack against the city itself beckoned, although its ultimate success was far from certain.

As Dix and his officers had discussed earlier, they had several options to consider in approaching Richmond in addition to the path Spear had followed to the bridges north a few days before. They could strike along the York River Railroad directly toward the city and attempt to force passage over the Chickahominy River or, alternatively, swing north through Henrico County, across the upper reaches of the Chickahominy, and approach the city via the Brook Turnpike or Meadow Bridge Road. Either of these approaches would bring Dix's attacking force in front of Richmond's three-tiered defense system. This network of fortifications was strong but not comprehensive and certainly not flawless. Further, the defensive works, regardless of their height and breadth, could provide protection only if they were actually occupied by adequate troops. If lightly manned or vacant at the point of assault, any of these positions would fall easily, allowing the attacking column to flood in behind other positions and open the door to the city. Dix and his officers surely considered these factors as they weighed their options.

When Dix asked his officers on June 29 about attacking Richmond, he did so without revealing his own view of the matter. All of them—Keyes, Getty, Gordon, Terry, Harland, Foster, and Peck—responded "promptly and unanimously" in the negative. Dix agreed immediately. Instead of an offensive against Richmond, he settled on a more modest plan. He chose to return to the railroad bridges north of the city by sending the bulk of his force against the RF&P bridge over the South Anna.[30]

His plan had two prongs. First, the main column, about 10,000 from the Seventh Corps led by Brigadier General George W. Getty and accompanied by Spear's cavalry, would march north through King William County and into Hanover to seize and destroy the RF&P rail bridge over the South Anna. Second, to cover General Getty's movement and ensure "its success," Erasmus Keyes would advance through New Kent County toward Richmond with a smaller force, about 6,000 troops from the Fourth Corps. Keyes would conduct a demonstration there, attacking the Confederates on the west side of the Chickahominy at Bottom's Bridge to prevent them from sending reinforcements to blunt Getty's operation. Under the plan, General Keyes would post his artillery on the east bank, shell the enemy, and hold his position there for two or three days until Getty had destroyed the railroad bridge in Hanover.[31]

Dix understood the advantage enjoyed by Richmond's defenders and realized the Confederates were on alert following Spear's raid on June 26. He estimated that the "insurgents," as he frequently called the Confederates, had gathered about 8,000 men to protect Richmond, not that far off from the approximately 13,000 actually there. He also still mistakenly thought Pickett's division was at Hanover Junction. Nevertheless, he knew that the Confederates, whatever their strength, would look to benefit from their interior lines. "Their telegraph and railroad lines," he wrote, "enable them to concentrate and move troops with great rapidity to different points in North Carolina and Virginia, to meet our movements." This neatly summed up the challenge the Federals faced. The Confederates could use rail cars, including those along the York line to the east and the Central and Fredericksburg tracks to the north, to rapidly shift troops from the defense lines east of the city, through downtown, and north to the railroad bridges. If the Federals threatened one location either at the Richmond defenses or north at the bridges, the Confederates could use their advantage of interior lines to speed units to the unthreatened sector and meet the danger.[32]

Despite these drawbacks, Dix had one clear advantage to overcome the Confederates' edge in this respect. He could choose when and where to attack the enemy's positions. To leverage this asset, he ordered Keyes to advance against Richmond's eastern defenses and provide a diversion from Getty's real attack against the South Anna bridges. Dix hoped the lunge by Fourth Corps at Bottom's Bridge east of the city would distract the Confederates, tie down their troops along the Williamsburg Road, and prevent them from moving men north to help repel Getty's attack. The plan's success depended on aggression and a convincing advance by Keyes that deterred the Confederates from sending railcars full of men to the South Anna. With this plan, Dix focused on the goal highlighted by Halleck in his earlier orders: the seizure and destruction of the bridges north of Richmond.[33]

Dix also appreciated the broader picture. He knew what was at stake in the crisis facing the Federal high command. "My officers and men are very anxious to contribute to relieve the country from the disasters with which it is threatened in Maryland and Pennsylvania," he reassured Halleck on June 29, "and everything that is possible will be done here, if thought best to retain this position, to inflict injury on the enemy and keep his forces fully occupied." However, there would be a bit more waiting. Dix did not want to commence his operation until Spear's cavalry, "having been a good deal jaded by their late hard work," had rested their mounts and were ready for active service. Accordingly, he arranged to wait and to send off his two infantry columns on Wednesday morning, July 1. Halleck, preoccupied with efforts to assist Meade, did not respond. Thus, Dix's main strike force would push off toward Richmond without any further guidance from the general-in-chief.[34]

"WE ARE DOING THE SAME THINGS NEAR RICHMOND"

Throughout the last days of June, President Lincoln and officials in Washington remained understandably focused on Lee's march into Pennsylvania as nearly everyone worked to rush troops and supplies to the point of danger. Halleck spent much of his time communicating with George Meade while Secretary of War Stanton monitored developments carefully. Gideon Welles, Lincoln's bewigged and amply bearded "Father Neptune," watched on with concern from his spot in the Navy Department as matters evolved. He worried that the Pennsylvania citizens were "inert and inactive, indisposed to volunteer to defend even their own capital," a problem he attributed in part to Halleck's "incompetency" to "concentrate effort, acquire intelligence, or inspire confidence." News also streamed in from the west where Charles Dana, Lincoln's eyes and ears embedded with Grant's headquarters, routinely submitted lengthy telegrams describing the events at Vicksburg.[35]

Despite the swirl of these other events, Dix's campaign against Richmond became the subject of considerable attention at the highest levels in Washington. Back on Sunday, June 28, as Dix developed his plan, Lincoln had convened a cabinet meeting at 10 a.m. on the second floor of the White House. The ensuing discussion touched on the efforts against the Confederate capital. As was his habit, Welles scribbled the highlights of the discussion in his diary. Lincoln began with the clamor in Congress about Clement Vallandigham and then moved on to address Joseph Hooker's departure from the command of the Army of the Potomac. An awkward exchange about Hooker's replacement followed during which Lincoln sought feedback on several possible candidates while eventually divulging that Meade had already been picked.[36]

News of Meade's ascent did not sit well with Secretary of the Treasury Salmon Chase, the rigid, balding abolitionist and, most pertinent to this meeting, a solid Joseph Hooker supporter. During the discussion, Chase was "disturbed more than he cared" to reveal, at least according to Welles, and suggested sending Hooker to replace Dix altogether and command the Richmond advance. Lincoln brushed off the proposal; Welles piped in and asked about the status of Dix's operation. Lincoln, who seemed keen on striking a blow against the Confederate capital, doubted Dix would accomplish much. In his diary, Welles noted that "though [Dix was] not much of a general, there were reasons why [Lincoln] did not like to supersede him," perhaps alluding to Dix's status as a high-ranking, loyal War Democrat. Nevertheless, during the discussion, Lincoln and Chase spoke highly of John Foster, the commander in North Carolina, whom they considered to be a "rising general" and a good candidate to manage affairs in Virginia. However, the meeting concluded with no change to Dix's status in Virginia or his mission against Richmond.[37]

The next day, Secretary Chase shared his thoughts on the matter with his daughter and informal political adviser Kate, a prominent figure in Washington circles. In a confidential note, Chase took a shot at Halleck, suggesting the general-in-chief had the capacity but "does not work, work, work, as if he were in earnest." Chase hoped Lincoln would put Benjamin Butler in Halleck's role, predicting the Massachusetts lawyer would seize the position "with a will." He also revealed his hopes for Dix's operation, explaining that, while the rebels "are doing these things near Washington, we are doing the same things near Richmond."[38] Chase may have sharpened his views following a recent communication from Daniel Butterfield, the Army of the Potomac's chief of staff, which repeated rumors of Richmond's weakness. Butterfield urged an immediate attack by Dix "from below" and a simultaneous advance by General Benjamin Kelley from West Virginia via Lynchburg.[39] On June 30, Chase wrote a friend to discuss the state of affairs, including the ongoing Pennsylvania campaign. He downplayed the appearance of J. E. B. Stuart's cavalry on the outskirts of Washington and doubted Lee would attack the national capital. He also expounded further on the potential of Dix's operation. He hoped Spear's South Anna raid was merely a prelude to a direct attack on Richmond itself. But Chase did not delve further, admitting it was idle for him to "speculate on military affairs," for Lincoln consulted only Stanton and Halleck on such issues.[40]

The cabinet convened again in the White House on Tuesday, June 30. However, with the president off at the War Department discussing the growing military crisis in Pennsylvania with Stanton and Halleck, it was not much of a meeting. Secretary Welles, already miffed by what he viewed as a Stanton–Halleck–Seward clique, believed the current conditions called for a "free and constant intercourse and interchange of views, and a combined effort," something unattainable with the handful of cabinet members in the room. During or shortly after this gathering, Chase informed Welles that both Lincoln and Stanton were anxious for "Dix to make a demonstration on Richmond." Of all the government officials mulling over the matter, Chase remained the primary proponent of such a strike. "This move on Richmond is cherished by Chase," wrote Welles on June 30, "and with a bold, dashing, energetic, and able general might be effective."[41]

Others were also eager for action. Gustavus Vasa Fox, Welles's deputy at the Navy Department, agreed that more could be done at Richmond. In a letter to his friend Admiral Samuel Phillips Lee, Dix's naval counterpart on the Peninsula, Fox recommended that General Foster, "a man of enterprise," should take charge of the Richmond operations. Fox also let on that both Lincoln and Stanton favored the move, but "a consultation with Genl Halleck to day [June 30] fails to satisfy him that it is at all feasible."[42] Admiral Lee apparently supported some sort of change in the Department of Virginia. Elizabeth Blair Lee, his wife and the sister of Postmaster General Montgomery Blair, wrote him this cryptic line in early July: "I think you are right about Dix as the P[resident] can if he will and he ought to do it." A few days later, she reported to her husband that "there is a universal revolt against Dix" in Washington.[43]

In his own letter to Admiral Lee, Fox put the issue in perspective. Conceding that Dix's men would be of great use in the North, he also saw promise in attempting a Richmond strike. If the War Department did not plan to order Dix's troops northward, Fox did not understand why those units could not "at least" march on the Confederate capital. In his estimation, Richmond was vulnerable, protected only by inexperienced units. However, Fox doubted Dix would do much because there were no generals of "enterprise" with him. He concluded observing that "every rash act of this war has been crowned with success and here is the most glorious opportunity ever afforded, yet Dix contents himself with raids that inflict no injury except upon the feelings of the enemy." Favoring John Foster for the Richmond operation, Fox then interjected some intrigue by asking Lee to involve Foster himself in an effort to convince Halleck to change commanders in Virginia. A few days later, Admiral Lee replied. While agreeing with Fox's sentiments, he doubted any good would come from his own "interference." To the contrary, he expected such machinations "would only produce a war upon me instead of the enemy." Fox's scheme apparently died there.[44]

In contrast to the enthusiasm expressed by Fox and Chase, there seemed to be little interest among other Washington officials about pushing the

Richmond operation. Even the plan's original architect, Henry Halleck, appears to have abandoned hope for meaningful results. In reflecting on Halleck's views at the time, Gideon Welles noted that Halleck, despite support for the demonstration from the president and Stanton, "does not respond favorably, whether because he has not confidence in Dix, or himself, or from any cause, I do not know." Postmaster General Blair, no admirer of Halleck ("good for nothing and knows nothing"), agreed that an operation against Richmond was not in the cards and expected Dix would soon march north to assist Meade. When Blair learned on June 30 that the Richmond plan was still on, he wrote the president to oppose it, focusing on the need to concentrate strength to meet Lee. "I think this would be so serious an error," he warned. To him, Richmond was "not scarcely of more importance than Alexandria" under the circumstances. He urged Lincoln to focus on destroying Lee's army first and snapping up the rebel capital afterward. In doing so, Blair signaled caution, arguing that an "army of reserve" (Dix's force) could protect "against disaster" or "pursue a victory to the destruction of Lee's Army if we gain the advantage."[45]

Gideon Welles also expressed reservations. He agreed with Lincoln that Dix was "not the man for such a movement" and concluded that the army, instead of seeking gains at Richmond, should gather every spare man to assist Meade in Pennsylvania. He also raised concerns about Halleck's focus on simply driving Lee out of the Keystone State. He took issue with Halleck's desire to push the rebels "back across the 'frontiers' instead of intercepting, capturing, and annihilating them." In Welles's view, Meade should attempt to cut off Lee and capture his army. "I don't want them to leave the State, except as prisoners," he wrote. He believed the chance for such a victory would increase should Lee cross over the Susquehanna and head farther east.[46]

Whatever their opinions, Welles, Chase, and Blair remained outside looking in as Confederate troops flooded across Pennsylvania. The real drivers—Lincoln, Stanton, and Halleck—apparently gave little additional attention to Dix's campaign and instead focused on the Confederate invasion. The day-to-day decisions fell to the president and the war secretary, with Halleck implementing the details. Based on his personal observations and discussions with other officials, Welles was not optimistic. According to him, Stanton lacked a firm grasp of the situation. "I come to the conclusion that he is bewildered, that he gets no light from his military subordinates and advisers, and that he really has no information or opinion as to the Rebel destination or purpose and the implementation of the response to Lee." Whether or not Welles was correct, the responsibility for managing the effort to repel the Confederate incursion fell to Henry Halleck.[47]

During the last days of June, Halleck diligently coordinated matters among the various military departments. He followed events at Charleston Harbor, monitored Rosecrans's efforts in Tennessee, and kept an eye out for news from Grant at Vicksburg. But it was the new army commander, George Meade, who drew most of his attention. The two kept up a nearly constant stream of correspondence, leaving the general-in-chief little time to attend to his amorphous plan to threaten Lee's communications (the scheme initiated through his June 14 directive to Dix).

Halleck's other efforts—the planned strikes in North Carolina and southwestern Virginia—remained stalled in their nascent stages. In the Old North State, John Foster's men had not left New Bern to damage the Wilmington and Weldon line. On June 30, Foster informed Halleck that "the continuous rainy weather has delayed the cavalry raid," but he expected his men would move within a few days.[48] In West Virginia, nothing had been done at all despite Halleck's June 25 directive for a small "mounted force" to "ascend the Great Kanawha, cross the mountains, and cut the Virginia & Tennessee Railroad."[49]

Given the lack of progress in these other sectors, Dix's advance on Richmond remained the principal element of Halleck's efforts against the Confederate lifelines. Even as Washington officials discussed the Richmond operations, Halleck did not send any further direction to the Peninsula. For better or worse, Halleck's inattention left Dix largely on his own. To his credit, Dix formed his own plans following Spear's raid and pushed ahead, with his infantrymen of the Department of Virginia preparing to embark on their mission. Many of these units had received limited opportunities to conduct active campaigning to this point in the war. Now was their chance. The historian for the 130th New York recalled that a "feeling of anticipation was shared alike by officers and men. It cheered our hearts and lightened our steps."[50]

12

Keyes's Advance to Bottom's Bridge

"SEND TO THIS PLACE ALL TROOPS NOT ABSOLUTELY REQUIRED"

THE MAELSTROM AT GETTYSBURG began on Wednesday, July 1, triggered in part by Lee's decision to consolidate his forces east of Chambersburg. Shortly after dawn, the Confederates of Henry Heth's division marched along the Chambersburg Pike and confronted the Union cavalrymen of John Buford's division west of Gettysburg. Additional columns of blue and gray converged on the town from nearly every point of the compass, and soon both armies became locked in a colossal engagement that, for many, would define the history of the entire war for generations to come.

While Heth formed his men that morning, John Dix's two columns, more than 150 miles to the south, departed from their camps at White House on the Pamunkey River. The main strike force, the 10,000 men led by Brigadier General George W. Getty, set off north into King William County and thence into Hanover County with orders to seize and destroy the RF&P Railroad bridge over the South Anna. The second column, a smaller force under Major General Erasmus Keyes, pointed south to demonstrate in front of Richmond's defenders east of the city. Unlike the clash in the rolling hills outside Gettysburg, neither Keyes's nor Getty's efforts would receive much attention from anyone.

Early in the morning on July 1, Keyes set out to conduct a convincing feint against the Confederate positions at Bottom's Bridge on the Chickahominy. For the mission, he brought an odd mix of units: Colonel Burr Porter's brigade (about 1,500) from Gordon's division, Colonel Robert M. West's independent brigade (also about 1,500) formerly with Brigadier General Rufus King's division, the 4th Delaware Regiment (about 500), Brigadier General Henry D. Terry's brigade (about 2,500) from the Seventh Corps, detachments of the 5th Pennsylvania and 6th New York Cavalry, as well as three of Captain James McKnight's batteries. Keyes's entire first division, under Rufus King (about 4,000 men), had remained at Yorktown and Gloucester Point. Why Dix and Keyes chose to assign such a jumbled set of units to the mission is unclear. Each of the three brigades hailed from a different division, and Henry Terry's came from an entirely different corps. Furthermore, and perhaps most important, none of these units had any significant experience operating together in large-scale combat operations. In any case, Keyes would head out on his demonstration with his column of more than 6,000, alone roughly half the size of the entire Confederate force defending Richmond.[1]

In orders communicated the previous day, Dix directed Keyes to "advance on the Richmond road, and attack the enemy," thought to be in "considerable force" on the west bank of the Chickahominy, near Bottom's Bridge. Dix expected Keyes "to post his artillery in position so as to command the bridge, . . . open fire on the enemy," and "hold his position for two or three days, until there was reason to believe that General Getty had accomplished his object." In digesting these orders, Keyes understood he was not expected to destroy the bridges across the Chickahominy but instead "engage the enemy with a view to detain him" while Getty operated against the South Anna bridges. Dix had picked Keyes for the task not only because of his major general's rank but also because Keyes had commanded troops near the Chickahominy the year before during the 1862 campaign. In a matter of hours, Dix would regret his decision.[2]

In wartime photographs, the fifty-three-year-old Keyes projected a distinguished air with his prominent Roman nose, dark, combed-back hair, and short, gray-speckled beard. One Connecticut soldier who had observed the general in the field described him as "a Yankee all over—tall, lank, and lean, with sharp features, and a slight sprinkling of whiskers." A Massachusetts native and West Point graduate, Keyes had commanded a brigade at First Bull Run. By the time George McClellan marched on Richmond in 1862, Keyes was a brigadier general and commanded the Fourth Corps in the Army of the Potomac. During the Peninsula Campaign, whispers of cowardice drifted through headquarters. However, Keyes performed creditably in fighting at Fair Oaks (Seven Pines) and commanded his men through more than half a dozen engagements during the campaign, including fighting at Bottom's Bridge.[3]

But Keyes, a New Englander, a Republican, and an abolitionist, had not impressed General McClellan, a conservative Democrat. After the fighting on the Peninsula in 1862, Keyes had been shunted aside and saddled with a post in the backwater of the Department of Virginia. Their antipathy was mutual. In his memoir, Keyes recalled instructing McClellan at West Point. While he remembered Little Mac's academic excellence, Keyes "did not forecast [McClellan's] love of popular applause."⁴ When Keyes received promotion to major general in March 1863, an unhappy McClellan described the New Englander as "of very moderate ability; very prissy, & entirely unfit to command a corps." Keyes, in turn, suspected McClellan's animus had more to do with political affiliations than military capacity.⁵

Early on Wednesday, July 1, the Fourth Corps camps were "alive and busy with the hum and motion of preparation" as Keyes's lead units departed White House Landing and tramped south toward the crossroads hamlet of Talleysville. Under cloudy skies, Colonel Robert M. West's brigade of New Yorkers and Pennsylvanians took the lead, along with about 100 men from the 5th Pennsylvania Cavalry. The rest of the troops, accompanied by Keyes and his staff, began the trek two hours later. The general's entourage included several officers, aides, his medical director S. S. Mulford, and an observant *New York Daily Herald* reporter, Stephen Hayes, who rode a captured Confederate horse. As the column marched south, George Gordon, staying behind to protect the base at White House, pushed a bit west down the railroad to Tunstall's Station with some artillery, a detachment of cavalry, the rest of his own division, and Francis Spinola's ailing, ill-equipped brigade from New Bern.⁶

At White House Landing, just as Keyes set off, Dix received a curious note from Halleck. "As soon as the expedition now terminates," wrote the general-in-chief, "you will draw in all your forces to Yorktown, Fort Monroe, and the defenses of Norfolk, and send to this place all troops not absolutely required for the defense of those three places." Halleck's dispatch, drafted while Meade's fortunes in Pennsylvania hung in the balance, marked a significant change. Instead of emphasizing operations against Richmond, Halleck now wanted Dix to transport his men north as soon as possible. His new message suggested Halleck, and others in Washington, now wanted to bring troops north rather than threaten the rebellion's capital. Halleck's July 1 note to Dix also conveyed a hint of panic. Washington's safety—not Richmond's fall—was now paramount.⁷

Halleck's new directive created a dilemma for Dix. For weeks he had followed, albeit slowly, Halleck's June 14 orders to threaten Richmond and strike Lee's communications.⁸ Dix had gathered his forces, pushed them up the Peninsula, overseen Spear's raid, and finally sent out two strong infantry columns. But the very morning Dix's infantry marched off to meet the enemy, Halleck had thrown cold water on the entire operation. The timing was awkward to say the least. However, there was nothing for Dix to do but sit and wait for news from Keyes and Getty about the fates of their expeditions.

Dix no doubt hoped to receive good news from Keyes during the day. The route to Bottom's Bridge was not long. About 12 miles separated White House and Bottom's Bridge, a distance the column was certainly capable of covering in a single day even in the warm weather. To aid the march, Keyes's men traveled light. Each regiment brought a single wagon, and each man carried only two days rations and 100 rounds of ammunition in their knapsacks and cartridge boxes. Keyes specifically ordered such arrangements so no excess baggage would encumber his force and impede "rapid movements and long marches."[9]

Stephen Hayes, the *New York Daily Herald* correspondent accompanying Keyes, filed a highly detailed, if somewhat muddled, account of the march on July 1 that provided a nearly minute-by-minute description of the advance. In his reporting, Hayes seemed somewhat confused about the purpose of Keyes's offensive. He mistakenly believed the general's mission represented "the fighting part of the programme" and the "more important project" compared to Getty's. Nevertheless, Hayes seemed to understand the immediate mission, which was, in his words, to find the Confederates "guarding the Chickahominy," draw them out beyond Bottom's Bridge, and then, "when an advantageous position offered, form in line of battle and attack."[10]

The march route covered ground Keyes had seen during campaigning the year before. A *New York Times* correspondent, who described this part of New Kent County during McClellan's campaign, had found few plantations of note and encountered a hodgepodge of architectural styles he considered "by no means pleasing to the eye." To him, the tattered collection of houses formed a "mass of tottering brick and wood, decayed by time, falling piece by piece" with no sign of any repair efforts or "that compound known as paint."[11] However, for the first few miles of their march on July 1, Keyes's troops saw little except for woods and a few open fields. In addition, the tree-covered portions of the path offered challenges. Rain-soaked ground in some locations diverted wagons, horses, and carts off the "badly rutted and cut up" path. In some places, the route's condition forced men to detour into the trees to keep their brogans out of the deep mud. Indeed, teamsters picked their lines carefully to avoid plunging their wagon wheels into the mire. Keyes later reported that the "roads were muddy, the weather oppressive, and the march . . . was one of the most fatiguing I have made on the Peninsula."

Eventually, however, the lead units emerged from the woods onto drier, more open ground. [12]

By 8 a.m., the summer sun emerged to warm the men as they tramped along in their blue woolen uniforms. About two and a half miles south of White House, the column passed the Old Quarter plantation and a nearby spring of the same name, which flowed from the base of a towering oak tree where, according to legend, Pocahontas had bathed her feet more than two centuries before. In another half-mile, the men passed a cherished landmark of the Revolutionary War era. St. Peter's Church, visible about 700 yards east of the march route, was known by many as the site for the wedding ceremony of George Washington and Martha Custis in 1759, though in reality the event may have taken place in the Custis House at White House Landing.[13] In any case, following the ceremony, Washington reportedly toasted his party at Old Quarter Spring. Many of the soldiers in Keyes's column caught a glimpse of this historical curiosity off in the distance to their left. "From time to time, as the church came in view," observed Hayes, "the veterans pointed it out to their younger companions, with an explanation of the interest attached to it." A mile beyond the church, the men tramped through Talleysville, also known as Baltimore Store, and then swung west for another 2 miles toward Crump's Crossroads, called by some "Baltimore Crossroads" or just simply "the Crossroads."[14] Keyes later noted the muddy roads and described the weather as so "oppressive" that soon all the ambulances with the column were filled with men overcome by the heat. Confederate pickets began to appear in greater numbers as well.[15]

At noon, the head of the column reached Crump's Crossroads, a small collection of houses more than a mile west of Talleysville. The regiments stopped, having covered a respectable 8 miles in nearly as many hours. The soldiers, who found the fires of Confederate pickets still burning where "they had cooked their coffee," spread out onto fields dotted with homes and buildings belonging to the extended Crump family, including Doctor Leonard C. Crump, whose house was one of the region's more impressive structures. A visitor to Crump's plantation the year before noted the property included "an elegant" home and "numerous out-buildings, in a fine condition of repair." The plantation had been in the thick of things during McClellan's campaign. Within the span of several weeks, both Confederate Joseph Johnston and Federal Daniel Sickles had taken up temporary residence there, the latter receiving a sizable bill from Crump before departing.[16]

Doctor Crump, an ardent secessionist, had owned forty-two slaves the

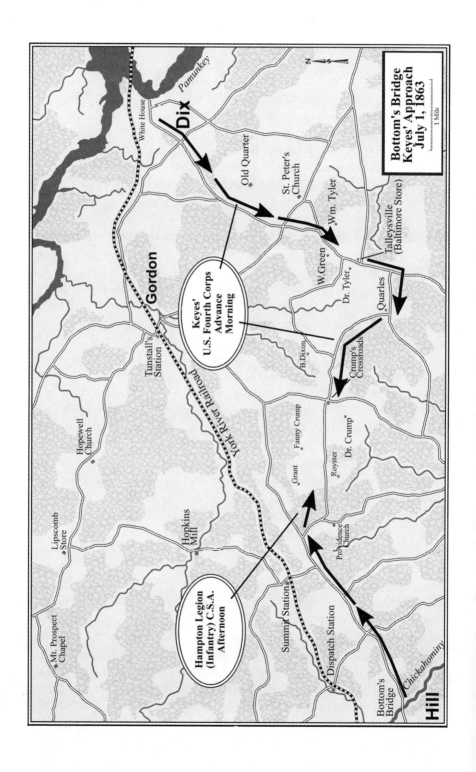

Bottom's Bridge
Keyes' Approach
July 1, 1863

1 Mile

N

Dix

Hill

Pamunkey

White House

Old Quarter

St. Peter's Church

Wm. Tyler

Talleysville (Baltimore Store)

W. Green

Dr. Tyler

Quarles

Gordon

Tunstall's Station

York River Railroad

Keyes' U.S. Fourth Corps Advance Morning

B. Dixon

Crump's Crossroads

Hopewell Church

Fanny Crump

Dr. Crump

Lipscomb Store

Hopkins Mill

Grant

Royster

Providence Church

Mt. Prospect Chapel

Summit Station

Dispatch Station

Hampton Legion (Infantry) C.S.A. Afternoon

Bottom's Bridge

Chickahominy

year before, at least sixteen of whom escaped to the Federal camps, or, as a *New York Times* correspondent put it, were not "come-at-able" at the plantation "owing to strange notions of being free." These refugees had made their way to Federal camps at McClellan's White House base, where officers hired them for various tasks. Distraught by the sudden change in his fortunes, Doctor Crump obtained a pass to visit the base, where he entreated his former slaves to return with appeals transparent to even the dullest observer. At least one freedman rebuffed his former owner's efforts and scoffed at Crump's nonsensical pleadings, so at odds with his habitual abuse and physical mistreatment on the plantation. During the exchange, the freedman reminded Crump of a blow the doctor had dealt him only a week before and displayed the wound to emphasize the point. Later, in front of the *New York Times* reporter, Crump wept over the loss of his slaves and complained how emancipation had destroyed much of his wealth.[17]

On Wednesday afternoon, Keyes seemed to have every intention of remaining at Crump's Crossroads. The general and his entourage arrived there around midday and hunkered down, apparently concerned the Confederates would launch a surprise attack against one of their flanks. Keyes seemed to have no inclination to march the remaining 5 miles west to Bottom's Bridge, his objective. In his report, he observed with apprehension that the enemy could pounce on this force at Crump's from the cover of woods at nearly every angle. The general also sought information about the Confederates in front. Once again, enslaved people stepped forward to aid a Federal operation. According to Keyes, a Black man warned that a rebel column had crossed Bottom's Bridge and had reached a house used by US troops the year before as a hospital.[18] Colonel West pushed forward some of his men, a mix of both cavalry and infantry, to discover what lay ahead. As West probed, danger lurked in the rear as well. For example, after the main column passed through Talleysville, Morgan Kupp, the quartermaster with the 167th Pennsylvania, lagged behind the column and became the prisoner of rebel bushwhackers. A detail under Second Lieutenant William Duryea of the 6th New York Cavalry rode back to rescue the captive without success.[19]

Early in the afternoon, Keyes established his headquarters at the Green House, a few hundred yards north of Talleysville and more than 7 miles away from Bottom's Bridge. Keyes found the position to be a "good one against a front attack" but believed the roads to the left and right rendered his flanks vulnerable. Ahead at Crump's Crossroads, he positioned Colonel West's three regiments—the 139th New York and 178th and 179th

Pennsylvania—in front. According to correspondent Hayes, the general selected these regiments based "on their experience in the field or his own knowledge of their reliability in any emergency," an odd statement given that West's units had no experience to speak of, having spent their short time in the service in uneventful duty at Yorktown, missing even the Suffolk Campaign. Around the Crossroads, the Federal cavalrymen also spread out to picket the various roads leading to the intersection to keep a watchful eye out for any Confederate advance from the Chickahominy. Facing west toward Bottom's Bridge, artillery crews manned their pieces at the front, and the infantry formed behind in line resting near their stacked rifles. Those cavalrymen not screening the roads stationed themselves on a "little plain on the right" with their horses "saddled and bridled, and the men ready to mount at the first trumpet-note."[20]

After reaching Crump's around midday, Keyes spent most of the afternoon arranging for defense. It was hot this day, and the following days would be even hotter, but even in the July heat there was time for his men to push the additional 5 miles to the bridge. In the afternoon, Keyes sent Colonel West's brigade out on a cautious probe down the Williamsburg Road in the fields west of the crossroads. During the approach, members of Keyes's command seized a horse from Beverly Dixon, a free Black farmer who lived about a mile east of Crump's Crossroads. He had aided Union troops during the Peninsula Campaign the year before by providing information about the local road network and, in one instance, hiding Union prisoners who had escaped through the rebel picket lines. Keyes's men repaid Dixon by taking his horse. He later stated:

> Some 8 or 10 soldiers came to my house and took the horse from the stable. There was an officer along, I took him to be a captain from his dress, who said he was on a raid, had lost his horse and must have one to take its place. They took a saddle from one of their horses that seemed lame, mounted mine and all rode off. There was a camp at the time about a mile off at Baltimore [Crump's] Crossroads and they went in that direction [and] I never saw my horse afterwards. It was six years old, large and sound.[21]

At 5 p.m., Keyes wrote Dix complaining about muddy roads and asking whether he should burn the bridges in his front across the Chickahominy. Dix's assistant adjutant general, D. T. Van Buren, responded a few hours later advising Keyes not to destroy the bridges, certainly wondering why he was not already at those crossings. Keyes's inaction was hard to explain. Concerned about his command's safety in rebel country and perhaps slowed by the mud and warm weather, he had moved deliberately, keeping his column compact and stopping well short of the Chickahominy. He seemed to assume that his mere presence in the middle of New Kent County would serve as the demonstration desired by Dix to divert Confederate attention from Getty's march to the South Anna. He was wrong.[22]

"ENEMY SAID TO BE LANDING"

In Richmond that day, the dark clouds gathering in the east over White House Landing had become unmistakable. Subsistence Department employee Herbert Claiborne noted in his diary: "Enemy said to be landing and moving up from White House. Richmond in danger, will always be so when Genl Lee is in Maryland."[23] Speculation about Federal plans filled the papers. The *Daily Richmond Examiner* reported that an elderly King William County resident arrived in the city with "awful accounts" of the enemy buildup and a prediction of an attack within three days. The rattled man reckoned the enemy troops at White House outnumbered McClellan's army the year before. A second herald swore his neighbor had seen 40,000 men at Hanovertown farther up the Pamunkey, and still another civilian claimed the enemy had appeared south of the city. But the *Examiner*'s editors admitted "our authentic intelligence is very limited." The *Dispatch* weighed in with rumors that the total force consisted of about 14,000, underestimating the actual strength by about 6,000, and expected this force would march north around Richmond to Gordonsville or Aquia Creek beyond Fredericksburg.[24]

In response to this news, the Confederates charged with protecting Richmond, D. H. Hill, Arnold Elzey, and James Seddon, began a juggling act with the troops already present in the city. All the while, the convoluted chain of command remained, raising questions about who was in charge and who had authority to make things happen. Nevertheless, word went out for members of the local defense units not already in the works to be ready "at a minute's warning." Hill and Seddon also cast about for more troops and managed to turn up 600 newly exchanged prisoners and nearly 1,800 more convalescents from the city's hospitals, including Chimborazo, Camp Winder, and Camp Lee. They looked to the south, too, and called on Alfred Colquitt, now at Goldsboro, to bring his brigade to Richmond "as soon as may be practicable." In addition, with

Montgomery Corse's brigade at Gordonsville ready to march north to join Robert E. Lee, Seddon suggested that a regiment from John Cooke's North Carolina brigade, perhaps including Cooke himself, head north to Hanover Junction and protect the vital points there, including the North and South Anna Bridges. Hill passed the proposition along to Elzey.[25]

D. H. Hill prepared his brigades—led by Jenkins, Ransom, and Cooke—to defend the city and the bridges to the north. He established his headquarters at Doctor Williams's house, near the York River Railroad and the Williamsburg Road.[26] Soon after his arrival in the capital, he had become concerned about the disposition of units manning the three defensive rings surrounding Richmond. Elzey had arranged his available men in tiers, a defense-in-depth that placed the convalescents on the outermost line of works, the bulk of Custis Lee's local defense troops in the intermediate line, and some artillery and other units in the inner batteries (the star-shaped forts). Custis Lee's command consisted of at least five battalions totaling about 1,700 men, augmented by newly organized companies that increased the total by a few hundred.[27]

Hill was not happy with Elzey's decision to place the inexperienced units in the outer line. In his view, the collapse of the exterior ring would turn "the whole advanced position" and put the "Yankees . . . in our camps and artillery parks." Hill also reached down into the details of the defensive arrangements. When he learned that some of Custis Lee's men had set up picket posts on the Richmond side of the Chickahominy, he asked Elzey to shift them across the river to Cold Harbor and Bethesda Church, where they could guard the roads approaching the Meadow and Mechanicsville Bridges.[28] Hill's instructions demonstrated his preference for an aggressive defense, which pushed troops out as far as possible to discourage the enemy, while also keeping units in reserve to move and strike at Federal advances. He also posted some of Colonel John A. Baker's cavalry at Old Church about a dozen miles from Dix's headquarters on the Pamunkey. From that position, these Tar Heel riders, many on fresh Yankee mounts captured at Winchester a few weeks before, could provide warning of any enemy column headed northwest for Hanover Junction. Hill also hoped to equip one regiment from Jenkins's South Carolina brigade with horses to picket the roads beyond the river. On the Richmond side of the Chickahominy, Matt Ransom's North Carolina brigade spent much of the morning working on the fortifications across the Williamsburg Road, each regiment taking half-hour shifts.[29]

As they deployed their units, D. H. Hill and his officers eagerly braced for word of an enemy advance. That news arrived Wednesday morning from the South Carolina cavalrymen of Colonel William P. Shingler's Holcombe Legion, who had scouted the roads of New Kent County east of the Chickahominy and Bottom's Bridge for the past several weeks. Shingler, a South Carolina slave owner, had produced a mixed record during the war highlighted by a reputation for brave conduct as well as a tendency to clash with superiors. Back in April, he had weathered General Henry Wise's charges of drunkenness and remained in service at the front. After the Federals' arrival at White House on June 25, Shingler's men conducted active reconnaissance of the region's roads. On July 1, to further develop the enemy's intentions, infantry under Lieutenant Colonel T. M. Logan from the Hampton Legion in Jenkins's brigade crossed Bottom's Bridge and ventured east toward Crump's Crossroads—the very spot Keyes had chosen to halt his force at about midday.[30]

"STRAY POPS OF MUSKETRY"

That afternoon, Colonel Robert West cautiously advanced his New Yorkers and Pennsylvanians along the Williamsburg Road in front of James McKnight's artillery batteries posted in the fields of Mrs. Fanny Crump's farm to the north. After West's men reached a slight elevation, they detected enemy skirmishers in a gap in the distant woods and in an orchard off to the right. These gray figures were Logan's South Carolinians pushing forward, as one of the them later put it, "to compel the [Federals] to develop" their numbers.[31] West's skirmishers pressed ahead, and "stray pops of musketry" soon echoed for several minutes through the evening air. However, West did not advance farther and quickly deployed Captain Charles E. Mink's battery (Battery H, 1st New York) near the front, which commenced a steady fire into the woods ahead supported by Colonel James Johnson's 178th Pennsylvania. General Keyes soon arrived at the scene and brought forward more units to form a solid line of battle supported to the rear by McKnight's battery (Battery M, 5th US) along with the 4th Delaware commanded by Colonel Arthur H. Grimshaw.[32]

Logan's Confederates, veterans of many engagements over the previous two years, kept up their fire for well over an hour. One of the Union cavalrymen on the left, Archibald Bennett from Company C of the 5th Pennsylvania, toppled dead from his horse when a bullet hit his left eye. Six more Federals received wounds. As the fire slackened on the skirmish line, Adjutant Frank Robinson, also from the 5th Pennsylvania, managed to capture a South Carolina soldier who had rushed out of the trees with "his musket at the aim and ready to fire." Robinson, revolver in hand, stepped forward with his orderly and directed the Southerner, who was attired in "a bright blue loose jacket and blue pants," to surrender. Keyes later learned from the prisoner that his unit had recently arrived in Richmond from the Blackwater River, screened various positions along the Chickahominy for several days, and crossed Bottom's Bridge that very morning.[33]

As the return fire from the Confederates gradually subsided, Mink's guns continued to lob shells into the woods. During the exchange, Lieutenant Colonel Logan sent a party of scouts behind the Union line; it discovered the size of Colonel West's force and concluded that the Federal operation was merely a probe. With that, Logan pulled his men back at dark to return across the Chickahominy River, his losses totaling only two wounded. Eventually, Colonel West also withdrew his troops from their advanced position and reformed on a slight rise just west of Crump's Crossroads.[34]

With the fighting over, General Keyes and his staff sat down in the grass to enjoy some "refreshment" and mulled over what to do next. But back at White House, Dix had become alarmed by reports that the Fourth Corps column had stalled at Crump's Crossroads. That evening, to ensure Keyes would not shrink back any farther, Dix's aide D. T. Van Buren sent another dispatch directing Keyes to "hold your own, unless the enemy shows himself in such force as to make it necessary to fall back." But Keyes had become anxious about what lay in his front and, instead of thinking about holding his own, worried about getting trapped. After midnight, he received a report from Colonel Alfred Gibbs that his scouts had picked up the sounds of artillery and troops crossing a bridge in the direction of the Chickahominy.[35]

Keyes continued to fret that the Confederates would emerge from the woods and conduct a devasting attack against his flank. He again shared his concerns with Dix. At 2:30 a.m., he wrote that the enemy might attack the rear of his position "without our knowing it, and a disaster may, therefore, ensue unless I fall back. I am not well enough acquainted with the country to feel sure."[36] His aide Oswald Jackson agreed, writing home later that Keyes's position was "rather exposed from the number of roads . . . leading around to our rear and the General did not care to risk his wagon train so we withdrew."[37] In short, Keyes was building a list of concerns—or possibly excuses. He worried that the enemy would attack him in his front, on his right flank, or against his left. But most of all, it seems, he stewed about the rebels appearing behind him and destroying his wagon trains. He consulted with his subordinates—"General Terry, Colonels West and Gibbs, and others." According to Keyes, all agreed the force was "in danger of having our trains cut off" if the column remained at the crossroads near Doctor Crump's.[38]

In the face of this perceived danger, Keyes folded and ordered his men to fall back to Talleysville, leaving the 4th Delaware and some of the 139th New York at Crump's Crossroads. The retrograde move began early in the morning on Thursday, July 2. Stephen Hayes, the *New York Daily Herald* reporter, confirmed that Keyes wanted "to get his command clear of the network of roads" branching from the Chickahominy and converging on his position. Keyes reestablished his field headquarters at a Doctor Tyler's in Talleysville, left Colonel West's regiments at Crump's, and extended pickets out to the west beyond. The 4th Delaware remained at "the post of honor and of danger."[39] At the crossroads, Francis Trowbridge of the 139th New York (Company D) wrote soon afterward that "we remained through the night in line of battle—the front rank lying down for two hours, and then the rear rank. One half was kept under arms all the time."[40]

In Stephen Hayes's estimation, Keyes had "no desire to bring on a general engagement" given the apparent strength of the enemy in his front, "with the advantage all on their side, and all the disadvantage on his." The *Herald* correspondent, apparently ignorant of any bigger picture, commended the "brave, skillful, and calculating" general for holding back and "declining to follow the enemy into unknown ambuscades." Hayes believed Keyes was instead coaxing the rebels into the open.[41] He applauded this stratagem. "What at first seemed a questionable Fabian policy proved to be the result of an astute understanding and a perfect comprehension of what even a few hostile troops could do in a country checkered with woods and small open fields." Hayes's own reconnaissance of the area around Talleysville and Crump's Crossroads had confirmed, at least in his mind, the position's vulnerability amid the innumerable roads "all debouching at numerous external points."[42]

It had not been an auspicious beginning. Dix's verbal orders had directed Keyes to reach Bottom's Bridge, post artillery there, and engage the enemy for two or three days. The operation's entire purpose was to generate a vigorous demonstration and prevent the Confederates from sending troops north to repel Getty's column at the railroad bridges in Hanover. Instead of carrying out this program, Keyes had halted about 5 miles shy of his target, stalled by a few skirmishers and a vague report of Confederate troops crossing the Chickahominy in force somewhere.

By morning, his units remained nearly as close to Dix's headquarters at White House as they were to their objective at Bottom's Bridge.

Keyes may have been seeking to bait the Confederates into attacking him. However, in his communications, he dwelled on his fears and spoke little of opportunities. His concern for his wagon train seemed odd given his own orders for the troops to march light. Further—and perhaps even more damning of his lack of action—supplies were not far away given the proximity of White House to the Chickahominy. In addition, Keyes's professed ignorance of the local terrain stood out as particularly curious given his presence there the previous year. In fact, Dix had handed Keyes responsibility for the mission partly due to his knowledge of the locality. Nevertheless, on the morning of July 2, Keyes informed Dix he had "never seen a country so intersected with roads and swamps, on which account my rear was extremely insecure."[43] But there were only so many roads and bridges, and it seems Keyes, armed with his prior knowledge of the topography as well as his ample skirmishers and scouts, could have done more. If the day's considerable heat had factored into his decisions, he did not say so specifically. Finally, given his fear of a Confederate attack, his troop dispositions seemed odd. He had split his forces, establishing headquarters at Talleysville while leaving a small, isolated force at Crump's in front 2 miles away. Such an arrangement seemed only to invite the sort of disaster he feared.

Back at White House, Dix and his staff did not welcome the news of Keyes's withdrawal to Talleysville. At 4:30 a.m. on Thursday, Dix's aide, D. T. Van Buren, probably exhausted and surely exasperated, implored Keyes to hold his position and drive the enemy back to Bottom's Bridge if possible.[44] Dix recognized that Keyes, by pulling most of his command back to Talleysville, threatened to expose a direct route to the base at White House. An operation initially intended to divert the Confederates now had opened opportunities for them to threaten the safety of his entire command. The Confederate capture of White House would impel Dix's scattered forces to find a way back to safety, either down the Peninsula, to West Point, or perhaps to Aquia on the Potomac. The political fallout of such a reversal in Virginia would be more than the commanding general surely cared to fathom.

To address the vulnerability created by Keyes, Dix first ordered Henry Gordon to send a regiment south from Tunstall's Station to guard against an enemy advance. Dix then wrote Keyes and directly underscored his concern: "It is of the utmost consequence that the enemy should not be allowed to advance in force this side of the Chickahominy during the next three days." He emphasized the importance of holding Crump's and covering the approaches from Long Bridge to the south. He also suggested Keyes could eliminate any concerns about his supply train by simply sending the wagons back to White House. Dix also offered to send Gordon's division along with Spinola's brigade in support, a move that would likely leave White House virtually undefended. In sum, Dix believed Keyes should protect his current position from attack and stand firm. Perhaps unwisely, he also conceded that Keyes should not "run any risks," advice that merely buttressed the New Englander's inclination for inactivity.[45]

The Confederates seemed confident. D. H. Hill sensed hesitation in his front, a hunch confirmed by the brief dustup that afternoon at Crump's Crossroads. Lieutenant Colonel Thomas Logan, back from his foray, reported that the Federal force at Crump's consisted of an infantry brigade, two cavalry regiments, and an artillery battery. While the actual strength was much greater—three infantry brigades, not one—the Confederates had accurately gauged Federal intentions. Colonel Shingler, in passing along Logan's report, suggested the Federals seemed to have "little disposition to advance." This assessment was accurate.[46]

13

The Fight at Crump's Crossroads

"FIGHT EXPECTED BETWEEN GENL HILL AND THE ENEMY"

ON THURSDAY, JULY 2, with temperatures edging into the eighties, Erasmus Keyes and his force remained idle. His inactivity contrasted sharply with events unspooling at Gettysburg to the north, where James Longstreet's massive assault would elevate sites such as Devil's Den, Little Round Top, and the Wheatfield into the popular memory of the war. East of Richmond, however, most of the day passed quietly in Keyes's camp. Early that morning, he provided some unsolicited advice to Dix, urging abandonment of the Richmond operation altogether. Beyond striking the rail bridges, Keyes had become convinced that any damage done outside the rebel capital was not worth holding back 20,000 men from supporting the Federal forces facing Robert E. Lee in Pennsylvania. Instead, Keyes asserted that, if he "were in the command of the department," he would prepare the men for transport north to protect the cities there. He ended his gratuitous note by informing Dix that "this I am convinced is the opinion of every thinking man under your command." There is no record of how Dix received this obnoxious dispatch. However, the next few days would reveal his increasing frustration with Keyes, who seemed more interested in offering his own opinions than in carrying out orders.[1]

On Thursday, unhurried and unwilling to trouble the enemy, Keyes made the rounds, visiting his officers and inspecting positions. Early in the afternoon, he checked on the picket posts ringing Crump's Crossroads.[2] He also sent two cavalry detachments south toward Long Bridge and north in the direction of the railroad to look for signs of the enemy.[3] The bulk of his men, however, waited for something to happen, understanding all the while their proximity to Richmond, its church spires visible to soldiers who ventured up into tall pines near the camps.[4]

Keyes's decision to remain at Talleysville throughout Thursday is puzzling. It is unclear whether he misunderstood his orders or believed he had achieved enough by simply getting there and staying put. Whatever the case, Keyes and Dix were not on the same page. Around 3 p.m., a manifestly irritated Dix feared the dawdling had deprived Getty's "movement of much of its value." In the afternoon, Dix again directed Keyes to advance the next morning, "unless prevented by an attack in force by the enemy." As Dix prodded and Keyes paused, Confederate commanders, namely D. H. Hill, had no interest in waiting and considered how to land a blow against the lethargic Yankees.[5]

In Richmond on July 2, the previous day's Federal advance was no secret. The *Daily Richmond Examiner* announced that after "much sifting of rumors, grave and ridiculous, all we have been able to satisfy ourselves is that the enemy yesterday advanced to the Cross Roads."[6] Following Wednesday's skirmish, many in Richmond anticipated a large battle in New Kent County on Thursday. In his line-a-day journal, Herbert Claiborne scribbled: "Fight expected between Genl Hill and the enemy."[7] From his desk at the Confederate War Department, John Beauchamp Jones also followed the events. He heard the "enemy were drawn up in line of battle this morning below the fortifications." The local defense forces, which included Jones's own son, gathered and marched out to the defenses. Word also circulated that the Confederate president was ill, an accurate story. Jones speculated Vice President Stephens would replace him should he expire, adding how "some would rejoice at it."[8]

As leaders in Richmond tried to predict the next Federal move, the command puzzle remained unsolved. Arnold Elzey, still in nominal control of the city's defenders, continued to shift units around the rings of fortifications. For his part, D. H. Hill recommended a mobile defense, which would allow him to keep his veterans in reserve ready to move to the point of danger. "The line of intrenchments is so long and so badly constructed that . . . it will be safer to concentrate our forces, and give fight outside our works," he explained to Secretary of War Seddon.[9] Elzey also placed pickets at the Chickahominy crossings where bridges no longer existed and ordered Custis Lee to send his local defense battalions east to the Charles City and New Market Roads. He cautioned Lee that the movement would be "slow work" given "the nature of the force." Finally, still concerned with the safety of the South Anna, Elzey planned to send 600 convalescents to Hanover Junction and bring Colonel Edward Hall's 46th North Carolina regiment southward to the river.[10] Seddon also engaged in the effort and searched for more men to defend the South Anna bridges from the pool of hospital convalescents, while Hill later recommended sending some of Custis Lee's troops to the South Anna Bridge.[11]

On July 2, Secretary Seddon finally met with the president, who still was suffering from dysentery. During the exchange, Davis objected to the expanded scope of Hill's responsibilities. Seddon quickly realized he had misunderstood the president's earlier guidance. Instead of giving Hill complete control, Davis wished to limit his assignment to the "forces operating in the field" outside the city, leaving the "defenses strictly" to Elzey, including the "trenches and local posts." If driven in, Hill would assume command of all forces in the city. Predictably, following this meeting, directives and guidance continued to stream from several different headquarters. It would take more time for order in the command structure to emerge.[12]

"A GENERAL SKEDADDLE"

By July 2, the defensive arrangements had evolved. Henry Wise's regiments manned the works along the Chickahominy to the northeast between Meadow Bridge and Bottom's Bridge. On the north side, some of Custis Lee's local defense troops protected the lines at the Brook Turnpike. To the east, beyond Richmond's outskirts on the Williamsburg Road, Matt Ransom and Micah Jenkins's brigades stood poised to meet any Union advance there, with Cooke's brigade in reserve. The Confederates looked for signs of an advance. Reports at Long Bridge, far downstream on the Chickahominy, suggested there was no threat there.[13] It was clear the immediate danger to the city stemmed from Keyes's column, a force stalled along the Williamsburg Road at Crump's Crossroads. During the day, Colonel W. P. Shingler again reported the enemy had not budged and remained at Crump's, where Lieutenant Colonel Thomas Logan had "left him yesterday."[14]

Sensing opportunity, D. H. Hill sought to seize the initiative from the Federals. Early in the morning on July 2, he departed his headquarters at the Williams House to observe matters at the front for himself. He soon ordered Ransom's and Jenkins's brigades forward toward the Chickahominy with Cooke's in reserve. To fill the void left by these units, some of Custis Lee's men filed into the works in the intermediate line at the Charles City and New Market Roads. Should the enemy move on Petersburg, Hill recommended that Henry Wise's brigade hurry there from Richmond.[15]

But Hill did more than simply shuffle men around to plug potential gaps. He considered an advance. There were many reasons to do so.

Richmond's defense line was imperfect—incomplete in some places, poorly mapped, and too long to adequately defend with the force at hand. The Confederates could not cover every possible route. They had a limited number of experienced troops for active operations: three brigades (under Jenkins, Ransom, and Cooke) amounting to about 7,000 that could head out and attack the enemy. Richmond's local defenders, the ragtag collection of office workers, hospital patients, and garrison troops, could not be counted on for anything but static defense. In addition, Hill did not know where all of Dix's men were. He only knew for certain that one Union column was now huddled at Crump's Crossroads and Talleysville with no apparent willingness to do much of anything.

Under these conditions, Hill chose to strike. He ordered his veteran brigades out of their camps and put them on the march across the Chickahominy, as the young Captain William Burgwyn from the 35th North Carolina put it, "to fight the Yankees as they would not fight us."[16] Later, another Tar Heel explained that Hill, "without waiting for them to approach nearer to his fortified line of defence, which he had not enough troops to adequately man, moved out rapidly upon them."[17] Undoubtedly, Hill believed a sudden sharp lunge would throw the Federals off-balance and further disrupt their operations.

Under Hill's direction, the attacking column marched out in force along Williamsburg Road to meet Keyes's troops. The South Carolinians in Micah Jenkins's brigade left their camps at dawn Thursday and tramped east over Bottom's Bridge past the old Federal earthworks built on the opposite bank the previous year. In addition, several guns from Major James Branch's artillery battalion—probably a dozen in all—and a squadron of cavalry from Colonel Shingler's Holcombe Legion joined the column. Matt Ransom's North Carolina regiments followed and John Cooke's North Carolina brigade accompanied the movement but remained in reserve.[18] Within a few hours, the column had crossed the river into New Kent County to "feel the enemy."[19] With the South Carolina regiments leading the way, Shingler's riders probed ahead and fanned out on both sides of the column.

Jenkins, a twenty-seven-year-old Edisto Island native, had led troops in the thick of many of the large 1862 engagements, including Seven Pines and Second Bull Run, where he received wounds. During the spring of 1863, he served with James Longstreet during the Suffolk Campaign. D. H. Hill, always candid in his assessments, held a high opinion of Jenkins. North Carolinian Matt Ransom, Jenkins's counterpart on Thursday's mission, was also a solid combat leader who had led the 35th North

Carolina in most of the major Virginia campaigns. The aggressive Carolinian earned the rank of brigadier general in early June and filled a vacancy created by the promotion of his brother, Robert Ransom. In commenting on Matt Ransom, one officer commended the Tar Heel for his "efficiency as disciplinarian and his skill and intrepidity on the field of battle."[20]

The Confederates pushed forward during the afternoon. Within a mile or two of Crump's Crossroads, the 24th North Carolina from Ransom's command advanced to support Jenkins's brigade.[21] As the column neared the enemy, Jenkins formed a vanguard out of select companies from several regiments and assigned Colonel J. M. Steadman from the 6th South Carolina to lead. Soon, a line of skirmishers pushed east through the woods toward the Crump plantation and arrived within sight of Keyes's line in the distance.[22]

On alert after the previous day's events, Union officers at the Crossroads looked out for the Confederates throughout the afternoon. At about five o'clock, a detachment from the 139th New York Infantry, supported by a section of Mink's battery, ventured out over the same ground they had fought over the evening before. The New Yorkers entered a patch of woods to the left of the road opposite Fanny Crump's house and emerged into an open space with the Royster homestead on the left and the Grant House across the road to their right. They advanced another 200 yards west toward a long tree line stretching across their entire front.[23] New Yorker Francis Trowbridge, ahead in the skirmish line, caught a glimpse of rebel pickets in front.[24]

The full Confederate force soon appeared, a battle line three men deep, debouching from the trees. The Federals halted, and the Southerners immediately opened the "most murderous fire." According to Trowbridge, the men in blue received an order to get down and threw themselves flat as enemy fire passed over their heads "faster than any hail stones ever fell."[25] "As I lay there," he recalled a few days later, "I made up my mind that [a] number of my men would be knocked off. As I sit down here and think of it, I cannot hardly realize that I am unharmed."[26] The New Yorkers managed to snap off two volleys but soon withdrew to avoid being swallowed by the oncoming battle line. Colonel West formed his infantrymen near the Crossroads with his entire brigade in line. Captain Andrew Fagan, 1st Pennsylvania Light Artillery, brought his guns forward. Additionally, a section of Mink's New York battery opened fire on Confederate skirmishers advancing across a slight ravine on both sides of the road about 900 yards away. According to correspondent Stephen

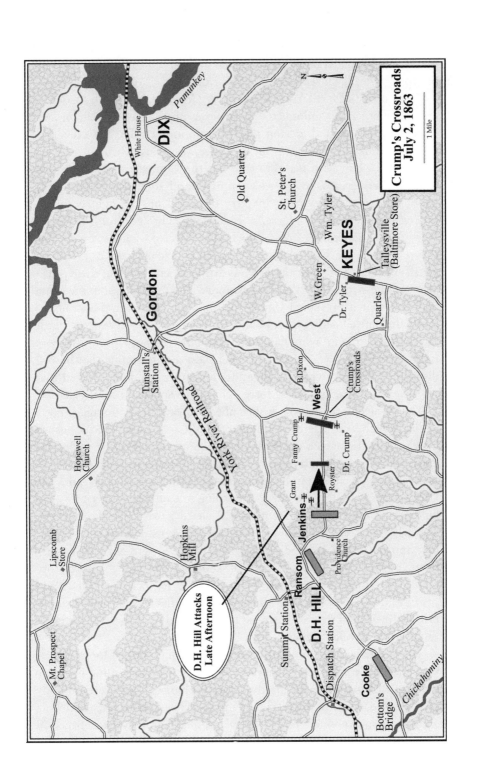

Crump's Crossroads
July 2, 1863

1 Mile

N

DIX

Pamunkey

White House

Old Quarter

St. Peter's
Church

Wm. Tyler

KEYES

Talleysville
(Baltimore Store)

W. Green

Gordon

Dr. Tyler

Quarles

Tunstall's
Station

B. Dixon

Crump's
Crossroads

West

Fanny Crump

Dr. Crump

Grant

Royster

Jenkins

Hopewell
Church

York River Railroad

Ransom

Providence
Church

D.H. Hill Attacks
Late Afternoon

Hopkins
Mill

D.H. HILL

Lipscomb
Store

Summit Station

Dispatch Station

Mt. Prospect
Chapel

Cooke

Bottom's
Bridge

Chickahominy

Hayes, the Confederate force numbered at least "one thousand strong," but to Trowbridge it seemed more like 7,000.[27]

From a tree-covered knoll west of the Crossroads, Branch's Confederate artillery crews unlimbered their pieces and shelled the Union line, tearing up the ground around the Federal guns. During the exchange, Captain Mink dismounted from his horse, drew his saber, and walked from gun to gun with his officers.[28] But the Confederates had at least eight artillery pieces, by Hayes's estimate, and soon gained the upper hand, though the New York infantry remained in "the fight with surprising readiness and coolness."[29] Francis Trowbridge, from the 139th New York, counted even more rebel guns—twelve—which "completely overpowered" the Federal line. The gunners exchanged fire for about a half an hour, but soon the Federal artillerymen limbered their pieces and withdrew to a less exposed position.[30] The rebels kept up their fire, so heavy that it prevented Union doctors from attending the wounded along the battle line.[31] Two miles away at Talleysville, Keyes could hear the sounds of the growing fight but apparently did not rush to the front right away. At 7 p.m., he sent Colonel West a note stating that he had dispatched Burr Porter's brigade and a few guns. He directed West that "if the enemy attacks in large force fight your way back to this place."[32]

The Confederate infantry pushed ahead toward the Crossroads. For a while, though, the Federals continued to hold up. Colonel Porter pushed forward two regiments into the battle line as Colonel West pulled his exhausted men back into reserve. But, regardless of how long or hard the Federals fought at Crump's Crossroads, the outcome was certain. The US force soon began to recede.[33] According to Confederate accounts, the fighting did not last long. Lieutenant Richard Lewis from the Palmetto Sharpshooters recalled that the Federals "gave us a few shots on our first approach, but as soon as they saw that we were not trifling with them . . . they commenced a general skedaddle movement, never stopping to exchange a single shot with us, but flying in great dismay and confusion."[34] The *Richmond Inquirer* reported that "[o]ur men, eager to test the [mettle] of the foe, hastened forward, and upon getting in musket range let fly a volley amongst them."[35]

The Confederates did not give the Federals high marks for their performance at Crump's. One believed the Yankee artillery did not fire more than four or five times during the entire exchange. They were similarly unimpressed with the blue-clad infantry. "They hardly remained long enough for our gunners to get the range, although they had formed in line of battle," wrote one Tar Heel. But such claims may have contained a large dose of Southern hyperbole. The fire from the US guns indeed exacted a toll. During the fighting, a Federal shell killed Private John G. Tate, waiting in reserve in the ranks of the 24th North Carolina of Ransom's brigade.[36] Another round came close to eclipsing the career of Colonel William J. Clarke, commander of Tate's regiment, when it exploded only a few feet away from him.[37]

Eventually, however, the entire Federal position collapsed under the weight of the Confederate advance. Colonel West and his force withdrew toward Talleysville, leaving eighteen men on the field in addition to those removed from the scene by the medical staff.[38] The Richmond newspapers described the Union withdrawal as a discreditable rout. According to the *Daily Richmond Examiner*, the Federals "broke and fled in great disorder . . . driven from their line of battle by the adventurous fire of our skirmishers alone," exhibiting a "feeble and spiritless resistance."[39] The *Richmond Enquirer* added that the Yankees "faintheartedly return[ed] the fire, and the clearing away of the smoke revealed the entire column and precipitate retreat." The *Enquirer* also reported that Jenkins ordered his men to pursue, and they stepped forward "roaring with shouts of laughter and enthusiasm."[40]

The Confederates pressed their pursuit. D. H. Hill ordered Colonel Shingler ahead with the Holcombe Legion to harass the retreating column. "Two hundred mounted troops made a most daring charge;" reported the *Richmond Sentinel*, and "three times the enemy ambushed him, firing volley after volley, but onward [Shingler] dashed," driving the enemy back for several miles. Adding to Shingler's riders, some of Jenkins's and Ransom's infantrymen joined in as well along with a portion of Branch's artillery. One member of Ransom's brigade described the affair as the "longest running fight that I saw during the war." Another, John Graham of the 56th North Carolina, reported his regiment arrived at the Crossroads after the fight only to see Federal prisoners there and then chased the enemy at the double-quick for 2 miles through "mud and water." During the pursuit, South Carolina infantrymen picked up several Union soldiers who had hidden away in the ravines along the road. But for the most part, the fleeing Yankees outpaced their pursuers. "We . . . gave up the chase as utterly hopeless, they being too expert on their heels for us," scoffed Richard Lewis.[41]

General Keyes eventually left his headquarters at Doctor Tyler's in Talleysville to find out what was happening at the front. According to the *Herald*'s Stephen Hayes, the general and his staff galloped toward Crump's Crossroads, passing retreating men along the way. It is not clear how far Keyes rode. At some point, he encountered Colonels Burr Porter and Arthur Grimshaw and ordered them to establish a new position near the Quarles House, on the road about a mile southwest of Talleysville.[42] During the withdrawal, Colonel Porter kept the rear guard intact and halted at Quarles as instructed. According to reporting by Hayes, the retreat was "persistently and hotly followed up by the rebels, who shelled them every yard of the road." Back at Talleysville, a member of Captain James McKnight's artillery recalled that "cavalry came in at full speed reporting the enemy near" and that the "matter looked rather dark." Before Porter's men reached Quarles, Confederate troops nearly cut them off, having followed a different route in pursuit. Hayes marveled that the Confederates' "perfect knowledge of the country enables them to move from one point to another with almost magical celerity."[43]

Back at Talleysville, Keyes planted a battle line in the woods at the edge of an open field near the intersection there. He hoped the advancing Confederates would expose their flank to his new position. His officers waited in anticipation, and orders passed along the line for the strictest silence. McKnight's gunners, shielded by the woods, readied to let loose their fire on the enemy. In Hayes's estimation, those minutes waiting for the Confederates to advance were the "most exciting few moments of my life." But D. H. Hill, or perhaps Jenkins, stopped the movement short and refused to take the bait. The decision impressed Keyes, who supposedly remarked that there was "a regularly trained soldier opposed to me there, whoever he is."[44]

Earlier in the afternoon, Dix had visited Keyes at Talleysville and then rode back north toward White House before the Confederate attack.[45] By the time D. H. Hill's lines hit Crump's Crossroads, the commanding general had returned to his headquarters on the Pamunkey. During the fighting, Keyes wrote for advice. "Shall I go forward with my whole force, or shall I consider the force now out as my advance, and this the battle-ground?" he asked. Once again, Keyes's caution alarmed Dix, who was doing everything he could to prevent his subordinate from abandoning the Talleysville position, falling back to White House, and inviting disaster. "You should fight the enemy on the ground you think most favorable to you," Dix snapped. He also emphasized the importance of regaining Crump's Crossroads and sealing off a direct route to the White House base. Dix was reluctant to send more men to Keyes and further weaken the garrison at this headquarters. That evening, General George Gordon visited Dix at White House, where dispatches from Keyes had piled up, full of excuses, questions, and concerns. As Gordon recalled,

Keyes's behavior baffled and exasperated Dix, who was as much "amused as disturbed" and expected Keyes would scamper back to White House by daylight. In any case, Dix ordered Gordon to prepare for a possible attack.[46]

Back at Talleysville that evening and into the morning hours, Keyes consolidated his position as members of his staff caught their breath. "We had quite a lively time for a while," noted Oswald Jackson, "but finally they withdrew & we retired to our virtuous coaches & ambulances, for we [have] been living in them altogether since we left White House & have altogether eschewed tents." At 11 p.m., Keyes wrote Dix again, this time explaining that Colonel Porter had dropped back to form a line at the Quarles House. At midnight, Van Buren replied, simply relaying General Dix's orders to "hold your position."[47]

For those in the thick of the fight on July 2, the small engagement was as harrowing as any other. "Now the excitement is over, my heart sickens at the thought of my situation and the awful scene around me," Trowbridge confessed. "The sharp crack of the rifle, the roar of artillery, the groans of the wounded and dying may be imagined but can never be described."[48] Casualties from the fight on July 2 were high relative to those engaged at the front but certainly low in comparison to the total forces on or near the field. According to D. H. Hill, Confederate losses amounted to two killed (one from the 24th North Carolina) and four wounded, mostly from Jenkins's brigade.[49] Confederate sources estimated that about twenty Federals had been killed, wounded, or captured. New Yorker Francis Trowbridge wrote home: "Of the forty advanced skirmishers of whom I was one, twenty-six were killed, wounded, or missing." One wounded US lieutenant reportedly had "both his legs shot off." Another account put the Federal loss at "some few" killed and about ten taken prisoner.[50] In addition to the casualties, the Confederates pursuing the retreating Federals discovered many "hats, coats, and everything that could impede their flight" littering the ground. In one field around the Crump Plantation, the rebels collected a partially butchered cow and many chickens tied up by their legs ready for slaughter, as well as two officer swords lying about the field.[51]

On Thursday evening following the engagement, Ransom and Jenkins turned their brigades around and marched back west to the Chickahominy.[52] In a later note to Seddon, D. H. Hill explained that his troops had driven the enemy steadily beyond the Crossroads until about 10 p.m., when the Federals was found too strong for a night attack. He admitted his men were tired from "throwing down intrenchments" in the city's fortifications the night before, "and the march of upward of 20 miles had worried them very much."[53] During the withdrawal, Micah Jenkins, realizing his men were exhausted from the day's fighting and marching, arranged for a train to come across the river on the rail line, perhaps at Dispatch Station or Summit Station, and ride the railcars back west to their camp. Ransom's Tar Heels, apparently not as lucky, marched back on the road across Bottom's Bridge, not reaching their camps until well after midnight.[54]

Hill had bested Keyes at Crump's Crossroads. His decision to march out and attack the Federal force reflected the stark difference between the attitudes of the opposing commanders. Hill believed his best approach lay in striking out against the US forces to blunt their movements and disrupt their plans. There was nothing subtle about Hill's tactics. He simply ordered his officers to form their men in line and push straight at the enemy. Hill's approach contrasted sharply with Keyes's. The Massachusetts general, cautious and conservative, had focused on preventing disaster. However, in doing so, he nearly managed to bring one about. By allowing Hill to drive him back so easily, Keyes damaged Getty's chances for success in his march to the South Anna. Indeed, Keyes's inaction convinced the Confederates there was no threat in New Kent County and gave Hill and his comrades breathing room to assess conditions outside Richmond and consider the Federals' next move.

Hill correctly determined that Keyes's operation was merely a feint to cover a more determined movement elsewhere. The anemic Federal advance had given Hill time to ponder. Late Thursday night, he reported to Seddon from Bottom's Bridge that the enemy had been driven back. He considered a new attack for the next day but decided against such a course after Jenkins and Ransom predicted the Federals would withdraw to White House or even retreat east to West Point. Hill also sought news from the north at Hanover Junction and planned to send Cooke's brigade there on the train Friday to aid Edward Hall. Not only had Keyes failed to pin the Confederates down; his lackluster performance appears to have tipped off the rebels to Getty's expedition into Hanover.[55]

The Richmond press rightly praised Hill. The small victory occurred at a time of great anxiety as officials and city residents waited for news from Pennsylvania and Vicksburg. Hill's neat, decisive win at Crump's Crossroads brought a modest measure of comfort. Recognizing the fight as a "small affair," the *Daily Richmond Examiner* found the engagement "in fact[] becomes ridiculous" when one considers "that this herd that fled so ignominiously at the first sound of our guns, was the greater part of the 'army, with banners,' hoping to walk right into Richmond." The newspaper heaped praise on Jenkins's and Ransom's brigades while not neglecting to take shots at the Federals. A report from another paper indicated prisoners taken by Hill's force "seem dissatisfied, and some of them say" the troops "are tired of the war, and weary of the folly of 'taking Richmond.'"[56]

"THIS SIDE OF BOTTOM'S BRIDGE"

On Friday morning, July 3, Dix once again ordered Keyes to advance, find the enemy, and gauge his strength. He stressed the importance of picketing the road north to Tunstall's Station as well as the "Mill Road," a narrow path that skirted Crump's Mill Pond west of Talleysville. Although Keyes had not fathomed the Confederate strength in his front, he took no chances. With the exception of a single regiment held in reserve, he placed every man either in the skirmish line or line of battle surrounding his position. He also asked Dix for more, including "a couple of good, strong regiments, under an active, enterprising man, to send out on a reconnaissance."[57]

Over the next few days, Keyes remained at Talleysville, doing little to either threaten the Richmond defenses or otherwise aid Dix's overall operation. He rested his men and continued to think defensively. He destroyed the small bridge at Crump's Mill to thwart any large enemy advance along the path passing that point on his right flank. He ordered his men to remain at their outposts and barricade all the roads leading to the Talleysville position. He also constructed a telegraph line strung from his field headquarters to White House, presumably to provide constant reports of his inactivity. He soon found that rebel bushwhackers cut the line so frequently that guards were needed to protect it from "end to end." In his late-morning dispatch to Dix on Friday, Keyes gave no hint of offensive plans and boasted that, if the enemy advanced again "day or night, I am prepared to receive him." But by midday, Confederate pickets had withdrawn from their forward positions and repositioned west near Bottom's Bridge, far away from Keyes's defensive enclave.[58]

By Independence Day, matters in Keyes's front had slowed to a crawl. With little going on, soldiers at Talleysville and White House looked for ways to kill time. At their picket posts, members of the 127th New York from Gordon's division feasted on blackberries, "which were very abundant, and which afforded an agreeable change from the salt horse and pork furnished by Uncle Sam." The men also helped themselves to the contents of a local icehouse, abandoned by a Confederate citizen who "left in too much of a hurry to be able to take his ice away with him," recalled a New Yorker.[59] According to aide Oswald Jackson, Keyes and his staff spent the days "at the large house on the top of the hill" at Talleysville and slept in their headquarters ambulances at night in a hollow behind the residence.[60]

As Keyes's front remained inert, Dix found other things to do. "Yesterday, Charlie [his son] and I were in front," he wrote his wife on Saturday, July 4, "and on our return last evening we visited a quaint old Church [St. Peter's], the one[] in which Washington is said to have been married. If he could have seen its present condition—deserted, stripped of all emblems of its sacred character . . . how would his heart have sunk . . . !"[61] With the sightseeing over, Dix could not escape further dealings with his subordinate. On Saturday evening, he visited Keyes once more and, after returning to White House, ordered him to attack the enemy "if we can find him this side of Bottom's Bridge." With his irritation unabated, Dix reminded Keyes that the attack should have happened on July 1, three days before, and that the instruction had been repeated "more than once." He even offered to relieve Keyes from responsibility for the operation if the enemy in his front was too strong. Otherwise, he urged Keyes to conduct a "rapid and decisive" movement by putting his "whole force in motion" the next morning to destroy Bottom's Bridge and the rail bridge just upstream. Keyes responded to this straightforward directive with more questions and equivocation. "Am I to understand that if I decide against making a movement on Bottom's Bridge, it will not be made?" he asked. A half-hour later, aide D. T. Van Buren wrote on Dix's behalf and clarified that the general expected an advance and that, if Keyes refused to do so, General Gordon would "be put in."[62]

Early Sunday morning, July 5, Keyes furnished an extraordinary response to the attack orders. Instead of drafting his own note, he forwarded a letter from his three brigade commanders—Terry, Porter, and West—prepared at 3 a.m. These officers had become convinced that the enemy had a strong position beyond Crump's Crossroads. They also concluded that no advance would be successful without additional troops and more ammunition.[63] This time Dix and Van Buren, surely dismayed by this wall of resistance, apparently gave up and simply directed Keyes to suspend the movement until further orders.[64]

In a bizarre turn of events only hours later on Sunday, Keyes wrote Dix raising the possibility of an advance, seeking advice, and hedging his bets.

But even in doing this, Keyes expressed concern the Confederate troops might appear again and stampede his column as it advanced on a single road. In Keyes's mind, Thursday's combat had been "the most persistent and long continued of any night attack I have witnessed during this war." To succeed in any upcoming effort, he proposed to move in two columns but believed an additional brigade would be necessary to do so. Without such additional troops, he feared success "would not be certain." He then sought further orders.[65]

Later that day, Dix was apparently finished with Keyes and suspended any movement against Bottom's Bridge. The potential utility of action in New Kent County had largely evaporated. In his communication, however, Dix reminded Keyes that he had always been at liberty to move in "two columns or one" according to his discretion. Dix also scoffed at Keyes's characterization of the Confederate attack on July 2. "The night attack you refer to was very fierce on the part of the enemy, so far as burning powder was concerned; but we did not lose a man." Dix was wrong about the casualty numbers, but he was correct in refusing to rank the engagement at Crump's Crossroads as a fierce, protracted battle. In any case, Dix concluded that Keyes's demand for another brigade "defeats the movement" by eliminating any reserves available for Getty and leaving White House completely unprotected. "The movement must, therefore, be abandoned," the commanding general concluded.[66]

Keyes did not let it go. The next day, still at Talleysville, he wrote: "I regret as much as you do that the move to Bottom's Bridge was not accomplished" and, perhaps anticipating formal reprimand for his inaction, added that "all testimony corroborates the correctness of our decision that another brigade was necessary."[67] He argued that a larger force was needed to overcome his "imperfect knowledge" of the local road network and the enemy's advantage operating in their home territory. Oddly, Keyes seemed to believe his efforts had somehow prevented the Confederates from sending troops north to help repel Getty's operation. "I certainly succeeded in diverting a large force from Getty as long as it was anticipated would be necessary." This was incorrect.[68]

By all measures, Keyes had failed. He had made little effort to engage and occupy the enemy and instead allowed the Confederates to dictate matters. D. H. Hill's troops had probed and fixed Keyes in place the first day, attacked aggressively and drove him back on the second, and finally ignored him almost entirely after it became clear the Federals in New Kent posed no credible threat to Richmond. Though his mission was limited, Keyes failed to even clear the low bar Dix had set for him. He had never come close to Bottom's Bridge or seriously threatened Confederate positions there. Once attacked, he pulled back to Talleysville and spent the next several days manufacturing explanations for his inaction in a torrent of dispatches to White House. His excuse-making oddly resembled that of his nemesis George McClellan the year before, who repeatedly conjured some reason to avoid attacking the Confederates in his front.[69] Keyes continually raised concerns about the safety of his command. Certainly, Hill's foray on July 2 only magnified that concern. His excuses were many, and he seemed content to do nothing. Ultimately, he simply did not possess the willingness to move forward, or perhaps he harbored a fundamental misunderstanding of what was needed from his command.

Conversely, D. H. Hill had outpaced Keyes at every turn. He refused to wait in a defensive shell and struck out with no hesitation. His brigades had marched out of the fortifications beyond the Chickahominy River into New Kent County to hit the enemy and rattle Union commanders, not unlike Lee at Mechanicsville and Gaines Mill the year before. After wiping away Keyes's line at Crump's Crossroads, Hill had been judicious in calling off his advance. His decisions brought the Federal demonstration to a grinding halt and fed the doubts already plaguing Keyes. By freezing the enemy column in place, Hill had bought time and space to deploy Richmond's defenders elsewhere to respond to other contingencies.

14

Getty's Expedition to the South Anna

"EQUAL TO EVERY DUTY AND POSITION"

BACK ON JULY 1, AS KEYES MARCHED toward Crump's Crossroads and Henry Heth pointed his division in the direction of Gettysburg, George Washington Getty set his command in motion for the South Anna River. The forty-three-year-old brigadier general and West Point graduate had served with the United States Army in Mexico with distinction, as well as in Florida and Kansas. Getty spent the first part of the war as an artillery commander, leading several batteries during the 1862 Peninsula Campaign before rising to become the Ninth Corps artillery chief during the Maryland Campaign. Late in 1862, he left the gunners for an infantry command and led a Ninth Corps division at Fredericksburg. Early in 1863, Getty joined Dix's force at Suffolk, where he commanded a division containing mostly New York and Connecticut units. He would later perform well in the Overland Campaign, in the Shenandoah, and at Petersburg.[1]

Despite his extensive experience and solid contributions during the war, Getty remains a somewhat overlooked figure. Few anecdotes or personal descriptions of the general appear in reminiscences and accounts. Theodore Lyman, a prolific diarist who later served on George Meade's staff, wrote: "He is a cool man, is Getty, quite a wonder." But even obituaries in Getty's hometown of Washington, DC, provided little or nothing to describe him beyond a long list of impressive accomplishments.[2] His obituary in a Vermont paper left this rather generic praise: A "true patriot; modest to a fault, ever faithful to duty, sharing danger with his men, as cool as he was brave in action, and equal to every duty and position."[3] However, not everyone had praise for the general. One Connecticut soldier who observed Getty early in the war painted an unflattering picture as part of a long series of short descriptions of dozens of officers, both famous and obscure. The man, whose views may not have been typical of the rank-and-file, found Getty "rough and exacting in the extreme," an officer who "never fails to give vent to his wrath in a torrent of oaths on the head of the offenders."[4]

On June 30, Getty gathered his force for the business end of Dix's offensive: the march north to Hanover County and the RF&P rail bridge over the South Anna. That evening, his officers shuttled artillery and wagons from White House across the Pamunkey on top of platform cars, while some of his infantry and cavalry also tramped along the span. Getty would follow the route Spear had taken on his return leg a few days before along the wide, less-exposed roads of King William County. Thirty-five miles stood between Getty's men and their objective, the RF&P bridge. For the mission, he brought a mix of troops totaling about 10,000 men. His own division, which had been detached from the Ninth Corps in the Army of the Potomac earlier in the year and absorbed into the Seventh Corps, formed the core of his command and contained three brigades: one under Colonel Samuel Alford (four New York regiments), another led by Brigadier General Edward Harland (four Connecticut regiments), and the third commanded by Colonel Michael T. Donohoe (two New Hampshire regiments and one from Rhode Island).[5] In addition, Getty brought along a "provisional brigade" (the 99th and 118th New York) commanded by David W. Wardrop, Brigadier General Robert S. Foster's brigade (13th Indiana, 112th and 169th New York, 165th and 166th Pennsylvania, and Battery G of the 7th Massachusetts), and Colonel Samuel Spear's cavalry, composed mostly of the 11th Pennsylvania.[6] Throughout Tuesday evening, Getty's artillery column continued to pass over the Pamunkey into King William County, with many of the wagons and much of the equipment reportedly placed aboard platform cars. By early the next morning, Getty's entire force made it over the river.[7]

Many of the men who crossed the river Tuesday night bivouacked on Pamunkey Island. That evening, it appears the troops helped themselves to 300 or 400 fence rails from Archie Miles's 35-acre farm to burn at their camp fires—though the precise timing of this destruction is not clear. The elderly Miles, a member of the Pamunkey Tribe, had served as a river pilot for the US gunboats the year before, much like William Bradby whose home had been torn down days earlier by Dix's troops. After the war, Miles's widow, Adelphia, would obtain compensation for the fence rails and other property from the US government through the Southern Claims Commission. At 8 a.m. on July 4, however, with the summer sun climbing, Getty's cavalrymen, foot soldiers, battery limbers, wagons, and ambulances formed up for the march north.[8]

"THE OBJECT OF THE EXPEDITION"

Dix's orders to Getty were thorough and touched on themes emphasized many times before. The instructions directed the column to pass through King William County via Lanesville, King William Court House, and Taylor's plantation ("Horn Quarter"). From there, Getty would pass over the Pamunkey on Littlepage's Bridge and proceed into Hanover County to "attack the railroad bridge of the [RF&P] over the South Anna, destroy it, and take up and twist or bend as many of the rails on the road as possible." Dix also urged Getty to capture the "insurgent troops guarding the bridge." Despite the fact that Halleck mentioned the bridges at the North Anna River in his original June 14 orders, it appears that, by this time, Dix had concluded the main target there, the rail line to Fredericksburg, was not worth the effort. Delving into the logistical details, Dix instructed Getty to take "five days' rations, two of which will be cooked," including "beef on the hoof," as well as five days' oats for the horses and mules.[9]

Predictably, Dix's orders exuded caution. To prevent the Confederates from throwing a force behind Getty's column, he wanted every bridge between White House and Taylor's plantation destroyed and all ferries along this stretch of the Pamunkey removed. He also ordered Getty to guard the remaining upstream spans (Taylor's and Littlepage's) and to leave all the wagons, except those carrying ammunition, in King William County. However, Dix's orders were not overly rigid, for they contained a proviso allowing Getty to stray from the instructions should conditions warrant, as long as "the object of the expedition" was met.[10]

Dix also demanded that Getty's men exercise moderation in dealing with the local population. As he had in all recent orders, Dix strictly prohibited undue harm to civilians or their property. "[A]ll pillaging is peremptorily forbidden," he admonished, explaining that such actions were both inconsistent with "the Rules and Articles of War" and a "violation of the principles of honorable warfare." Getty's men would take no private property unless under specific orders, and only then "for public use and as a military necessity." Dix even required Getty's officers during evening parade to read Article 52, the prohibition against treating enemy civilians as a "brigand or bandit," and Article 54, rules on hostages, from the Articles of War (the "Lieber Code").[11]

Although Dix's statements revealed his concern about property-holding Southerners, his orders did not mention the thousands of enslaved people in the region. In fact, he had mostly ignored these individuals throughout his tenure in southeastern Virginia. He found the Black refugees in and around his bases bothersome. "The contraband negroes who have been permitted to collect in great numbers at this fort and in this vicinity," he had complained in the fall of 1862, "have always been and are now a very great source of embarrassment to the troops in this garrison and in the camps hereabouts and to the white population in this neighborhood."[12] Unhappy with policies such as the Emancipation Proclamation, he had nevertheless performed his duty and complied, if unenthusiastically, with the various Federal directives and laws related to slavery. He had also sought to manage, in good faith, the influx of refugees streaming into the bases of his department. For instance, in December 1862, he wrote Secretary of War Stanton seeking to obtain payments owed freedmen for their labor due to an administrative error. He also sought to improve the conditions for women and children in the refugee camps. "The Government having adopted the policy of receiving these fugitives, and, by implication, promised them protection and security," he entreated, "it is respectfully submitted that some provision should be made for their intellectual and religious as well as for their physical wants."[13] However, such statements of concern about Black refugees were not common in his correspondence.

By not energetically engaging on these issues, Dix ignored what was in front of him. Over the course of the conflict, self-emancipated African Americans had aided the US military at nearly every turn. They had escaped from bondage, traveled to Federal bases, and contributed their labor. Early in the contest, Dix had not encouraged enslaved people to seek their freedom. In fact, he sought distance from the entire issue, writing in August 1861 that "we have nothing to do with slaves; that we are neither negro-stealers nor negro-catchers, and that we should send them away if they came to us."[14] Nevertheless, during 1862 and into 1863, Dix accepted the new policies and laws from Washington regarding Black refugees despite his personal views. Still, he did not seem to recognize the tangible contributions of Black people to the Union war effort.

Likewise, Dix did not demonstrate much enthusiasm for Black military recruitment. By the summer of 1863, his department had not conducted any significant efforts to enlist freedmen into the US ranks, even as such ventures were gearing up in other departments; neither did Dix aggressively cultivate the use of freedmen for intelligence gathering.[15] Tainted by his low expectations for such troops, he doubted the freedmen had much desire to enlist. In correspondence with President Lincoln on the subject in January 1863, for example, he reported his officers had experienced difficulty finding Black recruits. "The general reply was, that they were willing to work, but did not wish to fight." Dix also believed many freedmen did not have "cordial" feelings for the North because of voting prohibitions and "social prejudices" that effectively neutralized any "theoretical" political equality that might have been found in the law. Subsequent recruiting efforts in Virginia, however, would demonstrate that Dix was simply wrong.[16]

Dix fumbled several decisions related to refugees despite his considerable administrative and political skills. At the end of 1862, he informed Secretary Stanton that contact between Black refugees and the soldiers in the department was "injurious to both." His solution was segregation. He deposited formerly enslaved persons on Craney Island, 10 miles from Fort Monroe, pulling them away from housing they had constructed on the Peninsula and bringing them to a largely "barren" spot with inadequate quarters. In another instance, Dix managed to alienate potential allies in the North. At one point, he tried—in good faith, apparently—to encourage Northern governors to accept Black refugees from the South.[17] The suggestion and related correspondence appeared in newspapers throughout the country and ignited a small political firestorm that produced a torrent of ill-will aimed at Dix.[18] He moved beyond the dustup and concluded that the controversy would further discourage freedmen from joining the Federal ranks. Openly revealing the racism all too common among Federal officers, he remained doubtful that these men would measure up. In his view, the protection of crucial military positions such as Fort Monroe should not be "confided to any other class than the white population of the country," and the "inferior element" (i.e., Black troops) should be employed only "in very small proportion" in "services of secondary importance."[19]

Dix's prejudice formed a harmful blind spot. During the operations outside Richmond in the summer of 1863, he rarely, if ever, mentioned enslaved people in his orders, correspondence, or reports. However, in nearly every operation during the previous weeks—Gordon's occupation of West Point, the Aylett's raid, Spear's expedition to the South Anna, and Keyes's halting advance—Black refugees had escaped their captors to join Federal columns, provide crucial intelligence to his troops, and otherwise aided the US war effort. Nearly without exception, the operations of his men in enemy-controlled country drew refugees into the columns, creating opportunities for his command as well as significant logistical challenges in some cases. Dix, however, chose not to mention this issue at all in his directive to Getty, who was about to take 10,000 men through King William County and beyond, a region littered with slave plantations that had been rarely visited by Federal columns until that time in the war.[20]

"I NEVER SAW SUCH A COUNTRY FOR BLACKBERRIES"

Getty's column set out north on July 1, the same day Keyes had headed toward the Chickahominy. Early that morning, the 1,200 men in Spear's cavalry command fanned out ahead of the infantry column riding through Lanesville on its way to King William Court House. A plantation owner along the route recalled watching on as a long line of Union horsemen passed his land with two pieces of field artillery and one caisson. After traveling for 9 miles, Spear's men reached the courthouse and overran a small picket post there, capturing two rebels and some small arms. However, seven of the Southerners spurred their fresh horses away and escaped from the Yankees and their tired mounts.[21] In the afternoon, most of Spear's men broke off from the main column and headed west toward the Pamunkey to cover Getty's left flank, reaching the Drewry plantation, known as "Brandywine" (modern-day "Manquin"), where they captured two unlucky detectives from the Richmond police force, confiscated the pair's "papers, orders, horses, &c.," and sent them back to the rear under guard. Some of the cavalrymen camped that night near the Drewry property. Others headed toward the Pamunkey River to destroy the bridges, ferries, and boats there as far upstream as Hanovertown.[22] Companies A and E of the 11th Pennsylvania reached the ferry there, captured a Confederate wagon loaded with meal, and then rode upriver to Nelson's bridge, where the riders halted for the evening.[23]

The foot soldiers also made progress on Wednesday. The lead elements of Getty's infantry broke camp at 6 a.m. and marched all day under a hot sun that drove temperatures into the upper eighties. The morning departure, however, was apparently a leisurely one. A Connecticut veteran recalled having time to catch several large catfish in the Pamunkey from the railroad bridge after an elderly freedman recommended the use of "green" (fresh) cheese for bait.[24] Once on the road, the soldiers noticed a stark difference between the King William countryside and more war-torn locales. Hazard Stevens, a twenty-one-year-old who served on Getty's staff and was son of General Isaac Stevens, who had been killed at Chantilly the previous fall, found the region had "hitherto escaped the visitations of either army, and with them all is flourishing." The young Stevens marveled at the "splendid" wheat, which in one place covered "between 500 and 600 acres of land." "Such crops I never saw before," he marveled.[25]

The march itself was not particularly pleasing. The "air was oppressive" and "the traveling heavy from recent rains," recalled one New Yorker. Another soldier's diary noted the "very hot day" and recorded that "the boys were pretty well used up" by the end of the march. As the journey wore on, the men began to empty their knapsacks at each break, tossing aside overcoats, blankets, and other items that were quickly gathered by local inhabitants along the route.[26] To fend off the heat, the men scoured the fields along the road for berries. "I never saw such a country for blackberries," remarked one soldier; "the roads were lined all the way with them and [they] *were everywhere.*"[27] "Early fruits were in their prime, and the troops lived voluptuously," wrote a Connecticut veteran. Men accustomed to New England's "hard hills" plopped themselves on the ground and, without changing position, picked as many as they could eat. The Northeasterners in the expedition "had never before seen such a wealth of" the fruit. Some would fill their cups with berries, crush them with spoons, and soak their hard tack into them. Others would add them into their canteens, which made for "a far more palatable drink than that drawn from some puddle after the passage of a six-mule team."[28]

By midafternoon, following on the heels of the cavalrymen, much of the infantry column reached the King William Courthouse, a T-shaped structure built in 1725 that featured exquisite brickwork laid in Flemish bond, a pattern alternating bricks by their short and long sides. With the soldiers' trek complete for the day, many units halted in a field "to the left of the main road," having covered about 9 miles. Getty's staff set up their tents just outside the courthouse and used the building for their headquarters.[29] Back along the march, some Yankees did more than sample blackberries. According to one New Yorker, some soldiers committed depredations during the march, despite the "stringent orders for protection of property." The 118th New York, acting as the rear guard, made several arrests, but despite such efforts many local pigs, sheep, and poultry soon appeared in camp kettles, providing a "savory mess of provisions."[30]

A young member of Getty's staff, James Howard, recalled that while "here we had a great time—the people were rank Secesh and even impertinent." Ignoring General Dix's admonitions, Howard and his comrades spent much of their brief stay in the village plundering the locality. While searching for berries, they found a basket of fine, gilt-edge China hidden

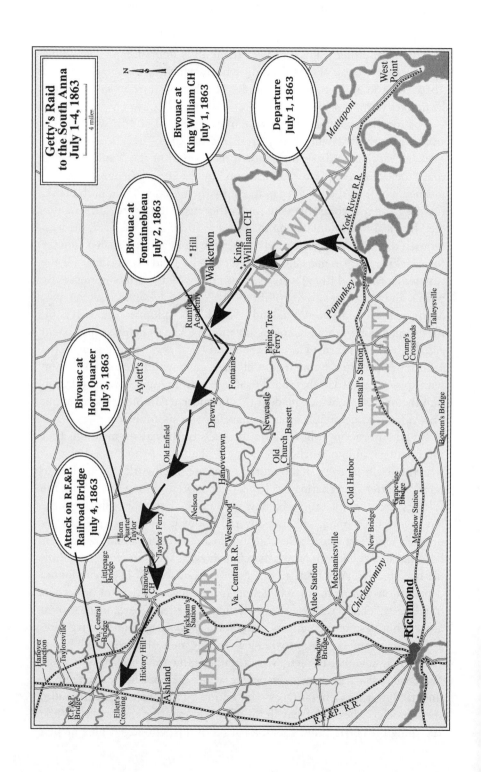

Getty's Raid
to the South Anna
July 1-4, 1863

4 miles

N

Bivouac at
King William CH
July 1, 1863

Departure
July 1, 1863

Bivouac at
Fontainebleau
July 2, 1863

Bivouac at
Horn Quarter
July 3, 1863

Attack on R.F.&P.
Railroad Bridge
July 4, 1863

West
Point

Mattaponi

KING WILLIAM

York River R.R.

Hill

Walkerton

King
William CH

Rumford
Academy

Pamunkey

NEW KENT

Talleysville

Crump's
Crossroads

Piping Tree
Ferry

Fontaine

Tunstall's Station

Aylett's

Drewry

Newcastle

Old
Church Bassett

Bottom's
Bridge

Old Enfield

Hanovertown

Cold Harbor

Grapevine
Bridge

Nelson

"Westwood"

Meadow Station

"Horn
Quarter"
Taylor

Taylor's Ferry

Va. Central R.R.

Mechanicsville

New Bridge

Littlepage
Bridge

Hanover
CH

Wickham's
Station

Atlee Station

Chickahominy

HANOVER

Hickory Hill

Meadow
Bridge

Richmond

Hanover
Junction

Taylorsville

Va. Central
Bridge

Ashland

R.F.&P.
Bridge

Ellett's
Crossing

R.F.&P. R.R.

in the bushes behind one of the nearby houses. Howard took a cup and saucer to send off to his family. He and his crew also uncovered two whiskey barrels tucked inside an icehouse, which "of course" they spilled on the ground to keep out of the hands of the rank-and-file. Later, they took two barrels of flour from a local store, one for the men and one for their officers, along with two heavy bolts of cloth. They dropped a third barrel into a nearby well along with eight bales of cotton. Howard would eventually sell some of the fabric and have the rest made into a tablecloth and sheets. Finally, to cap off his stay in the village, he entered the courthouse itself and pilfered an ink stand, a pile of "new pennies," and a pair of epaulets belonging to a "Lieutenant R. H. Hill." Howard also managed to scoop up four geese, two chickens, one duck, and a "good little" pup.[31]

While Howard and his associates perpetrated their spree, Edward Harland's Connecticut brigade camped in a clover patch west of the courthouse, turning loose horses from the column into "fields of juicy oats." According to one of the Connecticut soldiers, most of the owners of local properties seemed to be absent, "gone to an indefinite meeting at some indefinite place for some indefinite purpose."[32] A Rhode Island veteran later recalled camping nearby in a large field "filled with stacks of straw" that his comrades used as bedding. When the owner of the straw complained, officers ordered the men to return the bundles and stack them in a large pile at the center of the field. The men complied, but that night some returned to set fire to the straw. "It was all burnt up, much to the satisfaction of the whole force, and the great chagrin of the owner," noted the Rhode Islander.[33]

"SCARCELY HALTING"

Thursday, July 2, brought another warm day and more marching for Getty's men. "We were routed out," according to a Rhode Islander, and "had scarcely time to cook our coffee when 'Fall in' was heard, and again we took the dusty road."[34] To the west, Colonel Spear's cavalry continued their push up the Pamunkey and seized Taylor's Ferry as well as nearby Littlepage's Bridge, destroying bridges and ferries downriver. Companies A and E remained at Nelson's Bridge most of the day and, after burning that 70-yard span to the "water's edge" that afternoon, joined the rest of Spear's men at the Taylor plantation and its main house, Horn Quarter.[35]

Most of Getty's infantry began their march on Thursday at 6 a.m. As the men filed past the courthouse, members of Foster's brigade noticed

two women there on the steps openly "taking the number and description of the forces" and asking the men questions.³⁶ Getty's force marched
another 8 miles through the sticky air, some engaging in unpleasant verbal exchanges with local civilians.³⁷ "The blood-red sun, as it rose in
the heavens, shed its fiercest rays upon us," wrote George Allen of the
4th Rhode Island. "Man and beast suffered alike, but still the long line
stretched on through heat and dust, scarcely halting five minutes at a time
for rest."³⁸ The country, largely untouched by the war, overflowed with
goods; despite strict orders against straggling, many men stole away from
their units to see what they could find. Eventually, the head of the column
halted at Brandywine, the Drewry plantation, where some of Spear's cavalrymen had stayed the night before. The 112th New York, bringing up
the rear of the column, stopped for the evening farther back at Rumford
Academy in a grove of trees not far from the Mattaponi River.³⁹

In Richmond on July 2, Confederate officials tried to determine what
Dix and his forces were up to. Secretary of War James Seddon focused
on the safety of the railroad bridges and planned to send Edward Hall an
additional 500 men to augment his regiment, the 46th North Carolina,
that was already there. Seddon, guessing a real move was afoot against
the railroad, had also sent 600 convalescents from Richmond.⁴⁰ D. H.
Hill, who was busy snuffing out Keyes's advance, also understood the
danger north of Richmond and ordered Colonel John Baker's cavalry
to the North Anna at Morris Bridge. He recommended that Hall stay at
Hanover Junction and suggested J. C. Coit's and Samuel Wright's batteries reinforce the defenses there. Hill also considered whether Custis Lee
should send some of his troops to Hanover Junction or whether Montgomery Corse's brigade should backtrack from Gordonsville. In Hill's estimation, the resulting concentration of force could thoroughly "beat the
Yankees." Seddon wired Hall to "remain for the defense of the Junction
and the railroads, abandoning until further orders the idea of returning
here."⁴¹

"MANTELS, MIRRORS AND PICTURE-FRAMES, SMASHED TO FRAGMENTS"

Back in King William County on July 2, there was friction between Confederate citizens and Getty's men, leading to trouble. One regimental historian recalled that local civilians hurled insults at the US troops along
the march, triggering retaliation despite the strict orders prohibiting such

actions, a directive that had been emphasized over and over again.[42] Whether due to interactions with locals or for other reasons, parties of stragglers, "whose only excuse for loitering behind was mischief," plundered and then burned a few houses along the route.[43] Perhaps the expedition's most severe and well-known act occurred on Thursday about 7 miles west of King William Court House at "Fontainebleau," a property owned by William Spotswood Fontaine and his wife, Sarah Shelton Aylett, a granddaughter of Patrick Henry.

During the afternoon, Union soldiers reached the main house at Fontainebleau and found only enslaved people, some thirty or so there ranging in age from one to sixty-five.[44] When the soldiers arrived, Aylett and her daughters had hidden in one of the rooms and then managed to flee later without being seen. The soldiers ransacked the place. The destruction was extensive. According to a Connecticut veteran: "Every chair and table was broken, marble tables and mantels, mirrors and picture-frames, smashed to fragments." The Northerners also cut into an old family portrait "from top to bottom." The men broke open bureaus and scattered their contents, smashed jars of preserves against the house's "clean white walls," and destroyed "a splendid library," chopping books in two and stamping them to pieces. A veteran recalled that "nothing escaped the ax, or the butt of the musket: every room was strewn thickly with fragments and tatters, bedaubed and unsightly."[45]

The soldiers did not limit the destruction to the main house. They burned barns and outbuildings, destroyed crops, and slaughtered or took away all the cattle, horses, sheep, pigs, and chickens they could find. The mayhem reached a climax when the soldiers piled a large stack of debris in the middle of the house and doused it with kerosene. But before they could ignite the heap, an officer arrived who, with pistol drawn, forced the vandals to stand down. Years later, Fontaine's son, William, who served in the Confederate army during the war, penned an extensive account of the incident, which emphasized efforts of Fontainebleau's slaves to protect the property. In his story, the younger Fontaine also dwelled on his family's anger with General Getty, who should have known what was happening there, at least in their view. A letter of apology from the general, delivered a few days later, apparently did little to quell the family's outrage.[46]

Getty was, in fact, infuriated by the vandalism. He ordered guards posted at Fontainebleau and immediately began an investigation, arrested several men, and then held a drumhead court-martial under a large tree near the mansion. However, the evidence at hand apparently proved insufficient to support a guilty verdict for any of the accused.[47] The identity of the vandals remains unclear, though a Connecticut veteran later pointed to members of the 103rd and 117th New York Infantry Regiments. Another described the perpetrators simply as "bummers" acting out of revenge for something done or said, and still one more labeled the wrongdoers as "professional stragglers." Some members of the Connecticut brigade had picked up articles dropped "here and there" after the incident and "nearly came to grief from having some of these discarded trinkets in their possession." That evening, exhausted from marching and perhaps some mayhem, Getty's soldiers "fell like logs, went at once to sleep, in mud, on grass, anywhere, and it was next to impossible to wake them" in the morning. The column made only about 8 miles that day, progress impeded, according to George W. Pearl of the 117th New York, because of the destruction at the Fontaine House.[48]

"EXHAUSTED, FAINTING AND DYING OF FATIGUE"

On Friday morning, July 3, Getty's lead units departed the fields around the Brandywine plantation and other spots along the route at 7 a.m. and marched north toward Horn Quarter, the plantation of "rich secesher" George Taylor. Men at the column's rear, about 4 miles away near Rumford Academy, were ready to march at 3 a.m. but did not begin moving until three hours later due to what one veteran labeled "bad management." William Hyde, regimental historian for the 112th New York, later explained that "much of the suffering of the day [would have] been obviated" had the column moved earlier.[49]

It certainly turned out to be a difficult day. Accounts of the tortuous march would fill letters, diaries, and regimental histories.[50] Friday was indeed torrid, with temperatures climbing into the nineties, even hotter than the previous two days. The route the men followed offered little shade and exposed them to the "full influence of a broiling sun," and even in those few stretches that passed through trees, "the air was almost suffocating." "The heat and dust were intolerable, and the troops suffered exceedingly," wrote Getty. At noon, the column paused for an hour and then resumed and kept marching until 3 p.m. After another hour of rest, the miserable journey continued, stretching well past midnight for some units, "with only brief halts."[51]

During the occasional breaks, the men found more blackberry bushes, bursting with ripe fruit in the open ground near the road. Whole brigades spread over these sprawling patches and consumed all the berries they could find, filling "their tin cups" with the surplus and leaving enough left over for "another army to feast upon," according to William Hyde. He later concluded that the blackberries along the roads in King William County served as "a Sanitary Commission of itself," for many found the berries curtailed the chronic diarrhea that had afflicted them, a curious conclusion given the fruit's reputation for having the opposite effect.[52] Sergeant Major Robert H. Kellogg from the 16th Connecticut wrote that "the country through which we passed was a perfect garden, covered with corn and wheat fields—fruit trees of all kinds were loaded with fruit. We got all the cherries[] and blackberries that we could possibly eat."[53] Some of the men recalled the berries on the low bushes in the open fields were more tender and sweeter than those along the road.[54]

But the blackberries could only do so much to mitigate the effects of the summer weather. Many men made it through the morning, but by midday the march had become grueling. Sixty-five men from the 16th Connecticut fell out of line, fifteen with severe heat exhaustion. According to one account, four members of Harland's Connecticut brigade, which did not stop marching until 9 p.m., died right away, while scores of men fell out along the route suffering from sunstroke and exhaustion. Other units were hit hard as well. In his report, Getty singled out the greenhorns of the 165th and 166th Pennsylvania Militia from Robert Foster's brigade as particularly affected.[55]

Others suffered too. Colonel Michael Donohoe's brigade, the New Hampshire and Rhode Island regiments nearer the front of Getty's column, rose on Friday before dawn after only a few hours of sleep, as one veteran recalled, and waited in line without "any chance to make coffee, and there we stood in line for three hours with all our traps buckled on, waiting the order to 'Forward.'" They finally pushed on at 6 a.m. During the day, Donohoe's men suffered like all the others in Getty's command. "The heat was more severe, [and] not a breath of air was stirring," wrote George Allen of the 4th Rhode Island; "the dust kicked up by our feet hung in stifling clouds around us, and the line moved quicker than yesterday."[56]

Heatstroke (called "sunstroke" in the 1860s) had been recognized by physicians for centuries and was a common malady during active campaigning in the Civil War. The condition arises when the human body overheats due to exposure, physical exertion, or a combination of the two. Severe cases, which occur when a person's core temperature reaches 104 degrees or higher, can lead to fainting, confusion, nausea, headache, rapid breathing, elevated heart rate, and even death. Stories from the war suggest most soldiers, particularly veterans, understood the threat of sunstroke and the need for shade, rest, and water to mitigate the condition. However, men unaccustomed to active campaigning were less likely to take the necessary steps, such as rest and water consumption, to lower their body temperatures. A popular treatment involved "continuous dashing" of cold water on the patient until he revived. Medical personnel also urged stricken soldiers to drink water, loosen their clothing, and receive fresh air through fanning, the same steps recommended by modern medical practitioners. Some manuals of the day recommended the old practice of bloodletting, though it appears such procedures had fallen out of favor by the mid-nineteenth century.[57]

The July 3 march produced ideal conditions for the malady. Over the course of the day, temperatures increased into the nineties along an exposed route. Few of the units in the force had made many long marches during the past several months, and certainly not in such weather. Further, they were not dressed for comfort. Their woolen uniforms and packs would make even a short stroll on a warm day unpleasant. The weight of an unwieldy campaign kit—a knapsack, haversack, gun, canteen, bayonet, and cartridge box—made matters worse. The result was not surprising. Much later, James A. Mowris, a surgeon with the 117th New York and the regiment's historian after the war, described the ordeal. "As a source of suffering, a battle hardly exceeds a forced march during the warm season." The men "marched a distance which good pedestrians would not have fancied, even if untrammeled." Mowris, who made the journey on horseback, was dismayed to witness his miserable comrades in the ranks. He found it "very disagreeable duty . . . to be compelled to ride in rear of men thus suffering, with no consoling agent but well-meant words of encouragement."[58]

The soldiers looked to reduce the impacts of the wilting temperatures. A sensible member of the 16th Connecticut recalled that he withstood the heat by frequently soaking his cap with water throughout the march.[59] Sabin Stocking, a fifty-six-year-old surgeon in the 8th Connecticut, sought to help his comrades by gathering "all the horses, mules, carriages, and carts" he could find along the road to transport the loads of sick and fainting men. The effort produced a "motley collection of carts and gigs, of colts, toothless nags, and broken-down mules, uniform only in leanness and worthlessness." In attending to members of his regiment, Stocking himself became severely overheated. In camp that night, a comrade found him on "the ground completely exhausted and unable to help himself."

He could not walk or ride for the rest of the operation and would suffer from chronic blurred vision the rest of his life, a sacrifice that would earn special recognition from Congress in 1887.[60]

There was only so much that men like Sabin Stocking could do. Hundreds of infantrymen dropped down by the roadside delirious with heat. "O! the emptiness of words, when men are falling out and lying by the way-side, exhausted, fainting and dying of fatigue," wrote Mowris.[61] During the brutal march, men lost track of time, and some even fell asleep as they walked in the evening, colliding "against his file leader" when the column was called to halt. They also struggled to keep up, knowing that the rebel guerrillas swarmed in the darkness behind the column.[62] Some became prisoners. With darkness falling and the end of the tramp not yet in sight, New Yorkers in Wardrop's brigade began to sing "John Brown's Body," "which really helped the marching," recalled a member the 118th regiment.[63]

The attrition in Getty's force was severe. Scores fell out of the column, although the precise number of men afflicted by the heat is not known. According to data compiled by the Surgeon General's Office after the war, twenty men in Dix's department died of sunstroke in July. Most of these fatalities likely occurred during Getty's march. Soldier recollections suggest the numbers of men dead and injured from heatstroke were much higher, though the accounts varied considerably. George Allen of the 4th Rhode Island counted fifty victims, either dead or extremely ill, along the ground as he marched the route. He heard a rumor that six men from the 10th New Hampshire alone had died. In some cases, whole companies abandoned the march and ducked into the woods to wait for cooler evening air before finishing the day's journey. A Connecticut soldier estimated that about a dozen men fell dead, though it is unclear whether this applied only to his regiment or to Getty's entire command.[64] A member of the 117th New York wrote that his division lost 160 men (dead or missing) and twenty from his regiment alone. James Mowris, also from the 117th New York, estimated that only about 10 percent of the regiment was present when the column arrived at Horn Quarter that evening. Another New Yorker wrote he "had never known our regiment to be so utterly 'fagged'; but sleep came soon and sound, except to the unfortunate fellows detailed for picket."[65]

Eventually, the long July 3 march ended at Horn Quarter just east of the Pamunkey. By the end of the day, when the weary infantrymen made camp in the fields at the Taylor plantation, Getty's column had traveled a total of 28 miles in three days, hardly what anyone would consider a "forced march." Another 10 miles across the Pamunkey remained between Getty and his target: the RF&P rail bridge over the South Anna. Some units began arriving at Horn Quarter around sunset, while others did not reach there until midnight after suffering through hours of aggravating starts and stops. When the 118th New York completed their march, only about half of the brigade was present in line to stack their arms. According to William Hyde, one company in the 112th New York had only four privates left standing, and the largest company along the line counted only twenty. The missing men were strung out along the sweltering route, some struggling to continue the march and others curled up on the side of the road, having fallen out "by scores from sheer exhaustion." Many men who had left much of their clothing and equipment on the route during the day spread their blankets and "slept in the open air." Hyde's unit, which trudged onto the Taylor fields at midnight, received instructions from the regiment's commander, Colonel Jeremiah Drake, to stack arms—"boys, there's your wheat straw, grab it and camp down and go to sleep." Spear's cavalrymen fed their horses with the shocks of wheat and then, like the infantrymen, gathered more to make comfortable sleeping mats. The cavalrymen also helped themselves to the contents of a fully packed icehouse.[66]

George Taylor's plantation and its main house, Horn Quarter, proved to be somewhat of a curiosity for the Federal soldiers. An elegant, three-story mansion, the home exuded extravagance even by the standards of Virginia's slaveholding class. After their difficult march through a landscape dotted with other plantation dwellings, ubiquitous slave huts, and small yeoman farmer homes, the Yankees marveled at Horn Quarter with its fountains, formal gardens, and "indoor plumbing including water closets, baths, and basins." The house's "door yard" alone comprised 350 acres bordered by neat rows of cedars. The entire property consisted of about 3,000 acres, and Taylor had additional holdings elsewhere amounting to another 5,000. That summer, people enslaved at Horn Quarter had planted much of the farm with wheat, which had been reaped and lay stacked in neat piles.[67]

Despite Friday's devastating heat and punishing march, a sense of optimism emanated from the ranks as the men stacked arms and rested in the fields for the night. Some expected to attack Richmond the next day. "What was to hinder us?" Rhode Islander George Allen thought after hearing that "nothing but a small force of provost guards" shielded the city in a "state of alarm and confusion." Although Allen did not believe Richmond's capture was possible, he hoped his comrades would breach the city's defenses, if only for an hour, to free the prisoners at Libby, Castle Thunder, and Belle Isle and escort them back down the Peninsula. The effort would be, in his view, "well worthy our attempt." Around the campfires Friday night, men focused on these possibilities while "forgetting our tired limbs and blistered feet." As the regimental bands played, Allen and his companions fell asleep "to dream out our plans for the capture of Richmond."[68] Back at White House, John Dix dreamed as well. "The last 36 hours have been full of excitement," he wrote his wife. "We have been in contact with the enemy, & as I have sent off a considerable portion of my force on an expedition, he is attacking us."[69]

"NOT A MAN TO ASK FOR HELP WHEN NOT NEEDED"

In Richmond on Friday, July 3, no word had arrived from Robert E. Lee's army in Pennsylvania, but persistent rumors from King William County pointed to a Federal advance east of the city. That afternoon, the train arriving on the Richmond and York River line, which still operated unimpeded as far as Meadow Station, brought news of the previous day's fighting at Crump's Crossroads, making it clear the Federals still had their eyes on Richmond. With the threat increasing, the local defense troops under Custis Lee's command assembled early in the morning and marched out to their positions in the fortifications to the north as provost guards nipped at their heels and scooped up stragglers.[70]

Judging the Federals' anemic effort at Crump's the previous day, D. H. Hill correctly concluded the bulk of Dix's force was elsewhere. With any direct pressure on Richmond receding, he knew the South Anna would likely become the point of danger. Only two regiments protected the rail bridges there: Thomas Singeltary's 44th North Carolina from J. Johnston Pettigrew's brigade, which had lost Companies A and G to Spear's raid on the Virginia Central bridge, and Edward Hall's 46th North Carolina from Cooke's command. When Hall asked for more men, Hill offered to send additional regiments, telling Seddon that Hall "is not a man to ask for help when not needed." But Hill, knowing his men east of Richmond were exhausted from chasing Keyes the previous day, preferred sending the city troops north instead of another veteran regiment from Cooke's brigade.[71]

News of Getty's column reached the thirty-nine-year-old Colonel Hall on Friday, July 3, when reports arrived of a "large cavalry force" advancing into Hanover County. So far, Richmond's efforts to provide assistance had underwhelmed the colonel. He did the best he could with the troops he had been given. At the South Anna, he stationed the 46th North Carolina on the Fredericksburg Railroad (i.e., the RF&P). This crossing was the obvious target. With the Virginia Central span destroyed, the loss of the RF&P bridge would effectively sever direct connection to the railheads closest to Lee's army, those at Culpeper, Gordonsville, and Staunton. But Hall worried about his ability to protect this vital point with the men Richmond was sending him. For example, 300 former hospital patients under Lieutenant Colonel A. S. Cunningham had arrived with no ammunition, no tents, and no tent flies. Hall knew more men were on the way but hoped they would be better supplied.[72]

East of Richmond on Friday, D. H. Hill returned to his headquarters at the Williams House and looked for word from the South Anna. His assistant adjutant general, Archer Anderson, again requested that the military telegraph superintendent extend the lines from headquarters to allow for better communication. Hospital commanders in Richmond continued to shuttle their walking wounded up to Hanover Junction. During the day, 500 more armed convalescents headed north to assist Hall. Arnold Elzey, still in the command circle, knew the real danger lay there. "I am afraid we shall lose all at Hanover," he warned Hill. Seddon joined in as well, pleading with Hill to send one of Cooke's regiments to Hanover Junction. Hill agreed and resolved to get Cooke's entire brigade north. He also urged Secretary Seddon to order Montgomery Corse's brigade back from Gordonsville to Hanover. "If the Yankees establish themselves [in Hanover], they will be hard to dislodge. I have thought this might be their policy."[73]

Throughout the day on Friday, Hill and Elzey worked together to get Cooke's remaining regiments and R. L. Cooper's battery north to the South Anna. "If you can relieve Cooke on the picket line, I will order him to Hanover Junction," wrote Hill. The Tar Heels were exhausted, having marched nearly constantly over the past few days. According to Hill, these men were "in no condition to move, but I suppose it must be done." Still struggling with communications back to officials downtown, Hill asked directly that the telegraph line be run to his headquarters at Williams. "We may lose Richmond by these delays in the courier lines."[74]

Finally, on Friday afternoon as Getty reached Horn Quarter, Hill ordered a regiment of Cooke's brigade (the 15th North Carolina), General Cooke himself, and Cooper's battery to buttress Hall's 46th North Carolina at the South Anna. However, with rail transportation unavailable

Friday evening, Cooke and these reinforcements could not board a train until the next morning, July 4. As Cooke and his troops prepared to head north, Matt Ransom's brigade remained along the Williamsburg Road, with the 35th North Carolina in front, to watch for Keyes, who was still burrowed in at Talleysville. On Friday afternoon, William Burgwyn and his comrades in the 35th found time to take a swim in the muddy Chickahominy and escape the "very hot" weather smothering the region.[75]

In the midst of this activity, D. H. Hill remained confused about the command structure and the defensive arrangements for the Richmond fortifications. "I do not understand your disposition of forces," he complained to Elzey. "If we abandon the outer line at one point, it is abandoned at all." Though he had been at the capital nearly a week, Hill remained largely ignorant of details regarding the forts and trench lines ringing the city, having had no chance to inspect the fortifications since his arrival. Furthermore, the map he had received was incomplete, showing only portions of the existing works on the outer ring and completely omitting the intermediate line. "Does the outer line envelope the city on the left as well as the right?" he asked Elzey. Assuming that was the case, he urged his colleague to send some of Custis Lee's men to the outer line along the Brook Turnpike 5 miles north of downtown. Still unclear about the scope of his authority, he asked Elzey to issue the order to Custis Lee.[76]

Hill's confusion about the arrangement of the city's defense underscored the command dysfunction at Richmond. He was becoming exasperated with his lack of information and inability to coordinate efforts to repel the Federal operations. "Where is Hall? Where is Corse? Why is not Corse sent down to Hanover?" he asked Elzey.[77] To be sure, Hill was not truly in charge despite Seddon's earlier statement. Instead, his direct authority was limited to the three brigades from his own department. Otherwise, he seemed to be acting in an advisory role. All the while, his colleagues did not fill the void of command. The ailing Elzey mostly equivocated while Seddon tried to step in and manage the capital's defense in piecemeal fashion, certainly an unusual role for the secretary of war. But it was not unheard of for Confederate officials in Richmond, including the president himself, to dive into such minutiae.[78]

As the generals moved units around, Richmond's office workers remained on alert. On Friday evening, many marched northeast to defenses at the Meadow Bridge at the Chickahominy. Some of them found field service less than ideal. Gottfried Lange, a beer hall proprietor in his early fifties, had carried his rifle and a bag of bread with him out into the defenses with his fellow members of the local defense force. Rain and mud highlighted his tenure in the lines. He refused to eat the beans served to him, finding them infested with worms. He was not alone in his displeasure. Clerks in the War Department Guard complained about bad meat, moldy bread, and the fact that, despite previous assurances to the contrary, they found themselves well outside the city's inner defense.[79]

Like Hill, other Confederate leaders began to suspect that the US troops east of Richmond offered no significant threat. Hearing that Keyes had halted in New Kent County and knowing Cooke's regiments were headed to the South Anna, Seddon sought to pause Colquitt's movement from North Carolina, directing him to hold at either Petersburg or Weldon.[80] As usual, Confederate commanders faced multiple threats from all sides. If Colquitt moved north to gird the Richmond defenses, he would leave the Wilmington and Weldon Railroad largely unprotected. This was not lost on the officers in the Old North State. William Whiting, the commander at Wilmington and an inveterate complainer, believed his post was in the most danger. "I am not apprehensive about Richmond," he announced, but "am fearful for the railroad lines of this State."[81]

In Richmond, civilians and soldiers prepared. Late Friday, General John Cooke, along with the 15th North Carolina and R. L. Cooper's battery, stood ready to board train cars for the South Anna. That night, people in the city and the part-time defenders in the works heard the thud of cannon fire to the north in the direction of Hanover Junction and feared more Union troops were on the way. According to an account, an "awful continuous thunder shook the air and earth throughout the night." But the source of this din was in fact a huge summer storm that passed through Gordonsville, dumping buckets of rain and washing out a bridge on the railroad south of Culpeper. Nevertheless, despite the false alarm triggered by the squall, there was reason for continued concern. Getty and his 10,000 men were not far to the north at Horn Quarter preparing to march the remaining miles to the RF&P bridge.[82]

15

To the RF&P Bridge

"NUMBERLESS RUMORS"

ON SATURDAY, JULY 4, the Richmond *Daily Dispatch* published an extra edition filled with an array of stories from the North. There were many of them. Robert E. Lee's men were capturing towns in Pennsylvania. They were cutting railroads and burning bridges. They were headed for Philadelphia, Baltimore, and Washington. Out in the Richmond defenses, soldiers shared similar news. William Burgwyn, with Ransom's brigade at Bottom's Bridge, heard that Lee had maneuvered between Washington and Joseph Hooker's army and that New Orleans had been captured. He did not believe any of it, though. His skepticism was justified, for few of the rumors hit the mark. In fact, Lee's Army of Northern Virginia and Meade's Army of the Potomac had spent the past three days waging a massive battle at Gettysburg; the day before the stories appeared in the *Dispatch*, Federal forces had in fact gained a huge victory. Meade's army had crushed the last, desperate Confederate charge against the US position by a force that included Virginians from George Pickett's reduced division.[1]

As Richmond's newspaper editors waited for credible word from Pennsylvania, they sifted through the reports of Dix's offensive from Hanover and King William Counties. According to the *Daily Richmond Examiner*, a train conductor working the RF&P Railroad reported "numberless rumors, but no authentic information, of the movements and numbers of the Yankees." Other news arrived as well. "Some said [the Federals] were at Wickham's Farm, others that they were at the burnt Bridge, and others again that they were still on the left bank of the Pamunkey." Whatever the case, the city's newspapers remained defiant as Getty's column marched toward the South Anna. "The grand Yankee Army of the Pamunkey still continues a mysterious and ill-defined concern," mocked the *Examiner*'s editor, John Moncure Daniel. "It is, as at first, reported to be tremendously strong, but as far as it has been tested, it has been found weak, indeed, and much prone to flight." He estimated—quite accurately—that a force of about 6,000 remained near White House, and then he asserted—incorrectly—that the balance of Dix's force was conducting "a Negro stealing expedition in the county of King William."[2]

The Confederate officers orchestrating Richmond's defense knew the threat posed by the Federals marching through the countryside and continued their efforts to manage the crisis. As Hill and Elzey juggled the troops at the capital, the question of reinforcements from North Carolina remained unresolved. On July 4, Alfred Colquitt and his brigade had made it to Weldon, where the Georgians stopped and waited for further instructions.[3] D. H. Hill understood the danger posed to the Old North State and the consequences of losing the railroad there. But, by July 4, he also knew the Confederate high command faced a stark choice. "Richmond and Petersburg are richer prizes than Kinston and Goldsborough," he noted to Secretary of War Seddon. Furthermore, Hill expressed skepticism about the rumors coming up from the south about a Federal offensive there. "The Yankees are so fond of clap-trap, that I expect a general advance everywhere to-day—at Vicksburg, Tullahoma, Pennsylvania, [and] Richmond."[4]

Although the threat to Richmond remained, the safety of the rails and bridges to the north stood out as the immediate priority. After much back and forth on July 3, Hill, Elzey, and Seddon had finally sent General John Cooke, the 15th North Carolina, 500 convalescents, and R. L. Cooper's battery to the South Anna. Hill did not rest easy, however. He worried the regiment and the artillery would not reach the bridges in time. "I fear that, without a movable battery, [Hall] will be beaten and his artillery captured."[5] Cooke's detachment eventually arrived at the South Anna sometime early on Saturday, July 4, to augment the companies of Edward Hall's 46th North Carolina, scattered around the bridges and key positions in Hanover and Caroline Counties. With his limited troops, Hall had sought to protect several important points during the previous days, including the depots at Ashland and Hanover Junction, miles of track extending northwest to Gordonsville, and various culverts and small bridges along the routes. However, both Hall and the newly arrived Cooke knew that the most important position of all was the 600-foot span bearing the RF&P line over the South Anna River. The new reinforcements unloaded there and, now with Cooke in overall command, manned the batteries and rifle pits guarding the bridge.

In the midst of the shuffling, confusion persisted among officials in Richmond. D. H. Hill continued to complain about the ill-defined chain of command. On Saturday, he told Seddon that he never received confirmation of his authority to lead all forces at the city, an oversight that had forced him to contact Elzey before moving Cooke's men to Hanover. In so many words, Hill complained that the city's defense was being managed by committee. Characteristically confident in his own assessment, he asserted: "Had all this matter been in my own hands, Cooke's brigade would have gone up yesterday, and the Yankees would have been driven back to-day."[6] Later the same day, he sent another note to Seddon repeating his concern: "I am afraid this mixed command will result in evil." But in a rare moment of restraint, he apologized for the "freedom" of his remarks and assured Seddon he was not motivated by "desire to command" but rather simply by the wish to "secure an efficient organization and have one controlling mind," for he feared the existing arrangement might be "fatal."[7]

On July 4, unknown to Hill and Seddon, the crisis was coming to a head at the South Anna as Getty's troops prepared for the final leg of their march. In Richmond, the secretary of war digested Hill's remarks that day and continued to cast about for troops. Elzey had none to spare and, with most of the men already protecting either Richmond or the railroads, pointed back at Hill. A surely frustrated Seddon went ahead and ordered Colquitt's Georgians north from Weldon to Richmond "with all dispatch." But they would be too late to confront the impending threat. As Getty's column spilled into Hanover County, John Cooke and Edward Hall would have to make do with what they had at the South Anna.[8]

"THE ROAD IS BLUE WITH THEM"

The results at Gettysburg, still unknown to the combatants around Richmond, did not decrease the relevance and potential impact of George Getty's mission to the South Anna. Even if Lee withdrew his army to the relative safety of northern Virginia, he would need a secure line to cover a withdrawal over the Potomac and to supply his men as he confronted the pursuing Federals. A broken rail line from Richmond to the railheads at Culpeper and Staunton would hamper quartermaster and subsistence officials in their efforts to maintain the Army of Northern Virginia as it maneuvered south into the Shenandoah Valley around Winchester. Thus, a successful attempt to destroy the RF&P Railroad bridge over the South Anna would still offer potential benefits to the Union war effort.

On Independence Day, George Getty planned to get his column moving from Taylor's despite the damaging results of the previous day's scorching trek. All indications suggested the coming day would be just as hot. Getty informed Robert Foster that his brigade would depart at 4 a.m., only four hours after the fatigued men of the rear guard (the 112th New York) had stumbled onto the fields surrounding Horn Quarter. But Foster did not budge. All of his regimental commanders objected to the order, and Foster in turn informed Getty the 4 a.m. departure would be impossible for many of his units because hundreds of men still lay scattered along the previous day's route. Getty relented, and Foster's brigade did not leave the Taylor property until 10 a.m. To gather men who had fallen out of the column the previous day, a platoon of cavalrymen under Second Lieutenant Fletcher Blake from the 11th Pennsylvania tracked back on the march route and found nearly 800 exhausted infantrymen within 5 miles of Taylor's Farm.[9]

At Horn Quarter on July 4, Getty made an important decision. Instead of taking his full force toward the South Anna Bridge, he detached a good portion of it to guard his connections back to White House. He left Harland's entire brigade at Taylor's along with two batteries, a cavalry company, as well as the "sick, exhausted, and foot-sore."[10] In addition to the heat's impact, Getty may have considered Dix's admonition to cover the escape route and "strongly" guard the bridges into Hanover County. Whether or not in response to Dix, Getty's decision to leave men at Taylor's and at other locations throughout the day would severely decrease the strength of his striking column.[11]

Some of the soldiers left behind at Horn Quarter spent Saturday, as one Connecticut veteran later put it, assisting "Mr. Taylor in a proper celebration of Independence Day."[12] It had not been a happy few days for the plantation owner. His son, John Penn Taylor, a private in the 9th Virginia Cavalry, had traveled home the day before. He was absent without leave, at least according to documents in his service record. When the Union cavalrymen reached the farm, Connecticut veterans later recalled that several of Taylor's slaves revealed John's hiding place on the property as well as the location of "secreted treasures of meat, wine, grain, and stores." But on July 4, the elder Taylor became the focus of attention. Some of the Federals spoke with the old Virginian; one soldier described him as "keen, cruel, [and] sensual." He was a "wily, fluent, and vehement talker" and the son of a US senator. Taylor was firmly embedded in the web of the Virginia's slaveholding elite. His daughter, Lucy Penn Taylor, had married Robert E. Lee's brother in 1847.[13]

On Saturday, George Taylor did not hesitate to engage the Northern soldiers in political discussions while some of his 300 enslaved servants peered out of his mansion windows. Taylor lectured the Federal soldiers on the benefits of the institution and his "kindness" to those he had held in bondage. One of his unimpressed listeners recalled that Taylor emphasized his "paternal relation" to these people, which, as one of the soldiers wryly noted later, "in many cases[] was believed to be the exact truth." But many of these "trusted" servants had already escaped his grasp and headed for freedom. Every person on the property who "could hobble" gathered all they could carry to join the Federals, recalled one Connecticut veteran.[14]

Many of the soldiers in Getty's force were not fooled by Taylor's disquisition. All along the march, they had encountered Black civilians from nearby plantations, many affirmatively seeking their freedom from men such as Taylor. Though the official reports from officers did not dwell on the slaves encountered during the operation, the rank-and-file, who witnessed slavery's brutal effects firsthand, mentioned it often. A New Yorker told his parents that slaves would run out when his regiment passed a farmhouse and seemed "half . . . scart to death till they found out who we was and where we were going then the[y] would be as much pleased and tell us we could take Richmond sure." An elderly Black man told the soldier that there "couldn't be any folks left where we came from."[15] Robert Kellogg from the 16th Connecticut reported that the "contrabands flocked to us by scores, completely overjoyed to see us." At White House, Kellogg had seen a woman, who had been living in the woods since the Federal offensive the summer before, walk into the Union lines with hands "horribly broken" and twisted by the mistreatment of her former owner.[16]

As the elder Taylor chatted with his visitors, the rest of Getty's units continued to march westward after leaving more than 1,000 men in Edward Harland's brigade at Horn Quarter. The column pushed off west for Hanover Court House with the remaining brigades, under Alford, Foster, Wardrop, and Donohoe. If all went as planned, the day's trek would constitute the last leg of the expedition to strike the South Anna rail bridge. The depleted units headed out in light marching order. David Wardrop's two-regiment brigade of New Yorkers left its wagon train at Taylor's, along with the "tired-outs" and sick. The column marched for 3 miles to Littlepage's Bridge. There, Robert Foster's brigade halted long enough to allow the men to swim in the Pamunkey. Once across the river, the New Yorkers then rested in the woods along the road for several hours around midday. Some men, already overcome with exhaustion, wobbled back to the Taylor plantation. During the break, members of the 118th

New York visited a nearby cornmill, which, after some repairs, yielded a "hasty pudding" of salted meal for the hungry men.[17]

Before leaving Littlepage's Bridge, Getty cast off another brigade for guard duty. Michael T. Donohoe's command, consisting of the 10th and 13th New Hampshire and the 4th Rhode Island, remained by the river to protect the span. Later that afternoon, a large group of enslaved persons appeared at the picket posts manned by the New Hampshire soldiers. Some of these refugees had escaped from North Wales, Williams Carter's plantation, bringing with them their former owner's horses, mules, and carts. According to the historian of the 13th New Hampshire, the euphoric group "procured boards, laid them in the road, and sang and danced for a long time" to celebrate their freedom.[18]

The rest of Getty's column continued west beyond the Pamunkey with Spear's cavalrymen and Colonel Wardrop's foot soldiers in the lead. The troops reached Hanover Court House in the afternoon, the cavalry in front skirmishing with Confederate pickets along the way. A company from the 118th New York from Wardrop's force led the infantry.[19] Some of the rebels slipped away from the town into nearby woods. One of them hoisted himself into a tall tree and watched the proceedings. From his perch, he could see cavalrymen "going from house to house arresting all the men." Soon, the Union infantry and artillery appeared in the streets in a force he gauged to be about 10,000. In the village, Margaret Wight, who had witnessed Spear's raid a week before, recorded in her diary: "Another visit from the Yankees. They have come this time with Infantry as well as Cavalry—the road is blue with them." The Federal advance scooped up two young men from the Confederate Quartermaster's Office who had scrambled into an upstairs closet in Wight's house. By her observation, the Union officers kept their men in check, and the Northerners behaved "very well for enemies."[20]

While at Hanover Court House, Getty further diluted his force, leaving Colonel Samuel M. Alford's brigade to guard the crossroads there. By the time the column prepared to head off again, Getty had left more than half of his strength to guard three locations—Horn Quarter, Littlepage's Bridge, and Hanover Court House—all of which lay within 5 miles of one another. His target, the RF&P bridge, was still 6 miles to the west. His decision to shed two-thirds of his own division and another brigade left him with only Foster's fairly large brigade of mostly Pennsylvanians, Wardrop's two-regiment brigade of New Yorkers, one battery (7th Massachusetts Battery G, led by Captain Phineas A. Davis), and Spear's cavalry. In all, this remaining force consisted of about

5,000 men, about 4,000 of whom were infantrymen. At Hanover, Getty made another curious decision: instead of personally accompanying the attacking force on its last leg, he stayed behind at Hanover Court House and placed Brigadier General Robert Foster in charge of the advancing column. The reasons for this decision are unclear. Perhaps he wanted to manage the operation from a central location; perhaps he was ill from the heat. Whatever the rationale, he did not mention it in his report, and no explanation has appeared elsewhere. In Getty's absence, Foster took command of the remaining troops and sought to fulfill the primary objective of the entire operation.[21]

"BURN THE RAILROAD BRIDGE CROSSING THE SOUTH ANNA"

Brigadier General Robert S. Foster was now in charge of the expedition. A twenty-nine-year-old Indianan nicknamed "Sandy," he had commanded the 13th Indiana early in the war and fought at Rich Mountain as well as some of the engagements in the 1862 Shenandoah Valley Campaign. In the spring of 1863, he led a brigade in John Peck's command during the Suffolk Campaign and earned promotion to brigadier general in June. His orders from Getty on July 4 were "to proceed to a point of intersection of the Richmond and Fredericksburg Railroad and the county road, and, if possible without endangering the safety of the command, to burn the railroad bridge crossing the South Anna."[22] The caution injected by Getty in these instructions is puzzling. His men had struggled for four days through enemy country in the broiling heat to reach the key rail bridge over the South Anna. Now with his troops finally approaching the bridge, Getty's orders to Foster seemed to dampen expectations for the mission.[23]

As temperatures climbed to nearly 90 degrees on Saturday afternoon, Foster's column departed Hanover Court House led by Spear's cavalrymen on the River Road (Hickory Hill Road), the same route the troopers had used a week before. The horse soldiers clattered past Wickham Station and the Wickham plantation. The infantry followed. When New Yorkers in Wardrop's brigade crossed the Virginia Central Railroad, the men "soon began to see evidences of breakers ahead, in the form of horses killed by pickets, and the rapid movements of scouts and skirmishers and cavalry." Just beyond Hickory Hill, the column continued northwest, passing the turnoff to the Virginia Central bridge, and headed

Troop Dispositions: Getty Expedition

White House Landing

~10,000

Donohoe, Alford, Harland,
Wardrop, Foster, Spear (cavalry)

Horn Quarter

~10,000

Donohoe, Alford, Harland,
Wardrop, Foster, Spear (cavalry)

Harland's Brigade

Littlepage's Bridge

~8,500

Donohoe, Alford,
Wardrop, Foster, Spear (cavalry)

Donohoe's Brigade

Hanover Court House

~6,500

Alford, Wardrop,
Foster, Spear (cavalry)

Alford's Brigade

Ellett's Crossing

~5,000

Wardrop, Foster, Spear (cavalry)

All units except
4 companies

R.F.&P. Bridge at South Anna

~400

4 companies (118th and 99th New York)

west for the RF&P with Spear's horsemen, Phineas Davis's 7th Massachusetts battery, and the 99th New York from Wardrop's small brigade well to the front. Foster, with his own brigade temporarily commanded by Colonel Jeremiah Drake, lagged behind, apparently stopping to rest in a sunken segment of the road. As the balance of the force continued on, rumors began to circulate that the Confederates had reinforced the bridge ahead, manned strong earthworks, and planted batteries covering the approaches.[24]

During the advance, the Federal cavalrymen encountered a rebel picket post every few miles. In each instance, the men spurred their horses forward and drove the Confederates away. Less than a mile beyond the Virginia Central bridge, the Federals glimpsed the Winston plantation off to the right where J. E. B. Stuart's men had bivouacked during their remarkable 1862 ride around McClellan's army. Two miles more brought them to the RF&P line sometime after 6 p.m. at a spot called "Ellett's Crossing." The South Anna rail bridge stood about a mile along the rails to the north. Spear later described the structure as "of wooden trestle-work, about 100 yards long, and in the center about 70 feet high." The entire span stretched nearly 200 yards between abutments. Several hundred yards upriver and not far from Ellett's Crossing, Spear also found a wooden road bridge, referred to locally as "Ellett's" or simply the "county bridge."[25]

North of the bridges, Brigadier General John Cooke received word of the Federals' approach. The thirty-three-year-old, whose sister had married J. E. B. Stuart, had risen up the chain of command in 1862 but had suffered some bad luck in battle, receiving wounds at Antietam and Fredericksburg. At about 4 p.m., Cooke's pickets sighted the Union column "on our front across the river" moving "slowly and cautiously." The scouts estimated the force at 12,000 men, which was more than double its actual size. Colonel D. J. Godwin's riders brought in another report of US troops approaching from Hanover Court House, and some of John A. Baker's Tar Heel cavalry also tracked the column.[26]

To protect the crossing, the Confederates had constructed breastworks and rifle pits on both sides of the river and the rail line, though the exact size and extent of the works in July 1863 are uncertain. Confederate slave labor rolls show that enslaved workers had been sent to work at or near the "South Anna" bridges in 1862 and 1863.[27] Over the course of the war, the fortifications in the area would become quite extensive. Confederate engineer maps prepared later in the conflict show a large complex of batteries and trenches forming a massive rectangle that stretched all the way north to Taylorsville. However, in the summer of 1863, the works had not reached that size, though Edward Hall characterized the position as "strong" at the time. Weighing the various accounts, it appears that by July 4 the Confederates had prepared a few redans on the bluffs along the north bank and, to the south, a shallow trench or collection of rifle pits stretching across a cornfield straddling the rail line.[28]

The first elements of the Federal column reached Ellett's Crossing in late afternoon, probably around 6 p.m. Samuel Spear with his cavalry and Phineas Davis with his guns were first on the scene and concluded all the approaches to the railroad bridge posed severe challenges. The structure itself crossed the South Anna at the apex of a large bend in the river. If the Federals chose to approach the bridge directly along the rail line from the south, they would advance about a mile into the mouth of a large inverted "U," putting them into a pocket framed by the river, and most likely rebel batteries, on both flanks and in front. Alternatively, the force could attempt a flanking movement to the west via Ellett's Bridge.[29]

With General Foster still well back to the rear, Spear chose the second option and advanced to test the road bridge. Finding little resistance, he reached within 100 yards of the span while Captain Davis, leading the crews from the 7th Massachusetts Battery, followed and sought to find a "commanding position" for his guns. The Confederates did not take long to realize the Federals had arrived, and soon they opened fire with small arms and a 12-pounder howitzer from the opposite bank. Spear halted, dismounted his men, and deployed them for a more careful advance; rebel batteries upriver near the rail bridge began to fire as well.[30]

On the heels of Spear's cavalrymen, Colonel David Wardrop's infantry brigade arrived around 7 p.m. "Doing so," wrote a member of the 118th New York, "we were made aware of the presence of the enemy by volleys of musketry and the music of bullets."[31] With Foster still behind, Wardrop looked north and, in contrast to Spear, decided to send some of his men along the rail line toward the cornfield and the bridge. But instead of using most of his two regiments, Wardrop assigned only two companies from the 118th New York for the job. He directed Lieutenant Colonel Oliver Keese to command the detachment and "proceed cautiously down the railroad track, and, if possible, to reach the bridge and prevent the Confederates from crossing "at all hazards." Wardrop later wrote that the "object was to feel the enemy, and discover, if possible, whether he was in strong force."[32]

General Foster finally arrived sometime after 7 p.m. and passed Wardrop's position at Ellett's Crossing, no doubt learning that the two

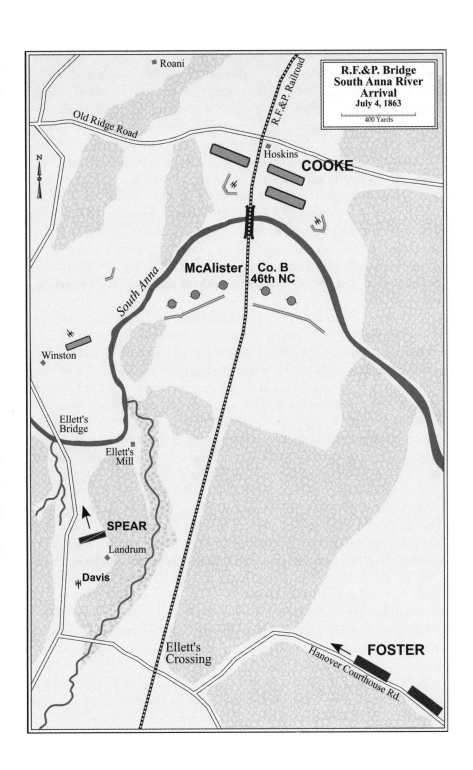

Roani

Old Ridge Road

R.F.&P. Railroad

N

**R.F.&P. Bridge
South Anna River
Arrival**
July 4, 1863

400 Yards

Hoskins

COOKE

South Anna

McAlister

**Co. B
46th NC**

Winston

Ellett's
Bridge

Ellett's
Mill

SPEAR

Landrum

Davis

Ellett's
Crossing

FOSTER

Hanover Courthouse Rd.

New York companies were headed north toward the rail bridge. He then rode farther west to Spear's position at Ellett's Bridge and found the cavalrymen ready to advance. Captain Davis was there as well, pushing his guns into position in a field near the road. Foster did not like what he saw and cancelled the effort against the western flank of the Confederate position, directing Spear and Davis to pull back to Ellett's Crossing. There, Davis searched in vain for a suitable gunnery position; Spear simply remained in reserve as ordered. Later, Spear stiffly noted that "General Foster then being in command, and I having reported to him, I acted under his orders." Spear's after-action report hinted at a clear dissatisfaction with Foster's decision. "Had not General Foster come up as he did, I should have opened fire in ten minutes." Foster's decision left Colonel Spear, one of the better officers in the entire department, out of the fight. The next several hours would reveal whether Spear's irritation was justified.[33]

Nothing in Foster's official report sheds light on his decision to reject Spear's plan. Perhaps he believed the western approach was overly circuitous or contained too many easily defended obstacles. Whatever his specific concern, he filled his report with general statements about the difficulty of the ground in the area, the reported size of the Confederate force, and the nature of the artillery arrayed against him. These observations suggest Foster may have concluded shortly after his arrival that any concerted attack would fail. Instead of giving Spear's turning movement a chance, he chose to wait and see how Wardrop's two companies would fair in their probe toward the railroad bridge.

Consistent with the orders and actions of his superiors, Foster's decision broadcast caution. His circumspection may have stemmed from local reports as well. A knowledgeable civilian, whose house overlooked the rail line, reported that the Confederates had spent the previous three days strengthening the "earthworks commanding the bridge" and bringing in reinforcements on trains, "two to four a day," "loaded with soldiers" from Richmond. According to the man, one of the trains transported eight artillery pieces. Whether influenced by this information or not, Foster focused on defense. "I . . . placed my command in a position to resist any onward movement or to make an aggressive movement, as I might under the contingency conclude to do," he explained. As the last of his regiments arrived and gathered at the broad, low hill south of the road, Foster ordered pickets to spread out and feel for the enemy in the darkness. He seemed preoccupied with what the enemy would do to his command, instead of how his men could destroy the bridge. Echoing Erasmus

Keyes's reports from New Kent County just days earlier, Foster explained that the "position I occupied was a very precarious one, as I was liable to an attack on all sides." Accordingly, he withheld most of his command to protect his position at Ellett's Crossing while committing only a small fraction of his force—a few hundred men from Wardrop's brigade—to the rail bridge's destruction.[34]

Back at Ellett's Crossing, most of Foster's units remained idle in the dark. Captain Davis, after thoroughly reconnoitering the area, finally found a workable position for his artillery "on a small compass of ground" between the woods and the railroad. It did not matter. His crews could not locate the enemy gun positions in the gloom, and, to avoid giving away his position or strength, Davis simply ordered his guns to stop firing. The infantrymen huddling in reserve had less success in minimizing their exposure. Foster's large brigade, strung out along the road, was "in a bad position," according to William Hyde of the 112th New York. Fortunately, the Confederate gunners could not pinpoint the location of the regiments. If they had, Hyde speculated, "our loss must have been heavy."[35]

The Confederates clearly held the advantage, their guns perched along at least three positions on the north bank. From these elevated spots, the rebel artillery swept the lower fields and woods to the south, where Foster deployed.[36] Although the exact number, type, and location of the gun positions are not entirely clear, the various accounts and reports suggest that the rebels likely had one upriver to Foster's left, another near the rail bridge, and a third on a bluff about 350 yards downstream to his right. The gunners sited the pieces to rake the woods to the south of the river and to command the county wagon road and Ellett's Bridge crossing. Judging from the sounds of the guns and the ammunition used, Colonel Spear later guessed that at least three types of field pieces furnished the Confederate barrage: a 12-pounder howitzer, an 18-pounder howitzer, and a 10-pounder Parrott gun.[37] Captain Davis counted two pieces opposite the county bridge, plus another five in "two positions farther down the river toward the right of the command."[38] The men from R. L. Cooper's battery also rolled their guns atop the north bank overlooking the ground to the south. Whatever their makeup, the Confederate batteries soon began a steady fire in the direction of Foster's troops huddled in the fields and woods near Ellett's Crossing. According to Davis, several 10-pounder Parrott shells whistling through the darkness landed close to his gunners but did no damage.[39]

In addition to the artillery, John Cooke's mixed command consisted

of the 15th North Carolina, 46th North Carolina, John A. Baker's 3rd
North Carolina Cavalry, and the ill-equipped convalescents wrung out
of Richmond's military hospitals. The entire force probably amounted
to about 3,000 men.[40] There were troops elsewhere in the area as well.
For instance, infantry companies from Thomas Singeltary's regiment, the
44th North Carolina, were spread out north toward Hanover Junction.
But Cooke and Hall knew the RF&P bridge over the South Anna was the
most likely target and had wisely concentrated their strength there. They
also understood that the terrain gave them the advantage. "Our position
is a very strong one, covering a bold bluff immediately in rear of the R.R.
bridge," one Tar Heel explained in a North Carolina paper, with artillery
"so posted as to subject the assailants to a crossfire, and effectively command all approaches."[41] After the battle, Cooke did not specify his troop
dispositions north of the river. He did, however, indicate that Baker's
cavalrymen shielded the western side of the Confederate line. However,
the exact positions of infantry from the 46th and 15th North Carolina are
not clear. South of the bridge on Foster's side of the river, Cooke deployed
a detachment of Tar Heels led by Captain Nathan Fleming's Company
B of the 46th North Carolina. These Confederates took a position in the
open cornfield straddling the railroad, about 300 yards south of the river,
and waited for the attack they knew would come soon.[42]

16

The Attack on the RF&P Bridge

"THE THRILL OF WHAT WAS BEFORE US"

THE FINAL APPROACH TO THE SOUTH ANNA BRIDGE had begun. When Wardrop's brigade first arrived at Ellett's Crossing, the regiment's acting adjutant general, Charles E. Pruyn, summoned the company commanders, Captain Josiah Norris (Company A) and Lieutenant John Cunningham (Company F), and joked that he was about to do them "a favor." He then broke the news of the mission. The adjutant's drollery did not amuse Lieutenant Cunningham, who "did not readily and enthusiastically appreciate" the gesture. Nevertheless, Cunningham soon formed up his tired men along the tracks. Despite the exhausting day, he recalled, "the thrill of what was before us made us forget our weariness." With that, Companies A and F of the 118th New York began their advance north through the darkness toward the rail bridge with only Nathan Fleming's Tar Heels standing in their way.[1]

The decision to send only two companies against the expedition's primary target underscored the anemic effort Getty's operation had become. Dix had given clear instructions to march north into Hanover County and destroy the RF&P bridge over the South Anna. Getty's force had taken four days to cover the 35 or so miles to the objective. Along the way, Getty had shed about half his strength at various locations, leaving units at Horn Quarter, Littlepage's Bridge, and then Hanover Court House. By Saturday evening, July 4, only Spear's cavalry, Davis's gunners, and the exhausted infantrymen in Robert Foster's brigade and Wardrop's small, two-regiment provisional brigade composed the attacking column. Further, Getty himself chose not to accompany this column for the final approach, sending young General Foster in his place. And then, Foster opted to remain near the rear of his force, leaving Colonels Spear and Wardrop to make initial dispositions at the South Anna, arrangements the cautious Foster then overruled upon his arrival. Finally, Foster chose to keep the bulk of his force idle and not send additional troops to support the two companies Wardrop had sent up the railroad.

The two New York companies advancing to the bridge had no combat experience to speak of. Organized at Plattsburg the previous summer, the 118th Regiment had served in the Middle Department manning the Washington defenses and then with the Seventh Corps during the Suffolk Campaign, where it saw no significant action and suffered no casualties.[2] Now, two of its companies, perhaps eighty men each, pushed out into the darkness to destroy a key link in Robert E. Lee's supply line.[3] As the small detachment proceeded along the rails, Wardrop focused on protecting the rest of his command around Ellett's Crossing by throwing "out pickets at every point" where danger could appear and forming the balance of his two regiments on a low rise south and west of the road.[4]

The New Yorkers proceeded into the night as their officers tried their best to guide by the tracks while avoiding a stream, Falling Creek, on their left. Norris's men in Company A advanced on the right while Cunningham's Company F lined up farther west on Norris's left. In a letter home shortly afterward, a New Yorker wrote: "Tramp, tramp, tramp, through the dark belt of wood and no sound is heard save the returning echoes of their measured tread." The men remained alert, expecting "to receive the murderous fire of the enemy's concealed artillery, or that superior numbers may spring from ambush upon them with resistless fury." Through the brush, the troops felt their way forward. After advancing for a short while, Captain Norris spread out his line and directed Cunningham to deploy the first platoon from Company F off to the left.[5]

The ground was not easy, especially in the dark. For 800 yards, the companies picked their way through a "swamp wood, tangled with brush" as well as a deep marsh on the left at one stretch, where Falling Creek veered within 100 yards of the tracks. The obstacle compressed the battle line and forced Cunningham to advance his men by the flank to narrow his front and avoid the morass. In the trees beyond the marsh, Cunningham redeployed his men into line and resumed the difficult advance. As the men moved forward, a few rebel pickets in the woods ahead fired off some rounds. The Yankees returned the favor.[6] Soon, the Confederate batteries across the river opened a steady fire, causing many of Cunningham's men to drop to the ground "as if they had all been killed." But, in the failing light, most of the projectiles missed, screaming over the New Yorkers' heads into the woods behind. However, not all of it flew high. In the barrage's initial stages, one round of solid shot hit Private Martin Sherman of Company A, inflicting a fatal wound.[7]

At the center, Captain Norris ordered his men to fix bayonets and sent skirmishers forward. After creeping north another 400 yards, the formation crossed a ditch and entered the open, mostly level cornfield. The men were now well inside the South Anna's large bend. On both flanks beyond the expansive cornfield, thick bushes and trees bordered the open space. From their elevated positions across the river to the north and west, the Confederate guns increased their fire, causing the Federal skirmishers to abruptly halt about 500 yards south of the bridge, with Company A still on the right and F on the left.[8]

During the course of the Federal advance, North Carolina pickets from Captain Fleming's company had given way steadily, letting loose a few scattered shots now and then. When the Yankees entered the cornfield, however, the rebel defense stiffened. In the distance, a makeshift rebel line waited for them. The position seemed to consist of stacked railroad ties, scattered rifle pits, and what looked to the Northerners in the darkness to be a small structure, perhaps a shed or barn. In a loud voice heard by his comrades on the bluffs across the river, rebel Captain Fleming directed his company to "commence firing." The resulting volley was a weak one. "Many of the enemy's guns did not go off, and the snap of percussion-caps was distinctly heard," noted Lieutenant Cunningham. Although much of the fire passed harmlessly over the New Yorkers, Corporal Cass C. Lapoint of Company A received a wound during this exchange. The Federals lay down and returned fire into the night, finding a little cover in the "the very few slight accidents of the field." Cunningham cautioned his men to "save their ammunition, and fire only when the flash of guns revealed the position of the enemy's skirmishers."[9]

The Confederate fire became more "severe and better directed." The artillery, which had been wildly off target earlier, began to land some rounds uncomfortably close to the New Yorkers. From across the river to the west, a few guns still sent many shells passing overhead into the trees behind them.[10] In addition, on the field's western edge, some Tar Heels who were tucked into a line of bushes began to push back the Federal skirmishers and threatened to wrap around the attackers' flank. In response, Lieutenant Cunningham, who could hear the words of the Confederates out in the darkness, spread out his line farther to the left.[11]

At the same time, Captain Norris heard shots on the right, which suggested the rebels had the same plan there. He paused to consider his next moves. In his report, he concluded the "fire now became very hot in front and also on my right and left, and I found that I could not make any farther advance without sacrificing my men, without accomplishing anything, without more assistance." Given the increasing resistance, Norris and Cunningham conducted a short consultation and concluded any

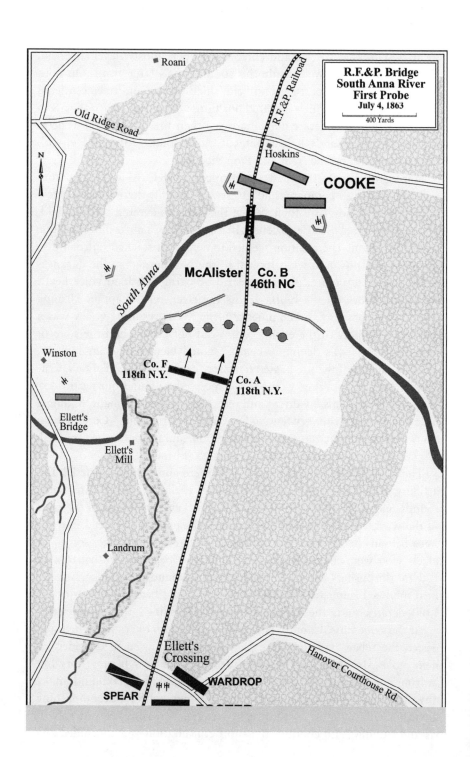

R.F.&P. Bridge
South Anna River
First Probe
July 4, 1863

400 Yards

Roani

Old Ridge Road

R.F.&P. Railroad

N

Hoskins

COOKE

South Anna

McAlister   Co. B
46th NC

Winston

Co. F
118th N.Y.

Co. A
118th N.Y.

Ellett's
Bridge

Ellett's
Mill

Landrum

Ellett's
Crossing

Hanover Courthouse Rd.

SPEAR

WARDROP

further effort was unwise. Norris ordered the men to pull back, leaving a small group to cover the withdrawal. The two companies fell back and deployed behind the ditch in the woods at the field's southern edge, a strong position that, according to Cunningham, "could have been held against great odds." But even a brilliant stand at the field's edge by the Yankees would not destroy the rail bridge.[12]

"READY TO GIVE THEM ANOTHER TRIAL"

When word of the difficulties in front reached the rear, Robert Foster considered sending more men to aid Companies A and F. He had plenty of troops with him, the better part of seven regiments clustered on the high ground near the rail line and "carriage road." But instead of gathering a large force to punch through to the bridge, he sent only two companies to aid Cunningham and Norris. The reinforcements, led by Major George F. Nichols, consisted of Company D of the 118th commanded by Captain Edward Riggs and Company E of the 99th New York. Leaving behind everything but their "arms and accoutrements," this small detachment advanced along the railroad at about 11 p.m. using the same route Companies A and F had followed earlier.[13] Major Nichols rode ahead and found Norris and Cunningham out in the darkness on the front line. After Nichols complimented the pair on their progress, the three resolved to attempt another advance. The new directive was quietly delivered to the men. Before stepping off, Nichols cautioned the troops to hold their fire unless they had the enemy in their sights. Soon, the reinforcements from Riggs's Company D reached their comrades and received orders to file left down the rail embankment and join Cunningham's left flank at the cornfield's western edge. Riggs placed half of his men in line at intervals of two or three paces and stationed the others in reserve. Company E from the 99th New York also arrived and formed to the right of Company A. Before pressing forward, the officers agreed that the "discharge of four guns in rapid succession from the reserve" would serve as the signal to withdraw and form back at the track.[14]

The moon rose around 11 p.m., bathing the field in a dim, eerie light. Officers on Company A's front passed along an order from Major Nichols to press "forward" slowly. "Each man was instantly on his feet, ready to give them another trial," according to Captain Norris. The entire force, four companies in all, resumed the advance. Once again, the New Yorkers climbed out of the ditch and into the open, crept forward

300 yards, and passed over a slight rise; once again, a "terrific volley" ripped through the night air, passing overhead. The rebel artillery also resumed its shelling. Norris counted at least four Confederate guns, "two of them near together and almost directly in front of my line, another near the railroad bridge (to our right), and the other beyond our left."[15]

The firing soon became general along the lines. "Shells and shot fly thick and fast," noted one Federal soon afterward. Several New Yorkers in Company A received wounds.[16] Despite the exchange, the attackers pressed forward, and Captain Norris brought up men from his reserve to extend into the woods on the left. The "line then advanced slowly," he wrote, "each alternate man then halting to load, as laid down in the instructions for skirmishers, with great regularity and precision, after the first or second time firing."[17] According to a Confederate account, the "Yankees fought with great obstinacy" and clawed their way within 50 yards of the defensive line on several attempts but were driven back each time. The combatants were so close that, at one point, Union soldiers reportedly called out and dared the rebels to emerge into the open field and fight.[18]

In the face of the continued pressure, most of the Confederates soon fell back to their rifle pits on the edge of the field. However, one group continued to man a spot near the center, a strongpoint of sorts that was apparently "entrenched or protected in some manner" and allowed the rebels there to keep up an "annoying" fire.[19] Apparently, the North Carolinians in this position had not received the order to withdraw. Adhering to earlier directives to "fall back under no consideration," they stuck to their post.[20] The Federals hoped to overrun the holdouts. In mulling over the options, Lieutenant Cunningham considered sending his entire line forward in a headlong charge. But twenty-two-year-old Second Lieutenant William H. Stevenson offered an alternative. He proposed to gather a few men, creep around the obstinate "bunch," and assault the position from behind.[21]

When Stevenson asked for volunteers, many within hearing distance raised their hand. From the eager pool, Stevenson chose Privates William D. Huff, Lewis Morse, Warren Monty, and Henry Wescott and Corporal John Cobb. The five loaded their rifles, fixed bayonets, and proceeded to make their way around the enemy position, which they soon realized was surrounded with timber, clumps of standing cedars, and bushes. Then, "with the yells of demons," they followed Stevenson and descended upon a group of more than a dozen Confederates. "Surrender or we'll murder every one of you!" demanded Stevenson. "Drop your guns!" Many complied at once, but a few ran north toward the river. The rest, with one exception, threw down their guns and surrendered. The single remaining holdout stubbornly refused to yield his weapon and was soon wounded by Stevenson.[22]

After the victorious Stevenson returned to the Federal line, he announced that he had "captured the whole d—d rebel army!" and then sent the prisoners on their way rearward escorted by a small guard.[23] Colonel Oliver Keese, commander of the 118th New York, later praised Stevenson's "courage and thoughtfulness" during the action.[24] As the captured Tar Heels headed to the rear, a Union shirker stepped out of his hiding place in the trees and clubbed one of the rebel prisoners across the captive's blanket roll, to little effect. An irritated Stevenson pushed the malcontent away, barking out: "These are my prisoners and you can't abuse them. If you want some for your own use, go out there and get them." The whole affair made a minor celebrity of the affable Stevenson. Years later, the unit's regimental history claimed one of the prisoners told Stevenson the next day: "Well, Lieutenant, you seemed a mighty sight bigger last night than you do now." The New Yorker supposedly replied: "I felt pretty big, myself, then." At some point after Stevenson's mission, a spent ball tumbling through the air hit Lieutenant Cunningham in the hip, causing a severe "contusion of the sciatic nerve vicinity." The blow knocked him down and out of the fight and would cause paralysis on his left side for years. Stevenson took Cunningham's place in command.[25]

Following Stevenson's small victory, Major Nichols and the other officers determined to press forward toward the rifle pits at the field's north edge. A forceful, successful push would put the Union men at the bridge trestle, which lay only about 300 yards behind the Confederate line. Captain Norris ordered his men in Company A to attach their bayonets and prepare to charge. The Federals resumed the advance. But the rebel resistance increased once again as the defenders poured in an intense fire from their works. Captain Riggs later speculated that more defenders had arrived because the firing became "more vigorous and frequent" and threatened the entire line. He was correct. Cooke had in fact ordered Major Alexander McAlister of the 46th North Carolina to take two additional companies across the river and reinforce Fleming's line.[26] The substantial increase in fire discouraged the Federal attackers. "It was distinctly apparent that we did not have force enough to even reach the railroad bridge," recalled Cunningham.[27]

The Confederate artillery barrage also became more intense. The batteries on the north of the river delivered "grape, or shrapnel," which,

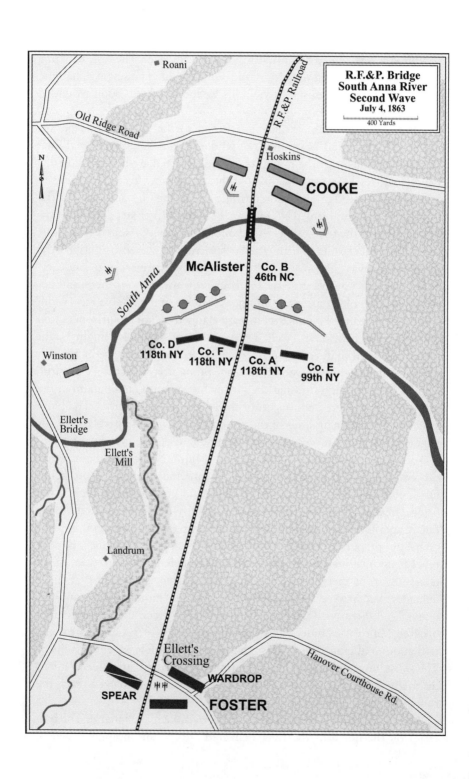

R.F.&P. Bridge
South Anna River
Second Wave
July 4, 1863

400 Yards

Roani

Old Ridge Road

R.F.&P. Railroad

N

Hoskins

COOKE

South Anna

McAlister

Co. B
46th NC

Co. D
118th NY

Co. F
118th NY

Co. A
118th NY

Co. E
99th NY

Winston

Ellett's
Bridge

Ellett's
Mill

Landrum

Ellett's
Crossing

Hanover Courthouse Rd.

WARDROP

SPEAR

FOSTER

according to Riggs, "seemed literally to fall in showers among us at every discharge." The pieces firing from the flanks also increased their cross-fire, becoming more accurate by the minute. Batteries that had sent shells harmlessly overhead earlier in the engagement now delivered rounds that exploded directly above and among the Northerners. Federal cartridge boxes lightened as ammunition ran low and overheated rifles forced some men to stop firing. Caught in the withering hail of lead, some of the New Yorkers expressed eagerness to charge ahead and engage the enemy at close quarters. But their officers deemed such an assault impractical in the dark against the reinforced enemy line. Furthermore, Major Nichols had given no orders sanctioning such a movement.[28]

Any such deliberations ended when orders to withdraw arrived from General Foster from his field headquarters back at Ellett's Crossing. The warnings from captured men may have triggered concerns about the safety of the position. Indeed, some of Stevenson's prisoners had apparently claimed that Cooke planned to surround the Federal "force and capture it." Foster may have also received word about the lack of progress at the rail bridge. Despite having several thousand unengaged troops with him, he chose to call off the limited operation. In his mind, it was time to go.[29] Soon, to the north along the rails, four consecutive rifle reports cracked the night air, signaling the Federal withdrawal. The New Yorkers at the front pulled back, formed up with the reserves, and headed south along the line, occasionally turning to fire until they entered the woods. Led by Major Nichols, the four companies returned to Ellett's Crossing and rejoined Wardrop's brigade.[30]

Throughout the evening, the soldiers at the crossing had waited and wondered what was happening as they watched the Confederate shells streak across the sky for hours. "The rebels shelled us the fore part of the night as we lay on the ground holding our horses," recalled George Cruikshank from the 11th Pennsylvania Cavalry. "It made a fine display of fireworks for the night of the Fourth of July." But Cruikshank did not watch the whole show. Not assigned to picket duty, he "made a bed of sheaf oats in a fence corner and slept soundly."[31]

When the four companies returned from their fight, Foster, Spear, and Wardrop gathered to discuss the situation and concluded nothing more could be done. Perhaps fearing his command's destruction by a rebel counterattack, Foster decided to "leave the place before daylight, with the satisfactory knowledge that it would be dangerous to remain longer, unless I received orders to the contrary." During the evening, George Getty, still at Hanover Court House, learned that Foster had found a large enemy force "with artillery mounted, commanding all the surrounding country and enfilading the roads." Foster reported his lack of progress, and Getty, upon confirming the information from local civilians and Confederate prisoners, sent a dispatch agreeing that the column should return to Hanover Court House by daylight.[32] Shortly after 3 a.m., Foster's men turned east and marched away, ending the attempt at the South Anna Bridge. The attack was over.[33]

The decision displeased many of the men in the ranks, who had marched hard to reach their objective. One New Yorker told his family back home that "dissatisfaction and chagrin is manifest, and all we can do is to keep marching and wondering why." As Foster departed Ellett's Crossing, he ordered two companies from the 169th New York (E and B) to destroy some of the track on the railroad in the direction of Richmond. They managed to tear up about 3 miles of the line, damage two culverts, and destroy some lumber stacked near the track.[34]

"MOTHER, GET UP, THE YANKEES ARE COME"

Hours before Robert Foster abandoned his efforts at the RF&P bridge, Getty sent Major Franklin Stratton with Companies G and M of the 11th Pennsylvania Cavalry southwest to the town of Ashland to destroy the railroad depot and buildings, storehouses, tracks, and any Confederate property there.[35] Around 8 p.m., civilians in the town had heard the rapid cannon fire in the direction of the South Anna Bridge. But danger soon arrived at their own doorsteps. In the eight-room cottage she shared with several families, a slumbering Judith McGuire woke when her daughter shook her and said, "Mother, get up, the Yankees are come." McGuire and her children quickly dressed and peered out the window. Looking across the moonlit street, she saw the cavalrymen break down the door of the telegraph office and throw the battery and other equipment into the street. McGuire detected little commotion, except for the occasional order "Be quick" or "Keep a sharp look-out."[36]

Major Stratton's riders had reached Ashland at 1:30 a.m., proceeding "at a walk, quietly and cautiously," and soon had taken positions on all the roads leading into the town. Once there, Stratton divided his men into four "working parties." Two groups tore up track; another headed a mile south to destroy the 50-foot trestle bridge over Stony Run; and the fourth remained in town to tend to the railroad buildings and equipment.[37] During their time at Ashland, according to one story in a North Carolina

newspaper, the Federal horsemen burned "all the public buildings, depot and all the property belonging to the railroad company," along with
"several hundred bushels of salt belonging to the county, for distribution
among the poor."[38] Four miles away at the South Anna River, Cooke and
his men could see the glow of flames from the town to the south.[39]

In his report, Stratton described the destruction in minute detail. In
addition to the ties burned, rails bent, and telegraph wires cut, his men
put the torch to station buildings, a warehouse filled with hay and tools,
a water tank, various rail switches, platforms, three freight cars, several
carloads of bridge timber, and a large woodshed. The troopers also ex-
tracted equipment from the telegraph office, including "a surgeon's compass." As the station and warehouse burned, flames came dangerously
close to a nearby private dwelling. Short on time and no doubt wary of
Dix and Getty's orders regarding private property, Stratton "impressed a
party of citizens, and ordered them to protect" houses in town. According to some locals, the Federal horsemen remained in a "terrible state of
alarm" throughout their stay, hurriedly mounting their horses and scam-
pering off several times in response to false reports that the Confederates
had arrived. After nearly three hours, the horse soldiers finally departed
for good and rode back to Hanover Court House, arriving around 6 a.m.
on Sunday, July 5. In Getty's judgment, Stratton performed in a "very
thorough and creditable manner."[40]

Judith McGuire witnessed the departure as the troopers rode off into
the night with "demoniac yells." Following the raid, the townspeople
emerged from their homes; according to McGuire, an "amusing group"
spilled into the streets. "Everyone had dressed in the dark, and all manner of costumes were to be seen—dressing-gowns, cravatless old gentle-
men, young ladies in curl-papers, collars pinned awry, etc." Some women
had donned their best clothes with lace collars, earrings, dress pins, and
watches to ensure their most-valued items would be on their person
should their houses burn.[41]

"THE SIGNS ARE YET VISIBLE IN THE CORNFIELD"

On Sunday, John Cooke sent Baker's North Carolina cavalry to find
where the enemy had gone. After confirming that his communications to
Gordonsville were still intact, Cooke surmised that the blue column was
headed back east the way it came. South of the bridge, evidence of the
night's combat remained. The station master at Ashland walked up the

tracks to Ellett's Crossing in the morning and found cut trees and loose traces, indicating a large group of horses had been tied there. Proceeding north along the tracks where the New Yorkers had advanced only hours before, the railroad man found bloodstains here and there.[42] One Tar Heel soldier also visited the site of the fighting. "The signs are yet visible in the cornfield where they dragged several dead bodies to the woods for burial," he reported to the *Greensboro Patriot*. His comrades also found unburied corpses under the trees, "belonging mostly to Company F, 118th New York." He also learned that several members of the 13th Indiana were among the casualties, a plausible claim, as that unit represented the lone Western regiment in Foster's brigade. The writer attributed the victory to a combination of the volume of artillery fire and the "severest shock" delivered by Fleming's infantrymen early in the contest.[43]

As was often the case, the estimates of casualties generated by the fight were spotty and inconsistent. Cooke identified seven prisoners from three different infantry regiments, plus one from Colonel Spear's command. Federal accounts estimated about twenty US casualties, including two killed. However, a story in the *Daily Richmond Examiner* claimed that eight dead Federals were found clumped together in the woods a mile south of the bridge. Another report, this one from a North Carolina paper, asserted that Baker's riders scooped up twelve prisoners and then found the same number of bodies in the woods.[44] Locals claimed the Federals pulled away three wagons loaded with wounded and two dead soldiers strapped to horses during their retreat.[45]

Official accounts of Federal combat losses were fairly low in absolute numbers but probably reflected about 10 percent of the men engaged. Wardrop reported losing two killed, ten wounded, and four missing in combat from his "provisional" brigade (the 99th and 118th New York). His force had captured twelve prisoners, though two managed to escape in the field.[46] In their reports, company commanders mentioned only a few casualties.[47] However, the *New York Daily Herald* published a detailed list of names and unit affiliations that included two killed (Martin Sherman and H. M. Mills, both from Company A of the 118th) and nearly twenty wounded or missing, spread evenly among Companies A and F of the 118th and Company E of the 99th.[48] The officers marveled at this low casualty count. Reflecting on the length of the fight (about two hours) and the fire's severity, Riggs observed that "it seems truly wonderful that no man of my company should have been killed or severely wounded." Cunningham also noted the "severe" fire, but, because most of it sailed high, few injuries resulted.[49]

The Confederate casualty count was low, a fact Cooke attributed to the rifle pits protecting his men. Cooke described his own losses as "very small" (one killed and six wounded). However, he made no mention of the men captured from Fleming's command in the cornfield.[50] Other sources provided further details. The *Greensboro Patriot* noted several wounded from Captain Fleming's unit (Company B), a few seriously: Abram Sloop, H. C. Owens, who had lost a finger at Fredericksburg six months before, and Thomas Terry. North of the river, a stray round hit Private P. B. Upchurch in the head and killed him instantly while his unit, the 15th North Carolina (Company D), supported a battery on the north bank. Finally, an unnamed member of the convalescent detail received a thigh wound while he crouched in the works with the other infirm members of Cooke's force.[51]

In letters home and official dispatches, the defenders reflected on the fight. Cooke was pleased with the fact his command had repulsed the enemy "repeatedly in handsome style." One of his men recalled the Federals made "three feeble charges during the night and retired completely foiled at daybreak" and that "groans from the wounded [could be] heard distinctly 250 yards off." Cooke also looked to future threats. He asked Richmond to send the rest of his brigade and replace the convalescents currently under his command. He also requested more ammunition for the guns attached to Baker's cavalry (a Blakely and a Napoleon) along with more rounds for his Parrott cannon and his infantrymen's Enfield rifles. Finally, he commended Edward Hall on the defensive arrangements at the South Anna and noted plans to expand on Hall's work in the coming weeks.[52]

Foster's men had little time for reflection. Exhausted from the previous night's operations at the South Anna, they struggled on the return march; Spear's cavalry covered the column's rear, to keep Baker's Confederate horsemen at a "respectful distance." Foster reached Hanover Court House early Sunday morning and, after joining Getty and the troops there, headed east toward King William County.[53]

During the withdrawal, more enslaved people managed to join the Federals. "Contrabands of every size & hue follow & accompany our teams on the way to freedom," recorded an assistant quartermaster in the 16th Connecticut. On the return early Sunday morning, the column again passed the Wickham plantation at Hickory Hill; some of the Yankees visited the property. "They went into the cellar and took a few bottles of brandy and wine," wrote William Wickham in his diary. But Wickham worried about more than his potent potables. "They carried off a great number of negroes and horses from the neighborhood," he lamented. "My loss is about 30 Negroes. . . . Had they [the Federals] remained longer near us, the probability is that a much larger number . . . would have left us." In addition, according to Margaret Wight in Hanover, the Federals carried away with them all the enslaved people from her neighbor's farm.[54]

Getty marched his column over Littlepage's Bridge while the 117th New York remained on the west bank until all the troops were across. Once Spear's rear guard passed over, the "match was applied and the bridge was soon in flames." But then, according to a veteran later, a tragic scene played out as a group of Black refugees came racing toward the burning span while Confederates in pursuit fired into the throng. The refugees took to the woods. One woman managed to cross the river downstream and rejoin the column, but the fate of the others was unclear.[55]

From Hanover Court House, Getty's column returned across the Pamunkey to George Taylor's plantation, arriving there early Sunday afternoon worn and exhausted, having accomplished next to nothing at the South Anna.[56] That day at Horn Quarter, three Union regiments fanned out into the countryside to "take all the beef, mules, horses, sheep, and salt. . . they could find." Whether the commanders viewed this activity as consistent with Dix's directives is not known. In any case, Getty's men stuffed their haversacks with the new supplies and prepared for the march to White House.[57]

The US soldiers also had some final, unpleasant interactions with George Taylor. According to the regimental historian of the 112th New York, an enslaved woman approached Colonel Jeremiah Drake, the unit's commander, complaining that Taylor refused to allow her to depart the plantation with her three-year-old child. Two men sent into the house by Drake found Taylor brandishing a revolver and threatening to shoot anyone who tried to enter. A group of soldiers from the 13th Indiana reentered the house and, deploying "persuasive arguments which they carried on their shoulders," forced the old slaveowner to deliver the child, making it clear that Taylor was in no position to make decisions about the youngster's fate.[58]

Getty's men departed Taylor's plantation on Sunday evening and marched until early the next morning, hurried along by rumors of a possible Confederate pursuit. Black refugees from the surrounding area joined the column in "large numbers"; Spear's cavalry again guarded the rear. As the soldiers and refugees marched through King William County on Monday, the heat of the previous week gave way to welcome clouds and frequent rain showers.[59] But the trek was not free of troubles. Rebel guerrillas nipped at the heels of the formation throughout much of the march, threatening to capture anyone who could not keep up. "The knowledge of this pursuit was quite a spur to quicken our march and prevent straggling," recalled a member of the 118th New York. One soldier who lagged behind and complained he could not "walk another step" could later be seen sprinting forward to rejoin his comrades after he caught a glimpse of rebel horsemen approaching in the distance behind him. When his commander said "I thought you couldn't walk another step," he replied: "Say, you don't call this walking, do you?"[60]

During the return, Getty's command took a different course, swinging through Mangohick to Aylett's on the Mattaponi River and avoiding the winding, irregular roads the column had used on the deadly, heat-plagued march a few days before. Much of the return route ran along the Ridge Road, which Getty found "dryer, more level, somewhat shorter, and altogether a much better road." Nevertheless, according to a Connecticut veteran, many of the men, exhausted from the past several days, "actually slept while marching," and when their unit halted early in the morning, "fell as if struck by lightning and were all sound asleep in two second's time."[61]

At noon on Monday, portions of Getty's command passed through Aylett's, the site of Lieutenant Colonel Tevis's raid several weeks earlier, and by evening encamped at King William Court House, covering in one day a distance that had consumed two full days on the way out. The pause created some anxious moments for James Howard and his fellow burglars, who had spent much of their time there several days before pilfering items from the locals. At the village Monday evening, Howard noted "considerable talk and inquiry . . . about [stolen] flour and things." But the civilians unknowingly brought their complaints to the very men responsible for the thefts. "The staff being in the secret and having been present at the examination," crowed Howard, "of course could find nothing." The next day, Tuesday, July 7, most of Getty's units marched away from King William Court House and reached White House, covering on the entire retreat in two days what had taken four days on their approach. "No annoyance was experienced from the enemy on the return," Getty reported.[62]

When Getty's force finally arrived at White House on July 7, it brought with it evidence of one of the expedition's few real accomplishments: the emancipation of hundreds of formerly enslaved people. The exact number of freed people who joined the column did not appear in official reports.

Neither Dix nor Getty mentioned them. However, an account from a Connecticut veteran recalled that the column arrived "in good spirits" with "five hundred thoughtless, careless, jolly contrabands swarming upon the flanks and rear."[63] Another Connecticut soldier indicated "a large number" accompanied the troops, seeking access to "Union territory."[64] Gurdon Robins, quartermaster of the 16th Connecticut, recorded his impression of the newly freed people in his diary: "The train was accompanied & followed by contrabands of all ages sizes & hues & on & upon almost all styles of conveyance." Women arrived in camp with "a full detail of progeny of relative heights from the nursling to the 12 yr. old," bringing their children to freedom. Robins also noticed that some of the women had adorned their heads with white handkerchiefs and extravagant bonnets, giving, in his words, "intimation of raids upon the wardrobe of their mistresses." His diary entry for that day also recorded the name that soldiers had already attached to the expedition. The operation "may fittingly be called the Blackberry raid," he wrote, "as this fruit was growing in great abundance in the fields by the road side."[65]

"WAS NOT ATTAINED"

Getty's expedition to the South Anna constituted one of the war's larger infantry raids up to that point. By almost any metric, it was a failure. The 10,000-man force had not touched the RF&P bridge at the South Anna and had inflicted only minimal damage elsewhere. Upon his return to White House, George Getty sought to put a positive spin on the results. Acknowledging that the bridge's destruction "was not attained," he asserted the "movement was practically successful, in that the railroad was broken at two points, and the track torn up and destroyed to such an extent that two weeks, at least, will be required for its repair." He commended all of his brigade and regimental commanders for their efforts to ensure the expedition's success. He singled out Edward Harland, David Wardrop, and Samuel Spear and highlighted Major Stratton's "exploit" at Ashland, labeling the late-night action in that town the "most brilliant" of the expedition. But it is unlikely these words fooled anyone. As many had come to understand, a few miles of torn-up track would have little effect on even the most inefficient railroad operation. In truth, the Confederates would repair the damage at Ashland and Ellett's Crossing in a few days.[66]

The officers who were on the front line during the engagement later expressed satisfaction with the performance of their troops. John Cunningham noted that his men, "although somewhat excited under the first fire, obeyed all orders with ordinary promptness and regularity." Each man fired off about twenty-five rounds in a manner that, according to Cunningham, was "more deliberate than hasty."[67] Edward Riggs wrote in his battle report that the men, after their first few shots, "were as cool and deliberate in loading and firing" as if conducting a skirmish drill. "I trust I shall be pardoned," he concluded "if I say I am proud of them and of their conduct in this their first trial."[68]

The fighting, experienced by a small fraction of Getty's entire force, represented only one of the threats involved with the expedition. In the end, heatstroke did the most damage to the soldiers and would stick in many minds as the most memorable aspect of the expedition. Although official medical records published after the war show that at least twenty men died from the heat during the operation, soldier accounts suggest the number may have been much higher. In addition, the heat incapacitated many hundreds marching under the hot July sun on their way to the South Anna, even though they may not have been officially identified on any sick lists. On July 3, for instance, the day's heat had rendered whole units ineffective, and no amount of blackberries could bring the units staggering onto the Horn Quarter fields back to combat effectiveness for the next day.

Several other factors beyond the heat had contributed to the ultimate failure of Getty's expedition. For one, the Confederates had ably shifted Cooke's force from Richmond to the South Anna just in time to fill the fortifications there. However, it is difficult to imagine how the Federals could have thrown a more feeble punch at the South Anna Bridge on the night of July 4. The decisions by Getty and Foster are puzzling. To be sure, Dix had advised Getty to protect the bridges in the rear of the column. However, over the course of the march to the South Anna, Getty repeatedly diluted his strength, ultimately cutting his numbers in half by leaving troops behind at Horn Quarter, Littlepage's Bridge, and Hanover Court House. He also chose not to accompany the shrunken strike force on its final leg, leaving that task to his young subordinate Robert Foster. Perhaps Getty, like many of his men, had fallen ill in the heat, though no mention of such a malady made it into his report; neither does any private account appear in his extant papers.[69] In addition, once the small force arrived at the river, Foster had deployed only four companies, probably a few hundred men, against the enemy while holding back several thousand in his immediate command. Granted, there were many uncertainties and challenges when the column reached the RF&P bridge. It was getting dark. The horseshoe formed by the river was potentially a dangerous place to send troops. The men were tired. The enemy's strength and positions were unknown. Victory was by no means certain. But neither Wardrop nor Foster seemed willing to give the attack a decent try.

Throughout the operation, Getty did not seem particularly focused on the mission's objective. He appeared to be more concerned about protecting his escape route than destroying the rail bridge. In his report, he demonstrated little concern about Foster's frail attack at the bridge. "[I]n abstaining from entering into a general engagement at the bridge over the South Anna," Getty wrote, "[Foster] displayed commendable prudence, and his course on that occasion was in accordance with my orders, and meets with my full approval."[70] No mention was made of Foster's decision to pull Spear away from an immediate attack at the road bridge. In general, Getty seemed content to go through the expedition's motions. Aside from the incidental accomplishment of freeing the enslaved persons along the way, his effort had no lasting impact. Indeed, Confederate railroad officials began to repair much of the damage soon after Getty's departure. The telegraph was back in operation on Sunday; crews were busy replacing the broken rails that day and, within a day or two, had put the rail line back into operation.[71]

PART FOUR
In Gettysburg's Wake

FOLLOWING THE FIGHTING AROUND RICHMOND and in Pennsylvania, Alexander Stephens, the Confederate vice president, concluded his enigmatic mission, generating more questions than answers about his endeavor. In addition, John Dix wrapped up his operations outside the Confederate capital. Following General-in-Chief Henry Halleck's orders, Dix would take his men back down the Peninsula and begin sending some north, leaving many to wonder what might have been done differently at Richmond. Finally, Halleck would continue to manage the US response to Robert E. Lee's invasion, overseeing raids in North Carolina and West Virginia during July even as the Army of Northern Virginia limped back into the Old Dominion following its defeat at Gettysburg.

17

The Peace Mission

"I AM ABOUT TO LEAVE ON THE BUSINESS WHICH BROUGHT ME HERE"

DURING GEORGE GETTY'S EXPEDITION to the South Anna, Alexander Stephens's diplomatic drama continued to unfold as Confederate leaders pressed for negotiations. Although the vice president prepared to discuss prisoner issues with US officials, he still harbored hopes for broader talks that might yield Confederate independence and leave slavery intact. However, once in Richmond, the vice president had become disenchanted with the enterprise after learning about Robert E. Lee's offensive into Pennsylvania. For him, the timing was simply off. But President Jefferson Davis and his cabinet remained intrigued by what the bargaining table might generate for their cause. Accordingly, in the first days of July, Stephens gathered his papers and packed his bags for Washington.

On Friday morning, July 3, still ignorant of the massive battle under way at Gettysburg, Stephens scrawled a short note to his brother Linton. "I am about to leave on the business which brought me here. I shall expect to be absent from the city for a few days."[1] At noon, he began his journey, accompanied by Robert Ould, the designated Confederate agent for prisoner exchanges. In the muggy air at Rocketts Landing not far from downtown, Stephens stepped aboard the *Torpedo*, a 90-foot screw tug commanded by Lieutenant Hunter Davidson. The boat steamed down the James and, with a truce flag hoisted aloft, reached US vessels the next morning near the Federal stronghold at Fort Monroe. Unknown to Stephens, much was happening elsewhere that day. George Getty's column approached the South Anna, Robert E. Lee's army had made its last lunge at Gettysburg, and John Pemberton was about to surrender the Confederate garrison at Vicksburg.[2]

As the *Torpedo* approached the US picket boats, the 40-gun steam frigate *Minnesota* appeared in the distance near shore, not far from the spot where it had fought the rebel ironclad *Virginia* the year before. The fully repaired frigate served as Acting Rear Admiral Samuel Phillips Lee's flagship. However, a much smaller craft, the tug *Lilac*, converged with Stephens's boat. A Federal officer stepped aboard the *Torpedo* and announced that standing orders prohibited the passage of any vessel past that point. After a brief exchange, Stephens handed over some letters, one for Admiral Lee and another for the "officer in command" of US forces at Fort Monroe. The *Lilac* reversed course and steamed back to the flagship.[3]

Stephens's dispatches began a protracted back-and-forth with Federal officials. In his letters, he identified himself as a "military commissioner" bearing a communication from Jefferson Davis and expressed his desire to "proceed directly to Washington City in the steamer *Torpedo*." He did not, however, hand over Davis's letter, which contained the Confederate president's complaints about the prisoner cartel, the treatment of noncombatants, and the execution of rebel prisoners—as well as an implied threat of retaliation should such issues not be resolved to his satisfaction. Ignorant of Stephens's aims, Admiral Lee immediately wired the request for a meeting to Secretary of the Navy Gideon Welles in Washington. At the same time, John Dix's staffer at Fort Monroe, William Ludlow, forwarded the other copy of Stephens's request to Secretary of War Edwin Stanton and offered a dispatch boat to escort Stephens's "small tug" to Washington.[4]

With the messages on their way, another Union vessel returned to the *Torpedo* with instructions for Stephens to head back upstream, take station there, and await further word. But the small rebel delegation aboard the *Torpedo* urgently requested passage down to the main Union fleet off of Newport News, explaining they had no anchor to sit and wait in the river. When offered an anchor, the Southerners said "they would get one from the hold," apparently laying bare their dissembling. The *Lilac*'s commander did not bend. He insisted that the *Torpedo* reverse course, head upstream, and remain off White Shoal Light off Newport News, about 8 miles west of the *Minnesota*.[5]

It was not a favorable start. The initial exchange annoyed Admiral Lee. A cousin of Robert E. Lee who had remained loyal to the United States, the admiral had reportedly quipped at the war's outset that "when I find the word Virginia in my commission I will join the Confederacy." He expressed a similar disdain for Stephens and his mission. He informed Gideon Welles on July 4 that to "allow the so-called Confederate States steamer to pass this blockade and display its assumed sovereign flag at the national capital was an act of recognition wholly at variance with my feelings and sense of duty."[6] Officials in Washington had similar views.

That evening, Secretary Stanton instructed Ludlow to "hold no communication with" Stephens or permit the rebel tug to leave the river or allow its passengers to otherwise enter the Federal lines.[7] Likewise, Welles
found the communication puzzling and showed it to Montgomery Blair,
who made no comment. Welles then discussed it with Stanton, "who
swore and growled indignantly." He also spoke to Secretary of State William Seward, who wanted nothing to do with Stephens or Davis. Welles
did not expect that Stephens intended "much good" with "the proposition," and he did not believe Stephens needed to come to Washington.[8]
Stephens's prospects did not improve when word of Meade's triumph at
Gettysburg arrived in Washington. "Our victory is complete. Lee in full
retreat," wrote Stanton to Ludlow on July 4.[9] The news from Gettysburg
would change many things, including the viability of Stephens's mission.

Despite the developments in Pennsylvania, Stephens's request kicked
off a flurry of deliberation in Washington. On Saturday, President Lincoln
was at the Soldiers' Home north of the city, where his family had been
summering. In the evening, he returned to the White House to discuss
Stephens's request with Edwin Stanton and others. During the meeting,
Lincoln shrugged off the whole matter and suggested pushing aside discussions until the next day. On Sunday morning at 11 a.m. with news of
Meade's triumph fresh in everyone's mind, Lincoln convened the cabinet
in his second-floor office to discuss Stephens's request. Welles described
the meeting's details in his diary. The president had mulled over the matter during the night. He opposed bringing the rebel envoy to Washington
but did see benefit in sending someone to talk with Stephens. Lincoln even
raised the possibility of making the trip himself, a suggestion that "startled" Seward and Stanton. The secretary of state was dead set against
any such face-to-face interaction with Stephens, believing the rebel vice
president to be a "dangerous man, who would make mischief anywhere."
Stanton and Chase agreed. Montgomery Blair also opposed a meeting but
expressed a willingness to "receive any communication" from Stephens.[10]

Discussions churned on in the White House. There were some tan-
gents, but most of the talk centered around a response to Stephens. Welles
proposed to string the matter along. He drafted a response to Admiral Lee, which simply stated that, without more information about the
content of Stephens's communication, he could not pass the blockade
with the *Torpedo*.[11] The other cabinet members did not embrace this
approach. At one point, Seward blurted out that "Admiral Lee should be
ignored," which Welles thought might reflect a judgment that Lee "was
incompetent, or not to be trusted." Throughout the discussion, Lincoln

sat next to Welles on one of the sofas. The president talked about sending a "special messenger" to meet with Stephens. But few present favored such an approach, perhaps reflecting a widely held distrust of the rebel vice president. Many urged Lincoln to simply reject Stephens's request summarily. Welles, however, found some of these concerns overblown and worried about the broader picture. He believed Stephens's gambit was a scheme "possibly for good, perhaps for evil," but he also feared that a "rude refusal" would hurt the administration in the North. He understood this to be a consideration for the president as well. The two recognized the potential political costs of rejecting Stephens outright. On one hand: "We must not put ourselves in the wrong by refusing to communicate with these people," mused Welles. "On the other hand, there is difficulty in meeting and treating with men who have violated their duty, disregarded their obligations, and who lack sincerity." Welles felt obliged to provide Admiral Lee with a response. However, Lincoln pushed the matter further off and decided to defer making any decisions until the next day.[12]

On Monday, July 6, at 9 a.m., the cabinet reconvened to discuss Stephens's request. This time, Seward brought a draft note simply informing the Confederate leader that his appeal was "inadmissible" and that any communication should go through "the prescribed military channel." Lincoln agreed and directed Seward, who had changed his views throughout the deliberations, to the telegraph office to ensure the note was "correctly transmitted."[13]

Back on the James River, little had happened. On Sunday afternoon, hours after Lincoln's cabinet meeting, the *Torpedo* shifted farther upstream but returned to White Point Light a few hours later. The next morning, Stephens, anxious for a response from Washington, instructed Davidson to take the *Torpedo* downriver once again. At noon, he passed a note over to the Union picket tug there asking: "Will Admiral Lee inform me, if he can, how long it will probably be before an answer will be made to my note of the 4th instant?"[14]

Stephens finally received his answer. At 2:30 p.m. on Monday, just a few hours after his latest plea, two small US vessels appeared in the distance steaming up the river. Both bore a separate dispatch, one from Welles of the navy and another from the army carried by Ludlow himself aboard Dix's truce boat, the *Henry Burden*. The messages were identical. "The request of Alexander H. Stephens is inadmissible. The customary agents and channels are adequate for all needful military communications and conference between the United States forces and the insurgents."[15]

Ludlow, who was aboard one of the boats, came over to the *Torpedo* himself and discussed exchange issues with Colonel Ould.[16]

That ended Stephens's mission. The *Torpedo* made its way back up the James to Richmond. The vice president returned to his temporary residence in the city and prepared to head back to Georgia. Before boarding the train home, he prepared a short report for Davis. He candidly acknowledged the mission's failure and concluded that the reasons for the Federals' rebuff "must be left to conjecture." He recognized Lincoln's rejection for what it mostly likely was: a refusal to discuss the broader issues of the war with him. In concluding his report, Stephens lamented the lost opportunity in his typical, long-winded style:

> Deeply impressed as I was with these views and feelings in undertaking the mission and asking the conference, I can but express my profound regret at the result of the effort made to obtain it, and I can but entertain the belief that if the conference sought had been granted mutual good could have been effected by it, and if this war, so unnatural, so unjust, so unchristian, and so inconsistent with every fundamental principle of American constitutional liberty "must needs" continue to be waged against us, that at least some of its severer horrors, which now so eminently threaten, might have been avoided.[17]

Stephens thus closed this obscure chapter of his largely ineffective career. He would revisit peace negotiations and even participate in a fruitless conference with President Lincoln aboard the steamer *River Queen* at Hampton Roads in February 1865. The failed mission aboard the *Torpedo* in July 1863 would foreshadow his unremarkable impact on the war's outcome and the fortunes of the Confederacy.

Stephens's failure did not remain a secret for long. Reports of the trip appeared in the Richmond papers on July 6.[18] Eventually, nearly all of the correspondence prepared by Stephens and Davis, as well as the dispatches between Stephens and Federal officials, appeared in the news over the next several weeks.[19] The deliberate disclosure of the correspondence may have reflected an attempt by rebel officials to peg Lincoln and his administration as unreasonably opposed to negotiations. But Davis's refusal to directly raise the possibility of peace talks in his letter to Lincoln certainly muted any public relations benefits. Apparently, Stephens viewed the omission as a lost opportunity. In his view, a more direct peace proposal would have allowed the Confederates to blame the war's prolongation on the Lincoln administration and, perhaps in the bargain, dampen Northern war enthusiasm and erode Lincoln's electoral chances in 1864. As Stephens explained a year later, peace terms "could have been published and of course ought to have been if rejected." He predicted the Northern "masses would have been made to understand them. The war spirit would have been broken."[20]

Neither Stephens nor Davis completely put the episode behind them. During the remainder of the war, animosity between the two would continue to brew. Near the end of 1863, the Confederate president angered Stephens when he suggested, in a letter to Governor Zebulon Vance of North Carolina, that he had approved the mission to humor the vice president. By this time, Stephens's general displeasure with Davis had grown, and the president's remark sent him down a rabbit hole of conspiracy. In a long letter drafted for his brother Linton but never sent, Stephens accused Davis of orchestrating the peace mission's failure through an elaborate scheme. In the Georgian's imagination, Davis had supported Robert E. Lee's march into Pennsylvania, pushed for John Hunt Morgan's raid into Ohio, and allowed the capture of the correspondence between Davis, Cooper, and Lee in late June—all to give the Federals warning of Stephens's mission and contrive the best means to reject his entreaties. These decisions, in Stephens's estimation, were part of a Davis plot to prolong the war, concentrate power, and remain in office as long as possible. However, nothing supports the fantastic assertions set out in the draft, and since Stephens never sent the letter containing the accusations, it is not clear what to make of them. In any event, Stephens's disenchantment with Davis, as well as with the war as a whole, would endure.[21]

The real goals and other details behind Stephens's mission remain murky. Observers at the time found the whole affair puzzling. The Northern press, at least the papers that took note of the event, sniffed a deeper purpose behind the mission and suspected there was more to the failed diplomatic effort than an attempt to mend the prisoner exchange cartel. The *Philadelphia Inquirer* acknowledged the Confederate vice president would have "improved all the chances for opening negotiations on other subjects" beyond the stated prisoner concerns had Lee succeeded in Pennsylvania. But the editors believed Stephens desired more than to discuss merely the cartel. "We are satisfied that some trivial affair about prisoners or retaliation would have been put forward as the pretext of this visit." In their view, the mission's timing belied "some deeper scheme" connected to Lee's invasion.[22] Furthermore, the notion that Stephens wanted to bargain broadly for peace seemed to be common knowledge in Washington. Elizabeth Blair Lee, Admiral Phillips Lee's spouse, reported that the "City is quite excited by the Refusal of the President to receive Mr. Stephens & his message in making peace overture as it is called here."[23]

The mission generated additional speculation in the newspapers. One account in the New Orleans *Times-Picayune* claimed Stephens planned to announce a Confederate–French alliance to Lincoln. Another, from Kentucky, argued the rebel vice president was really a true "Union man" under it all and that restoration of the country was his real goal. Still one more report asserted, without elaboration, that Lincoln knew the "real" reason behind the mission and chose to reject Stephens's entreaty. In the Confederate War Department, observant clerk John Beauchamp Jones heard various stories. In one, Stephens had headed for Washington to simply propose peace terms. In another, he had sought a "definitive understanding" with the Lincoln administration about "whether or not property is to be respected" during the war. Without such an assurance, General Lee, according to the rumor, would proceed to "desolate the Northern States."[24]

One of the more sensational explanations for Stephens's mission appeared in the *New-York Tribune* on July 31. Penned under the pseudonym "Randolph," the column purported to reveal Stephens's true intent in engaging the Lincoln administration. It contained a remarkable claim, summarized by the *Tribune* editorial page as such: "The Confederates are alarmed and indignant at our arming the negroes to fight them, and desired to send Mr. Stephens to Washington to enter an imposing remonstrance against it, and give our government fair notice that, if we did not give it up, they would also embark in it with all their might, and arm ten negroes to our one."[25] According to the letter, Stephens certainly hoped to discuss measures "to lighten the troubles of prisoners, and alleviate the pains of the wounded," but his real object, emphasized "Randolph," was to protest "against the mustering and the arming of the blacks" by the Federals and to threaten to arm Southern slaves in retaliation. The letter acknowledged that Confederate units included "body servants" (i.e., enslaved persons), who became prisoners from time to time. However, it also confirmed that "not one single regiment or corps of negroes has ever been brought into Confederate service, to be turned against you." But Stephens, according to the letter from "Randolph," planned to threaten the Federals with a broad effort to fill Confederate armies with enslaved soldiers. The South had 750,000 "able-bodied fellows, loving and trusting their masters," wrote "Randolph," who would be ready to "follow them up to the mouths of their cannons" after three months of drilling. "Randolph" predicted doom for the North should this come about.[26]

Regardless of its accuracy, the *Tribune* story is remarkable not only because it attributed this proposal to the Confederate vice president but also because the proposal itself predated the full Confederate debate on arming enslaved men by nearly two years. Talk of such measures had cropped up occasionally from the war's first days. But the "Randolph" letter appeared a full five months before Major General Patrick Cleburne's provocative suggestion to place slaves in the Confederate ranks. Cleburne's radical proposal in late 1863 created somewhat of a scandal in the army and was promptly swept under the rug by his superiors. It was not until the fall of 1864 that the notion of arming slaves began to gain traction in public debate, eventually leading to the formation of a few small units only weeks before the war's end.[27]

The source of the "Randolph" piece makes the whole matter even more intriguing. The story arrived at the *Tribune* by way of reporter John Williamson Palmer, a well-traveled native of Baltimore and a Confederate sympathizer. After receiving his medical degree from the University of Maryland, he served as a doctor in San Francisco and Hawaii and then traveled farther east to work as a surgeon for the East India Company during the Second Burmese War. Following stints in China and India, he proceeded to New York, where he abandoned medicine to become a journalist. After several different jobs, he landed a post as a feature writer for the *New-York Tribune*. Despite Palmer's extensive reporting for Northern newspapers, he would later be best known for an unflinchingly pro-Confederate poem, "Stonewall Jackson's Way," which was put to music and released in 1863 by a Richmond publisher, J. W. Randolph.[28] During 1862 and 1863, Palmer traveled throughout the mid-Atlantic states, sending stories to his editor at the *New-York Tribune*, Sydney Howard Gay. By the summer of 1863, Palmer had become of one of the *Tribune's* most "valued and shadowy" contributors.[29]

During the Gettysburg Campaign, he chased the armies throughout Pennsylvania and eventually filed an informative report with the *Tribune* about Lee's retreat. Several weeks after Gettysburg, Palmer sent the mysterious "Randolph" letter to the *Tribune*. Before mailing it to New York, however, he had talked up the piece to Gay, calling it a story of "truly great importance . . . derived from the highest official sources." When the piece did not appear in the *Tribune*, Palmer complained: "I am distressed that you have not published the Richmond letter today. It is genuine—upon my sacred honor." He claimed Lincoln's cabinet was well aware of these details and that it reflected Stephens's message "exactly." "For Heaven's sake, don't hesitate to publish it," he implored Gay and even suggested he would take it elsewhere, noting that the *Herald* would give $500 for the letter. After a few days of silence from New York, Palmer began to regret his aggressive tone and, in a frantic July 27 missive, walked back some of his bombast and again sought to assure Gay that the Stephens account was genuine. In the end, he was much relieved when Gay finally printed the letter. On the day it appeared, he wrote Gay to thank him and provided some further corroboration.[30]

On the editorial page accompanying Palmer's story in the July 31 *Tribune*, Gay wrote at length about the implications of Stephens's alleged hidden purpose. He found the reported threat absurd. "But, then, if the Rebels arm their negroes, they must FREE them. That is inevitable." He doubted the Confederates would find success in their gambit. "It is the easiest thing in the world to arm slaves (provided you have the arms); to disarm them is quite another matter." Gay doubted Stephens really believed such an effort was possible. "The Confederates, then," he concluded, "will not arm their slaves, because that would insure their defeat and overthrow in one way or another."[31]

Other newspapers were not sure what to make of the story in the *Tribune*, which was excerpted and mentioned in several Northern papers, flagged mostly as a curiosity.[32] The *Alexandria Gazette* reported "there is considerable doubt as to the truth of the whole story."[33] Neither Stephens nor anyone else in the Confederate government addressed the assertions made in the "Randolph" letter. As Stephens's correspondence from June and July 1863 demonstrates, the vice president was indeed preoccupied with issues involving US Black troops. In addition, his correspondence in late June vaguely referenced threats of retaliation in relation to negotiations with the Federals. Thus, the notion that Stephens would raise the threat of arming slaves in negotiations with Federal officials cannot be dismissed out of hand. However, outside of the *New-York Tribune* piece, no clear evidence has emerged that he planned to do so. In any event, within weeks of Stephens's aborted diplomatic mission, the speculation about its purposes faded away from the newspapers and from the public mind, swallowed by new events and developments.[34]

18

The End at Richmond

"THE DESIGN ON RICHMOND WAS NOT A FEINT BUT A FAINT"

NEWS OF THE RESULTS AT GETTYSBURG was slow in reaching Richmond. A day after Robert E. Lee's disastrous charge against the Federal center in Pennsylvania, anxious Confederate officials still waited for word of Lee's fortunes while also keeping an eye on the Union movements at the city's doorstep. All the while, commanders kept men stationed in the fortifications ringing the city. Ransom's North Carolinians continued to block the Williamsburg Road and watch Bottom's Bridge to the east. To cover the Chickahominy to the northeast, Custis Lee's battalions occupied the partially completed works at Meadow Bridge. The amateur soldiers remained throughout the night and then moved to Stewart's Farm on the Brook Turnpike overlooking Brook Run the next day. It had been a chaotic period for these factory workers and office clerks. They had marched out to the entrenchments and remained there for several days, shuttling from point to point. Custis Lee shared in the experience. A clerk in the Department Guards, a unit made up of War Department officer workers, encountered Lee earlier in the week and found him "looking well, after sleeping on the ground the first time in his life, without a blanket."[1]

Major Josiah Gorgas, the chief of ordnance, visited the defense lines on a special mission in response to concerns expressed by President Jefferson Davis about the defenses and "their condition of preparation." On July 4, Gorgas promptly rode out to examine the curtains, ditches, redans, and redoubts for himself. In his journal, he described the inner line's star forts as "works of considerable strength . . . well constructed and in good order, commanding all the principal avenues of approach to the city." Further out at the intermediate line, he found a continuous string "of rifle pits, or covers, with places for field batteries" on the high ground. Given the number of men available for defense, Gorgas recommended the use of the inner line.[2] The works in this sector had also drawn the interest of the Confederate engineer corps. On the same day, Colonel Walter Stevens wrote his superiors about the need to impress as many as 500 free Black men in the city and force them to work on a gap in the intermediate line on the Mechanicsville Road.[3]

On Sunday morning, July 5, D. H. Hill and others in Richmond learned about Cooke's successful defense at the South Anna the night before.[4] Hill's own courier, who had traveled to Hanover Junction to gather all the information he could find, reported that "a considerable battle" had occurred resulting in a Yankee repulse. Looking east, Hill pondered John Dix's next move and concluded the danger had mostly passed. In a buoyant note to Secretary of War James Seddon, he included one of his more memorable wisecracks: "Where have the Yankees gone? The design on Richmond was not a feint but a faint." However, he did not believe the campaign was over and suggested the Federals might still march west toward Gordonsville and Staunton, then north down the Valley, "doing much mischief." Alternatively, he guessed Dix would move units north to reinforce Washington. Hill confessed to Seddon that the whole affair had been somewhat embarrassing. "It is mortifying to have them play around us as they have done," he explained. However, given "imperfect information" and a "defective system of scouting," he doubted more could have been done, especially given Federal control of the rivers. Hill also worried about events in North Carolina and expressed particular concern that John Foster would soon conduct a raid to destroy the arsenal at Fayetteville.[5]

Over the next few days, more reports arrived about the South Anna Bridge fight. An account from a railroad employee described the damage done by Union cavalry at Ashland. The papers also relayed stories of Cooke's victory and reported the enemy column had left Hanover Court House and crossed back into King William County. A witness had caught a glimpse of the Federal wagon train in retreat, extending over a mile in his estimate. By the middle of the week, the papers confirmed the Union expedition had returned to White House.[6] The *Richmond Sentinel* gave well-deserved praise to Cooke:

Our success is attributable, in a great measure, to the ready and soldier-like manner in which Gen. Cooke handled his forces. He is every inch a General. He arrived here only yesterday (Saturday) morning, and it was wonderful with what facility and quickness he became thoroughly acquainted with the position and the geography of the country.[7]

On July 8, the *Dispatch* reported that a train on the Fredericksburg line arrived in the city with seventeen Union prisoners captured at the South Anna. In addition, the Confederate press did not neglect the reports of Yankee depredations. The *Richmond Daily Dispatch* passed along stories from an "exiled" citizen of King William County who spoke of "squads of thieves . . . scattered throughout the county, taking whatever they can find, and destroying what is not convenient for them to remove." Neither did the papers fail to warn that the invaders had sought to stir up a slave revolt, a favorite dread of the Confederate press. "They are also endeavoring to incite the Negroes to insurrection," advised the *Dispatch*, claiming that one enslaved laborer had been offered a company command as an inducement to leave with the Federals. "The Negroes, under these influences," asserted the *Dispatch*, "are said to be very insubordinate, and some are even boasting, of their freedom and ability to maintain it." The paper also claimed the force with Getty contained Black cavalrymen, who seemed "to be on a perfect equality with their white skinned comrades, cavorted about furiously, and anathematized fiercely the 'd—d rebels.'"[8]

Such stories reflected deep-seated Confederate fears. The growing emancipatory aspects of the US war effort had produced much apprehension. Many Confederates had frequently warned that Union policies would produce slave insurrection and speed slavery's demise. They also worried about the new African American units then forming in Northern cities and Union-controlled enclaves in the South. Black regiments such as the 54th Massachusetts, which reached South Carolina in late May, were already at the front. But there is no evidence Dix's command contained any African American units in the summer of 1863. Nevertheless, the Confederate press understood the existential threat posed by these aspects of the Union war effort. No doubt fueled by such concern, the *Dispatch* spat its venom in a wide stream, proclaiming that the "truth is, even the free Negro, as low as he is in the scale of humanity, is not as degraded nor abominable, in the sight of Heaven or mankind, as the degenerate and debauched descendants of the old New England Puritans, who are carrying on this war."[9]

On July 6, with no more signs of a US advance outside Richmond, Arnold Elzey ordered Custis Lee to dismiss the city battalions and other local defense forces. D. H. Hill was not happy with the decision. He hoped to do some damage to Dix's command while it remained near Richmond. "I wished to be free to move with my own brigades, having the roads guarded by the local force," he told Elzey.[10] But the local defense troops stood down. The clerks of the Department Guard, which included diarist

John Beauchamp Jones's son, returned to the city "sun-burnt and covered with dust." Some of the part-timers had been out on the lines for several days—sleeping under the open sky without tents, dining on small quantities of unappetizing victuals, and waiting for an attack that never came.[11] On July 6, Seddon looked for aggressive action to completely eliminate the Union threat around Richmond.[12] But no tremendous clash would occur. Out in New Kent County near Talleysville, D. H. Hill's forces continued their low-intensity standoff with Keyes, including a cavalry skirmish at the Quarles House on July 6.[13]

"ALL OTHER INTERESTS ARE SWALLOWED UP"

As the Confederate leaders observed Dix's force, they also waited for definitive news from Pennsylvania. Vague, unconfirmed reports of fighting at Gettysburg had begun to trickle down to Richmond. On July 5, a truce boat at City Point brought word that a "great battle" had occurred. "The Yankee papers, I am told, claim a victory, but acknowledge a loss of five or six generals," recorded John Jones. The next day, newspapers arriving in Richmond from Baltimore and New York provided "loose" accounts of the battle, calling it "indecisive." As they waited for news from Lee's army, Richmonders seemed to lose interest in Dix's Federals, who were still only a few miles from the city's door. A line in the *Daily Richmond Examiner* captured the mood: "All other interests are swallowed up by that grand battle fought and fighting in the heart of Pennsylvania. Is Gettysburg another Antietam?" Rumors of a Lee victory raised spirits. On Sunday evening, William Burgwyn wrote that he had "heard the glorious news" of a victory for Lee's army and the capture of 40,000 Federals.[14]

But the bad news for Confederate Richmond eventually arrived. On July 7, Jones at the War Department received definitive word of the defeat in Pennsylvania. Confirmation of Vicksburg's capture came a day or two later. Over the next week, stories from Gettysburg and Vicksburg along with long lists of casualties crowded newspaper columns. The crisis outside Richmond began to fade as well. With Lee withdrawing back to Virginia and Dix seemingly uninterested in moving against the city, the Confederates increasingly diluted their strength in the surrounding defenses. On July 7, Seddon ordered Montgomery Corse to leave Gordonsville for Winchester in the Valley to support Lee. From his headquarters at the Williams House east of Richmond, D. H. Hill continued to manage his troops and tend to the city fortifications, bluntly urging Seddon to send troops and engineers, "minus their kid gloves," to improve the works at Brook Turnpike, River Road, and Staples Mills. Brushing away Hill's tone, Seddon agreed, and that day Chief Engineer Jeremy Gilmer directed his staff to look into matters. Hill also kept an eye on Dix's force at White House. He predicted the "Army of the Pamunkey, or the Monkey army," as he sarcastically labeled it, would move its base to Washington or Petersburg. He expressed particular concern about the rail junction at the latter. His fear was well-founded, for Petersburg would become the target of Ulysses S. Grant's operations the next year. As Hill mused, other Confederate leaders at Richmond continued to speculate about Dix's intent and future operations.[15]

"A GOOD DEAL CHAGRINED"

News of the Federal victory at Gettysburg had reached John Dix several days before it became commonly known in Richmond. The Gettysburg triumph seemed to convince Secretary Stanton that Dix's operations had a renewed importance. He informed Dix: "Whether [Lee] ever gets to Richmond may depend much upon your success in breaking his communication." Word of George Meade's success elated Dix, who was still waiting for word of Getty's South Anna expedition. "Many thanks for the glorious news," he wired the secretary. The next day, Stanton confirmed Lee was retreating south. But, despite Stanton's vague musing about further efforts at Richmond, neither he nor Henry Halleck urged Dix to resume the advance against the rebel capital. In fact, no additional orders arrived overriding Halleck's previous directive for Dix to send many of his troops to Washington upon Getty's return. Two days later, adding to the tidings of Meade's victory, Stanton informed Dix that "a dispatch from Grant confirms Vicksburg's surrender."[16]

With word of these tremendous successes elsewhere, Dix grappled with the mixed results of his own operation. On the same day news of the Vicksburg victory arrived at White House Landing, he informed Halleck of Getty's return. Dix tried to put a good face on the expedition's failure. In his telling, Getty had found the RF&P bridge "guarded by about 8,000 men[] with fourteen pieces of artillery" and, "deeming an attack too hazardous," had settled for destroying 3 miles of track and dismantling the depot at Ashland. Unaware the damage would be repaired in a day or so, Dix believed the results would force the Confederates to supply Lee using the railroads running through Danville, Lynchburg, and Charlottesville instead of along the Virginia Central via Gordonsville. With his operations over, Dix planned to send three of his Pennsylvania regiments to Washington and would ship more men the next day.[17]

Dix's report produced some harsh words from Washington. "We feel a good deal chagrined at the slight results of the late operations in your department," wired Stanton. The secretary, relying on the captured correspondence between Davis and Lee, correctly asserted that Getty had likely exaggerated the enemy's strength at the South Anna by "two or three times." Stanton then concluded his missive with this cutting remark: "The great murmuring in every quarter at the waste of force in your command will probably be a good deal aggravated by this last disappointment." Part rebuke and part rumor, this line in the letter managed to convey Stanton's disapproval while suggesting that others, including President Lincoln himself, were disappointed with Dix's performance.[18]

A surely mortified Dix responded the next day. He described his commanders Getty, Foster, and Spear as "three of my best officers," implying the trio had not exaggerated the size of the Confederate force in their fronts. Dix failed to explain, however, that Getty was not present at the South Anna fight, or that Foster and Spear had conducted most of the operation in the dark, or that Foster with only a few companies committed to the fight had not pressed his men close to the rebel positions. In fact, Dix and his subordinates were wrong in the estimates of enemy strength. Cooke had two infantry regiments (the 15th and 46th North Carolina), a cavalry regiment (Baker's 3rd North Carolina), a battery (Cooper's), and about 500 walking wounded from the Richmond hospitals. These troops probably did not amount to more than 3,000. For certain, this was a sizable force, surely enough men to repel a slow advance by four companies in the dark. In addition, there is no doubting that the ground in front of the bridge was difficult. However, Cooke simply did not have the numbers imagined by Getty and Foster.[19]

Duly chastised, Dix focused on his command's departure from White House Landing. On the morning of July 8, he wrote Halleck in cipher from Yorktown, leading with: "Thank God for giving us Vicksburg!" He then reported his men were breaking up their camps along the Pamunkey and that he was departing "with great regret." But he held on to the possibility of additional operations. His engineers had placed wooden planks along the railroad bridge across the Pamunkey, allowing the passage of artillery and supply trains there. Once again, he indirectly suggested further operations against the Confederate capital. "If Lee is broken up, and I can have 20,000 men, I can go into Richmond." He then offered this clarification: "I have not delayed a compliance with your order, but hoped that changed relations might keep me here."[20]

But there were no "changed relations" in Washington, and there were no revisions to Dix's orders. Halleck still wanted all available men sent north. The rear of Getty's wagon train crossed over the Pamunkey to White House at sunset on July 7, and at sunrise the next day, Dix hurried his entire command toward Yorktown over roads muddied by the recent rains. The next day, Halleck emphasized the directive: "It is important that the troops be pushed forward with all possible dispatch, and also that they arrive here ready for the field," his wire to Fort Monroe read. "Another great battle is pending, and I wish to get them in time to take part." Surely crestfallen, Dix prepared his men to leave.[21]

The Confederates soon learned that Dix's operation was over. On July 8, D. H. Hill urged Seddon to send a column to White House to determine the number of enemy troops still there and attack them if possible. But later that day both Elzey and Cooke reported that the Federals were gone. John Dix's force, the units of the Fourth and Seventh Corps, was already headed down the Peninsula. Some loaded onto transports and floated down the Pamunkey's muddy waters, escorted by gunboats. The rest of the men, artillery, supply wagons, and ambulances headed overland along roads enveloped once again by Virginia's thick summer heat. A Connecticut veteran recalled that he and his comrades eventually returned quietly to their former camps, "cheering over the news from Gettysburg and Vicksburg, and resolutely subduing their feelings of pride as they rehearsed the achievements of 'The Blackberry Raid.'" John Dix's campaign against Richmond was over.[22]

19

Halleck's Bootless Plans

"AN OPPORTUNITY TO DO THE REBELS MUCH INJURY"

THE WITHDRAWAL OF DIX'S FORCES signaled the stuttering end to the centerpiece of Henry Halleck's half-formed plan to threaten Robert E. Lee's communications during the Gettysburg Campaign. But, despite Dix's departure from Richmond, Halleck's entire effort was not over. Throughout early July, he had focused on the threat in Pennsylvania and coordinated the Federal reaction to Lee's incursion, remaining in constant contact with various department commanders. However, while he tended to matters in Pennsylvania, he continued to pursue other means to cut Confederate communications while Lee was still miles away from ally-controlled railheads. Specifically, he kept his eye on North Carolina and western Virginia, where he hoped raids would break the vital Wilmington and Weldon Railroad and the Virginia and Tennessee line.

Into early July, Halleck waited in vain for word from Brigadier General Benjamin F. Kelley in the new Department of West Virginia. Back on June 25, he had ordered Kelley to send Brigadier General Eliakim Scammon on a mounted raid "to ascend the Great Kanawha, cross the mountains, and cut the Virginia & Tennessee Railroad" in southwestern Virginia. Nothing had come of it. On July 4, Halleck asked Kelley about the raid's status, noting the reported absence of rebel troops in the void between Lee's army and Richmond. He urged Kelley to lose no time pushing the expedition forward. He also directed Kelley to concentrate additional units on the Baltimore and Ohio Railroad and operate on Lee's western flank as the Virginian withdrew from Pennsylvania. In response, Kelley explained that his scattered force would require a few days to concentrate, although he had ordered Scammon to move. It did not sound promising.[1]

Halleck was also anxious for news from North Carolina, where John Foster had provided no update on plans to break the Wilmington and Weldon Railroad. Back on June 21, Foster had offered to help efforts to repel Lee's offensive. And then on June 30, he had informed Halleck that a planned cavalry raid, delayed due to "continuous rainy weather," would depart in a few days. On July 5, Halleck prodded. He pointed to the recently captured Confederate correspondence to Lee from Davis and Cooper detailing troop strength at Richmond and speculated that few rebel troops remained in North Carolina. "I think . . . you will have an opportunity to do the rebels much injury, even with your small force."[2]

When Halleck wrote those words, Foster's men were already on the move. On July 6, he informed the War Department that "in obedience to orders from General Halleck" a cavalry raid of about 700 men "is now out for the purpose of cutting and destroying the Wilmington and Weldon Railroad." Indeed, a few days before, Lieutenant Colonel George W. Lewis had left New Bern with 640 cavalrymen riding west toward the rail line. Behind Lewis, a 2,000-man infantry force under Brigadier General Charles Heckman also departed to protect the cavalry's line of retreat and prevent Confederates at Kinston from intercepting the raiding column. To distract the rebels, units to the north at Plymouth would move overland and along the Roanoke River to attack Confederate positions near Williamston. Reveling in the encouraging news from the North, Foster found overall prospects "most cheering" and predicted Meade's results would "fulfill the most sanguine expectations." He also planned to do more in the coming weeks by sending a force to cut the railroad north of Goldsboro.[3]

On Friday, July 3, Lieutenant Colonel Lewis left New Bern with the 3rd New York Cavalry, two companies of the 23rd New York Cavalry, Company L of the 1st North Carolina Union Volunteers, and a section of the 3rd New York Artillery. The column reached Trenton that evening and rode through Comfort and then Hallsville the next day, brushing aside pickets along the way. The "route was very low and thickly wooded, deep fords occurring every few miles," reported Lewis. Nevertheless, the raiders made good progress in the Carolina backwoods with assistance from local Unionists. Although not mentioned in Federal reports, Confederate sources later confirmed that freedmen from the region served as guides for the column, ensuring the Federals could navigate the countryside between New Bern and the railroad even at dark.[4]

Lewis's force pushed on throughout July 4 and arrived that night at Kenansville, the site of a small armory owned by Louis Froelich, a Bavarian immigrant. Confederate pickets had spread news of the approaching Yankees, but apparently no one in the garrison there, commanded by Captain W. K. Lane, received or heeded the warning.[5] The Federals rode into town and found the defenders asleep and quickly "captured all but about half a dozen" and moved on to the armory and saddle manufactory, burning the former and destroying the contents of the latter. According to Foster's report, the armory contained "some 2,500 sabers and large quantities of saber bayonets, bowie knives, and other small-arms, a steam-engine and implements for manufacturing arms." A local report stated that the troopers also put the torch to stores of bacon, flour, and corn and took $80,000 from the town in addition to "horses, negroes, &c."[6]

On Sunday morning, after four hours of sleep, the cavalrymen rode farther west and, at 8 a.m., reached Warsaw, a station on the Wilmington and Weldon line. A civilian, who witnessed their arrival and recorded her impressions under the pseudonym "Quelqu'une" ("Someone"), wrote that the "first Yankee dashed through our street to the rail road, quickly followed by another on another street, and then thicker and faster they came till there was nothing but blue coats, fire arms, and dust to be seen." The onlooker claimed the force included "a company of contrabands," but Union reports make no mention of such a unit with Lewis. These may have been scouts, guides, or refugees assisting the raiders. Among the riders, the townspeople recognized one of the Tar Heels from Company L of the 1st North Carolina Union Volunteers, a white laborer from Duplin County who spoke to a freedman in the town by name.[7]

The Federals went to work cutting telegraph wires, tearing up track, and destroying the depot and warehouses with their contents of corn, flour, bacon, rolling stock, and 1,000 tar and turpentine barrels. Luckily for the townspeople, there was no breeze that morning to spread the fire to nearby homes. According to one account, the Federals did not burn everything. In an incident omitted from official reports, some of the cavalrymen, not wanting to see the bacon burned "when so many needed it," pulled out large amounts and handed it to local civilians watching nearby.[8]

The Yankee cavalrymen remained busy in Warsaw during their short stay. "There was no stopping them anywhere," noted the local chronicler. "It was a constant, run turn and dash off." Another witness wrote immediately afterward that a squad "were breaking open the stores and destroying everything they could." At the local homes, the Federals pleaded for milk, asked for water, stole a few pies, and no doubt purloined other items. They also broke into any safe they could find looking for money and valuables and managed to locate some whiskey. "Some of the boys who are over fond of the 'critter,'" reported a New Yorker, "came out very 'blue' having discovered a large quantity of what we call apple-jack, but they came out all square." According to the civilian account, the riders

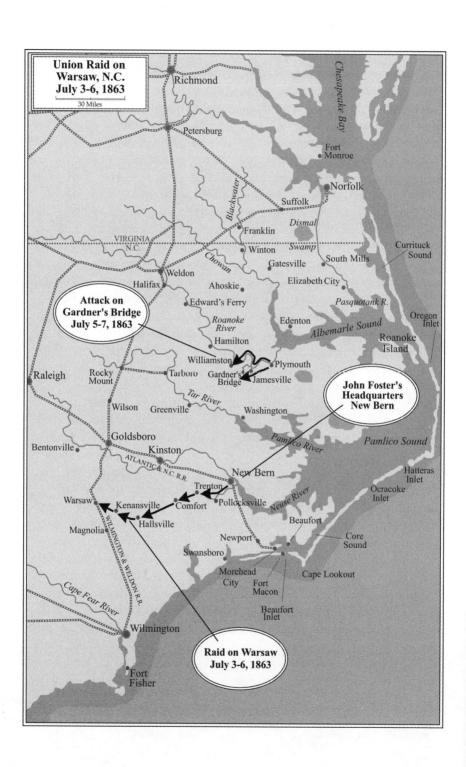

**Union Raid on Warsaw, N.C.
July 3-6, 1863**

30 Miles

Richmond

Petersburg

Fort Monroe

Norfolk

Blackwater

Suffolk

Dismal

Franklin

VIRGINIA
N.C.

Winton   *Swamp*

Currituck Sound

Chowan

Gatesville   South Mills

Weldon

Halifax   Ahoskie

Elizabeth City

**Attack on
Gardner's Bridge
July 5-7, 1863**

Edward's Ferry

Pasquotank R.

Roanoke River

Edenton

Oregon Inlet

Hamilton

Albemarle Sound

Roanoke Island

Williamston   Plymouth

Raleigh   Rocky Mount   Tarboro   Gardner's Bridge   Jamesville

**John Foster's
Headquarters
New Bern**

Tar River

Wilson   Greenville   Washington

Goldsboro

Pamlico River   *Pamlico Sound*

Bentonville   Kinston

ATLANTIC & N.C. R.R.

New Bern

Hatteras Inlet

Trenton

Ocracoke Inlet

Warsaw   Kenansville   Comfort   Pollocksville   *Neuse River*

Magnolia   Hallsville

Beaufort

Core Sound

WILMINGTON & WELDON R.R.

Newport

Swansboro

Morehead City   Fort Macon

Cape Lookout

Cape Fear River

Beaufort Inlet

Wilmington

**Raid on Warsaw
July 3-6, 1863**

Fort Fisher

Chesapeake Bay

also took tobacco and cut some of it into fragments or gave it to some enslaved people standing there, "thus inducing them to plunder to their fullest desire." Lieutenant Colonel Lewis, however, openly apologized for burning the warehouse—blaming the whiskey his men had imbibed—and reportedly handed $10 to the owner of a potato patch damaged by the artillery crews. The local witness noted that Lewis "seemed disposed to be very correct in his dealings and to replace damages done to private citizens," although surely not everyone in town shared this view. [9]

Soon, however, Lewis received a warning about approaching Confederates bent on putting a stop to his raid. Indeed, a train with fourteen empty cars had headed south to Wilmington for troops. In addition, four infantry companies and an artillery battery from Magnolia, 10 miles to the south of Warsaw, were concentrating nearby at Rusk's Bridge. Another force, Claiborne's Partisan Rangers (7th Confederate Cavalry), was speeding for Warsaw itself. To underscore the danger, rebels in the distance began to fire on Lewis's pickets posted on the roads leading into town. In the face of these threats, Lewis ordered his men back to Kenansville at 1 p.m., where he found "pickets and a strong reserve"; after an exchange that killed a horse and wounded one of the Carolina Unionists in Company L, the rebels withdrew west to Magnolia and Lewis's men rode on, taunted by civilians along the route who predicted they would never make it back. [10]

At Hallsville on Sunday evening, Lewis bivouacked for a few hours. But at 1 a.m. on Monday, July 6, he had his men back in the saddle headed for Trenton after hearing new rumors that an enemy force, J. H. Nethercutt's 8th Battalion North Carolina Partisan Rangers, lay in their path. But they found only a courier and some guerrillas in the woods. Lewis pushed on and camped for the night near Pollocksville, making it back to New Bern at noon the next day, July 7. His men had traveled 170 miles in five days and "during that time been out of the saddle less than twenty hours." In addition to destroying some property, they captured about fifty prisoners, 100 horses and mules, and brought along about 500 newly free people, including men, women, and children. [11]

The small raid increased Confederate anxiety in North Carolina and produced a round of finger-pointing. "There appears to have been a lamentable want of energy in dispatching information on the movement," concluded the *Fayetteville Observer*. The Confederates had tried to blunt the raid, albeit ineffectively. Major General William Whiting at Wilmington had attempted to organize a response, sending men under Brigadier General James Martin to pursue the Federal cavalrymen. Nethercutt's

battalion, Samuel Bunting's battery, and the 42nd North Carolina engaged Charles Heckman's rear guard at Free Bridge west of Trenton.
However, these efforts failed to bag the Yankee troopers, thanks in large
part to Heckman's efforts to protect the line of retreat.[12]

The tangible results of the raid and associated operations, however,
were limited. To the north, the diversionary strike out of Plymouth did
not yield much either, foiled by a strong current in the Roanoke River
that delayed the boats and ruined any coordination during the operation.[13] After Lewis returned to New Bern, a small controversy erupted
regarding the extent of damage done to the railroad at Warsaw. In his
report, Lewis claimed his men had destroyed "the rails for between 3 or 4
miles in both directions." However, a memorandum from Captain H. W.
Wilson, an engineer who accompanied the raid, suggested Lewis and his
men had done little to accomplish the raid's principal purpose, namely
to disable the primary artery supplying the Confederates in Virginia.[14]
Confederate accounts tended to lend credence to the engineer's report
and further signaled the futility of raids that managed to tear up only
short sections of track. The anonymous civilian in Warsaw wrote that,
"after terrible tugging and prizing," the raiders "succeeded in getting up
a few irons and sills in these places, but gave up in despair—declaring
that it was 'the damndest hard packed road'" they had ever encountered.
According to another account, the blue troopers complained that it was
"too infernal hot to tear up railroads!" Later reports also suggested the
raid had caused minimal damage. A note from a rail superintendent in a
Richmond paper confirmed that only a quarter-mile of the line had been
destroyed. In addition, according to multiple reports, the damage had
been repaired by 3 p.m. the next day, Monday, and trains were already
running that evening.[15]

"A VERY CLOSE AND HOT FIGHT"

As Foster conducted these operations in North Carolina, Kelley remained
inactive in West Virginia, much to Halleck's annoyance. The Confederates
there, however, had not been quiet. To support Lee's move north, John
Imboden's rebel cavalry had severed the Baltimore and Ohio Railroad in
late June and destroyed key bridges along that line. In addition, hoping
for a "real attack" in West Virginia, Lee urged Major General Samuel
Jones to push out and threaten Federal positions west beyond the Valley. The suggestion led to a July 1 engagement at Beverly, where, during

two days of skirmishing, Union forces under Colonel Thomas M. Harris repulsed about 2,000 Confederates under Colonel William L. Jackson.[16]

Unlike Lee, Halleck was getting no results from his own commanders in West Virginia. Finally, after a weekslong delay that was never fully explained, a raiding force departed Charleston for the Virginia and Tennessee Railroad on July 13. Colonel John Toland, leading the 34th Ohio Infantry (Mounted) and several companies from the 1st and 2nd West Virginia Cavalry, marched south toward Wytheville, a stop on the railroad in southwestern Virginia. For three days, the force struggled through the mountainous terrain, passing Oceana Court House and Tazewell (Jeffersonville) while fending off ambushes by small pockets of Confederate troops. On July 18, Toland finally reached Wytheville, only to find rebel forces waiting there for him.

Word of the raid had reached Confederate officials beforehand. From his headquarters to the east at Dublin, Samuel Jones commandeered a passenger train and sent two inexperienced militia companies and railroad employees (about 130 men in all) to Wytheville, where they were joined by armed civilians. When Toland's Federals entered the town, they rode straight into a fight. For forty-five minutes, the two sides exchanged fire, with many of the Confederates, reportedly including some women from the town, firing from inside houses on Main Street. The Federals gained ground in their initial charge but soon found the defenders too much for them. "It was a very close and hot fight, and our men and horses were falling fast," wrote a West Virginia officer. Many of the Federal cavalrymen broke under the fire, abandoning their horses and seeking personal safety. Their effectiveness declined further when their commander, Colonel William H. Powell, received a bullet in his back, perhaps the result of friendly fire. Command devolved to Lieutenant Colonel Freeman E. Franklin. Soon, the 34th Ohio arrived to support the advance and pushed forward against the rebels firing from the courthouse and nearby buildings. During the fighting, a ball also killed Colonel Toland while he was mounted and directing his troops.[17]

The Federals controlled Wytheville, at least temporarily, and some riders even reached the train depot. But soon news arrived that fresh rebel forces were near. Lieutenant Colonel Franklin, believing his entire command was in jeopardy, chose to withdraw, having accomplished next to nothing in the way of destroying railroad lines. On the return, Franklin led his command along mountain paths to avoid the pursuing Confederates and finally arrived back in camp on July 25, having lost eighty-six men (nine killed, thirty-two wounded, seventeen captured, and twenty-six missing). In contrast, the Confederates suffered about five killed and several wounded. The raid, widely reported, was viewed as a failure caused by resourceful Confederates. However, little or no attention was paid to how the operation fit into the larger context of the Gettysburg Campaign.[18]

In any event, the Wytheville Raid sounded the final echo of Halleck's effort to threaten Lee's supply lines during the Virginian's offensive into Pennsylvania. Occurring nearly a month after his original orders and weeks after the Confederate defeat at Gettysburg, it would have had little of its intended effect, even if successful. In North Carolina, Foster continued to harass the Confederate lifeline there. As the Wytheville Raid ran its course, Foster conducted another strike against the Wilmington and Weldon Railroad. This one, led by Foster's chief of staff, Brigadier General Edward Potter, headed for Rocky Mount, north of Goldsboro, and did more damage than the Warsaw foray. In addition to tearing up more track, Potter's men managed to destroy an ironclad under construction at Tarboro. But, like all the other recent efforts, the raid only caused temporary harm and did little to affect conditions in Virginia.[19]

PART FIVE
Conclusion
Looking Back

IN THE SUMMER OF 1863 during the Gettysburg Campaign, Dix's advance on Richmond captured the attention of political and military leaders at the highest levels as they weighed the operation's potential to generate dramatic results. However, in the wake of the failed effort, discussions would swiftly move to other concerns. In the months and years that followed, few would examine the operation's relationship to the Gettysburg Campaign, the possibilities it generated for the Union war effort, or its place in the context of the overall conflict.

20

The Forgotten Campaign

"ALL DAMAGE POSSIBLE"

AFTER MAJOR GENERAL JOHN DIX'S TROOPS headed back down the Peninsula to Yorktown, the public and private debates about his campaign at Richmond commenced. Even before the Fourth and Seventh Corps departed White House, Secretary of War Edwin Stanton had already weighed in back on July 7 when he informed Dix that administration officials "feel a good deal chagrined" at the operation's "slight results." In his stinging conclusion, the secretary had complained about Dix's "waste of force" and shared his aggravation over "this disappointment."[1] In doing so, Stanton appeared to reveal an understanding, shared in Washington by some, that Richmond's capture had been the expedition's primary goal.

In response, Dix took issue with Stanton's assertions and sought to tamp down any suggestion that taking the rebel capital had been the campaign's object. In his official report filed a few weeks later, he focused on the precise wording of Henry Halleck's June 14 orders, repeating the general-in-chief's directive, which had read: "All your available force should be concentrated to threaten Richmond by seizing and destroying their railroad bridges over the South and North Anna Rivers, and do them all the damage possible." In his summary, Dix highlighted the operation's modest accomplishments and obscured its failures. He emphasized the efforts to cut the rail lines and did not dwell on the fact that the RF&P bridge had been left untouched. Dix's report and later correspondence also steered clear of any suggestion that an attack against Richmond had been a serious consideration and omitted any mention of his various war councils to discuss an assault on the city. Instead, Dix focused on three goals that, in his opinion, encapsulated Halleck's orders: "(1) To threaten Richmond; (2) to destroy the railroad bridges over the South and North Anna Rivers, and do the enemy as much damage as possible; and (3) to occupy a large force of the enemy." In reflecting on these, Dix concluded he had met "the first and last of these objects" and had "at the time . . .

completely cut off Lee's communications." In his view, he had substantially accomplished the mission by effectually breaking the railroad connection between "Lee and Richmond," occupying "a large force of the
enemy," and inflicting a "very severe injury . . . on him."[2]

Although Dix remained unhappy with the criticisms from Washington,
he soon had new issues to worry about. After his return to Fort Monroe,
he consolidated his remaining forces at key locations in his department
and dutifully shuttled troops north to help Meade. A few days later, his
tenure as commander in Virginia came to an abrupt end. To the north,
after draft riots tore through New York City, officials turned to Dix,
looking for a steady hand to help quell the crisis. On July 16, he received
orders to assume command of the Department of the East, which encompassed New York, New Jersey, and New England. To replace Dix
in Virginia, the War Department installed John Foster, the commander
in North Carolina.[3] In New York, the largely administrative post suited
Dix's skills, much more so than a field command. It proved a good fit,
and Dix would ably oversee matters there through the end of the war. All
the while, he continued to vigorously support President Lincoln and the
Union war effort, putting aside any personal reservations he might have
had with some of the administration's policies.[4]

Despite Dix's successful move to New York, the friction between Dix
and Halleck regarding the Blackberry Raid persisted well beyond the former's departure from Virginia. In November, Halleck prepared an annual
report that summarized military operations over the course of 1863. In
commenting on Dix's Richmond campaign, Halleck echoed Stanton's rebuke from the previous summer. He wrote that, as Lee moved into Pennsylvania, Dix had marched all his available men up the Peninsula "for
the purpose of cutting off Lee's communications with Richmond, and
of attacking that place, which was then defended by only a handful of
militia." In Halleck's opinion, Dix's "expedition . . . failed to accomplish
a single object for which it had been fitted out."[5]

Halleck's annual report appeared in newspapers a month later and
triggered some political squabbling in the press. The solidly Republican
New-York Tribune, which called the memo a "very belligerent document" and branded Halleck "a Hunker Democrat of the most case-hard-
ened Pro-Slavery type," concluded that Halleck had refused to take any
responsibility for the military setbacks of the previous year.[6] The Dem-
ocratic-leaning *New York World* fired back and defended the general-
in-chief.[7] However, in the midst of this fracas, no one seemed confused
by Halleck's words about Dix's operations. "Gen. Dix is sharply rapped

over the knuckles for his campaign against Richmond," concluded the *New York Times.*[8]

The official censure by Halleck predictably displeased Dix, who was by then in New York tending to his newly acquired department. In a December letter, he took issue with the report, once again emphasizing the actual wording of the June 14 orders. "It will be perceived that an attack on Richmond was not a part of the plan," he explained. "That city is understood to be nearly as strongly fortified as Vicksburg, and only to be taken by regular siege." He also objected to an assertion in Halleck's report that "only a handful of militia" defended Richmond. Dix correctly observed that the letters between Lee and Richmond officials captured in late June revealed that the city not only contained Wise's brigade and the usual local defense troops but also three veteran brigades under D. H. Hill. Dix then added that, by destroying the Virginia Central bridge and tearing up portions of the RF&P line, his men achieved the campaign's object to cut Lee's communications. "To myself, this correction of a statement, which I am sure is inadvertent, is of less consequence than to the gallant troops under my command," he concluded. "For their sake I ask permission to give publicity to this letter, or to my report of the expedition."[9]

In a response prepared several days later, Halleck declined to authorize Dix's note for publication but suggested Congress would release it officially at a later date. He regretted any offense. "I certainly had no intention to reflect upon you, or to find any fault with you as the commanding general of the department," he pleaded. However, Halleck dug in on his overall assessment and emphasized that, in his view, Dix had simply not accomplished the mission's objectives. Halleck acknowledged he should have used the word "threaten" instead of "attack" in his discussion about Richmond but otherwise brushed the issue aside, claiming one word implied the other and, in any case, he had no time to pore over the reports or otherwise discuss the controversy. In wrapping up, he sought to smooth Dix's feathers, saying that "while much disappointment was felt here at what was considered a failure of the expedition, no blame whatever was attached to you . . . [and] perhaps no blame should have been attributed to any one."[10]

In the spat with Halleck, Dix managed to have the last word. His memoir, prepared by his son and released in 1883 after the general's death, contained a previously unpublished memorandum defending his performance during the Blackberry Raid. The document, written in the third person but probably drafted by Dix himself, repeated arguments in his original campaign report and his December 1863 letter to Halleck. It stressed that the operation "was never designed to attack Richmond" but instead was conducted to "engage the attention of the enemy and prevent him from sending re-enforcements to General Lee, and to destroy his railroad communications over the South Anna." The memorandum also addressed at some length questions about the size of the forces involved in the campaign. Although the piece correctly pointed out that others had underestimated the Confederate strength at Richmond, it wrongly asserted the opposing sides were equal. In fact, Dix did have more men, about 20,000 to the rebels' approximately 13,000. The memorandum also emphasized the interior lines and superior communications enjoyed by the Confederates, which allowed them to concentrate troops and prevent a coup-de-main.[11] But, as with his official report, it provided no mention that Dix had seriously considered an attack on Richmond itself, despite his contemporary correspondence and accounts revealing otherwise.

"ACCOUNTABILITY FOR THIS MISFORTUNE"

As Halleck and Dix argued, the Northern press weighed in on the operation against Richmond. In the effort's immediate wake, newspaper accounts tended to praise Dix or simply pass along assessments from him or his staff. A short piece in the *Boston Post* and other papers, for instance, noted Dix arrived at Fort Monroe on July 9 and reported "that the expedition had been a perfect success . . . having effectually destroyed all communication between Richmond and Lee's army."[12] Editors of the *New York Commercial Advertiser* also concluded that Dix had conducted an effective feint, managing to "amuse and play upon the fears of the rebels," and had understandably refrained from throwing his men against the "bristling battlements of a second Fredericksburg,"[13] *The Cavalier*, the Williamsburg newspaper published by officers in Erasmus Keyes's command, amplified the ovations, concluding that Dix's achievements furnished "ample compensation for the outlay of life, time and money."[14]

Not surprisingly, a political element infused the reporting. Because some observers viewed Dix as a viable Democratic candidate to challenge President Lincoln in the upcoming election of 1864, many watched the general's military performance closely for signs that might shape his fortunes in such a contest. Assessments of Dix followed a pattern. The *New York World*, known for its Copperhead views, praised Dix's performance outside Richmond, explaining that the "affair has resulted in as much legitimate damage to the rebel government and cause . . . as possible under the circumstances." The newspaper also commended Dix for his prudence. Although such an assault "might be brave," one *World* editorial explained, it "would have been fool hearty, when equal forces were waiting in deep and strong entrenchments for his approach." The *World* concluded that the expedition had "resulted in what it was intended for, excepting the failure to destroy the last bridge over the South Anna."[15] In addition, in line with Dix's own reports, W. H. Stiner, a *New York Daily Herald* correspondent, suggested Dix had "added fresh laurels to his fame as a far-sighted and able commander."[16]

But newspapers of other stripes took a dim view of Dix's efforts at Richmond. The solidly Republican *Semi-Weekly Wisconsin* declared that the "right kind of General" would have captured the rebel capital, but it did not expect such a result from Dix, "who is one of the most cautious of men, and would make no venture where there was a doubt of success." William Cramer, the paper's Republican editor, labeled the general an "incipient candidate for Presidency" belonging to the "war democracy," whose members "claim they are entitled to the next Union candidate."[17] Horace Greeley's *New-York Tribune* also criticized the operation, though the paper went straight at Henry Halleck and largely bypassed Dix. "General Halleck cannot escape his share—and it is a large one—of accountability for this misfortune," declared Greeley's editorial page. Halleck was to blame for "the imbecile strategy which kept the forces of Gen. Dix promenading on the Peninsula, while a decisive struggle was pending in Pennsylvania." Dix's presence outside Richmond was "useless," Greeley's paper added, because the destruction of Lee's army would have transformed the rebel capital into "a ripe apple waiting to drop into our hands."[18]

The campaign also received some attention during congressional hearings in 1864 held by the Joint Committee on the Conduct of the War, a forum for Republican senators to buoy Joseph Hooker at George Meade's expense. When asked about the best use of Dix's troops during Lee's offensive, Hooker was characteristically full of ideas. On one hand, he confirmed that nothing prevented Dix's force from coming north to operate against the Army of Northern Virginia. On the other, he viewed an attack on the Confederate capital as a real possibility. There was nothing "to prevent [Dix's] troops going into Richmond." Hooker asserted, albeit incorrectly, that "Richmond had been stripped of everything but a police force" and that no other troops were "within two or three days' march of there." And, once Dix's men left the Peninsula to aid Meade, Hooker testified that "the proper place to have sent these men . . . would have been on the south side of the Potomac, for the purpose of preventing Lee's army from crossing."[19]

"NOT A GREAT SOLDIER, NOR A MAN WHO COULD GET ENERGETIC"

Over time, any laurels attached to the campaign wilted. The glowing assessments printed immediately after Dix and his men marched back down the Peninsula were overtaken by unfavorable conclusions when veterans and historians mentioned the Blackberry Raid in their books, articles, and letters. Although the event was largely forgotten among the slew of other, more prominent campaigns and operations, it occasionally received attention.[20] In 1908, for instance, *National Tribune* editor and staunch Republican John McElroy wrote a scathing assessment of the operation as part of a series on the Chancellorsville and Gettysburg Campaigns. Echoing the criticisms made by Stanton and Halleck decades before, McElroy, himself a veteran, wrote that Richmond's capture should have been "an easy matter" if only Dix and his officers had handled their troops "with boldness and skill" against the weak enemy garrison. He contended that a more "energetic commander" would have brought more men with him, would not have dallied at White House, would not have advertised his plans to the enemy, and would not have hesitated to march on Richmond. McElroy, who viewed Dix's efforts as a "mortification to the Administration," added that Dix was "not a great soldier, nor a man who could get energetic, effective service out of the subordinates given to him."[21]

In reviewing the results and accounts of the campaign, McElroy found Dix's report "full of the old familiar excuses employed when an incompetent commander attempts to get results out of incompetent and unwilling subordinates." He saved some acid for Keyes and that officer's "long story" full of excuses related to exhaustion, warm weather, the lack of supplies, and other explanations often raised by "non-performers."[22] A similar assessment appeared five years later in an unattributed, stock column published in newspapers across the country. The piece concluded that the "almost characterless" operation conducted with "so little dash and energy . . . was productive of discontent and disappointment" in Washington.[23]

Other veterans reflected on the campaign. Most of the regiments in the Fourth and Seventh Corps never gained the fame enjoyed by other units during the war. In the summer of 1863, many were either newly formed or had spent most of the conflict in backwater commands, and few observers considered them frontline troops. Only weeks after the operation's conclusion, the War Department disbanded both the Fourth Corps and the Seventh Corps and reassigned their component regiments to the Eighteenth Corps, a formation that had been created a few months before from units stationed in North Carolina. In 1864, the Eighteenth Corps would participate in the Richmond–Petersburg Campaign as part of the Army of the James.[24]

In recalling the Blackberry Raid, these veterans looked back with a mix of bitterness and regret. During the operation, many in the rank-and-file expected to capture Richmond. But the miles of miserable, unproductive marching and the operation's limited results deflated them.[25] "The expedition was substantially a failure," recalled a Connecticut veteran, "and the troops felt disheartened as they turned their faces again to the rear."[26] William Hyde, in his history of the 112th New York, lamented the fact that more had not been done during the campaign. He called out Keyes in particular and generally concluded that the "men capable of executing a plan requiring so much vigor and system[] had not yet appeared in the Department of Virginia."[27] To James Mowris, writing about the 117th New York, the "most notable features of this expedition, so far as the soldiers were concerned, were the severity of the march, and the profusion of blackberries."[28]

The regimental historian for the 130th New York, J. R. Bowen, addressed the expedition extensively in his unit's history. He knew historians and other observers were of different minds about the campaign. For instance, *New-York Tribune* editor Horace Greeley considered the effort a "bona fide" attempt to capture Richmond, while Joel T. Headley, historian and onetime editor of the *Tribune*, viewed the operation merely as a feint to hold Confederates in the city. Bowen himself had a decidedly negative impression of the offensive and tended to agree with those who labeled it "one of the most illy advised, worst executed, and fruitless military movements of the war." He was also highly critical of Dix's and especially Keyes's leadership. "Instead of a bold and determined attack, our timorous general only puttered around," Bowen wrote, "skirmishing a little here and there, and accomplished nothing worthy [of] the cost of the movement." In his view, Colonel Samuel Spear had been the operation's saving grace.[29]

Some of the old soldiers also dwelled on the opportunities lost. There was "no time during the war when a bold and rapid dash would have secured us a victory, as on that occasion, and none where it was so foolishly thrown away" reflected Colonel Samuel Tolles of the 15th Connecticut. "Nine days were consumed in doing what should have been done in two." Sheldon Thorpe, the regiment's historian, added that "Dix's poor leadership" had prevented one of the war's "grandest successes." By the end of the campaign, failure was "written all over the enterprise" and "made this once proud command hang its head in humiliation." For the members of the regiment, their impression of Dix's 1863 Richmond campaign evolved over the following years into a "theme of banter ridicule."[30]

21

Questions of Supply

"SAFELY ACROSS"

ALTHOUGH SOME VETERANS AND HISTORIANS would discuss the merits of Dix's Richmond campaign in the weeks, months, and years following its conclusion, few weighed the operation's actual impacts on Robert E. Lee's campaign into Pennsylvania. Much of the postmortem focused on whether Dix should have attacked Richmond directly, or whether his forces should have inflicted more damage to the rails and bridges north of Richmond, or whether Halleck should have directed Dix to conduct the operation in the first place. There was no examination into whether the campaign's most tangible result—the destruction of the Virginia Central bridge at the South Anna on June 26, 1863—had affected Lee's operations before and after the Battle of Gettysburg. In other words, did the campaign make any difference?

After Dix's withdrawal from White House and Lee's retreat from Gettysburg, the Army of Northern Virginia remained vulnerable. With Lee's force still largely untethered well north of Richmond, the impact of Dix's operations on the railroads outside Richmond retained relevance in the days and weeks that followed. A few days after the battle, Lee's column made it to the Potomac at Williamsport; it remained there for nearly a week, trapped on the north bank by a rain-swollen river. Packed into a strong line of earthworks, Lee's men waited until the waters began to recede and finally crossed on a pontoon bridge at Falling Waters just below Williamsport on July 13 and 14. George S. Bernard, a private in the 12th Virginia, recalled the affair: "By midday Tuesday the rear guard was safely across. How rejoiced we were at the idea of being once more on Confederate soil."[1]

Throughout the standoff at Williamsport, George Meade held back and did not assault the strong earthworks shielding Lee's beleaguered forces, a decision that disappointed President Lincoln and War Department officials who had hoped the Gettysburg victory would lead to the Army of Northern Virginia's annihilation. Once over the Potomac, Lee's units filtered into the Shenandoah Valley and would consume another two weeks making their way over the Blue Ridge and back to their positions on the Rappahannock. During this period, a cautious Meade kept his units east of the Blue Ridge, shielding Washington and shadowing the gray columns while looking for chances to drive through mountain passes and cut the rebel army in two. Such an opportunity arose on July 23 when William French's Third Corps sliced through Manassas Gap and attacked units from Richard Anderson's Confederate division at Wapping Heights east of Front Royal. But the engagement led to nothing, and by July 24 most of Lee's army had safely reached Culpeper behind the Rapidan River.[2]

Throughout this dance in late July, Lee's communications remained exposed. His most direct line ran through the mountain gaps and roads linking the Valley to the railheads at Gordonsville and Culpeper. In addition, he continued to rely on the Valley connection to the depot at Staunton, with its link to Richmond via Charlottesville and Gordonsville. As Meade's army lumbered south, it threatened these connections but never managed to seriously imperil the Army of Northern Virginia. Other Federal units posed risks to Lee's army as well. Throughout much of July, Halleck and Stanton repeatedly urged Brigadier General Benjamin Kelley in West Virginia to attack the retreating Confederate forces in the Valley.[3] However, when Kelley emerged from the mountains with 6,000 men, he could do little more than skirmish with Confederate cavalry near Martinsburg and soon withdrew to Cherry Grove on the Potomac to preserve his line of retreat.[4] By July 25, the bulk of Lee's army safely arrived in Culpeper and resumed its positions behind the Rappahannock, a posture it would maintain until active operations resumed during the Bristoe Campaign in October.

"BUSILY EMPLOYED REPAIRING"

After Dix's campaign at Richmond faded into the past, few considered whether the Federal efforts at Richmond had harmed Lee's army during the Gettysburg Campaign. In the end, it was clear that the Federal effort to cut Lee's communications had failed to generate decisive results. None of Halleck's schemes could be considered a success. The raids against Wytheville in southwestern Virginia and Warsaw in North Carolina inflicted little more than superficial wounds, causing only minor damage to

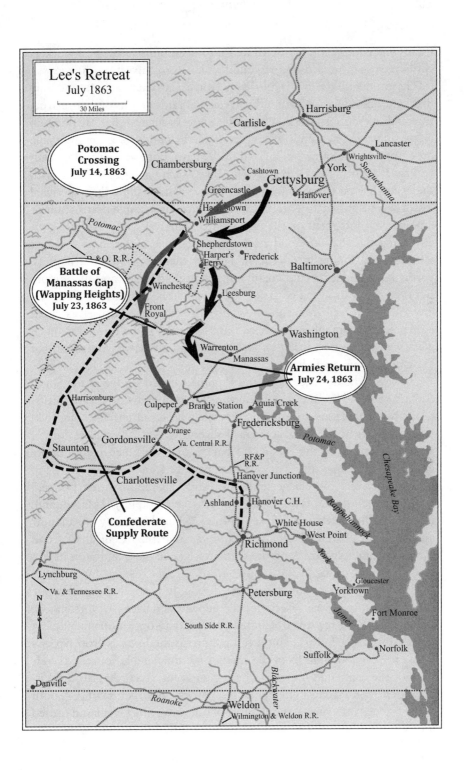

Lee's Retreat
July 1863

30 Miles

Potomac
Crossing
July 14, 1863

Battle of
Manassas Gap
(Wapping Heights)
July 23, 1863

Armies Return
July 24, 1863

Confederate
Supply Route

N

Harrisburg
Carlisle
Lancaster
Wrightsville
Chambersburg
Cashtown
York
Greencastle
Gettysburg
Hanover
Hagerstown
Williamsport
Shepherdstown
B.&O. R.R.
Harper's
Ferry
Frederick
Winchester
Baltimore
Front
Royal
Leesburg
Washington
Warrenton
Manassas
Harrisonburg
Culpeper
Brandy Station
Aquia Creek
Orange
Fredericksburg
Gordonsville
Va. Central R.R.
Potomac
Staunton
RF&P
R.R.
Charlottesville
Hanover Junction
Ashland
Hanover C.H.
White House
Rappahannock
West Point
Chesapeake Bay
Richmond
York
Lynchburg
Va. & Tennessee R.R.
Gloucester
Petersburg
Yorktown
Fort Monroe
James
South Side R.R.
Suffolk
Norfolk
Danville
Blackwater
Roanoke
Weldon
Wilmington & Weldon R.R.

tracks and equipment. Confederate railroad administrators and workers easily repaired the torn-up lines and the damaged culverts within days.

These operations in Virginia and North Carolina in June and July highlight questions about the effectiveness of raids on railroad infrastructure and operations. The results of these forays suggest that breaking up a few miles of track and burning a couple of buildings generally made little impact. The same can be said of the harm done at Ashland by Federal cavalry during Dix's expedition. Unless such damage coincided with the enemy's vital troop movements or crucial shipments, the superficial losses served mostly to harass. In the absence of massive destruction or a permanent lodgment on the line, Confederate railroad personnel, usually using slave labor, could repair track sections within hours. Target selection and timing were crucial. The destruction of larger structures, particularly bridges, could create longer-lasting damage and disruption. But even the destruction of major bridges could be mitigated with ferries and alternative rail routes, and usually the structures themselves could be repaired in a manner of weeks. But ultimately, while there was much glamor in such raids, it is reasonable to wonder what impacts many of these operations really had.

However, the destruction of the Virginia Central Bridge at the South Anna by Samuel Spear's cavalry on June 26, though by no means devastating to Confederate operations, may have been more than a pinprick. Bridge repairs at the river consumed several weeks. As early as July 9, reports appeared in the Richmond papers that workmen were "busily employed repairing" the span.[5] In fact, engineers and laborers were unable to complete the bridge until late July. "The South Anna Bridge," noted the *Staunton Spectator* on July 7, "is being rapidly replaced, and, is hoped, will in a few weeks be completed."[6] Finally, on July 28, a report appeared in the *Daily Richmond Examiner* that the "Central Railroad is again running its trains on the regular schedule time, and with its full complement of trains."[7]

Ultimately, the loss of the bridge during July affected Confederate operations, though the severity of the impacts is unclear. Unfortunately, the few surviving records of Confederate railroad operations in Virginia during July 1863 fail to paint a full picture of the impacts from Spear's raid. However, judging from the smattering of available sources, the effects of the campaign may have been significant. According to the Virginia Central Railroad's 1863 annual report, the destruction of the South Anna Bridge "interrupted the running of trains to some extent and caused a loss of revenue." The company further reported that trains were "run on the track of the Richmond, Fredericksburg, and Potomac Railroad Company, between Richmond and Hanover Junction, until July 25th." The company report, however, did not specify when such an arrangement began.[8]

Other evidence points to disruption of service along the line. Specifically, a July 7 notice in the *Staunton Spectator* informed readers that the bridge's destruction had completely stalled railroad service from the capital. "We have had no trains from Richmond since Friday last, and no telegraphic communication, as the Yankees have destroyed a bridge and cut the wires." In addition, a few extant records from officials in the Confederate Quartermaster Department suggest grain shipments may have halted altogether for a few weeks following Spear's raid. Those records show no shipments received at locations north of the South Anna, such as the stations at Beaverdam and Gordonsville, during that period— although reasons other than the bridge's destruction, such as the lack of demand at those stations at the time, may have played a part. After July 17, the official quartermaster reports reveal that grain shipments resumed but generally in reduced quantities, at least until the end of the month.[9] In addition, *The Cavalier*, the newspaper run by Federal troops in Yorktown, reported that "all communication of the rebel army of Lee with Richmond was temporarily, at least, severed."[10] Furthermore, other reports suggest supply problems arose as Lee withdrew to Culpeper. On July 24, the Quartermaster Department in Richmond informed officials to the south that forage was "indispensably necessary here for General Lee's army. Send forward all grain rapidly in your reach."[11] These various accounts, however, do not definitively establish an extended break in service. In fact, other information suggests that the railroad continued to operate. For example, a few brief notices in the *Richmond Enquirer* refer to passengers arriving in the capital by train from Staunton in the week after Spear's raid. These newspaper stories, however, did not clarify whether freight was running at the time along the line.[12]

Whether or not Dix's operations disrupted service, it seems unlikely the destruction of the South Anna Bridge seriously affected Lee's army. Once in Pennsylvania, the Confederates freely foraged from local farms, so much so that the army not only fed itself but also allowed subsistence officers and quartermasters to send supplies by the wagonload back into Virginia. Lee's declaration to Davis in late June that he had abandoned his lines of communication and would no longer rely on supplies from the south reveals his confidence in the Pennsylvania stores. However, at the same time, Lee did not intend to cut loose his army completely from his supply connections. Although his army could pilfer food from the Pennsylvania farms, he could not obtain artillery shells or troops there. In fact, Porter Alexander noted that the intense barrage preceding Pickett's Charge on July 3 threatened to deplete the ordnance on hand.[13] Accordingly, following the battle, Lee needed to maintain a connection to Virginia to ensure that ammunition could reach his army.[14]

Ultimately, any ammunition shortage following Gettysburg did not impair Lee's army because Lee's force received ample ammunition after the battle and the army did not fight any large engagements for the rest of July. Indeed, ordnance shipments from Richmond continued to reach Lee during much of his foray north. At least until June 26, Lee's army received supplies from material off-loaded onto wagons at the Staunton rail depot and driven north along the Valley Turnpike to the Potomac.[15] After the Army of Northern Virginia crossed north over that river, Lee received at least two large ordnance wagon trains to augment what his troops originally carried into Pennsylvania. Both shipments managed to reach Staunton before Spear's attack on the South Anna Bridge.

First, a "large number of wagons and teams" captured at Winchester were sent back along with ammunition wagons to "Staunton to be filled," according to William Allan, Richard Ewell's chief ordnance officer. Allan sent instructions to Josiah Gorgas in Richmond "to secure ammunition to fill them," and within a few days such supplies were sent by railroad to Staunton, where a "large train was loaded and brought back to the army" and arrived at Chambersburg "some days before the battle." "I cannot recall the number of wagons but it was large and the supply obtained very considerable," wrote Allan. The fresh ammunition was distributed throughout the army.[16]

Second, at least one other wagon train carrying ordnance made its way down the Valley to Lee sometime in late June. The 54th North Carolina, from Robert Hoke's brigade, had remained in the Valley to guard the prisoners captured at Winchester. At some point following the battle there, the regiment escorted the prisoners to Staunton and then accompanied them on the train to Richmond. The Tar Heels eventually returned to Staunton and marched for several days north along the Valley Turnpike, reaching Winchester on July 3. The next day, the regiment, along with the 58th Virginia, received orders to guard a large ordnance train that had traveled to Winchester from Staunton.[17] The wagons and the regiments reached Williamsport on July 5 just as Lee's force reached the swollen Potomac and began to exchange fire with the pursuing Federals.[18] John Imboden recalled that, when one of the Confederate batteries ran out of shells at the river, "two wagon-loads of ammunition" from an ordnance train that had arrived from Winchester "were ferried across the river and run upon the field behind the guns, and the boxes tumbled out, to be broken open with axes. With this fresh supply our guns were all soon in full play again."[19]

Other evidence points to ordnance shipments rolling through the Valley during the campaign. On June 30, an Augusta County resident's diary entry indicates that "wagon trains going from Staunton to Winchester are now required to be guarded. A train is waiting till a guard of five hundred men can be formed of convalescent soldiers."[20] In addition, a July 9 report circulated in various newspapers that an ordnance train had made it to Martinsburg, about 30 miles north of Winchester.[21]

These wagon trains arriving during Lee's withdrawal back into Virginia no doubt significantly improved matters for his army. In all likelihood, the wagonloads replaced a substantial portion of the rounds expended during the three days of intense fighting at Gettysburg. On July 10, Lee confirmed as much when he informed President Davis that the "army is in good condition, and we have a good supply of ammunition."[22] Accordingly, these shipments from Staunton certainly helped fill limber chests and cartridge boxes as Lee's units wound their way through the Valley and the Blue Ridge gaps on their way back to the Rappahannock.

While these various reports clearly demonstrate that Confederate supplies trundled north from Staunton during Lee's campaign in Pennsylvania, it is not clear whether any of these shipments reached Staunton after the South Anna Bridge was destroyed. In the end, though, it did not matter. The troops under Lee appear to have had adequate supplies throughout July. Ultimately, the loss of the Virginia Central bridge at the South Anna seems to have been little more than an inconvenience to Confederate subsistence and quartermaster officers, mostly because ample shipments were already on their way to Lee's army prior to Spear's raid and, after Gettysburg, Confederate forces used up little ammunition in July. However, if George Getty's force had managed to eliminate the RF&P span and if significant fighting had occurred during Lee's retreat, Confederates officials would have faced serious difficulties in supplying the Army of Northern Virginia. In the end, no such break occurred.

22

The Broader Scope

"HISSED AND HOOTED AS HE RODE ALONG THE LINE"

AFTER THE WAR, HISTORIANS AND VETERANS would occasionally mention John Dix's Richmond offensive. However, few recognized that the operation formed part of Henry Halleck's loose effort to threaten the supply lines feeding Virginia and Robert E. Lee's army during the Gettysburg Campaign. In isolation, the raids against the South Anna bridges, the tracks at Warsaw, and the depot at Wytheville resembled dozens of other expeditions conducted during the conflict. On the face of it, there was little to signal that these particular operations actually formed the diverse elements of Halleck's half-hearted scheme to threaten Lee's communications as the Army of Northern Virginia advanced into Pennsylvania. In cobbling together these disparate efforts, Halleck sought to respond to Lee's incursion indirectly and to do more than simply react to the Virginian's movements and funnel reinforcements north to protect Washington.

Halleck's plan, if it can be called that, had promise. In ordering Dix to move on Richmond, approving Foster's raid in North Carolina, and calling for a strike against the railroad in western Virginia, he sowed the seeds of a promising counterblow. However, he never cultivated these various elements into a coherent, effective program. If there had been greater urgency, more aggressive officers, additional men, more specificity in orders, or greater commitment from Washington, perhaps these efforts would have yielded more. In the end, these operations were indifferently coordinated, inadequately managed, and for the most part poorly executed.

To be sure, there were many other priorities at the time. Halleck's focus on the details of managing the Army of the Potomac and its new commander, George Meade, not to mention the various departments responding to Lee's incursion, may have prevented him from developing and coordinating a more effective counterstroke to the Confederate invasion. Alternatively, Halleck and other administration officials may have simply believed that the need to repulse Lee's army crowded out consideration of nearly all else. In any event, the spare results of Dix's efforts highlight the absence of any effective, harmonized approach at the time. Halleck, in particular, had much to juggle in June 1863 as he tracked Grant's progress at Vicksburg and coordinated the response to Lee's offensive, which had triggered a full crisis in Washington. He was undoubtedly distracted, a fact reflected in his infrequent communications with the commanders in the Virginia and North Carolina Departments—Dix, Foster, and Kelley.

Halleck's dispatches to Dix suggest he never settled on a clear goal for the mission at the Confederate capital. As the campaign heated up in Pennsylvania, Halleck became increasingly concerned about bringing more troops north to support Meade and the Federal army there. He did not push the operation at Richmond or send additional troops to that location, aside from a handful of weak regiments from New Bern. In addition, his orders never clearly identified Richmond's capture as a priority. Furthermore, in the first days of July, Halleck's communications revealed that he no longer had serious expectations for the rebel capital, effectively eliminating any sense of urgency for Dix's effort.

Overall, the entire campaign at Richmond demonstrated a cautiousness emblematic of similar Federal operations in the war's first years. More aggressive oversight from Halleck, coupled with more troops from other departments (e.g., a larger share of the 20,000 troops then in North Carolina) and additional support, might have yielded a different result. However, given the conditions and information available to Halleck and other Union officials at the time, a full, committed operation against Richmond did not qualify as the prudent approach in light of the eminent threat posed by Lee's offensive. Following the Blackberry Raid, Halleck remained in his role as general-in-chief until early the next year, when Lincoln would give Ulysses S. Grant overall command of US forces. Grant's ascension would shift Halleck into the position of "chief of staff," where he would attend to the logistical and administrative details of managing the various armies and departments—a role perhaps better suited to his skills and personality. After the war, he would remain with the army, serving in various low-profile posts in California and the South.

While Halleck may have furnished only vague directions and may not have poured energy and resources into the operation, John Dix's performance was not without its own blemishes. Ultimately, Dix chose the cautious path by not attempting a direct attack on Richmond, an approach consistent with a narrow, literal interpretation of Halleck's orders. In addition, he and his generals failed to fully achieve the more modest objective of destroying both rail bridges at the South Anna. His decision to forgo an attack on the city reflected a focus on avoiding defeat at the expense of possible victory, a victory that would have likely changed the war's course. Instead of moving aggressively against the Confederate capital and risking a repulse and perhaps high casualties in the process, he chose to minimize his own liabilities and limit his operations. Indeed, Assistant Secretary of the Navy Gustavus Fox was perhaps not far off when he complained that "Dix contents himself with raids that inflict no injury except upon the feelings of the enemy."[1]

Dix's prudence extended beyond the battlefield. Throughout June and July, he remained concerned about civilian property and stuck to his belief in moderation in dealing with Confederate civilians.[2] Dix's warning against unnecessary destruction no doubt tempered the aggression of operations during the Blackberry Raid, forcing his officers to make judgments in the field about what property qualified as legitimate targets and to constantly police their troops to prevent and punish the type of destruction that occurred during Getty's march in King William County. Debate over these issues would continue throughout the war as Grant, William Sherman, Phil Sheridan, and other commanders began to apply a more aggressive "hard war" approach to the conflict in the following years.

This is not to say, however, that Dix was clearly wrong or unreasonable in his decision to limit his operations to the rail bridges; neither is it clear that his policies toward civilians and their property materially affected the campaign's outcome. Spear's initial failure to destroy the RF&P bridge at the South Anna left a portion of Dix's mission unfulfilled and may have discouraged him from committing to a strong, direct strike against Richmond itself. Dix also correctly surmised that the number of troops defending Richmond was greater than many in the North estimated.[3] In fact, Dix did not enjoy the advantage imagined by the detractors at the time and afterward. During the operation, he brought about 20,000 to White House and faced about 13,000 defenders in and around Richmond, including three veteran brigades. Such odds did not create an overwhelming advantage for the attacker, particularly against defenders in strong fortifications. As such, a drive against Richmond's lines would have been a gamble. But Dix was not a gambling man, and he chose the more cautious approach. His decision to limit his attacks to the railroad bridges reflected the conservative strategy often employed by Federal commanders in Virginia up to that point in the war. Given this track record and Dix's mindset, the results of the campaign are not surprising.

However, Dix was off the mark in his subsequent assertions that an assault against the city was never contemplated. In fact, he understood that an attack on the capital was in the cards, a fact exposed by his decision to hold several councils of war at his White House base to weigh that very possibility. He did not hide those discussions at the time. In his official report, however, he omitted any mention of those deliberations. Instead, in an apparent effort to parry critics in Washington who expected more, Dix's report and subsequent communications focused on the specific wording of Halleck's June 14 orders and proceeded, over the course of many pages, to catalog how he had successfully threatened the city, tied up its defenders, and partially cut its rail lines.

To be fair, Dix was hampered by Halleck's somewhat vague orders, which never clearly identified Richmond as the operation's target. Neither Halleck nor anyone else in the high command gave Dix an unequivocal directive to seize the city. In fact, even as Getty pushed off toward the South Anna, Halleck began urging Dix to wrap things up and send more men north to help concentrate strength there. Further, Dix, like Halleck, understood that there were priorities elsewhere. A Confederate victory in the Pennsylvania countryside or, worse yet, the capture of a major Northern city such as Philadelphia or Baltimore, could have dealt a fatal blow to the Union war effort. Accordingly, in early July, Dix certainly understood that a strike against Richmond was becoming less and less of a priority given the need to drive Lee and his Army of Northern Virginia back south. Therefore, the limited scope of his offensive stemmed as much from competing Federal priorities as it did from his innate conservatism.

However, whether or not Dix should have directly attacked Richmond, it is important to underscore that his force achieved only partial success in its limited mission to destroy both rail bridges at the South Anna, a fact obscured by larger debates. In short, Dix left the RF&P bridge intact. Ultimately, in light of this failure, it appears that the operation suffered from a deficit of urgency and resolve among US officers in the field in meeting those objectives. At nearly every turn, the Federal commanders—many of whom had only limited battlefield experience—acted cautiously. On June 26, Samuel Spear, perhaps Dix's most aggressive commander at the time and rightly lauded for reaching and destroying the Virginia Central bridge, chose not to press on to the RF&P bridge after hearing unconfirmed, ultimately false reports that a large Confederate force was there. Spear's decision forced Dix to return to the South Anna and spoiled the element of surprise for any further attempts at the vital rail span.

In addition, Erasmus Keyes conducted an astonishingly feeble demonstration during his effort to threaten Bottom's Bridge in New Kent County. When faced with the slightest opposition, he recoiled and ensconced his command at Talleysville, a precipitous withdrawal that endangered Dix's supply base at White House Landing. Keyes's reflexive caution prevented him from getting anywhere near his objective and helping the Union offensive. His bumbling would have allowed even the most thickheaded Confederate commander to conclude that the Federals were conducting only a feint in his front. D. H. Hill was not fooled and managed to strike out at Keyes while sending ample reinforcements to the South Anna.

George Washington Getty, who would excel later in the war, also made questionable decisions during his expedition to the South Anna in the first days of July. Apparently concerned with securing his return route or perhaps overly mindful of Dix's orders to guard the bridges in his rear, he dropped off large numbers of men along the march at Horn Quarter, Littlepage's Bridge, and Hanover Court House. By the time his command reached its final target, it only carried a third of its original strength. Getty's bread-crumb strategy reflected a conservative, conventional course of action that ensured his safe return. However, alternative approaches were certainly possible. That summer in the Mississippi Valley, for instance, Grant and Sherman were perfecting a different course, one they would employ to good effect in campaigns the following year. Instead of spreading their strength along the route to cover their communications, Grant and Sherman showed no hesitation in driving large, concentrated forces into enemy country with little regard to securing their lines of communication behind them, often because they did not return the way they came. The pair would follow or recommend such a strategy not only at Vicksburg but also during the Meridian Campaign, in Grant's proposed but unrealized operation into North Carolina (the so-called Suffolk Plan), in Georgia, in the Carolinas, and in Grant's lunge at Five Forks outside Petersburg. Such ideas were not particularly novel. In fact, one of Dix's officers, George Gordon, had suggested marching the raiding column to the South Anna and then continuing north to the Federal depot at Aquia Creek. Such a move would obviate the need to guard bridges in the rear. However, neither Dix nor Getty embraced the proposal, and Getty, in conformance with Dix's plan, chose to leave about half of his strength along the route of march behind his attacking column.

Getty made other questionable calls. He chose not to accompany the sharp end of his operation and instead placed a young, less-experienced officer, Robert Foster, in charge. In addition, he did not adequately communicate urgency to Foster, who appeared only to go through the motions at the RF&P bridge, limiting his effort to a four-company probe while leaving several whole regiments, all his artillery, and most of the cavalry—including the most aggressive commander in Dix's entire department, Samuel Spear—idle in the darkness by the side of the road.

In the wake of the Blackberry Raid, Dix's subordinates went their separate ways. The campaign would prove fatal to Erasmus Keyes's military career. During the march back down the Peninsula, his men "hissed and hooted as he rode along the line," at least according to an unhappy veteran years later.[4] In the summer of 1863, Keyes would not remain in command for long. In August, with Dix off to New York, the War Department broke up the Fourth Corps, leaving Keyes without any troops to lead.[5] Over the coming months, he occupied himself with various administrative duties and served for a stint on a retirement board for disabled officers. Finally, realizing he would never receive another command, he resigned in early May 1864. After the war, he moved to California, where he served as an executive for a gold-mining company, established the Edge Hill Vineyard, and helped form the vine-culture society. He spent the last years of his life wintering in southern France and summering on Lake Geneva.[6]

George Getty continued to serve in Virginia throughout the war, commanding troops in the Sixth Corps at Petersburg and during Philip Sheridan's Valley Campaign, where he performed well in contrast to his efforts in the summer of 1863. He remained with the army until his retirement in the 1880s.[7]

Samuel Spear, who commanded the only successful effort of the campaign, also stayed with the army. Despite his extensive war experience, little has been written about him. After the conflict, he served in the Irish Republican Army within the Fenian Movement along with fellow Department of Virginia veteran Charles Carroll Tevis, the commander of the Aylett's raid. After his death from "rheumatic gout" in 1875, the following sad note appeared in several obituaries: "His wife and little daughter and a few old friends were the only mourners in the cheerless little room, and a stranger read the burial service."[8]

"HE IS A REAL HERO"

For all the Federals' mistakes, the Confederates had something to do with the campaign's failure. The rebels acted with urgency because they had to. The loss of Richmond would have most likely shortened the life of the rebellion significantly, shrinking the Confederacy's size, severing Robert E. Lee's logistical net, and displacing the seat of government. Outnumbered and operating in their own territory, Confederate commanders took chances, acted aggressively, and sought to seize the initiative wherever they could. While Arnold Elzey and Custis Lee juggled the city's defense, Secretary Seddon and even President Davis delved into the tactical details of operations. And even though these men certainly contributed to Richmond's protection, D. H. Hill and his brigade commanders served as the heart of the defensive effort. Hill, deftly using Ransom's, Jenkins's, and Cooke's brigades, operated assertively. Hill chose to march the bulk of his command east across the Chickahominy and hit Keyes's column at Crump's Crossroads on July 2. Then, using the interior lines provided by the railroads, he nimbly transferred many of John Cooke's Tar Heels to the South Anna in time to repulse Getty's expedition there two days later. During these engagements, troops from Lee's army left behind to protect Richmond, such as Jenkins's brigade from Pickett's division, had provided valuable service.

In contrast to Northern observers, the Confederates had little to say about the Blackberry Raid. Awash in alarming accounts of the disastrous losses at Gettysburg and Vicksburg, Southern editors and correspondents may not have viewed the repulse of Dix's offensive and its relatively bloodless engagements worthy of the column space. The campaign was not completely ignored, though. Accounts of the events appeared in the weeks after the operation as well as decades later.[9] Hargrove's defense of the Virginia Central bridge at the South Anna on June 26 drew particular attention. The heroic stand by the men from the 44th North Carolina would receive well-deserved plaudits for years to come.[10] But beyond occasional stories of the bridge fight, other events during Dix's campaign garnered little note. Hill's successful preemptive attack on Keyes at Crump's Crossroads on July 2 and Cooke's repulse of Getty at the RF&P railroad on July 4 would receive only scattered mentions here and there over the years.

Like his Federal counterparts, D. H. Hill did not remain in Richmond after the campaign. In the days after Dix turned his men back down the Peninsula, Jefferson Davis had a new assignment for the outspoken commander. The president arrived at Hill's headquarters outside Richmond and ordered him to pack his bags and head south to join Joseph Johnston's force in Mississippi. Although Hill had performed well in defending Richmond over the previous several weeks, not everyone was sad to see him go. Robert Kean, an official in the War Department, reflected on the transfer and offered a damning commentary on Hill: "A worse appointment could hardly be made for a people whose loyalty is shivering under the pressure of expected occupation," penned Kean. "Harsh, abrupt, often insulting in the effort to be sarcastic, he will offend many and conciliate none."[11]

That fall, Hill would command a corps in the bloody fighting at Chickamauga. But his open opposition to Braxton Bragg, coupled with his abrasiveness in Virginia no doubt, left him without a command to lead. Hill approached the War Department in late 1864 expressing his "desire to be placed in any position." Efforts by friends and allies to get him back into the field were largely unsuccessful. In October 1864, Governor Zebulon Vance of North Carolina urged President Davis to give Hill, then "at home without employment," command of forces in his state. Robert E. Lee did not object to such an arrangement but warned of mixing Hill with Bragg. "I fear there may be a want of harmony between the two," Lee dryly remarked. Finally, during Sherman's campaign in North Carolina in 1865, Hill volunteered his services and participated in the Battle of Bentonville.[12]

Tazewell Hargrove, the defender of the Virginia Central bridge during Spear's raid, spent the rest of the war as a prisoner. His bravery during the fight would earn him much praise. After the conflict, he became a leader in the Republican Party, aligning against the political interests of most former Confederates, a decision that reduced his stock among Lost Cause adherents. As North Carolina's attorney general in the 1870s, he supported rights for Black citizens and condemned the terrorism of the Ku Klux Klan. But the conservative press in the Old North State considered him a "degenerate son and a disgrace to the white race," according to one contemporary. Still, even his political opponents grudgingly commended his record in the war. In 1889, the *Wilmington Messenger* recounted the South Anna fight and mentioned Hargrove's decision to align with the Republicans. "He is of good Granville stock—good Whig stock before the war, and how he could ever identify himself with the party he did has always been inexplicable to us. But he is a real hero."[13]

In addition, Rooney Lee's saga would drag out for months as the prisoner cartel disintegrated over the summer of 1863. Some in the North viewed this high-profile prisoner as a valuable bargaining chip in the controversy over the reported mistreatment of captured Black US soldiers and their officers, practices presaging the numerous murders of Black captives by Confederates on battlefields in the coming months. "We have now the means in our hands of checking the cruel measures of the Jeff. Davis government toward officers who command negro regiments," declared a Milwaukee newspaper.[14] Acrimony between Confederate and Union officials escalated during Rooney Lee's stint at Fort Monroe and later at New York. Only weeks after Rooney Lee's capture, officials threatened to execute him as part of a spiral of retaliation and threats on both sides. But the controversy cooled somewhat, and in March 1864 he was exchanged and returned to Confederate service to fight out the rest of the war while commanding his cavalry division in his father's army.[15]

Finally, Alexander Stephens's peace mission rarely earned more than a passing mention in most studies of the Gettysburg Campaign. Buried in obscurity, the vice president's errand reveals the optimism Davis and his cabinet members embraced as the Army of Northern Virginia marched into Pennsylvania. Few disputed that the mission's publicized goal—to discuss the prisoner exchange and civilian treatment—was nothing more than a pretense to cover a more ambitious agenda. Immediately after the war, Edward Pollard, editor of the *Daily Richmond Examiner*, asserted that the "prisoner exchange" rationale offered by Davis and Stephens did not add up. The combative Pollard scoffed at the "absurd futility" of traveling to Washington "merely to protest against the enemy's cruelties in conducting the war." For him, Stephens's purpose was likely "to sound the Washington Government on the question of peace."[16]

Pollard's conclusion seems well-founded. Stephens certainly held grave concerns about the existing prisoner exchange system. Its failure hurt Confederate military chances and subjected rebel soldiers to long-term imprisonment. However, by nearly all indications, Stephens and Davis had more in mind for the mission. Stephens clearly hoped to broach issues of war and peace with Lincoln administration officials and had vaguely suggested as much in his initial correspondence with Davis. But the precise scope of the matters he planned to discuss with Union officials in July, particularly his strategy for the bargaining table, remains murky. He may have simply sought to leverage expected military success in Pennsylvania to yield a cessation of hostilities and give the Confederacy breathing room. Whether he planned to wield threats at the bargaining table is even less clear. Finally, no additional substantiation has been found to support the assertion in the *New-York Tribune*'s "Randolph" letter that Stephens planned to threaten the Lincoln administration with arming slaves, though the circumstances surrounding the mystery letter are intriguing. Overall, regardless of Stephens's particular bargaining strategy, there is little doubt he hoped to negotiate a peace cementing Confederate independence. In any event, Stephens would try his hand at the bargaining table again without success, and throughout the rest of the war his distaste for Davis and the administration's policies would only grow.

"CONSTANT CONTACT AND REGULAR COMMUNICATIONS"

The campaign against Richmond in the summer of 1863 also shed light on other issues underlying the entire war. Accounts of the Blackberry Raid and operations in North Carolina confirm that enslaved and free Black people, even when they were not under arms, made frequent, crucial contributions to the efforts of the US military—a pattern observed at other times and locations throughout the war.[17] In June 1863, African Americans had no formal role in military events taking place within the Department of Virginia. John Dix had helped to see to that. He had not embraced the war for abolition and, doubting that freedmen would make good soldiers or even desired to serve, had not aggressively pursued Black recruitment in the months after the Emancipation Proclamation (though to be sure such efforts were only just beginning in most other departments). But Dix's disdain and neglect did not prevent Black people in the region from aiding the Federal cause, a fact revealed repeatedly in accounts of the campaign.

However, beyond passing references in official correspondence, private letters, and newspaper stories, detailed accounts of the actions of Black participants, particularly from freed people themselves, during the operations outside Richmond are frustratingly few. What remains are snippets here and there about the contributions of African Americans during the campaign. In 1937, for instance, eighty-eight-year-old Robert Ellett, born into slavery at the Sweet Hill plantation in King William County, sat down for an interview with staff from the Works Project Administration and provided a rare, brief description of events outside Richmond seven decades earlier. During the interview, Ellett, who had arrived with his mother at Federal camps on the Peninsula in June 1863, recounted his recollections of the war in the region. In referring to the Blackberry Raid, he stated that "General [Dix] made a raid . . . and brought back everything he could pick up such as animals, food and all the colored men to put them behind the Union lines where they could help fortify the place, cook food, and work for the officers."[18]

For the most part, what is left of the African American experience during the operation comes from brief references in the accounts of white participants. Nevertheless, it is clear that enslaved people, although largely neglected or referred to as nameless figures in official reports and dispatches, aided Dix's commanders at nearly every turn. They guided troops along obscure roads, identified Confederate units in the area, reported the location of bridges and fords, and warned of approaching Confederate columns. There is no doubting the earlier observation of General Henry Wise of the Confederacy that the region's slaves were in "constant contact and regular communications with the enemy."[19] However, although Blacks' contributions in June and July 1863 remain a mostly hidden aspect to a largely obscure campaign, reports confirm that such aid was the rule and not the exception during the war in Virginia. Similar actions had also occurred during the Peninsula Campaign the previous year and elsewhere. During the 1862 operations, for example, freed people contributed labor and furnished intelligence that shaped Union military efforts and helped build support in the North for emancipation.[20]

Not only did African Americans in the counties east and north of Richmond assist Federal units; they also acted aggressively to gain their own freedom. Following Getty's expedition to the South Anna, fire-eater Edmund Ruffin jotted in his diary that "both in King William, & at Hanover C.H., they [the US soldiers] were quite near enough for our slaves to abscond to them, if so inclined."[21] US troops had begun operating in the region a year earlier during the 1862 operations, and many enslaved people had taken advantage of the Federal presence to escape their bondage then. However, accounts of the Blackberry Raid demonstrate that many still lived on the region's plantations well after the Emancipation Proclamation. During Dix's campaign, many hundreds—perhaps thousands—of enslaved people left local plantations to escape with the blue-clad infantry and cavalrymen and gain their own freedom.

Many Federal officers and soldiers approached the issue of slavery in the region with ambivalence and even exhibited open hostility to African American refugees living and working at the Federal posts. John Dix, who had never warmly embraced emancipation as part of the war effort, did not identify the freedom of local enslaved people as an objective in his mission orders during the summer of 1863. Furthermore, many of his subordinates most likely viewed the hundreds, if not thousands, of enslaved people burdening their columns simply as an unsought, collateral consequence of their operations. However, not all Federal officers and enlisted men involved with the campaign held such opinions. For instance, during the operations at West Point, George Gordon had worked aggressively to help enslaved people escape their bondage and welcomed them into his camps. In addition, the letters and diaries of many soldiers during Dix's campaign—men who saw the conditions of these people firsthand as they marched past plantation after plantation—took joy in witnessing the new freedom gained by the enslaved and pride in the army's role in securing it during the operations. Although Dix may not have specifically sought such results, in the end his force helped create the conditions for many enslaved people to leave their plantations to a new life.

Accounts about the Blackberry Raid underscore how complicated the process of emancipation was. It involved more than individuals merely walking away from plantations. Individuals seeking to gain their freedom had to weigh a host of factors involving timing, opportunity, and personal circumstances. Although the presence of Federal soldiers at their homes or in the local vicinity provided a window for many to escape, others had to consider issues of family, infirmity, or other factors that might incline them to stay in their place of bondage.[22]

Once free, many refugees worked for the Federal army as laborers, cooks, servants, and dockhands. Formerly enslaved men from New Kent, King William, Hanover, and other counties would eventually enlist in Federal regiments in Virginia and elsewhere. Data compiled by historians LaVonne Allen and Camilla Tramuel reveal that at least forty men born in New Kent County enlisted in more than two dozen different regiments and that fifty-six from King William County and the town of West Point did the same, also into multiple units. In addition, partial data shows that at least 100 United States Colored Troops recruits hailed from Hanover County. Most enlisted after 1863, signing up at recruiting stations all over Virginia and other states in both the North and the South.[23] Some of these men returned home after the war. William Henry Winston, for example, who had been held in slavery at North Wales near Hickory Hill, enlisted in the 2nd United States Colored Cavalry in December 1863 and participated in operations against Richmond the next year, receiving a serious wound in the process. After the war, he returned to Hanover County and became a community leader and a church deacon.[24] The residents of these counties would see significant change as Virginians experienced emancipation, Reconstruction, the resurgence of conservative political control, the brief reprieve of the Readjuster movement, and the eventual stranglehold of Jim Crow segregation.[25]

"WHAT ITS PURPOSE WAS"

Ultimately, beyond all the various issues and considerations, the fact remains that a large US force had marched on a lightly defended Richmond during the Battle of Gettysburg and accomplished close to nothing. Put simply, Dix's Richmond operation—whether due to vague design, poor execution, or competing priorities—was not a success. Nevertheless, the campaign still had its lessons to offer, whether or not anyone paid attention. For the Confederates, it confirmed the wisdom behind the approach, first adopted by Robert E. Lee, to conduct a mobile, aggressive defense in shielding the capital. Confederate commanders would continue to follow this course in larger operations outside Richmond and Petersburg in 1864 and 1865. For the Federals, the Blackberry Raid's disappointing results highlighted the risks of saddling inexperienced commanders with hazy goals and little guidance. Matters would change with the arrival of Ulysses S. Grant in Virginia the next year, who would implement a broader, clear-eyed plan for winning the war. In addition, Grant, Sherman, Sheridan, and other commanders would demonstrate a willingness to wage "hard war" and use emancipation as a tool to bleed Confederate strength and fill the Federal ranks.

A look at Dix's campaign also reveals insights than can be gleaned from a close examination of lesser-known military events—those movements, battles, and skirmishes that fail to rank among the few dozen larger campaigns so dominant in most military studies of the war. Barren of decisive results and crowded out of the headlines by Gettysburg and Vicksburg, the Blackberry Raid has never gained purchase in the popular memory of the war. The campaign did not generate the large battles or significant casualties to draw the attention of observers at the time or historians later. Furthermore, the principal commanders on both sides were either obscure, unpopular, or both. Nevertheless, a detailed consideration of the campaign provides a look at the summer of 1863 within a broader context and demonstrates how renowned events such as Gettysburg were part of a larger, expansive landscape. The consideration of Dix's operation also reveals how events that are now considered minor drew substantial attention from military and political leaders at the highest levels of government on both sides.

Over the years, these operations have not received much attention. Indeed, few but the most dedicated students of the conflict know that, as Meade and Lee fought at Gettysburg, 20,000 Federals had gathered within a few miles of Richmond and were ready to strike. However, the

Blackberry Raid qualifies not only as an intriguing lost opportunity for the Federals but also as a largely forgotten one. Although it may have presented possibilities for the Union cause, it is impossible to determine what conditions—more troops, more resolve, a different commander, less determined defenders—would have led to a different result. Speculation aside, it is no stretch to posit that the conditions outside the Confederate capital in June and July 1863 offered a chance for a decisive blow to the rebellion. Gustavus Fox, the deputy navy secretary quoted at the very beginning of this volume, may have had a point when he wrote that "every rash act of this war has been crowned with success and here is the most glorious opportunity ever afforded."[26] Although a Union victory at Richmond in the summer of 1863 was by no means guaranteed with the forces available, it is certain that neither Halleck nor Dix acted rashly.

In the end, the campaign is the story of failure, a breakdown not only in execution but also in conception, design, and communication. When the weary troops of the Fourth and Seventh Corps tramped away from White House back down the Peninsula, they understood that their efforts had not generated, as one Connecticut soldier put it, "any very brilliant results."[27] During the march, with the taste of defeat lingering in their mouths, they encountered more heat, more misery, and more blackberries. John Lovell Cunningham, one of the New Yorkers who had fought under the moonlight at the South Anna on July 4, captured the feeling of many of his comrades as well as observers for years to come when he wondered "what our expedition meant" and "what its purpose was."[28]

APPENDIX A:
FEDERAL ORDER OF BATTLE

ORA 27(3):450.

United States Army, Department of Virginia
Maj. Gen. John A. Dix, commanding

FOURTH ARMY CORPS
Maj. Gen. Erasmus D. Keyes

First Division
Brig. Gen. Rufus King
  First Brigade, Brig. Gen. Hector Tyndale
    2nd Massachusetts Cavalry (battalion), Maj. Casper Crowninshield
      [detached to Spear's cavalry]
    2nd New York Cavalry (battalion), Maj. John E. Naylor [detached to
      Spear's cavalry]
    169th Pennsylvania, Col. Lewis W. Smith
    8th New York Battery, Lieut. Peter Morton
  Second Brigade, Col. George E. Church
    5th Pennsylvania Cavalry (detachment)
    11th Rhode Island, Lieut. Col. J. Talbot Pitman
    1st Pennsylvania Light Artillery, Battery E, Capt. Thomas G. Orwig
    2nd Wisconsin Battery, Capt. Charles Beger
  Third Brigade, Col. Charles Kleckner
    168th New York, Col. William R. Brown
    173rd Pennsylvania, Lieut. Col. James A. Johnson

Second Division
Brig. Gen. George H. Gordon
  First Brigade, Col. William Gurney
    127th New York, Lieut. Col. Stewart L. Woodford
    142nd New York, Col. N. Martin Curtis
    143rd New York, Col. Horace Boughton
    144th New York, Col. David E. Gregory
  Second Brigade, Col. Burr Porter
    22nd Connecticut, Col. George S. Burnham
    40th Massachusetts, Maj. Joseph M. Day
    141st New York, Lieut. Col. William K. Logie

Artillery
4th Wisconsin Battery, Capt. John F. Vallee
Reserve Artillery, Capt. James McKnight
   1st New York Light, Battery F, Capt. William R. Wilson
   1st New York Light, Battery H, Capt. Charles E. Mink
   1st Pennsylvania Light, Battery H, Capt. Andrew Fagan
   5th United States, Battery M, Capt. James McKnight
Miscellaneous
Independent Brigade
Col. Robert M. West
   139th New York, Col. Anthony Conk
   178th Pennsylvania, Col. James Johnson
   179th Pennsylvania, Col. William H. Blair
Not Brigaded
   4th Delaware, Col. Arthur H. Grimshaw
   6th New York Cavalry (3d Battalion), Maj. William P. Hall
   5th Pennsylvania Cavalry, Lieut. Col. William Lewis

SEVENTH ARMY CORPS
Maj. Gen. John A. Dix

First Division
Brig. Gen. Michael Corcoran
  First Brigade, Brig. Gen. Henry D. Terry
    26th Michigan, Col. Judson S. Farrar
    1st New York Battalion Sharpshooters, Capt. Joseph S. Arnold
    130th New York, Col. Alfred Gibbs
    152d New York, Lieut. Col. George W. Thompson
    167th Pennsylvania, Col. Joseph D. Davis
  Second Brigade, Brig. Gen. Robert S. Foster
    13th Indiana, Lieut. Col. Cyrus J. Dobbs
    112th New York, Col. Jeremiah C. Drake
    169th New York, Lieut. Col. John McConihe
    165th Pennsylvania, Col. Charles Buehler
    166th Pennsylvania, Lieut. Col. George W. Reisinger
    7th Massachusetts Battery (G), Capt. Phineas A. Davis
  Third Brigade (Irish Legion), Col. Mathew Murphy
    10th New Jersey, Col. Henry O. Ryerson
    155th New York, Col. William McEvily
    164th New York, Col. James P. McMahon
    170th New York, Col. James P. Mclvor
    182nd New York, Lieut. Col. Thomas M. Reid

Artillery
  Capt. Frederick M. Follett
    1st Delaware Battery, Capt. Benjamin Nields
    19th New York Battery, Capt. William H. Stahl
    4th United States, Battery D, Capt. Frederick M. Follett
    4th United States, Battery L, Capt. R. V. W. Howard
  1st New York Mounted Rifles, Col. Benjamin F. Onderdonk
  99th New York, Company I (detachment)

Second Division
Brig. Gen. George W. Getty
  First Brigade, Col. Samuel M. Alford
    3rd New York, Lieut. Col. Eldridge G. Floyd
    89th New York, Col. Harrison S. Fairchild
    103rd New York, Col. William Heine
    117th New York, Lieut. Col. Alvin White
  Second Brigade, Brig. Gen. Edward Harland
    8th Connecticut, Col. John E. Ward
    11th Connecticut, Col. Griffin A. Stedman Jr.
    15th Connecticut, Col. Charles L. Upham
    16th Connecticut, Lieut. Col. John H. Burnham
  Third Brigade, Col. William H. P. Steere [Col. Michael T. Donohoe on
      July 4, 1863]
    21st Connecticut, Maj. Hiram B. Crosby
    10th New Hampshire, Lieut. Col. John Coughlin
    13th New Hampshire, Col. Aaron F. Stevens
    4th Rhode Island, Lieut. Col. Martin P. Buffum
  Artillery
    1st Pennsylvania Light, Battery A, Capt. John G. Simpson
    5th United States, Battery A, Lieut. James Gillis

Independent Commands
  Provisional Brigade
    Col. David W. Wardrop
    99th New York, Lieut. Col. Richard Nixon
    118th New York, Lieut. Col. Oliver Keese Jr.
  Wistar's Brigade
    Brig. Gen. Isaac J. Wistar
    9th Vermont, Col. Edward H. Ripley
    19th Wisconsin, Col. Horace T. Sanders
    18th New York Battery, Capt. Frederick L. Hiller
  Spinola's (Keystone) Brigade
    Brig. Gen. Francis B. Spinola
    158th Pennsylvania, Col. David B. McKibbin

168th Pennsylvania, Col. Joseph Jack
171st Pennsylvania, Col. Everard Bierer
Cavalry
11th Pennsylvania, Col. Samuel P. Spear*
*(command included men from 2nd Massachusetts, 2nd New York, and 12th Illinois)

Camp Hamilton (at Fortress Monroe)
Capt. Franz Von Schilling
3rd Pennsylvania Heavy Artillery, Company B, Capt. Franz von Schilling
11th Pennsylvania Cavalry, Company C, Lieut. William T. Camac

Fort Monroe
Col. Joseph Roberts
3rd Pennsylvania Heavy Artillery (eight companies)

Norfolk
Brig. Gen. Egbert L. Viele, Military Governor
148th New York, Col. William Johnson
173rd Pennsylvania, Col. Daniel Nagle
177th Pennsylvania, Col. George B. Wiestling
1st New York Mounted Rifles, Company K, Lieut. Silas E. Reynolds
7th New York Battery, Capt. Peter C. Regan

APPENDIX B:
CONFEDERATE ORDER
OF BATTLE

ORA 27(3):1057–1068.

Richmond Defenses
  Col. T. S. Rhett
    10th Virginia Battalion of Heavy Artillery, Maj. J. O. Hensley
    18th Virginia Battalion Heavy Artillery, Maj. M. B. Hardin
    19th Virginia Battalion Heavy Artillery, Maj. N. R. Cary
    20th Virginia Battalion Heavy Artillery, Maj. J. E. Robertson
    Alexandria Light Artillery, Capt. D. L. Smoot
    Caroline Artillery, Capt. T. R. Thornton
    Nelson Artillery, Capt. J. H. Rives
    Surry Artillery, Capt. J. D. Hankins

Chaffin's Farm
  Lieut. Col. J. M. Maury
    Gloucester Artillery, Capt. T. B. Montague
    King and Queen Artillery, Capt. A. F. Bagby
    Lunenburg Artillery, Capt. C. T. Allen
    Pamunkey Artillery, Capt. A. J. Jones

Drewry's Bluff
  Maj. F. W. Smith
    Johnston Artillery, Capt. B. J. Epes
    Neblett Artillery, Capt. W. G. Coleman
    Southside Artillery, Capt. J. W. Drewry
    United Artillery, Capt. Thomas Kevill

Godwin's Cavalry
  Col. D. J. Godwin
    Three Companies (42nd Virginia Cavalry Battalion) (ORA 27(3):1066)
    Co. F, L.W. Allen' Company
    Co. E, Captain R. R. Hord (Hord's Company)
    Co. C, Company C (Captain John K. Littleton's Company of Virginia
      Partisan Rangers, also known as "Chesapeake Rangers")

Baker's Cavalry
   3rd North Carolina (41st North Carolina State Troops), Col. John A. Baker

Richmond Local Defense Troops
   Gen. G.W. Custis Lee (*ORA* 27(3):950)
   Five battalions (Brown's, Downer's, Henley's, Minor's, and Waller's)

Wise's Brigade
   Brig. Gen. Henry A. Wise
      26th Virginia, Col. P. R. Page
      46th Virginia, Col. R. T. W. Duke
      59th Virginia, Col. William B. Tabb
      4th Virginia Heavy Artillery, Col. J. T. Goode
      Holcombe Legion (Cavalry), Col. W. P. Shingler
      10th Virginia Cavalry, Company D, Capt. L. J. Hawley
      15th Virginia Cavalry, Company C, Capt. E. W. Capps
      32nd Virginia Battalion, Maj. J. R. Rob
      Stark's Artillery Battalion. Maj. A. W. Stark

Troops at Richmond from the Department of North Carolina
   Maj. Gen. Daniel Harvey Hill
   Cooke's Brigade (assigned to Department of Richmond in late June)
      Brig. Gen. John R. Cooke
         15th North Carolina, W. MacRae [at RF&P bridge at South Anna on
            July 4]
         27th North Carolina, Col. John A. Gilmer Jr.
         46th North Carolina, Col. E. D. Hall
         48th North Carolina, Col. Robert C. Hill
         Claytor's Battery, Capt. R. B. Claytor
         Cooper's Battery, Capt. R. L. Cooper
   Jenkins's Brigade (assigned to Dept. of Richmond in late June)
      Brig. Gen. Micah Jenkins
         1st South Carolina (Volunteers), Col. F.W. Kilpatrick ("Hagood's First
            South Carolina")
         2nd South Carolina (Rifles), Col. Thomas Thomson
         5th South Carolina, Col. A. Coward
         6th South Carolina, Col. John Bratton
         Hampton Legion, Col. M. W. Gary [T. M. Logan]
         Palmetto Sharpshooters, Col. Joseph Walker
   Ransom's Brigade
      Brig. Gen. Matt Ransom
         24th North Carolina, Col. William J. Clarke
         25th North Carolina, Col. Henry M. Rutledge

35th North Carolina, Col. John J. Jones
49th North Carolina, Col. Lee M. McAfee
56th North Carolina, Col. Paul F. Faison
Detached Army of Northern Virginia
  Corse's Brigade (Pickett's Division)
    Brig. Gen. Montgomery D. Corse
      15th Virginia, Col. T. P. August (detached)
      17th Virginia, Col. M. Marye; Lieut. Col. A. Herbert
      29th Virginia, Lieut. Col. James Giles
      30th Virginia, Col. A. T. Harrison (absent); Lieut. Col. R. S. Chew
  From J. Johnston Pettigrew's Brigade (Heth's Division)
    44th North Carolina, Col. T. C. Singeltary

ACKNOWLEDGMENTS

THROUGHOUT THIS PROJECT, I've gained further greater appreciation of what can be learned from the examination of lesser-known operations during the war. As my friend John Selby aptly noted when he read an early draft, "I like the notion that even what we now consider sideshow events were objectively important and viewed as important by the commanders and officials at the time—but are too often overshadowed by the big 20 or so battles in studies." I wholly agree. The potential of Dix's offensive against Richmond during the Gettysburg Campaign was not lost on the leaders in Washington and Richmond at the time. The city's capture in early July 1863 would have ended the war, or at least significantly altered its course. This fact alone warrants a good look into these events.

Over the course of this project, many people have stepped forward to offer invaluable help as I lumbered along to a final product. National Park Service Historian Bobby Krick, whose vast knowledge of Richmond during the war includes the Blackberry Raid, is one of the few bona fide experts on the campaign. Early in my efforts, he shared a trove of material about the operation collected over many years. When I had scratched out an early, ugly draft, he generously plowed through it and offered key suggestions and saved me from many mistakes.

I also want to thank several others who took the time to review drafts of the manuscript and offer their feedback. They include: Jeff Harris, educator, coach, and friend, who was the first reader out of the gate and made some important observations and provided constant encouragement on this project; John Selby, author of an excellent George Meade biography and a long-time collaborator and friend; Bob Helferty, an old friend with a new interest in the Civil War; William Marvel, the acclaimed author and researcher who has consistently provided me over the years with what every author needs—unflinching, unvarnished feedback; Will Kurtz, friend and former managing director of the University of Virginia's Nau Center; Stran Trout of New Kent Historical Society; Michael Snyder, who read through a late version of the manuscript; and author David Bright who provided insights based on his extensive knowledge of Civil War railroads. I would also like to thank veteran researcher Bryce Suderow, who suggested that I look into these events in the first place. Finally, I'd like to thank my father, Dickie Newsome, for reviewing the whole manuscript and lending his spot-on insight and never-ending encouragement.

Many thanks are also due to others for their help with research and other aspects of the project. These individuals include: Natalie Slater, who conducted extensive research for the project in New York repositories; Shannon Pritchard, who kindly gave me a personal tour of Hickory Hill, his home and the site of Rooney Lee's capture; Cecily Zander of Southern Methodist University who trained an eagle eye to the page proofs; William Griffing whose excellent Spared & Shared website contains a vast trove of period letters; Wade Sokolosky, author, North Carolina expert, and good guy; Edward Alexander, author and mapmaker; LaVonne Allen and Stran Trout of the New Kent County Historical Society; Chris Meekins of the N.C. Office of Archives and History; author Chris Hartley, who is working on a biography of D. H. Hill; Anne McCrery of the Virginia Museum of History & Culture; Leslie Harris, my friend who shared her expertise on garden design; Lauren Ziarko and Christopher Sanders of Manhattanville College Library; Sarah Hedlund, Montgomery History; McKenzie Lemhouse of South Caroliniana Library; Ethan Rafuse of the US Army Command General Staff College; Amy Folk of the Oysterponds Historical Society; Bill Sheild, RF&P RR Historical Society; Elisa Ho of the Jacob Rader Marcus Center of the American Jewish Archives; Sabina Beauchard of Massachusetts Historical Society; Andy Trudeau, author of one of the few articles on the Blackberry Raid; Andrew Duppstadt of the N.C. Department of Natural and Cultural Resources; Hang Nguyen of the Iowa Department of Cultural Affairs; Terry Reimer of the National Museum of Civil War Medicine; Adam Domby of Auburn University; Glenn Brasher, author of *The Peninsula Campaign and the Necessity of Emancipation*; Arthur Taylor of the Hanover Historical Society; Skip Riddle; Robert Rice of Aylett; Joseph Ledford; Jody Lynn Allen of William & Mary; Rodney Foytik of the US Army Heritage and Education Center; Sierra Dixon and Connecticut Historical Society; Melissa Mead of the University of Rochester; Nathan Verilla and Thomas Crew of the Library of Virginia; Margaret Best of St. Peter's Church; Malgosia Myc of the University of Michigan; Lauren Gray of the Kansas Historical Society; and Timothy Hodgdon at University of North Carolina—Chapel Hill. I also want to express my appreciation for the past work of Martin Lichterman and John Brumgardt, whose unpublished dissertations on John Dix and Alexander Stephens respectively provided invaluable insights and sources for this project.

I would also like to thank the staff at University Press of Kansas for all their work and support throughout this project, including Joyce Harrison, who has now guided me through three book projects; Kelly Chrisman Jacques, who steered this volume to its completion; Derek Helms, who graciously fielded my many requests and questions; and sharp-eyed copy editor Jon Howard, who caught more mistakes than I could count and offered excellent substantive suggestions that improved the manuscript.

Finally, many thanks and much love to Margot, Jake, and Silas for their support and encouragement.

NOTES

ABBREVIATIONS

DMRL	David M. Rubenstein Rare Book and Manuscript Library, Duke University
ECU	Joyner Library, East Carolina University
LOC	Library of Congress
NARA	National Archives and Records Administration
NCOAH	North Carolina Office of Archives and History
NHHC	Naval History and Heritage Command
NYSMM	New York State Military Museum
ORA	US War Department, *The War of the Rebellion: A Compilation of the Official Records of the Union and Confederate Armies*, series 1 (unless otherwise noted)
ORN	US Navy Department, *Official Records of the Union and Confederate Navies in the War of the Rebellion*, series 1 (unless otherwise noted)
OR Supp.	Hewett, *Supplement to the Official Records of the Union and Confederate Armies*
RG	Record Group
SHC	Southern Historical Collection
SLNC	State Library of North Carolina
UNC	University of North Carolina
UVM	University of Vermont Libraries
VMHC	Virginia Museum of History & Culture

INTRODUCTION

1. Cruikshank, *Back in the Sixties*, 39; Shirley, "A Raid of the 11th Pa. Cav." According to official reports, the US vessels assigned to operations on the Pamunkey included the *Commodore Barney*, *Commodore Morris*, *Morse*, and *Western World* (transport). It appears the latter three escorted the flotilla on the morning for the 25th because the *Commodore Barney* did not arrive until much later that day. However, a reporter with the *New York Daily Herald*, accompanied Spear's force and noted the *Smith Briggs* was present too. Lee and Crosby Reports, *ORN* 9:82–84; *New York Daily Herald*, June 30, 1863. The transports included the *City of Albany*. *Daily Alta California*, August 10, 1863.

2. George Cruikshank letter, June 30, 1863, George L. Cruikshank Civil War Letters, State Historical Society of Iowa.

3. *New York Daily Herald*, June 30, 1863; Unidentified Newspaper Clipping (130th New York), June 28, 1863, 1st Regiment of Dragoons New York Volunteers, Civil War Newspaper Clippings, New York State Military Museum (blackberries); Lee to Davis, June 25, 1863, ORA 27(3):930–931 (Lee opposite Williamsport).

4. Dix to Halleck, June 14, 1863, 12 m, ORA 27(3):111.

1. LEE HEADS NORTH

1. Frye, *12th Virginia Cavalry*, 36. For more on the Battle of Brandy Station, see Davis and Wittenberg, *Out Flew the Sabres*; Wittenberg, *The Battle of Brandy Station*.

2. "Memorial Addresses on the Life and Character of William H. F. Lee," United States Congress, 52nd Cong., 1st Sess., Mis. Doc. No. 320, at 93 (remarks of M. C. Butler).

3. *Lincoln Courier*, August 1, 1890 (account of W. A. Graham, 2nd North Carolina Cavalry).

4. *Lincoln Courier*, August 1, 1890; Guelzo, *Gettysburg: The Last Invasion*, 56–57; Hartley, *Stuart's Tarheels*, 131; Quincy, *History of the Second Massachusetts Regiment of Infantry*, 13; *Annual Reunion*, United States Military Academy at West Point, 111.

5. Von Borcke, *Memoirs of the Confederate War for Independence*, vol. 2, 278.

6. Beale, *A Lieutenant of Cavalry in Lee's Army*, 223; Lee, *Recollections and Letters of General Robert E. Lee*, 95.

7. Hooker informed Halleck he planned to go after Stuart's cavalry movement to "break it up in its incipiency." Hooker to Halleck, June 6, 1863, ORA 27(1):33.

8. For single-volume monographs covering the Gettysburg Campaign, see Coddington, *The Gettysburg Campaign*; Trudeau, *Gettysburg: A Testing of Courage*; Sears, *Gettysburg*, and Guelzo, *Gettysburg: The Last Invasion*.

9. Lee to Seddon, April 9, 1863, ORA 25(2):713–714; LeGear, "The Hotchkiss Collection of Confederate Maps."

10. Lee to Davis, April 16, 1863, ORA 25(2):724–725; Reagan, *Memoirs*, 150–153.

11. Lee's surviving dispatches with Richmond officials in June betray little of his plans. In addition, his discussions with Cabinet officials are poorly documented. Even as he drove his army north following the Brandy Station fight, his correspondence gave few hints of his movements and intentions. Any evidence of his aims comes from the bits and pieces of his letters and reports as well as accounts of conversations between the general and his officers at the time and afterward. For a thorough discussion of Lee's goals in moving north, see Hartwig, "The Army of Northern Virginia and the Gettysburg Campaign." In attempting to divine Lee's motivations, some historians have focused on supply, while others have looked to political factors. As discussed by Hartwig, those who have pointed to Lee's hope to bring change to political conditions in the North include Stephen Sears, Craig Symonds, Edwin Coddington, and Andre Trudeau. Those who have

emphasized Lee's desire for supply include Kent Masterson Brown, Douglas Freeman, Wilbur Nye, and Clifford Dowdey. See Dowdey, *Death of a Nation*; Tucker, *High Tide at Gettysburg*; Nye, *Here Come the Rebels*; Brown, *Retreat from Gettysburg*; Coddington, *The Gettysburg Campaign*; Craig Symonds, *American Heritage History of the Battle of Gettysburg*; Trudeau, *Gettysburg: A Testing of Courage*; Sears, *Gettysburg*; Roland, "Lee's Invasion Strategy." At least one student of the campaign has emphasized a desire by Lee and his generals to wreak havoc on Northern lines of communication, means of production, and even natural resources (e.g., the iron ore mines of Pennsylvania). See Kegel, *North with Lee and Jackson*.

12. Jones, *A Rebel War Clerk's Diary*, vol. 1, 351.

13. Historian Scott Hartwig concluded that the campaign's "principal goal was to maneuver the Army of the Potomac out of Virginia, break up the enemy's plans for a summer campaign, and hopefully compel them to withdraw forces then operating along the Atlantic coast." Hartwig, "The Army of Northern Virginia and the Gettysburg Campaign," 44. See also, Lee to Davis, June 25, 1863, ORA 27(3):931–933 (Lee says his movement will prevent the Federals from reinforcing the Peninsula).

14. Trimble, "The Battle and Campaign of Gettysburg," 121.

15. Lee to Seddon, June 8, 1863, ORA 27(3):868–869.

16. Lee to Mary C. Lee, April 19, 1863, *Wartime Papers of R. E. Lee*, 438.

17. See Klement, *The Limits of Dissent*.

18. Lee to Seddon, May 10, 1863, ORA 25(2):790 (two dispatches).

19. Lee to Seddon, June 8, 1863, ORA 27(3):868–869.

20. Seddon to Lee, June 10, 1863, ORA 27(3):382.

21. Beauregard to Johnston, July 1, 1863, ORA 28(2):173–174. Alexander, *Military Memoirs of a Confederate*, 366; Stoker, *The Grand Design*, 293–294. As was his tendency, Beauregard urged a grand concentration of troops in Middle Tennessee with units from his own department along with the Army of Northern Virginia to defeat Rosecrans there and then move west to defeat Grant outside Vicksburg.

22. Keyes to Hooker, June 2, 1862, ORA 18:739; Sharpe to J. McEntee, June 4, BMI, RG 393, NARA; *Richmond Daily Examiner*, June 6, 1863 ("The northern press teems with reports . . .").

23. Hooker to Lincoln, June 5, 1863, 11:30 a.m., ORA 27(1):30; Lincoln to Hooker, June 5, 1863, ORA 27(1):31.

24. *Richmond Enquirer*, June 6, 1863; *Philadelphia Inquirer*, June 1, 3, and 4, 1863 (speculates Lee was making a demonstration toward Washington before heading into the Valley and thence to Maryland and Pennsylvania).

25. Lincoln to McClellan, October 13, 1862, ORA 21:97–98. Lincoln explained to McClellan that, if Lee were to recross the Potomac in full force, "he gives up his communications to you absolutely, and you have nothing to do but to follow and ruin him."

26. Halleck to Burnside, January 7, 1863, ORA 25(2):13.

27. Lincoln to Hooker, June 10, 1863, The Reports of the Committees of the Senate of the United States for the Second Session Thirty-eighth Cong., 1864–'65. Washington: Government Printing Office, 1865, 255.

28. Marvel, *Lincoln's Autocrat*, 290.

29. Alexander, *Fighting for the Confederacy*, 276. Whether Lincoln was reasonable in such a conclusion is unclear. By the summer of 1863, Federal intelligence efforts had largely debunked the notion that Lee had overwhelming numbers, and officials in Washington knew of the problems in manning the defenses at Richmond.

30. Hooker to Halleck, June 13, 1863, 7 p.m., *ORA* 27(1):38.

31. Lincoln to Hooker, 5.50 p.m., June 14, 1863, 5:50 p.m., *ORA* 27(1):39.

32. Sears, *Gettysburg*, 86.

33. Johnston, *Virginia Railroads in the Civil War*, 118 (effected lines in southeastern Virginia included the eastern segments of the Norfolk and Petersburg as well as the Seaboard and Roanoke).

34. Mordecai, *A Brief History of the Richmond, Fredericksburg and Potomac Railroad*, 33.

35. Turner, "The Virginia Central Railroad at War, 1861–1865," 524 (in 1863, two trains per day left Richmond). Other lines ran south and west from Richmond and connected with Lynchburg and Charlottesville, but these roads offered a circuitous route to the Valley and ran over several different lines with inconsistent gauges.

36. Turner, "The Virginia Central Railroad at War, 1861–1865," 524; and Freeman, *R. E. Lee*, vol. 3, 77.

37. Confederate officials would investigate Ruth during the war, and afterward he would win recognition for his efforts from US officials. See Stuart, "Samuel Ruth and General R. E. Lee."

38. See *ORA* 11(1): 35, 37, 200, 680, 683, 686, 690–693; Stuart, "Samuel Ruth and General R. E. Lee," 67 n. 103.

39. J. J. Pettigrew to Elzey, May 4, 5 p.m., 1863, *ORA* 18:1044; Sears, *Chancellorsville*, 368–370.

40. Pettigrew to Elzey, May 14, 1863, 1 p.m., *ORA* 18:1060–1061.

41. Lee to Cooper, June 15, 1863, *ORA* 27(3):890.

42. Lee to Longstreet, June 15, 1863, *ORA* 27(3):891. Porter Alexander expressed doubts about moving into Pennsylvania given the exposure of the wagon route for ammunition and supplies to Staunton. Alexander, *Military Memoirs of a Confederate*, 365.

43. See *Weekly Raleigh Register*, July 15, 1863; Murchison Report (54th North Carolina), August 5, 1863, *ORA* 27(2):487–488 (guarded prisoners from Staunton to Richmond and then "the regiment returned to Winchester on July 3, when, in conjunction with a Virginia regiment, it was ordered to guard an ordnance train to the army, then in Pennsylvania"); Hoffman Report (31st Virginia), *ORA* 27(2):488–490. (left Winchester on June 17 to escort prisoners to Staunton, arriving June 22; four companies accompanied prisoners on train to Richmond. Returned to Staunton and escorted a wagon train down the Valley, arriving in Winchester on June 18). Wise, *The Long Arm of Lee*, 400 ("A large supply of ammunition arriving from Richmond.") It is likely that this ordnance train traveled by rail to either Gordonsville or Staunton.

44. Murchison Report, August 5, 1863, *ORA* 27(2):487–488; Lee to Davis, June 25, 1863 ("Opposite Williamsport"), *ORA* 27(3):931; Lee to Davis, June

25, 1863 ("Williamsport"), *ORA* 27(3):932; See also Wynstra, *At the Forefront of Lee's Invasion*; Brown, *Retreat from Gettysburg*.

45. On June 23, Lee requested that Richmond officials send reinforcements via rail to Culpeper, where they could march to Winchester via Chester Gap. Lee to Cooper, June 23, 1863, *ORA* 27(3):925–926.

46. Within Virginia, the rail network also had challenges. The Virginia and Tennessee, South Side, and Richmond and Danville Railroads had broad-gauge tracks. All other routes in Virginia, however, employed the smaller standard gauge. For details on Virginia's railroads during the war, see Johnston, *Virginia Railroads in the Civil War*.

47. Wadley to Seddon, April 15, 1863, *ORA*, ser. 4, vol. 2, 486–487.

48. Lee to Randolph, October 25, 1862, *ORA* 19(2):681.

49. *Virginia & Tennessee Railroad Eighteenth Annual Report*, 77.

50. Garfield, *The Wild Life of the Army*, 70; see also, Noe, *Southwest Virginia's Railroad*, 115; Hayes, *Diary and Letters of Rutherford B. Hayes*, vol. 4, 184 (called the Southwest Railroad "the jugular vein of Rebeldom").

51. Johnston, *Virginia Railroads in the Civil War*, 11; Wadley to Seddon, April 15, 1863, *ORA*, ser. 4, vol. 2, 486–487; Nowland, *A Unique Hell in Southwestern Virginia*, 39. Additional lines crisscrossed the Commonwealth and served as the Confederates' diminished internal rail network. One of them, the Richmond and Danville road, stretched southwest from the capital into South Side Virginia but terminated there, at least in 1863. Later in the war, the completion of a new segment, known as the "Piedmont Railroad," would connect the Danville line to North Carolina. Another line, the South Side Railroad, ran west from Petersburg to Lynchburg. Finally, to the east, the Federal capture of Norfolk early in the war effectively eliminated the Seaboard and Roanoke line as a useful route for the Confederates. See Burke, *Wilmington & Weldon Railroad*; Johnston, *Virginia Railroads in the Civil War*; Black, *Railroads of the Confederacy*.

52. *ORA* 18:733 (Department of Virginia return, May 31, 1863); *ORA* 18:736 (Department of North Carolina return; May 31, 1863); *ORA* 27(3):450 (West Virginia); *ORA* 25(2):589 (Middle Department, 8th Army Corps return, May 31, 1863; Third Division under Scammon at Charleston, West Virginia, and the Fourth Separate Brigade led by Averell at Beverly, Buckhannon, Bulltown, Clarksburg, Parkersburg, and Weston). The Department of West Virginia was created on June 28, 1863.

53. *ORA* 27(3):299.

54. "Troops in the Middle Department," May 31, 1863, *ORA* 25(2):589. Union troops manned outposts at Philippi, Buckhannon, Weston, Beverly, Bulltown, Clarksburg, and Fayetteville.

55. Return for Department of Western Virginia, *ORA* 27(3):960. Samuel Jones stationed his 7,000 troops along a line of outposts shielding the Virginia and Tennessee Railroad stretching from Huntersville in the mountains southwest through Lewisburg, Beckley, and Abingdon.

56. *ORA* 27(3):960.

57. Examples of such operations include a December 1862 Union cavalry raid under Samuel Carter near Bristol and a Confederate raid under John Imboden in the spring of 1863 against the Baltimore and Ohio Railroad near Grafton;

well-prepared railroad officials deployed their engineers and highly efficient laborers to repair extensive damage to tracks and trestles within days. See Collins, *The Jones–Imboden Raid* (William "Grumble" Jones also commanded riders during Imboden's raid); Longacre, *Mounted Raids of the Civil War*.

58. Tri-monthly return for Department of North Carolina, May 31, 1863, ORA 18:736.

59. Jones, *A Rebel War Clerk's Diary*, vol. 1, 303.

2. JOHN DIX AND THE DEPARTMENT OF VIRGINIA

1. Troops in the Department of Virginia, June 30, 1863, ORA 27(3):450–454.

2. *Memoirs of John Adams Dix*, vol. 2, 104. Voegeli, "A Rejected Alternative," 765–790. There is no published biography of John Dix. For the most comprehensive unpublished study of Dix, see Lichterman, *John Adams Dix, 1798–1879*.

3. Lichterman, 78, 118, 629.

4. Dix to Anderson, January 21, 1861, Dix Papers, Columbia University.

5. Dix, *Memoirs of John Adams Dix*, vol. 1, 371 (Dix dispatch, January 29, 1861).

6. *Philadelphia Inquirer*, February 8, 1861; *The Tennessean*, February 10, 1861; *Richmond Enquirer*, February 8, 1861; *Chicago Tribune*, February 4, 1861; *New York Times*, February 8, 1861. See also, Roosevelt Civil War Envelopes Collection, Manuscripts Collection, Booth Family Center for Special Collections, Georgetown University Library.

7. Dix to Shattuck, April 20, 1820, *Proceedings of the Massachusetts Historical Society*, vol. 50. 139–141.

8. Dix, *Memoirs of John Adams Dix*, vol. 1, 118–199; Lichterman, *John Adams Dix, 1798–1879*, 48.

9. Lichterman, 475 (referencing Dix to Blair letter, December 4, 1861).

10. Nevins, *The War for Union*, 422.

11. Dix to Tilden, December 3, 1861, *Letters and Literary Memorials of Samuel J. Tilden*, vol. 1.

12. Dix to Lincoln, January 15, 1863, Lincoln Papers, Library of Congress.

13. Voegeli, "A Rejected Alternative," 765–790.

14. Dix to Tuckerman, January 18, 1862, John A. Dix Collection, Syracuse University.

15. Work, *Lincoln's Political Generals*, 165 (quoting Dix to Seward, April 15, 1863, William Seward Papers, University of Rochester).

16. For scholarship on "hard war" policies and moderation, see, e.g., Grimsley, *The Hard Hand of War*; Neely, *The Civil War and the Limits of Destruction*; Rafuse, *McClellan's War*; Sheehan-Dean, *The Calculus of Violence*.

17. Getty Report, July 11, 1863, ORA 27(2):837–839; Van Buren to Getty, June 30, 1863, ORA 27(2):840.

18. John Dix to Catherine Dix, July 3, 1863, Dix Papers, Columbia University.

19. John A. Dix, *Letter from John A. Dix to the War Democracy of Wisconsin*, September 10, 1863 (in Dix, *Memoirs of John Adams Dix*, vol. 2, 343); Work, *Lincoln's Political Generals*, 215.

20. Lichterman, *John Adams Dix, 1798–1879*, 14.

21. Johnson, *Twentieth Century Biographical Dictionary of Notable Americans*, vol. 3, 1898, 277–280. See also, Lichterman, *John Adams Dix, 1798–1879*.

22. Johnson, "Blockade or Trade Monopoly?"; Futrell, "Federal Trade with the Confederates States" (author estimates large quantities of bacon passed through Norfolk to Lee's troops).

23. Department of Virginia Returns, November 30, 1863, *ORA* 18:467. A *New York Daily Herald* correspondent listed Dix's staff as follows: Colonel D. T. Van Buren, Assistant Adjutant General; Lieutenant Colonel C. W. Thomas, Chief Quartermaster; Surgeon Rufus H. Gilbert, Medical Director; Major Charles Seafort Stewart, Chief Engineer; Major Charles Temple Dix, Aid-de-Camp; Captain G. Von Eickstedt, Aid-de-Camp; Captain Charles S. Davis, Chief Signal Officer; Lieutenant F. R. Kent, Acting Chief Ordnance Officer; and Lieutenant Charles Worret, Topographical Engineer. *New York Daily Herald*, June 30, 1863.

24. Dix to Halleck, April 23, 1863, *ORA* 18:649–650.

25. Halleck to Dix, December 13, 1862, *ORA* 18:479.

26. Dix to Halleck, December 13, 1862, *ORA* 18:479–480.

27. Department of Virginia Returns, May 31, 1863, *ORA* 18:733.

28. Cooper to Longstreet, April 30, 1863, *ORA* 18:1032.

29. Halleck to Dix, May 14, 1863, *ORA* 18:718. Longstreet's departure and the subsequent US withdrawal raised questions about the purpose of defending the town in the first place. In discussing the matter with Dix, Halleck oddly asserted that Suffolk was "a most ill-chosen position for defense . . . why it was ever occupied I do not know."

30. Halleck to Dix, April 17, 1863, *ORA* 25(2):225–226.

31. Dix to Halleck, April 23, 1863, *ORA* 18:649.

32. *Dix to Gordon, May 7, 1863, ORA* 18:705; *Richmond Dispatch*, May 16, 1863.

33. Itinerary of the Second Division, Fourth Army Corps, May 1–June 1, *ORA* 18:372–373; Gordon, *A War Diary of Events*, 55. Engineering drawings of the West Point works reveal several redans connected by two curtains, all covering the railroad and county road leading east. At the landing itself, Gordon's command also constructed several batteries covering the York River downstream. "Map of West Point, Va., with defensive works constructed by Gordon's Division between May 7 and June 1 1863. Capt. G. W. Cooper, 127th New York," George H. Gordon Papers, Civil War Correspondence, Diaries, and Journals, Massachusetts Historical Society; McGrath, *The History of the 127th New York Volunteers*, 46.

34. Dix to Halleck, May 8, 1863, 10 a.m., *ORA* 18:707; *Richmond Dispatch*, May 16, 1863.

35. Gordon Report, May 16, 1863, *ORA* 18:357; Gordon, *A War Diary of Events*, 65–66.

36. Itinerary of the Second Division, Fourth Army Corps, May 1–June 1, 1863, *ORA* 18:372–373.

37. Ruffin, *Diary of Edmund Ruffin*, vol. 1, 657 (May 15, 1863). Following the raid, General Gordon received a packet of letters delivered by a "tremulous little boy" containing a series of requests from several local widows hoping for the return of their horses, mules, and livestock. Gordon, *A War Diary of Events*, 59; McGrath, *The History of the 127th New York Volunteers*, 47.

38. McGrath, *The History of the 127th New York Volunteers*, 46.

39. Gordon, *A War Diary of Events*, 57.

40. Gordon, *A War Diary of Events*, 63–71; Wallace, *Framingham's Civil War Hero*.

41. Gordon, *A War Diary of Events*, 63–71.

42. Gordon, 63–71.

43. See *ORA*, ser. 3, 1:937–938 (related to amendments to Articles of War); and Pub. L. 37-195 (Second Confiscation Act).

44. Gordon, *A War Diary of Events*, 63–71.

45. Gordon, 63–71.

46. Lee to Pettigrew, May 11, 1863, *ORA* 18:1056; Lee to D. H. Hill, May 25, 1863, *ORA* 18:1071.

47. Pettigrew to Elzey, May 14, 1863, 1 p.m., *ORA* 18:1060–1061. Later in the month, Lee suspected the enemy troops at West Point had arrived from Foster's command in North Carolina. Lee to D. H. Hill, May 25, 1863, *ORA* 18:1071; Lee to D. H. Hill, May 28, 1863, *ORA* 18:1075–1076.

48. Davis to Lee, May 31, 1863, *ORA* 18:1083–1084.

49. Dix to Halleck, May 26, 1863, 11 p.m., *ORA* 18:727–728; McGrath, *The History of the 127th New York Volunteers*, 48; Dix to Hooker, May 31, 1863, *ORA* 18:733. Dix commended Gordon on his "prompt and efficient" withdrawal. Dix to Gordon, June 2, 1863, Gordon Papers, Massachusetts Historical Society.

50. By June 2, Confederate officials were aware of the withdrawal. Seddon to Lee, June 2, 1863, *ORA* 18:1090.

51. Lee to Davis, June 15, 1863, 7 a.m., *ORA* 27(2):295.

52. Johnston, *Virginia Railroads in the Civil War*, 160; Coddington, *The Gettysburg Campaign*, 100. Angus Johnston, in his study of Virginia railroads during the Civil War, concluded that Lee saw the West Point withdrawal as the green light to march north. However, while Johnston's assertion seems plausible, there is no clear evidence the Federal withdrawal from West Point specifically triggered Lee's campaign north.

53. Dix to Hooker, June 9, 1863, *ORA* 27(3):44; Dix Report, *ORA* 27(2):820.

3. THE UNION RAID ON AYLETT'S FOUNDRY

1. Kurtz, "An American Condottiere"; Hutto, *A Poisoned Life*, 45–49; *Argus and Patriot*, April 27, 1854; *Milwaukee Daily News*, March 24, 1855.

2. Gillis Report, June 6, 1863, *ORN* 9:60–61. Today the town is known as "Aylett." Union reports, as well as Virginia newspapers at the time, generally referred to it as "Aylett's."

3. Keyes Orders, June 4, 1864, *ORN* 9:62; S. P. Lee Report, *ORN* 9:59.

4. Keyes's Report, *ORA* 27(2):777–778; Dix to Lockwood, November 11, 1861, *ORN* 5:424–425.

5. Bauer, *Register of Ships of the U.S. Navy, 1775–1990*, 96; Abstract Log of Commodore Jones, *ORN* 9:63 ("colored pilot").

6. Claim of Terrill Bradby (6306), Deposition of Bradby, Southern Claims Commission Case Files, RG 217, NARA (Bradby deposition).

7. Claim of Terrill Bradby (#51404), Deposition of Adelphia Miles, Southern Claims Commission Case Files, RG 217, NARA; Babcock Report, December 24, 1863, *ORN* 9:373–374 (refers to Bradby as "Tinell Bradley"); Claim of Terrill Bradby (6306), Summary Report, Southern Claims Commission Case Files, RG 217, NARA ("In June '63 he was a pilot on an Expedition under Gen'l Dix—was at White House. At the same time, U.S. troops of Gen. Getty's command of White House landing on the island + made camp there.").

8. Tevis Report, June 6, 1863, *ORA* 27(2):778–780.

9. Tevis Report, June 6, 1863, *ORA* 27(2):778–780; Gillis Report, June 6, 1863, *ORA* 27(2):781–783.

10. *Richmond Sentinel*, June 19, 1863.

11. Pollard, *Memoirs and Sketches of the Life of Henry Robinson Pollard*, 104.

12. Wise Report, June 6, 1863, *ORA* 27(2):783. Major John R. Bagby led Company K of Colonel Thomas Goode's 4th Virginia Cavalry.

13. Wise to Elzey, June 5, 1863, 10:30 a.m., *ORA* 27(3):861; Wise Report, *ORA* 27(2):783.

14. Elzey to Wise, June 5, 1863, Elzey Service Record, RG 109, NARA (Elzey directed Wise to put his forces on the west side of the Pamunkey and to block a crossing there).

15. Wise to Elzey, June 5, 1863, *ORA* 27(3):861; Elzey to Wise, June 5, 1863, *ORA* 27(3):861–862; and Elzey to Pettigrew, June 5, 1863, *ORA* 27(3):861 (asking Pettigrew to request that Pickett respond to the raid). Wise countermanded some of his orders and sought more guidance from Richmond. Elzey wrote back clarifying that Wise should do whatever was needed to combat the incursion ("exercise your judgment according to the movements of the enemy"). Pettigrew to Elzey, June 6, 1863, *ORA* 27(3):862 (two dispatches).

16. Lee Report, June 6, 1863, *ORA* 27(2):780–781.

17. *Richmond Sentinel*, June 19, 1863.

18. McGuire, *Diary of a Southern Refugee During the War*, 166 (though McGuire claimed "faithful servants" moved the horses to safety).

19. Ruffin, *The Diary of Edmund Ruffin*, vol. 2, 4.

20. Bagby, *King and Queen County, Virginia*, 175.

21. *Richmond Sentinel*, June 19, 1863.

22. Tevis Report, June 6, 1863, *ORA* 27(2):778–780.

23. *Richmond Sentinel*, April 18, 1863 (Williams Report); *OR Supp.*, vol. 27 (ser. 43–44) 475; Wise Report, June 6, 1863, *ORA* 27(2):783 (details of casualties and officers involved; claims three Federals killed and one Confederate wounded).

24. Tevis Report, June 6, 1863, *ORA* 27(2):778–780. The corporal, William Bamford, was paroled and rejoined the regiment. William H. Dickerson and William Bamford Personal Files, Record Group 94, NARA.

25. Tomblin, *Bluejackets and Contrabands*, 55; Tevis Report, June 6, 1863, *ORA* 27(2):778–780; Gillis Report, June 6, 1863, *ORA* 27(2):781.

26. Gillis Report, June 6, 1863, *ORA* 27(2):781; Abstract Log of the Commodore Jones, *ORN* 9:63.

27. *National Tribune*, May 16, 1901 (Nelson, 169th Pennsylvania).

28. *Richmond Sentinel*, April 18, 1863 (Williams's report indicated that thirty to forty horses and three or four wagons were left on shore).

29. *National Tribune*, May 16, 1901 (Nelson, 169th Pennsylvania); Lee Report, June 6, 1863, *ORA* 27(2):780–781. According to one postwar account, the Native Americans at Indian Town "were all Union people." Claim of Terrel Bradby, Deposition of Adelphia Miles, Southern Claims Commission Case Files, RG 217, NARA.

30. Bagby, *King and Queen County, Virginia*, 175.

31. Gillis Report, June 3, 1863, *ORA* 27(2):781.

32. Abstract Log of the *Commodore Jones*, *ORN* 9:63.

33. A 1912 report from the Virginia Division of Mineral Resources indicated that the bluff at Mantapike Landing was 20 feet high. "Between Wakema, right bank (Frazier's Ferry), and Indian Town there is a high bluff about 75 feet in height which is said to be the highest bluff on the river." Bulletin, Issue 4, Virginia Division of Mineral Resources, Charlottesville: University of Virginia, 1912, 137.

34. Mitchell Report, June 6, 1863, *ORN* 9:61–62; Gillis Report, June 6, 1863, *ORA* 27(2):781.

35. See *ORA* 18:124 (expedition to White House, January 7–9), 260 (April 7, 1863, expedition to Gloucester Court House), 359–361 (May 19–22, 1863, combined expedition into Matthews County conducted by Gillis and Judson Kilpatrick).

36. Keyes to Dix, June 8, 1863, John A. Dix Papers, Columbia University (Keyes raised concerns that Pickett, reported to be at Newtown, would join with Wise's force to attack).

37. See, Davis Report, *ORA* 18:32 ("contrabands" warned of approaching Confederate force).

38. Wise to Councill, December 12, 1862, *ORA* 18:798–799.

39. Dix to Lockwood, November 11, 1861, *ORA* 5:424–425.

40. *ORA* 27(2):778. See also, Reports from Matthews County Expedition, *ORA* 18:359–361; "Expedition to Robinson's Plantation in King and Queen County," *ORA* 18:357.

41. Tevis Report, April 12, 1862, *ORA* 18:341 and 343. Tevis followed up this raid with another on April 27. For additional discussion of "hard war" policies and eastern Virginia, see Grimsley, *The Hard Hand of War*, 54–55, 111.

42. Gordon Report, May 16, 1863, *ORA* 18:357.

43. Keyes to Dix, June 16, 1863, OR 27(3):168–9 (Dix's initial letter is not extent).

44. Keyes Report, *ORA* 27(2):777–778.

45. Tevis to "General," April 10, 1866, and Tevis to "Adjutant General," February 20, 1867, Letters Received by the Adjutant General, 1861–1870, RG 94, NARA (on July 16, 1867, designated Brevet Brigadier General for "gallant and meritorious service in the war" backdated to March 13, 1865). Perhaps in support of this procedural maneuver, Tevis requested copies of the official reports for the Aylett's Raid from the War Department in 1866 and again in 1867. Tevis File, Compiled Service Records of Volunteer Union Soldiers Who Served in Organizations from the State of Maryland, RG 94, NARA.

46. Kurtz, "An American Condottiere."

47. Seddon to Lee, June 9, 1863, *ORA* 27(3):874–876.

48. Wise Report, June 6, 1863, *ORA* 27(2):783–784. Wise noted the slaves

escaped from several plantations including Gregg, Robbins, Edwards, Croxton, and Cooke. Bagby, *King and Queen County, Virginia*, 175.

49. *Daily Richmond Examiner*, June 4, 1863.

50. *Semi-Weekly Richmond Enquirer*, June 12, 1863; Jones, A *Rebel War Clerk's Diary*, vol. 2, 313; *Daily Dispatch*, June 17, 1863; Ruffin, *Diary of Edmund Ruffin*, vol. 2, 22; *Fayetteville Observer*, June 25, 1863. Another story claimed that about forty slaves who had walked off the Gregg Plantation during the raid later drowned in the Chesapeake when a boat captain threw them overboard suspecting a smallpox outbreak. The Richmond press labeled the alleged incident an example of "Yankee cruelty."

51. *Richmond Sentinel*, June 19, 1863.

52. Wise to Elzey, June 9, 1863, *ORA* 27(3):876–877. Wise also announced his intention to post men between the Pamunkey and Mattaponi Rivers in King William.

53. Wise Report, June 6, 1863, *ORA* 27(2):783; Jones, A *Rebel War Clerk's Diary*, vol. 1, 343 (June 8, 1863, entry).

54. Davis to Lee, June 6, 1863, *ORA* 51(2):721; Lee to A. P. Hill, June 8, 1863, *ORA* 27(3):869; S. P. Lee Report, June 7, 1863, *ORN* 9:59–60 (Admiral Lee speculated that the West Point evacuation had lulled the Confederates into complacency); Dix to Hooker, June 6, 1863, 8 p.m., *ORA* 27(3):20.

55. Hooker to Dix, June 4, 1863, *ORA* 27(3):6; Dix to Hooker, June 9, 1863, *ORA* 27(3):44.

4. HALLECK'S PLANS TO COUNTER LEE'S INVASION

1. Gordon, A *War Diary of Events*, 137.

2. Stanton to Halleck, July 11, 1862, *ORA* 11(3):314.

3. A generally negative view of Halleck's performance as general-in-chief in directing operations, particularly his tendency toward indecision, remains the convention. See, e.g., Marszalek, *Commander of All Lincoln's Armies*; Ambrose, *Halleck*; Pryor, "Conflict, Chaos, and Confidence Abraham Lincoln's Struggle as Commander in Chief;" and Marvel, *Burnside*. However, others have offered more positive assessments. See, e.g., Hattaway and Jones, *How the North Won*; Hattaway and Jones, "'Old Brains' Was Brainy After All," in *The Ongoing Civil War*; Shutes, "Henry Wager Halleck." Halleck frequently expressed a preference for troop "concentration"; see, e.g., Halleck, *Elements of Military Art and Science*, 40–45 ("celerity of movement is less important than concentration" and "the first and most important rule in offensive war is, to keep your forces as much concentrated as possible"); Reardon, *With a Sword in One Hand & Jomini in the Other*, 29; Halleck to Pope, January 27, 1863, *ORA* 8:528 ("[W]e will get time to concentrate and organize our forces").

4. Lincoln to Halleck, January 1, 1862, *ORA* 21:940.

5. Welles, *Diary of Gideon Welles*, vol. 1, 180 and 216; Gordon, A *War Diary of Events*, 137 (during a Washington visit in December 1863, Gordon found Halleck obnoxious and imperious).

6. Haupt, *Reminiscences of General Herman Haupt*, 177. In later 1862, Halleck also wrote: "I have always, whenever it was possible, avoided giving positive

instructions to the commanding generals . . . leaving them the exercise of their own judgement, while giving them my opinion and advice." Halleck to Wright, November 18, 1862, *ORA* 20(2):67.

7. Marszalek, *Commander of All Lincoln's Armies*, 150; Strong, *Diary of George Templeton Strong*, vol. 3, 258 (September 24, 1862, entry).

8. Halleck to Dix, June 14, 1863, 12 p.m., *ORA* 27(3):111; Halleck to Dix, June 14, 1863, Dix Papers. Columbia University. In the handwritten version of Halleck's note in the Dix papers, there is no comma between "Richmond" and "by." It also says "occupy a large force," not "find occupation for a large force of the enemy."

9. Dix to Foster, June 8, 1863, *ORA* 27(3):36–37. Hooker also saw an opportunity in Dix's quarter. On June 15, he wrote the president suggesting, among other things, that Dix could "be re-enforced from the south to act on their rear." Hooker to Lincoln, June 15, 1863, 10 p.m., *ORA* 27(1):43.

10. In ordering Dix to move against Richmond, Halleck chose not to bring troops from the Department of Virginia north to concentrate at Washington—a move arguably at odds with the fundamental Jominian principle of concentration, a notion he stressed in his own writings and at other times during the war. For instance, in rejecting a plan by Grant to conduct a large-scale raid in North Carolina in early 1864, Halleck complained that the Federals had been too often focused on "cutting the toenails of our enemies." Halleck, *Elements of Military Art and Science*, 40–45 ("celerity of movement is less important than concentration" and "the first and most important rule in offensive war is, to keep your forces as much concentrated as possible"); Ambrose, *Halleck*, 125; Reardon, *With a Sword in One Hand & Jomini in the Other*, 29; Halleck to Pope, January 27, 1863, *ORA* 8:528; Ambrose, *Halleck*, 6; Hattaway and Jones, *How the North Won*, 13; Newsome, *The Fight for the Old North State*, 47.

11. Stanton to Dix, June 14, 1863, 11 a.m., *ORA* 27 (3):110.

12. Dix to Halleck, June 14, 1863, *ORA* 27(3):111.

13. Stanton to Dix, June 14, 1863, 11 a.m., *ORA* 27 (3):110.

14. During the meeting, Lincoln apparently made no mention of his direct orders requiring Hooker to track Lee's movement north. When Welles suggested Hooker could pitch in to Lee's rear, the president replied that it "would seem so" but warned that his commanders knew little of the situation. Welles, *Diary of Gideon Welles*, vol. 1, 328–329.

15. Dix Report, *ORA* 27(2):820; Dix to Hooker, June 9, 1863, *ORA* 27(3):44. In June 10 correspondence with President Lincoln, Hooker questioned Dix's approach against Richmond, predicting that Dix, by splitting his forces, had ensured neither column would be successful. Hooker recommended the columns "unite at City Point, or below, and move on the north bank of that river." Hooker to President, June 10, 1863, *ORA* 27(1):34–35.

16. Peck to Dix, June 6, 1863, *ORA* 27(3):20; Dix to Halleck, June 14, 1863, *ORA* 27(3):111; Corcoran to Dix, June 18, 1863, *ORA* 27(3):207; McEvily Report, *ORA* 27(2):789.

17. Keyes to Gordon, June 11, 1863, NARA RG 393; Lee Report, June 16, 1863, *ORN* 9:70; Keyes to Gillis, June 10, 1863, *ORN* 9:68; Ruffin, *Diary of Edmund Ruffin*, vol. 2, 12; Lee Report, June 16, 1863, *ORN* 9:70–71 (complaining

about Keyes and urging better interservice cooperation in future missions); Welles to Lee, June 27, 1863, *ORN* 9:72 (stressing that "neither branch of the service commands the other").

18. Keyes to Dix, June 16, 1863, NARA RG 393, Department of Virginia. On the morning of June 14, 1863, men from the 40th Massachusetts led by Colonel Burr Porter overran the Confederate pickets from the 59th Virginia at the Diascund Bridge, which carried the main road to Richmond and was the site of a Revolutionary War engagement, "without serious resistance." Dix to Hooker, June 11, 1863, *ORA* 27(3):66; Keyes to Gordon, June 14, 1863, RG 393, Fourth Corps, Letters Sent, NARA; Ruffin, *Diary of Edmund Ruffin*, vol. 2, 12. Gordon, *A War Diary*, 96; Keyes to Gordon, June 24, 1863, 4th Corps Letterbook, NARA.

19. Gordon, *A War Diary*, 100; Letter written by D. Shannon from near Richmond, Virginia, to his wife on June 21, 1863, American Civil War Collection, Hamilton College.

20. *Daily Richmond Examiner*, June 13 and 16, 1863; Hume Report, Scout on the Peninsula, VA, *ORA* 27(2):791; Jones, *A Rebel War Clerk's Diary*, vol. 1, 305; *Daily Richmond Examiner*, June 17, 1863 (details operations of Company A of the 59th Virginia ["McCulloch's Rangers"] during the Federal advance).

21. *Daily Richmond Examiner*, June 18, 1863; *Carolina Standard*, June 17, 1863 ("considerable excitement").

22. Ruffin, *Diary of Edmund Ruffin*, vol. 2, 22.

23. Halleck to Dix, June 18, 1863, 10 a.m., *ORA* 27(3):206.

24. Dix to Halleck, June 18, 1863, *ORA* 27(3):206.

25. There were two main overland routes running west over the Peninsula to Richmond: the Old Stage ("Williamsburg") Road running just south of and parallel to the York River, and another road to the south, which passed over the Diascund Bridge and through Providence Forge.

26. Lee Report (June 25, 1863), *ORN* 9:82–83; Halleck to Dix, June 14, 1863, 12 p.m., *ORA* 27(3):111; Halleck to Dix, June 14, 1863, Dix Papers, Columbia University.

27. Department of Virginia Returns, *ORA* 27(3):451–454. Despite Dix's efforts to transfer men to the Peninsula, many units still remained at Suffolk in mid-June, held over for the advance to the Blackwater.

28. See Dix Report, *ORA* 27(2):820; Dix to Corcoran (and Dix to Getty), June 20, 1863, *ORA* 27(3):241.

29. Gordon, *A War Diary of Events*, 110.

30. Keyes to Dix, June 16, 1863, *ORA* 27(3):168–169.

31. Lee to Welles, June 25, 1863, *ORA* 9:82–83 ("that if he had 10,000 more men").

32. Welles, *Diary*, 331.

33. *New York Daily Herald*, June 17, 1863. The *Herald* article was reprinted and referenced in the Richmond papers. See, e.g., *Semi-Weekly Richmond Enquirer*, June 23, 1863.

34. *New York Daily Herald*, June 23, 1863; Ruffin, *Diary of Edmund Ruffin*, vol. 2, 27.

35. Van Buren to Spear, June 23, 1863, *ORA* 27(2):795.

36. See, e.g., Circular, Head Quarters 4th Army Corps, Near 9 Mile Ordinary,

June 24, 1863, 4th Corps Letterbook, National Archives; Gordon, *A War Diary of Events*, 110; Keyes to Gordon, June 22, 1863, and Whitehead to Gordon, June 23, 1863, Gordon Papers, MHS.

37. *History of Battle-flag Day, September 17, 1879*, 163.

5. RICHMOND'S DEFENDERS

1. Lee to Davis, June 10, 1863, *ORA* 27(3):880–882; Lee to Davis, June 25 (two letters), 1863, *ORA* 27(3):930–933.

2. Lee to Davis, June 10, 1863, *ORA* 27(3):880–882.

3. Lee to Davis, June 25, 1863, *ORA* 27(3):930–931. In this June 25 dispatch ("Opposite Williamsport"), Lee thanked Davis for a June 19 letter and stated he was "much gratified by our views in relation to the peace party of the North." Lee also referred to the prisoner exchange controversy. See also, *The Papers of Jefferson Davis*, vol. 9, 230.

4. Cleveland, *Alexander H. Stephens in Public and Private with Letters and Speeches, Before, During, and Since the War*, 718.

5. See Dew, *Apostles of Secession*.

6. Avary, *Recollections of Alexander H. Stephens*, 323; Brumgardt, *Alexander Stephens and the Peace Issue in the Confederacy, 1863–1865*, 10–11.

7. See, e.g., *Philadelphia Inquirer*, July 14, 1869.

8. For Stephens's career generally, see Schott, *Alexander H. Stephens of Georgia*.

9. Jones, *Rebel War Clerk's Diary*, vol. 1, 306.

10. Stephens, *A Constitutional View of the Late War Between the States*, vol. 2, 558.

11. See, e.g., Pierce, *The Effects of the Cessation of Exchange of Prisoners During the Civil War*.

12. A. P. M., "The Capture of the Maple Leaf," *The Southern*, vol. 9 (July–December 1871), 302. See also, Witt, *Escape from the Maple Leaf*; and *Daily Dispatch*, June 25, 1863 (eyewitness account from captured Confederate officer including full list of officers involved).

13. Hunter to Davis, April 23, 1863, *ORA* 14:448.

14. Stephens, *A Constitutional View of the Late War Between the States*, vol. 2, 558.

15. Stephens, 558; Raburn, "A Letter for Posterity," 13.

16. Stephens, *A Constitutional View of the Late War Between the States*, vol. 2, 561.

17. Lee to Davis, June 23, 1863, *ORA* 27(3):930–931; *The Papers of Jefferson Davis*, 229.

18. A. Stephens to L. Stephens, June 22, 1863, Stephens Papers, Manhattanville College; Stephens, *A Constitutional View of the Late War Between the States*, vol. 2, 563–565. In his memoir, Stephens recalled that he left Georgia on June 19 and arrived on June 22 or 23. His correspondence with Linton, however, clearly shows he was still in Georgia on June 22 and arrived in Richmond on June 26.

19. L. Stephens to A. Stephens, June 26, 1863, Stephens Papers, Manhattanville

College. To Linton, Stephens referred generally to some correspondence "between the President and myself" related to the upcoming visit. He left some documents for Linton at Liberty Hall and urged his brother to read the packet. Linton did so several days later on a visit to Crawfordville with his family but resealed the document without revealing any more details in his subsequent correspondence.

20. *Times-Picayune*, April 27, 1861.

21. Brock, *Richmond During the War*, 25; *Evening Telegraph* (Philadelphia), October 14, 1867.

22. *Richmond Dispatch*, July 19, 1885 (account of John E. Edwards).

23. *Daily Dispatch*, June 29, 1863.

24. *Greensboro Patriot*, July 2, 1863.

25. *Daily Richmond Examiner*, June 20, 1863.

26. *Daily Dispatch*, June 27, 1863 (reports of Ewell crossing into Maryland on June 17); *Daily Richmond Examiner*, June 22, 1863; *Daily Dispatch*, June 24, 1863. These reports were not far off. In fact, Rodes's men entered Greencastle, Pennsylvania, on June 22 and reached Chambersburg two days later.

27. *Richmond Dispatch*, March 14, 1863.

28. For scholarship on the Richmond Bread Riot, see Chesson, "Harlots or Heroines?"; Titus, "The Richmond Bread Riot of 1863"; McCurry, *Confederate Reckoning*.

29. *Richmond Daily Dispatch*, July 6 and 11, 1863. Confederate officials suspected espionage in the city but had limited success in tamping it down and never caught Van Lew.

30. Varon, *Van Lew*, 105; *Semi-Weekly Richmond Enquirer*, July 21, 1863 (arrest of Mary C. Allan). In one letter, Allan lamented General Stoneman's lack of aggression during his recent raid, labeling him a "white-gloved general." In her view, the raiders should have burned James Seddon's Goochland Plantation. Her legal defense would outlast the Confederacy, and she herself would outlast most of her contemporaries, dying in 1927 at the age of ninety-three.

31. Hess, *Field Armies and Fortifications in the Civil War*, 171–173. Gilmer also coordinated the efforts on various construction projects throughout Confederate-controlled Virginia.

32. "Map of the Vicinity of Richmond made under the direction of Capt. A. H. Campbell, Chief of Topographical Dept.; Ch'f Engineer's Office D.N.V., Col. J. F. Gilmer, Ch'f. Eng'r, March 21, 1863," Small Special Collections, University of Virginia Library.

33. Pettigrew to Elzey, May 14, 1863, *ORA* 18:1060–1061; Hall to Seddon, June 3, 1863, *ORA* 18:1091.

34. *ORA* 18:1086 (Field Return for Department of Richmond).

35. Elzey to Cooper, May 13, 1863, *ORA* 18:1059; Field Return for Department of Richmond, *ORA* 18:1086 (did not include any brigades from Lee's army or D. H. Hill's department). Returns in May showed the total number of troops in Richmond to be about 8,000, due in part to the presence of Johnston Pettigrew's large infantry brigade at the time.

36. For more on D. H. Hill, see Bridges, *Lee's Maverick General*.

37. Haskell, *Haskell Memoirs*, 40; Stiles, *Four Years Under Marse Robert*, 65–66.

38. *Western Sentinel*, April 3, 1863; Bridges, *Lee's Maverick General*, 153; D. H. Hill Report, *ORA* 19(1):623; D. H. Hill to Seddon, February 23, 1863, *ORA* 18:890–891.

39. Newsome, Horn, and Selby, eds., *Civil War Talks*, 59; Bridges, *Lee's Maverick General*, 85–87; Stovall, *Statesman, Speaker, Soldier, Sage*, 257.

40. D. H. Hill Report, *ORA* 11(2):629; D. H. Hill Report, *ORA* 19(2):1018–1030.

41. Lee to Davis, August 17, 1862, *ORA* 51(2):1075–1076.

42. Lee to Seddon, May 20, 1863, *ORA* 18:1066.

43. Department of North Carolina Returns, *ORA* 18:1086.

44. Cooper to D. H. Hill, May 15, 1863, *ORA* 18:1061–1062.

45. Lee to D. H. Hill, May 16, 1863, *ORA* 18:1063–1064 (offers to exchange Junius Daniel's brigade for one of Hill's).

46. Lee to Davis, May 30, 1863, *ORA* 25(2):832.

47. Lee to D. H. Hill, May 25, 1863, *ORA* 18:1071; D. H. Hill to Lee, May 27, 1863, *ORA* 18:1074–1075; Whiting to Hill, May 28, 1863, *ORA* 18:1076–1077 (Whiting shared Hill's concern, fearing for the railroad's safety following Ransom's departure).

48. Davis to Lee, May 29, 1863, *ORA* 18:1077.

49. Lee to Davis, May 30, 1863, *ORA* 18:1078–1079. "This army has been diminished since last fall by the brigades of Jenkins, Ransom, Cooke, and Evans. It has been increased by Pettigrew's. I consider Colquitt's exchanged for Daniel's."

50. Lee to D. H. Hill, May 30, 1863, *ORA* 18:1079.

51. Davis to Lee, May 31, 1863, *ORA* 18:1083–1084.

52. D. H. Hill to Isabella Hill, June 25, 1863, D. H. Hill Papers, North Carolina State Archives. Although D. H. Hill he may not have objected publicly to Lee's offensive, his aggressive efforts to retain troops in his department in May and into June undoubtedly cost him in terms of his reputation with Lee and with others.

53. Davis to Lee, May 31, 1863, *ORA* 18:1083–1084.

54. Cooper to Hill, May 31, 1863, *ORA* 18:1084–1085.

55. Department of North Carolina and Department of Richmond Returns, *ORA* 18:1086.

56. Lee to Davis, June 23, 1863, *ORA* 27(3):924–926.

57. Lee to Davis, June 25, 1863, *ORA* 27(3):930–931. Lee had made a similar request during the Maryland Campaign when he asked that Bragg head north from Tennessee. See also Alexander, *Fighting for the Confederacy*, 276–277 (Union officials were "insanely afraid of our capturing" Washington); *ORA* 27(3):906; Kean, *Inside the Confederate Government*, 88 (Davis and Cooper's replies were captured by the Federals and printed in the papers); *The Papers of Jefferson Davis*, vol. 9, 247.

58. See Norris to Davis, June 20, and Davis to Elzey, June 21, 1863, *ORA* 41(2):724–725; and Elzey dispatch, June 21, 1863, *ORA* 27(3):910–911.

59. D. H. Hill to Seddon, June 21, 1863, *ORA* 27(3):911. Micah Jenkins to Caroline Jenkins, June 22, 1863, Micah Jenkins Papers, South Caroliniana Library, University of South Carolina.

60. Pickett to Chilton, June 21, 1863, *ORA* 27(3):910.

61. D. H. Hill to Seddon, June 21, 1863, *ORA* 27(3):911.

62. *Richmond Dispatch*, May 20, 1863; Driver, *Richmond Local Defense Troops*, 2–11. By June 1863, the notion of forming a larger militia force floated around the Confederate government. In May, following Stoneman's raid, the City Council approved a plan for the organization of Richmond's civilians, including employees of the War Department.

63. Jones, *A Rebel War Clerk's Diary*, vol. 1, 344 (June 9, 1863, entry).

64. Jones, 347–348 (June 14, 1863, entry). Tension between Confederate and state officials stemmed, in part, from Davis's declaration that the force would report to Confederate, not state, commanders.

65. Jones, 348–354 (June 19, 1863, entry).

66. McGuire, *Diary of a Southern Refugee during the War*, 165.

67. *Daily Examiner*, June 24 and 25, 1863.

68. *Daily Dispatch*, June 23, 1863.

69. *Daily Richmond Examiner*, June 25, 1863.

70. William Walter Cleary Diary, June 24, 1863, entry, VMHC. William Augustine Claiborne Diary, VMHC; *Daily Richmond Examiner*, June 25, 1863.

71. *Daily Richmond Examiner*, June 25, 1863. Letcher also urged the listeners to remember Virginia's "proud position" in the Revolutionary War.

72. William Walter Cleary Diary, June 24, 1863, entry, VMHC.

73. Andrews to S. S. Lee and Tabb to Wise, June 25, 1863, *ORA* 27(3):934–935.

74. *Fayetteville Weekly Observer*, July 13, 1863 (letter by Murdoch John McSween, a member of the 35th North Carolina, writing under the pen name "Long Grabs").

75. *Richmond Sentinel*, June 26, 1863.

76. Seddon to D. H. Hill, June 25, 1863, *ORA* 27(3):933; D. H. Hill to Seddon, June 25, 1863, *ORA* 27(3):936; *Greensboro Patriot*, July 2, 1863.

6. DIX BEGINS HIS PENINSULA CAMPAIGN

1. *Semi-Weekly Richmond Enquirer*, June 26, 1863 (Vicksburg reports).

2. *Daily Dispatch*, June 25, 1863.

3. Halleck to Hooker, June 15, 1863, 2 p.m., *ORA* 27(1):41–42.

4. Hooker to Lincoln, June 16, 1863, 11 a.m., *ORA* 27(1):45; Lincoln to Hooker, June 16, 1863, 10 p.m., *ORA* 27(1):47.

5. Halleck to Hooker, June 16, 1863, 10.15 p.m., *ORA* 27(1):47.

6. Marszalek, *Commander of All Lincoln's Armies*.

7. Hooker to Halleck, June 27, 1863, 1 p.m., *ORA* 27(1):60 (Hooker's request to be relieved); Halleck to Hooker, June 16, 1863, 10.15 p.m., *ORA* 27(1):47; Marszalek, *Commander of All Lincoln's Armies*.

8. Halleck to Dix, June 18, 1863, 10 a.m., *ORA* 27(3):206.

9. Foster to Halleck, June 20, 1863, 9 p.m., *ORA* 27(3):242.

10. Eighteenth Corps, Department of North Carolina Returns, *ORA* 18(1):736.

11. For operations in North Carolina during the first three years of the war, see Barrett, *The Civil War in North Carolina*; Sauers, *The Burnside Expedition in North Carolina*; Newsome, *The Fight for the Old North State*.

12. Halleck to Potter, June 22, 1863, *ORA* 27(3):265.

13. Foster offered about ten regiments, all of them "nine months" men, for immediate transport north to Fort Monroe or to Baltimore. Foster to Halleck, June 20, 1863, 9 p.m., *ORA* 27(3):242.

14. For example, the 45th Massachusetts, whittled down by fever to 350 effectives, arrived at Fort Monroe on June 25, just twelve days before their scheduled departure from the army. The regiment's commander, Colonel Charles Codman, informed Halleck he hoped to return to New England if they were not needed in Virginia. Codman to Halleck, June 25, 1863, *ORA* 27(3):332. See also Mann, *History of the Forty-fifth Regiment, Massachusetts Volunteer Militia.* Foster himself traveled north, accompanied by about half a dozen more Massachusetts infantry units (3rd, 5th, 8th, 43rd, 44th, 46th, and 51st), all under General Henry Prince. Three Pennsylvania infantry regiments (158th, 168th, and 171st) commanded by Francis Spinola followed closely behind. Foster to Halleck, June 28, 1863, *ORA* 27(3):394–395; Department of North Carolina. Returns, *ORA* 27(3):454; Dix to Halleck, June 29, 1863, *ORA* 27(3):412.

15. Foster to Halleck, June 28, 1863, 1 a.m., *ORA* 27(3):394–395; Foster to Halleck, June 30, 1863, *ORA* 438–439 (rainy weather has delayed cavalry raid).

16. Halleck to Kelley, June 25, 1863, 1:29 p.m., *ORA* 27(3):330.

17. At nearly the same time that Halleck sent his dispatch, Daniel Butterfield, Hooker's chief of staff, also suggested a similar move against Lynchburg. *Joint Committee on the Conduct of the War at the Second Session Thirty-Eighth Congress, 1864,* 294 (Butterfield to Chase, June 27, 1863).

18. Kelley to Halleck, June 25, 1863, 1:29 p.m., *ORA* 27(3):330.

19. Shirley, "A Raid of the 11th Pa. Cav."

20. Cruikshank, *Back in the Sixties,* 39.

21. John C. Lee to Dix, June 24, 1863, Dix Papers, Columbia University.

22. Dix Report, July 1863, *ORA* 27(2):820; Skelly, John A. Letter, June 30, 1863.

23. John Dix to Catherine Dix, June 25, 1863, Dix Papers, Columbia University.

24. Lee Report (June 25, 1863), *ORN* 9:82.

25. John Dix to Catherine Dix, June 25, 1863, Dix Papers, Columbia University.

26. Dix to Halleck, June 25, 1863, 4 p.m., *ORA* 27(2):793.

27. *Daily Alta California,* August 10, 1863; Crowninshield to Mammy, July 2, 1863, Caspar Crowninshield Papers, Massachusetts Historical Society; *Orangeburg News,* September 26, 1874 (article about Company I, 11th Pennsylvania); Skelly, John A. Letter, June 30, 1863; George Cruikshank letter, June 30, 1863, George L. Cruikshank Civil War letters, State Historical Society of Iowa (baggage transported on the *Maple Leaf*); Roper, *History of the Eleventh Pennsylvania Volunteer Cavalry,* 75; *New York Daily Herald,* July 1, 1863 (Colors of 11th Pennsylvania lost off transports at Yorktown).

28. *Burlington Times,* June 9, 1866; Peck to Dix, June 10, 1863, *ORA* 27(3):53; *National Tribune,* September 13, 1906 (reminiscences of J. N. Flint).

29. *Public Opinion Weekly* (Chambersburg), May 4, 1875; *Daily Commonwealth* (Topeka) May 13, 1875; *Morristown Gazette,* July 7, 1875; *The Times* (Phil.), April 26, 1875.

30. *New York Daily Herald,* June 30, 1863; Shirley, "A Raid of the 11th Pa. Cav.," January 19, 1884; Skelly, John A. Letter, June 30, 1863; George

Cruikshank letter, June 30, 1863, George L. Cruikshank Civil War letters, State Historical Society of Iowa.

31. *History of the Eleventh Pennsylvania Volunteer*, 75.

32. *Daily Alta California*, August 10, 1863; *New York Daily Herald*, June 30, 1863; Spear to Van Buren, 7:30 a.m., June 25, 1863, Dix Papers, Columbia University (mix of infantry and cavalry).

33. *Semi-Weekly Richmond Enquirer*, June 30, 1863; Spear to Van Buren, 12:00 p.m., June 25, 1863, Dix Papers, Columbia University; *Semi-Weekly Richmond Enquirer*, June 30, 1863 (separately, a detachment of Californians also fanned out into the countryside on foot but failed to find any additional sign of the enemy); *Daily Alta California*, August 10, 1863; George Cruikshank letter, June 30, 1863, George L. Cruikshank Civil War letters, State Historical Society of Iowa; *New York Daily Herald*, July 1, 1863.

34. *New York Daily Herald*, June 30, 1863.

35. Spear to Van Buren, 12:00 p.m., June 25, 1863, Dix Papers, Columbia University; Corbett Diary, Bancroft Library, Berkeley.

36. Diary of Gurdon Robins (Lt. AQM, 16th Conn.), University of Connecticut Special Collections.

37. NARA M653; Eighth Census of the United States (1860 population schedules).

38. Richardson, *Southern Generals*, 53.

39. Spear to Van Buren, 12:00 p.m., June 25, 1863, Dix Papers, Columbia University; *Daily Alta California*, August 10, 1863. One of the boats was apparently left without unloading rations and forage. George Cruikshank Letter, June 30, 1863, George L. Cruikshank Civil War Letters, State Historical Society of Iowa.

40. Keyes to Dix, June 16, 1863, ORA 27(3):168–169.

41. See Longacre, *Mounted Raids of the Civil War*, 12.

42. Stuart, "Samuel Ruth and General R. E. Lee"; Johnston, *The Virginia Railroads in the Civil War*, 68–72, 117, and 150–155.

43. Pettigrew to Elzey, May 14, 1863, 1 p.m., ORA 18:1060–1061 (recommending the construction of fortifications to protect the South and North Anna River rail bridges); Hall to Seddon, June 3, 1863, ORA 18:1091; Gilmer to Stevens, Aug 5, 1863 (Gilmer calls for improvements to South Anna works) ORA 29(2):626; *New York Daily Herald*, August 5, 1863 (excerpt from *Daily Richmond Examiner* reporting South Anna bridge repaired); Lee to Seddon, March 25, 1863, ORA 25(2):683–684; Virginia Central Railroad Records, Library of Virginia ("The Virginia Central Railroad promises to pay in current funds at their office in Richmond to [slave owner] or assigns, the sum of [__] Dollars, being for hire of [__] slave named [__] said Slave to be employed on the Virginia Central Railroad, and to be returned well clothed in the usual way, and with a Hat and Blanket.").

44. Seddon to Lee, March 31, 1863, ORA 25(2):693.

45. Daniel to Seddon, August 1, 1863, ORA 51(2):747.

46. Lee to Cooper, June 23, 1863, ORA 27(3):925–926; Lee to Longstreet, June 15, 1863, ORA 27(3):891.

47. See, Lee to Davis, June 25, 1863 ("Opposite Williamsport"), ORA

Notes to Pages 88–91

27(3):930–931; Lee to Davis, June 25, 1863 ("Williamsport"), *ORA* 27(3):931–933. See also, Wynstra, *At the Forefront of Lee's Invasion.* The ammunition for Lee's army was limited to whatever his supply wagons could carry, augmented only by whatever his men could capture from Federal garrisons along the way.

48. Although supply shipments continued to run along the Virginia Central from Richmond to Staunton in the latter part of the month, no comprehensive records survive for those shipments in June and July, making it difficult to precisely gauge Lee's reliance on the railways during June.

49. Marshall, *An Aide-de-Camp of Lee*, 218–220; Marshall, "Events Leading Up to the Battle of Gettysburg," 226. For shipments, see, e.g., *Weekly Advertiser*, July 15, 1863 ("Dispatch from Martinsburg dated July 9 . . . an ordnance train has just passed to Lee who is waiting for it."); *Weekly Raleigh Register*, July 15, 1863 (" . . . an ordnance train had just passed Martinsburg on its way to our army"). See also, Wise, *The Long Arm of Lee*, 400. See chapter 21 for additional discussion of these issues.

7. SPEAR'S RAID TO THE SOUTH ANNA

1. William Fanning Wickham Diary, Wickham Family Papers, VMHC.
2. Special Order A, No. 1, *ORA* 27(2):795.
3. Special Order A, No. 1, *ORA* 27(2):795.
4. Crowninshield to Mammy, July 2, 1863, Caspar Crowninshield Papers, Massachusetts Historical Society.
5. Cruikshank, *Back in the Sixties*, 40. Many of the men in Company A, 11th Pennsylvania were from Iowa.
6. Longacre, *Mounted Raids of the Civil War*, 14; *Republican & Sentinel*, July 27, 1863; William Fanning Wickham Diary, Wickham Family Papers, VMHC (fine weather and then some rain); Cruikshank, *Back in the Sixties*, 40; George Cruikshank letter, June 30, 1863, George L. Cruikshank Civil War Letters, State Historical Society of Iowa; *New York Daily Herald*, July 1, 1863; Ruffin, *Diary of Edmund Ruffin*, vol. 2 (Shattered Dream), 32.
7. *Richmond Dispatch*, June 27, 1863; Spear's Report, *ORA* 27(2):795–797.
8. *New York Times*, July 6, 1863 (says column encamped at "Barrett" about 10 miles from Richmond; period maps show no such property but do show a "Bassett" farm on Spear's path); *History of the Eleventh Pennsylvania*, 76–77; *Daily Alta California*, August 10, 1863 (large field). The regimental history for the 11th Pennsylvania says the forces stopped for the night in the "vicinity of Hanovertown." However, other accounts make it clear that they stopped somewhere to the south, probably southeast of Old Church. Confederate States of America, Army, Department of Northern Virginia, Chief Engineer's Office, and Edward Porter Alexander. *Map of the counties of Charles City, Goochland, Hanover, Henrico, King William, New Kent, and part of the counties of Caroline and Louisa, Virginia.* [Chief Engineer's Office, D.N.V, 1864] Map, Library of Congress.
9. Cruikshank, *Back in the Sixties*, 40.
10. Cooper to Lee, June 29, 1863, *ORA* 27(1):75–76; Corse to Elzey, June 15, 1863, *ORA* 27(3):893–894.
11. Picket to Chilton, June 21, 1863, *ORA* 27(3):910. Pickett headed north

with only three infantry brigades—Armistead's, Garnett's, and Kemper's—totaling fewer than 5,000 men.

12. Singeltary Report, *ORA* 27(2):797.

13. Wise to Elzey, June 25, 1863—4 p.m., *ORA* 27(3):936; Wise to Chestney, June 25, 1863, *ORA* 27(3):935 (Colonel is identified in dispatch as Shingler); *Fayetteville Semi-Weekly*, June 29, 1863 (excerpt from *Richmond Dispatch*).

14. *Daily Alta California*, August 10, 1863; Ruffin, *Diary of Edmund Ruffin*, vol. 2, 32, 37 and 55.

15. *Staunton Spectator*, July 7, 1863; *New York Daily Herald*, July 1, 1863.

16. Ruffin, *Diary of Edmund Ruffin*, vol. 2, 32; *Richmond Sentinel*, June 27, 1863.

17. McGuire, *Diary of Southern Refugee*, 67; *Richmond Sentinel*, June 27, 1863.

18. Crowninshield to Mammy, July 2, 1863, Caspar Crowninshield Papers, Massachusetts Historical Society; *OR Supp.*, vol. 27, 130.

19. Eighth Census of the United States, 1860, vol. 1, United States. Census Office (total free Black population in Hanover County listed as 257).

20. Spear's Report, *ORA* 27(2):795–797; *Daily Alta California*, August 10, 1863; Roper, *History of the Eleventh Pennsylvania Volunteer Cavalry* (Phil. 1902), 76; Cruikshank, *Back in the Sixties*, 40.

21. Shirley, "A Raid of the 11th Pa. Cav.," January 19, 1884.

22. Spear Report, *ORA* 27(2):795–797; *Daily Alta California*, August 10, 1863; *History of the Eleventh Pennsylvania Volunteer Cavalry*, 76; Cruikshank, *Back in the Sixties*, 40; Shirley, "A Raid of the 11th Pa. Cav.," January 19, 1884.

23. *Daily Alta California*, August 10, 1863; *History of the Eleventh Pennsylvania Volunteer Cavalry*, 77; Skelly, John A. Letter, June 30, 1863; George Cruikshank letter, June 30, 1863, George L. Cruikshank Civil War letters, State Historical Society of Iowa (says another train had reportedly passed through an hour before).

24. *New York Times*, July 6, 1863. According to William Shirley from Company G (11th Pennsylvania), one of the Pennsylvanians was killed in the charge and a few were wounded. Shirley, "A Raid of the 11th Pa. Cav."

25. *Daily Alta California*, August 10, 1863; *History of the Eleventh Pennsylvania Volunteer Cavalry* (Phil. 1902), 77; Skelly, John A. Letter, June 30, 1863; George Cruikshank letter, June 30, 1863, George L. Cruikshank Civil War letters, State Historical Society of Iowa.

26. Haas and Talley, *A Refugee at Hanover Tavern*, 94; *Greensboro Patriot*, July 2, 1863 (Wight describes theft and destruction and reports that they "carried off several negroes, both male and female—especially the female.").

27. *Greensboro Patriot*, July 9, 1863.

28. Spear's Report, *ORA* 27(2):795–797. *Daily Alta California*, August 10, 1863; *History of the Eleventh Pennsylvania Volunteer Cavalry*, 76; Cruikshank, *Back in the Sixties*, 40; Shirley, "A Raid of the 11th Pa. Cav."

29. Skelly, John A. Letter, June 30, 1863.

30. Godwin to Seddon, June 26, 1863, *ORA* 27(3):938. Captain L. W. Allen passed on to his commanding officer, Colonel D. J. Godwin, reports of the enemy "advancing toward Richmond in three columns—one by Diascund Bridge, on

the James City, one by Barhamsville, on the Williamsburg Road, and one by the White House, each column estimated at from 5,000 to 7,000 strong."

31. *Wilmington Morning Star*, March 10, 1897; *ORA* 27(2):798 (Godwin Report).

32. *ORA* 27(2):798 (Godwin Report). Allen's cavalry company would become part of the 40th Virginia Cavalry Battalion in July and then part of the 24th Virginia Cavalry regiment later in the war.

33. See also, Jordan, *North Carolina Troops*, vol. 10, Raleigh: North Carolina Office of Archives and History, 1985, 399.

34. *Wilmington Morning Star*, March 10, 1897; *ORA* 27(2):798 (Godwin Report).

35. *Asheville Citizen-Times*, June 24, 1923 (account of Robert Bingham); *Henderson Daily Dispatch*, May 8, 1926 (Peace account); Jordan, *North Carolina Troops*, vol. 10, Raleigh: North Carolina Office of Archives and History, 1985, 399.

36. Peace, "Fighting at Great Odds."

37. Devine, "Defense of the South Anna Bridge," *Confederate Veteran*, vol. 40, 178–182.

38. Peace, "Fighting at Great Odds"; Devine, "Defense of the South Anna Bridge," ("thirty thousand stands of arms and a large depot of supplies of ammunition and food").

39. *Oxford Public Ledger*, September 24, 1903; NARA M270; *Wilmington Messenger*, August 23, 1889; Winston, Robert, "A Rebel Colonel," 84. Hargrove was born in Townesville, North Carolina.

40. The Hanover Court House Road was also known as the River Road; today it is Hickory Hill Road. See Map of Hickory Hill in Cemetery, *Hickory Hill Slave and African American Cemetery*, DHR No. 042-5792, National Register of Historic Places Registration Form; and Map of W. F. Wickham's Plantation Known as "Hickory Hill," February 1878, Hickory Hill, Private Collection.

41. *Semi-Weekly Richmond Enquirer*, June 30, 1863; *Greensboro Patriot*, July 2, 1863 (account says that "three" trains approached).

42. *Richmond Sentinel*, July 1, 1863 (the men included Lieutenant McKnight, Sergeants George Summers and John Mills, George Millan, a man named Simpson of the Fairfax Rifles, and another named Baxter of the Prince William Rifles); Cruikshank, *Back in the Sixties*, 41; Shirley, "A Raid of the 11th Pa. Cav."

43. *Asheville Citizen Times*, June 24, 1923 (Bingham account); Godwin Report, *ORA* 27(2):798–799; Cruikshank, 41; Shirley, "A Raid of the 11th Pa. Cav.," January 19, 1884 ("no artillery"); Skelly, John A. Letter, June 30, 1863. Accounts vary on the number and nature of the earthworks at the position on June 26, 1863. Most identify a trench line just west of and perpendicular to the rail line. Others identify more. See Shirley (two forts); John Skelly (three forts; "Dirt forts had been constructed on the north side, but these were too far from the bridge for occupation"); *Henderson Daily Dispatch*, May 8, 1926 (Alexander Peace account); George Cruikshank letter, June 30, 1863, George L. Cruikshank Civil War letters, State Historical Society of Iowa ("there were several earthworks this side of the river but they were deserted, on the other side, the rebels are

[inside] a house and line of rifle pits on each side of the R.R."); *Chatham Record,* March 11, 1897 (Stedman article; breastwork on the south side of the bridge built to be manned by no fewer than 400 men).

44. Shirley, "A Raid of the 11th Pa. Cav."

45. *Henderson Daily Dispatch,* May 8, 1926 (Peace account).

46. *Republican & Sentinel,* July 27, 1863 ("drawing the fire"; says advance guard was led by Lieutenant Ramsey); *Asheville Citizen Times,* June 24, 1923 (Bingham account); Godwin Report, *ORA* 27(2):798–799; Cruikshank, *Back in the Sixties,* 41; Shirley, "A Raid of the 11th Pa. Cav."; *Henderson Daily Dispatch,* May 8, 1926 (Peace account); Singeltary Report, *ORA* 27(2):797.

47. Crowninshield to Mammy, July 2, 1863, Caspar Crowninshield Papers, Massachusetts Historical Society; *Richmond Sentinel,* June 29, 1863 (at about 2 p.m.); *Daily Alta California,* August 10, 1863; *Asheville Citizen Times,* June 24, 1923 (Bingham account).

48. *Daily Alta California,* August 10, 1863; *Republican & Sentinel,* July 27, 1863 ("shots did little damage"); *New York Times,* July 6, 1863; *Asheville Citizen Times,* June 24, 1923 (Bingham account); *Richmond Sentinel,* June 29, 1863.

49. Peace, "Fighting at Great Odds," 370–371; *Semi-Weekly Richmond Enquirer,* July 21, 1863; *New York Times,* July 6, 1863; *Asheville Citizen Times,* June 24, 1923 (Bingham account; says two companies were A and G); *Daily Alta California,* August 10, 1863 (saying ford was above the bridge but all other sources say below); Cruikshank, *Back in the Sixties,* 41; *History of the Eleventh Pennsylvania Volunteer Cavalry,* 76; John A. Skelly, Letter, June 30, 1863 (one of three Skelly brothers in the regiment—John, James, and Joseph; Skelly's name is sometimes spelled "Skelley").

50. *Asheville Citizen Times,* June 24, 1923 (Bingham account).

51. *Oxford Public Ledger,* September 24, 1903; *The Land We Love,* March 1867, 375 (letter from Robert Bingham). The first name of private "Cates" is unknown. Records for the 44th North Carolina show about twenty individuals named "Cates" serving in the regiment as well as half a dozen privates of that name in Company G captured at the South Anna on June 26. Compiled Service Records of Confederate Soldiers Who Served in Organizations from the State of North Carolina, RG 109, NARA.

52. *National Tribune,* August 23, 1883.

53. *Daily Alta California,* August 10, 1863 (saying ford was above the bridge but all other sources say below); Cruikshank, *Back in the Sixties,* 41; *History of the Eleventh Pennsylvania Volunteer Cavalry,* 76; *New York Times,* July 6, 1863. *Republican & Sentinel,* July 27, 1863 ("Had they charged firmly, the enemy must have surrendered, and the fight would have closed."); Shirley, William, "A Raid of the 11th Pa. Cav." According to Bingham's recollection long after the war, Skelly made two other unsuccessful attacks, but other Union sources do not mention that. *Asheville Citizen Times,* June 24, 1923 (Bingham account).

54. *Annual report of the Adjutant-General of the Commonwealth of Massachusetts,* 935 (Lieutenants [William M.] Rumery, [John F.] Richards, and [John W.] Sim also led in the advance); *Republican & Sentinel,* July 27, 1863.

55. John A. Skelly, Letter, June 30, 1863; *Daily Alta California,* August 10,

1863. More men with Roper may have also "crossed the river at a shorter distance below the bridge" and dismounted the men under the cover of thick bushes. *History of the Eleventh Pennsylvania Volunteer Cavalry*, 76.

56. *Daily Alta California*, August 10, 1863; Crowninshield to Mammy, July 2, 1863, Caspar Crowninshield Papers, Massachusetts Historical Society.

57. Cruikshank, *Back in the Sixties*, 41.

58. *Republican & Sentinel*, July 27, 1863.

59. *Record-Union*, July 3, 1898; *Henderson Daily Dispatch*, May 8, 1926 (Peace account).

60. Crowninshield to Mammy, July 14, 1863, Caspar Crowninshield Papers, Massachusetts Historical Society. For a recent discussion of close-quarters fighting in the Civil War, see, Steplyk, *Fighting Means Killing*, 90–118.

61. The multiple, conflicting accounts, drawn from various perspectives and recorded at different times after the battle, make it difficult to piece together the engagement's details, particularly the melee at the end. Some of the more detailed accounts of the brutal hand-to-hand fighting appeared well after the war. The various accounts of the South Anna Bridge fight underscore the difficulties in piecing together multiple recollections of a single event. The various locations of the participants, personal and political biases, the stress of combat, and, most of all, the imperfection of memory all dilute and distort accounts recorded after any traumatic event.

Most of the sources agree on the basic chain of events. Colonel Spear's cavalry arrived at the bridge. The Confederates withdrew to the north bank. Some Federals conducted an initial, unsuccessful charge after crossing the ford downstream from the bridge. Spear then ordered a two-prong attack, one mounted and one dismounted. This effort overwhelmed the Confederates, and Spear's men captured the bridge after intense hand-to-hand combat. Beyond this basic story line, the many accounts reveal disagreements, inconsistencies, and omissions. Accounts differ on the number of earthworks in the vicinity, the duration of the hand-to-hand fighting, and the details of the Federal river crossing near the bridge.

62. Peace, *To Tranquillity*, 149 (Alexander Peace to W. K. Peace, June 29, 1863); *Asheville Citizen Times*, June 24, 1923 (Bingham account). After the Federals closed with Company A, Bingham ordered his men to cease firing to avoid hitting their comrades.

63. Cruikshank, *Back in the Sixties*, 41.

64. *Asheville Citizen Times*, June 24, 1923 (Bingham account); *Henderson Daily Dispatch*, May 8, 1926 (Peace account); and Peace, *To Tranquillit*, 149.

65. *Henderson Daily Dispatch*, May 8, 1926 (Peace account); Peace, *To Tranquillity*, 149; *Asheville Citizen Times*, June 24, 1923 (Bingham account); *Oxford Public Ledger*, September 24, 1903; *The Land We Love*, March 1867, 375 (letter from Robert Bingham).

66. *Henderson Daily Dispatch*, May 8, 1926 (Peace account); *Oxford Public Ledger*, September 24, 1903 (Peace account). See also, Jordan, ed., *North Carolina Troops*, vol. 10, 401. However, Robert Bingham, who wrote of Cash's involvement soon after the war and years after, did not mention Cash's encounter with Spear. Peace's is probably more credible since Bingham did not participate in the fight at the watchman's hut. See *The Land We Love*, March 1867, 375 (letter

from Robert Bingham) and *Asheville Citizen Times*, June 24, 1923 (Bingham account).

67. *Henderson Daily Dispatch*, May 8, 1926 (Peace account).

68. *Henderson Daily Dispatch*, May 8, 1926 (Peace account); first names from Compiled Service Records, RG 109, NARA.

69. *Daily Alta California*, August 10, 1863.

70. *History of the Eleventh Pennsylvania Volunteer Cavalry*, 76 (1st Sergeant of Company B killed after surrender); *OR Supp.*, pt. 2, vol. 57, 161 (McFarlan killed).

71. *New York Times*, July 6, 1863 (ten minutes); Skelly, John A. Letter, June 30, 1863 ("took the whole force after a hand-to-hand fight of about 20 minutes"); *Daily Alta California*, August 10, 1863; *Republican & Sentinel*, July 27, 1863 ("shots did little damage"); *Henderson Daily Dispatch*, May 8, 1926 (Peace account). "The enormous disproportion in strength made the contest very short. It lasted only half an hour." *Richmond Sentinel*, June 29, 1863. See also, Shirley, "A Raid of the 11th Pa. Cav."

72. *Daily Alta California*, August 10, 1863.

73. Spear Report, *ORA* 27(2):795.

74. Spear and Dix Reports, *ORA* 27(2):794–797. Samuel J. Corbett, a Californian in Company A, in his diary put the Union loss at three killed and five wounded and Confederate loses at thirty killed and wounded. Corbett Diary, Bancroft Library, University of California, Berkely; *Republican & Sentinel*, July 27, 1863 (anonymous account from New Yorker—Confederate—ten killed; eighteen wounded); Godwin Report *ORA* 27(2):798–799 (Confederates at the bridge—five killed, nineteen wounded [Confederate]; Godwin's cavalry—two men and one horse shot [Captain Allen's]; Federal—six killed and thirteen wounded).

75. Singeltary Report, *ORA* 27(2):797 (says fifty men in Company A and forty in Company G were in the fight). Colonel Godwin, who commanded Confederate cavalry in the area, put the losses at five killed and nineteen wounded from his side and six killed and thirteen wounded for the Federals. Godwin Report *ORA* 27(2):798–799.

76. *Daily Alta California*, August 10, 1863; *OR Supp.*, pt. 2, vol. 57, 161 (R. McFarlan, Co. B, 11th Pa., killed by bayonet to heart). Casualties among the Californians included Private Joseph A. Burdick and Richard S. Ellet, both of San Francisco. Parson, *Bear Flag and Bear State in the Civil War*, 60.

77. *Republican & Sentinel*, July 27, 1863; Singeltary Report, *ORA* 27(2):797.

78. *Richmond Sentinel*, June 29, 1863. For an extensive discussion of prisoner experiences from 44th North Carolina, see *Asheville Citizen Times*, June 24, 1923 (Bingham account). *Old Homes of Hanover County*, 103–104; "[Map of Hanover County, Va.]," G3883.H3 186-.M2, Library of Congress Geography and Map Division, Library of Congress (location of South Wales—marked "E. Winston"—home of Edmund and Sarah Terrell Winston).

79. Various postwar recollections from Confederate veterans and secondary accounts include: Devine, "Defense of the South Anna Bridge"; Bingham, "North Carolinians at South Anna Bridge," 455–458; Bingham, "A Reminiscences of 1863," n.p., 1916; Peace, "Fighting at Great Odds," 370–371; Bingham, "We Saved Gen. Lee's Communications with Richmond," *Civil War Times Illustrated*,

5:22–25; T. H. Pearce, "Defenders of the South Anna Bridge," *The State*, January 1984 (Vol. 51, No. B), 76–78; Hess, *Lee's Tarheels*, 109.

80. *Daily Alta California*, August 10, 1863; *Oxford Public Ledger*, September 24, 1903; *The Land We Love*, March 1867, 375 (letter from Robert Bingham); *Henderson Daily Dispatch*, May 8, 1926 (Peace account); *Asheville Citizen Times*, June 24, 1923 (Bingham account).

81. Confederate reminiscences contain various quotes about their performance attributed to Spear. See, e.g., *Chatham Record*, March 11, 1897 (Charles Stedman article; Spear supposed "he was fighting four hundred infantry instead of eighty").

82. Godwin Report, *ORA* 27(2):798.

83. Spear Report, *ORA* 27(2):796–797.

84. *Richmond Dispatch*, June 27, 1863.

85. Godwin to Elzey, June 26, 1863, 10 p.m., *ORA* 27(3):938. Hargrove's reports reached Captain Bingham at Taylorsville and then Colonel Godwin at Hanover Junction, who sent Allen's cavalry in support. Godwin would later wire General Elzey in Richmond that he "had driven the enemy off; can't say how far"—adding news about the burned bridge and casualties. He finished his short dispatch with three words: "Send the re-enforcements."

86. *Richmond Dispatch*, June 27, 1863; Cooke to Gilmer, June 26, 1863, *ORA* 51(2):728; Singeltary Report, *ORA* 27(2):797; *Charleston Mercury*, June 30, 1863 (letter from "Hermes").

8. ROONEY LEE'S CAPTURE

1. See Williams Carter Wickham Correspondence (Folder 4 of 6), Wickham Family Papers, VMHC (contains detailed Brandy Station account).

2. Michel, "From Slavery to Freedom," 109–110.

3. *Hickory Hill Slave and African American Cemetery*, DHR No. 042-5792, National Register of Historic Places Registration Form; and "Map of W.F. Wickham's Plantation Known as "Hickory Hill," February 1878, Hickory Hill, Private Collection.

4. Lee, *Recollections and Letters of General Robert E. Lee*, 97–100.

5. Henry T. Wickham, Address Delivered Before the Joint Session of The General Assembly of Virginia (Richmond, Va., February 23, 1940). The rounds referred to in Wickham's account may have been those known as "Williams 'cleaner' bullets," which contained a zinc washer at the base designed to expand and "engage" the barrel's rifling. The zinc fragments would often break off in a wound, causing complications. Hasegawa, *Villainous Compounds*, 116.

6. Lee, *Recollections and Letters of General Robert E. Lee*, 97–100. See *Survey of Historic Resources, Hanover County Virginia, 1990*, 18 (identifies outbuilding "office"); see also Hickory Hill, National Register of Historic Places, Inventory-Nomination Form, September 17, 1974.

7. Anne Butler Carter Wickham to Charles Carter Lee, June 27, 1863, reprinted in Pryor, *Reading the Man*, 362–363.

8. According to her husband (W. F. Wickham), who was in Richmond that day, the cavalrymen arrived at noon. William F. Wickham to Robert E. Lee, June

28, 1863, The Papers of Robert E. Lee, 1830–1870, Albert and Shirley Small Special Collections Library, University of Virginia. Lee, *Recollections and Letters of General Robert E. Lee*, 97–100.

9. Lee, *Recollections and Letters of General Robert E. Lee*, 97–100.

10. Anne Butler Carter Wickham to Charles Carter Lee, June 27, 1863, reprinted in Pryor, *Reading the Man*, 362–363; Lee, *Recollections and Letters of General Robert E. Lee*, 97–100.

11. Shirley, "A Raid of the 11th Pa. Cav.," January 19, 1884.

12. Anne Butler Carter Wickham to Charles Carter Lee, June 27, 1863, reprinted in Pryor, *Reading the Man*, 362–363.

13. Lee, *Recollections and Letters of General Robert E. Lee*, 97–100. Anne Wickham, July 30, 1863. Account from Anne Butler Wickham, Wickham Family Papers, VMHC; *National Tribune*, June 4, 1896 (Tripp account); and Shirley, "A Raid of the 11th Pa. Cav.," January 19, 1884.

14. Anne Butler Carter Wickham to Charles Carter Lee, June 27, 1863, reprinted in Pryor, *Reading the Man*, 362–363.

15. William F. Wickham to Robert E. Lee, June 28, 1863, The Papers of Robert E. Lee, 1830–1870, Albert and Shirley Small Special Collections Library, University of Virginia.

16. The most detailed eyewitness accounts of the incident may be lost. According to a letter housed at the University of Virginia from Lucy Wickham to her husband, Williams Carter Wickham, Wickham children "Henry, Annie, & Frank—all wrote long and circumstantial compositions of the Yankees second raid." However, no such accounts were found in the Wickham papers. Wickham Family Papers, 15753 Box 12 L. P. W., [Lucy Penn Taylor Wickham] to my husband [Williams Carter Wickham], July 25, 1863, Small Special Collections, University of Virginia.

17. *Eleventh Pennsylvania Cavalry*, 76–77.

18. Shirley, "A Raid of the 11th Pa. Cav.," January 19, 1884. Shirley continued, incorrectly, to recount that the cavalrymen captured Rooney Lee in the carriage. However, most accounts indicate that Lee was captured as Spear's men returned from South Anna. Crowninshield to Mammy, July 2, 1863, Caspar Crowninshield Papers, Massachusetts Historical Society.

19. Lee, *Recollections and Letters of General Robert E. Lee*, 97–100. Nearly eighty years later, Henry Wickham identified Lee's servant as "Scot Davis." "Henry T. Wickham, Address Delivered Before the Joint Session of The General Assembly of Virginia" (Richmond, VA, February 23, 1940). *Senate Document No. 10, Richmond, Division of Purchase and Printing*, 1940.

20. "It is possible a negro betrayed his whereabouts." *Richmond Dispatch*, October 28, 1897.

21. *National Tribune*, June 4, 1896 (account Stephen Tripp, Capt., 11th Pennsylvania).

22. Lippincott, George E., "Lee-Sawyer Exchange," *Civil War Times Illustrated*, June 1962, 39.

23. Anne Wickham, July 30, 1863. Matthew Butler Wickham, Wickham family papers, VMHC.

24. William F. Wickham to Robert E. Lee, June 28, 1863, The Papers of

Robert E. Lee, 1830–1870, Albert and Shirley Small Special Collections Library, University of Virginia (transcription by Colin Woodward).

25. *New York Daily Herald*, June 30, 1863.

26. *National Tribune*, June 4, 1896 (Tripp account).

27. *New York Daily Herald*, June 30, 1863.

28. "Instructions for the Government of Armies of the United States in the Field" (prepared by Francis Lieber), Adjutant General's Office, April 24, 1863, Washington 1898: Government Printing Office. Article 49 read: "A prisoner of war is a public enemy armed or attached to the hostile army for active aid, who has fallen into the hands of the captor, *either fighting or wounded*, on the field or in the hospital, by individual surrender or by capitulation" (emphasis added).

29. Fremantle, *Three Months in the Southern States*, 144.

30. *Daily Independent*, October 26, 1891; *Charlotte Democrat*, October 23, 1891.

31. Lee, *Recollections and Letters of General Robert E. Lee*, 97–100; Daughtry, *Gray Cavalier*, 144 ("Lee's faithful servant Scott").

32. According to Henry Wickham's 1940 speech, the two slaves reported that US cavalrymen had visited the North Wales Plantation, the home of Williams Carter (Anne Carter Wickham's uncle) just across the river from Hickory Hill and, finding no horses there, "got very rough, and had beaten him [Carter], injuring him severely." Henry T. Wickham, "Address Delivered Before the Joint Session of The General Assembly of Virginia," (Richmond, VA, February 23, 1940), Senate Document No. 10, Richmond, Division of Purchase and Printing, 1940. However, contemporary accounts do not specifically mention any such injuries, suggesting that Henry Wickham may have not accurately recalled those events. See Anne Carter Wickham to Mary Carter, July 30, 1863, Wickham Family Papers, VMHC; William F. Wickham to Robert E. Lee, June 28, 1863, The Papers of Robert E. Lee, 1830–1870, Albert and Shirley Small Special Collections Library, University of Virginia; Wickham Diary, Wickham Family Papers, VMHC; Lucy Penn Wickham to Williams Carter Wickham, July 25, 1863, Papers of the Wickham Family, Albert and Shirley Small Special Collections Library, University of Virginia.

33. Anne Butler Carter Wickham to Charles Carter Lee, June 27, 1863, reprinted in Pryor, *Reading the Man: *, 362–363.

34. William Fanning Wickham Diary, Wickham Family Papers, VMHC.

35. Anne Wickham to Mary Carter, July 30, 1863, Wickham Family Papers, VMHC.

36. *Richmond Sentinel*, June 29, 1863.

37. *The Bee* (Danville, Va.), February 23, 1940.

38. Haas and Talley, *A Refugee at Hanover Tavern*, 94.

39. *History of the Eleventh Pennsylvania Volunteer Cavalry*, 76.

40. Crowninshield to Mammy, July 2, 1863, Caspar Crowninshield Papers, Massachusetts Historical Society; Parson, *Bear Flag and Bear State in the Civil War*, 60.

41. *National Tribune*, June 4, 1896 (account Stephen Tripp, Capt., 11th Pennsylvania).

42. Cruikshank, *Back in the Sixties*, 42; Shingler Report, *ORA* 27(2):799; *Richmond Sentinel*, July 1, 1863. Cruikshank refers to the captured man as "Olcutt." This was most likely Private "George Olcott" of Fort Dodge, Iowa. See, *History of the Eleventh Pennsylvania Volunteer Cavalry* 199 (Olcott captured on June 26).

43. Spear Report, *ORA* 27(2):796–797. According to the *New York Daily Herald* (July 1, 1863), Spear's men burned Nelson's bridge next to widow Nelson's plantation. However, Spear does not mention this in his report. Lowe, *Meade's Army*, 179.

44. *Spirit of the Age* (Raleigh), July 6, 1863. The story came from a Raleigh, North Carolina, resident who was visiting Hanover County on June 26 and was detained by Spear. Later, the Union cavalrymen released the civilians during the march back through King William County.

45. *National Tribune*, June 4, 1896 (account Stephen Tripp, Capt., 11th Pennsylvania).

46. *New York Daily Herald*, July 1, 1863.

47. *National Tribune*, June 4, 1896 (account Stephen Tripp, Capt., 11th Pennsylvania).

48. Spear's Report, *ORA* 27(2):795; Crowninshield to Mammy, July 2, 1863, Caspar Crowninshield Papers, Massachusetts Historical Society; Corbett Diary, Bancroft Library, University of California Berkeley; Shirley, "A Raid of the 11th Pa. Cav.," January 19, 1884 (Co. G); *Vermont Journal*, July 11, 1863; *New York Daily Herald*, July 1, 1863.

49. *Richmond Dispatch*, June 27, 1863.

50. *Greensboro Patriot*, July 2, 1863.

51. Compiled Service Records of Confederate soldiers from North Carolina Units, M270, RG 109, NARA.

52. *Weekly Era* (Raleigh), June 6, 1872 (reprint from *Wilmington Post*; "The Colonel [Hargrove] is an able, logical, and extremely fluent speaker"); Winston, "A Rebel Colonel," 84.

53. *Oxford Public Ledger*, Sept 24, 1903.

54. *Richmond Enquirer*, July 3 and 21, 1863; *Greensboro Patriot*, July 9, 1863. See also, *Daily Progress*, June 29, 1863 (claims Singeltary's men defended the bridge while Richmond's local defense troops were pursuing their "usual avocations" unrelated to fighting).

55. *Fayetteville Semi-Weekly Observer*, July 13, 1863.

56. Ruffin, *Diary of Edmund Ruffin*, vol. 2, 35.

57. *New York Daily Herald*, July 1, 1863; *Philadelphia Inquirer*, July 1, 1863.

58. They also burned two thousand bushels of wheat in a warehouse in Hanover. *Spirit of the Age* (Raleigh), July 06, 1863.

59. *Richmond Sentinel*, June 27, 1863; Ruffin, *Diary of Edmund Ruffin*, vol. 2, 32, 37, and 55; Corbett Diary, Bancroft Library, University of California Berkeley; Dix Report, *ORA* 27(2):794.

60. Brasher, *The Peninsula Campaign and the Necessity of Emancipation*.

61. Browning, *Shifting Loyalties*; Reid, *Freedom for Themselves*.

62. Dix Report, *ORA* 27(2):794; *New York Times*, June 29, 1863; *New York Daily Herald*, July 1, 1863.

63. *Republican & Sentinel*, July 27, 1863; Crowninshield to Mammy, July 2, 1863, Caspar Crowninshield Papers, Massachusetts Historical Society.

64. Confederate Papers Relating to Citizens or Business Firms, RG 109, NARA (C. S. Nitre and Mining Service, June 26, 1863); Jones, *Rebel War Clerk's Diary*, vol. 1, 360.

65. Annual Report of the Virginia Central Railroad Company, 1863, Small Special Collections, University of Virginia, 16.

66. *Fayetteville Semi-Weekly*, June 29, 1863 (excerpt from the *Richmond Enquirer*).

67. *Evening Star*, June 29, 1863; *Baltimore Sun*, June 29, 1863.

68. Halleck to Dix, June 14, 1863, 12 m., ORA 27(3):111.

9. REBEL DIPLOMACY

1. Halleck to Meade, June 28, 1863, 3:30 p.m., ORA 27(1):63.

2. Burnett, "Letters of a Confederate Surgeon," pt. 2, 159–190.

3. Lee to Cooper, July 31, 1863, ORA 27(2):307–311.

4. Lee to Cooper, January 20, 1864, ORA 27(2):316–317.

5. Marshall, *An Aide-de-Camp of Lee*, 218–220. See also, Marshall, "Events Leading up to the Battle of Gettysburg," 226.

6. As part of Lee's plan to concentrate the Army of Northern Virginia, Ewell's corps would head south and west from Carlisle and York while Longstreet and Hill would head east and over the mountains from Chambersburg. Marshall, *An Aide-de-Camp of Lee*, 218–220.

7. According to Charles Marshall, the news of the Union advance north eliminated any concerns Lee had that the Army of the Potomac would turn south and attack Richmond. Marshall, *An Aide-de-Camp of Lee*, 218–220.

8. Stephens to Linton Stephens, June 26, 1863, Alexander Stephens Collection, Manhattanville College. Stephens said the "plan," which he learned from a "man of high character in NC," had been discovered in captured correspondence between John Foster in North Carolina and James Montgomery on the Georgia coast. Thomas, *The Confederate State of Richmond*, 23.

9. Stephens, *A Constitutional View of the Late War Between the States*, vol. 2, 558–564; Rabun, "A Letter for Posterity," 13.

10. Stephens, 558–564; Rabun, "A Letter for Posterity," 13. In his memoir, Stephens misremembered the date of his arrival in Richmond. According to his memoir, he arrived on the "22nd or 23rd," but his correspondence with his brother makes it clear he arrived on the night of June 26. His memoir also claims that he first heard of Lee's offensive when he reached Richmond. His letters from 1863 and 1864 make it clear that he learned of the movement sometime before reaching the capital. Stephens to Linton Stephens, June 26, 1863, Alexander Stephens collection, Manhattanville College; Rabun, "A Letter for Posterity," 13.

11. Johnston and Browne, *Life of Alexander H. Stephens*, 442; Stephens to Linton Stephens, June 27, 1863, Alexander Stephens Collection, Manhattanville College.

12. Stephens to Linton Stephens, June 28, 1863, Alexander Stephens Collection, Manhattanville College.

13. Stephens to Linton Stephens, June 30 and July 1, 1863, Alexander Stephens Collection, Manhattanville College.

14. Gorgas, *The Journals of Josiah Gorgas, 1857–1878*, 72; A. Stephens to Linton Stephens, July 1, 1863, Stephens Collection, Manhattanville College.

15. A. Stephens to Linton Stephens, July 1, 1863, Stephens Collection, Manhattanville College; Rabun, "A Letter for Posterity," 13.

16. Stephens, *A Constitutional View of the Late War Between the States*, vol. 2, 558–564.

17. A. Stephens to Linton Stephens, July 1, 1863, Stephens Collection, Manhattanville College; Augustus S. Montgomery to Major General Foster, May 12, 1863, *ORA* 18:1068–1069. Vance to Davis, May 21, 1863, *ORA* 18:1067–1068 (Vance reports Federal plan for slave uprising).

18. Davis to Stephens, July 2, 1863, *ORA*, ser. 2 6:75–76.

19. Jefferson Bradford to Jefferson Davis, June 5, 1863; and Anna Farrar to Davis, June 20, 1863, *The Papers of Jefferson Davis*, vol. 9, 231–232.

20. Davis to Lincoln, July 2, 1863, *ORA*, ser. 2, 6:75–76.

21. See Stephens, *A Constitutional View of the Late War Between the States*, vol. 2, 558–564; Stevenson, "The Southern Side; Or, Andersonville Prison," 237. Stephens's statements appear in the form of an interview with an unidentified, perhaps fictitious, "Prof. Norton."

22. Stephens, 558–564.

23. Reagan, *Memoirs*, 166.

24. See, Rabun, "A Letter for Posterity," 15. Months later Stephens would admit to Linton that the Confederates had "made a blunder in refusing to exchange" Black prisoners and their officers. In the same breath, he pointed at Federal officials for making "a much greater blunder" in threatening to retaliate when Confederates planned to send "recaptured slaves" back into slavery. Stephens viewed the Federal threats to retaliate as at odds with the "universally acknowledged principles of the laws of nations."

10. RICHMOND PREPARES

1. Lee to Davis, June 23, 1863, *ORA* 27(3):924–926.

2. Davis to Lee, June 28, 1863, *ORA* 27(1):76–77.

3. Davis to Lee, June 28, 1863, *ORA* 27(1):76–77.

4. Cooper to Lee, June 29, 1863, *ORA* 27(1):75–76.

5. Butterfield to Halleck, July 3, 1863, *ORA* 27(1):75.

6. Halleck to Kelley, July 4, 1863, 11:30 a.m., *ORA* 27(3):528; Stanton to Thomas, July 4, 1863, 4:40 p.m., *ORA* 27(3):526.

7. Thomas to Stanton, July 4, 1863, 10:30 p.m., *ORA* 27(3):526.

8. *New York Times*, July 4, 1863; *Philadelphia Inquirer*, July 6, 1863; *New York Times*, July 30, 1863; *Evening Star*, July 30, 1863.

9. Herbert Augustine Claiborne Diary, Claiborne Family Papers, VMHC.

10. Causey to Norris, June 26, 1863, *ORA* 27(3):939.

11. The 13,000 figure should be treated as a general estimate. It is based on returns from the North Carolina and Richmond departments during June and July. Such returns were sometimes incomplete and usually reflected only

the units present on the precise date attached to the report. For example, the Richmond returns for the end of July, several weeks after Dix's campaign, show 2,075 men with Custis Lee's local defense force. For the purposes of deriving an early July estimate, it is assumed this number roughly reflects the men commanded by Custis Lee earlier in the month during Dix's operations. Returns for Richmond and North Carolina Departments, *ORA* 27(3):947–950 and 1065; Custis Lee to Chestney, July 5, 1863, *ORA* 27(3):971–972. Custis Lee had been promoted to brigadier general on June 25, 1863. Compiled Service Records of Confederate General and Staff Officers, and Nonregimental Enlisted Men, RG 109, NARA. The other units from D. H. Hill's command were positioned as follows: "Clingman's brigade is near Wilmington; Colquitt's, Kinston; Martin's, nominally on railroad (Weldon, &c."). Davis to Lee, June 28, 1863, *ORA* 27(1): 76–77.

12. Lewis, *Camp Life of a Confederate Boy*, 51.

13. Micah Jenkins to Caroline Jenkins, June 22, 1863, Micah Jenkins Papers, South Caroliniana Library, University of South Carolina.

14. Gilmer to Hill, June 27, 1863, *ORA* 27(3):941. Jeremy Gilmer, the chief Confederate engineer, declined the request, explaining that, while his bureau already had used a "large body" of slaves, the War Department had returned them to their owners in April to labor on the plantations.

15. See, e.g., Hill to Seddon, June 25, 1863, *ORA* 27(3):936.

16. Seddon to Hill, June 25, 1863, D. H. Hill Papers, Library of Virginia.

17. Seddon to Hill, June 25, 1863, *ORA* 27(3):933.

18. Hill to Seddon, June 25, 1863, *ORA* 27(3):933.

19. Henry Brantingham and W. H. S. Burgwyn Diary, Private Collections, State Archives of North Carolina.

20. Causey to Norris, June 26, 1863, *ORA* 27(3):939. In addition, the Federals had apparently conducted a ruse, embarking troops onto transports to lend the impression that Dix was sending men north to support the Army of the Potomac.

21. Seddon to D. H. Hill, June 26, 1863, *ORA* 27(3):938.

22. D. H. Hill to Seddon, June 26, 1863, *ORA* 27(3):939.

23. Colquitt to Hill, June 29, 1863, D. H. Hill Papers, Library of Virginia. Colquitt surmised Dix would "raid to plunder, to destroy, and to harass our long lines of communications will be their policy."

24. Hill to Seddon, June 27, 1863, *ORA* 27(3):939.

25. Seddon to Corse, and Seddon to Hill, June 27, 1863, *ORA* 27(3):940; Seddon to Corse, June 28, 1863, *ORA* 27(3):944; Taylor to Pickett, June 29, 1863, *ORA* 27(3):944–945.

26. Vance to Seddon, June 30, 1863, *ORA* 27(3):946.

27. Lewis, *Camp Life of a Confederate Boy*, 51–52. See also, Baldwin, *The Struck Eagle*; Thomas, *Career and Character of General Micah Jenkins*, 1903; Micah Jenkins to Caroline Jenkins, June 22, 1863, Micah Jenkins Papers, South Caroliniana Library, University of South Carolina.

28. *Charleston Mercury*, June 30, 1863.

29. *OR Supp.*, vol. 48, 810 (Record of Events, 25th NC).

30. Lewis, *Camp Life of Confederate Boy*, 53; *OR Supp.*, vol. 64, 606, 616 (Record of Events, 6th SC, Jenkins Brigade); Letter of J. W. Calton, 56th North

Carolina, Richmond National Battlefield Park; *Fayetteville Weekly Observer*, July 13, 1863 (letter from "Long Grabs," i.e., Murdoch John McSween).

31. *Fayetteville Weekly Observer*, July 13, 1863 (letter from "Long Grabs").

32. Burgwyn Diary, 35th NC, Ransom's Brigade, Henry Brantingham and W. H. S. Burgwyn Diary, Private Collections, State Archives of North Carolina.

33. *Fayetteville Weekly Observer*, July 13, 1863 (letter from "Long Grabs"); John A. Graham to William Graham, July 5, 1863, in Williams, *Papers of William Alexander Graham*, vol. 5, 503–505.

34. Hill to Seddon, June 28, 1863, ORA 27(3):944 (two dispatches).

35. Elzey to Hill, June 29, 1863, ORA 51(2):728; and Seddon to Adjutant General, June 29, 1863, ORA 27(3):945. Seddon to Adjutant-General, July 1, 1863, and Special Orders No. 156, ORA 27(3):948.

36. Hill to Seddon, June 30, 1863, ORA 27(3):945.

37. Burgwyn Diary, Henry Brantingham and W. H. S. Burgwyn Diary, Private Collections, State Archives of North Carolina. The next day (June 29) under rainy skies, Ransom's brigade dismantled fortifications built the year before by Union forces. Clark, *Histories of the Several Regiments*, vol. 3, 329–330.

38. *Richmond Dispatch*, June 29, 1863; Driver, *Richmond Local Defense Troops*, 17–20.

39. *Richmond Daily Examiner*, June 29, 1863.

11. DIX PREPARES THE SECOND WAVE

1. Meade to Halleck, 7 a.m., June 28, 1863, ORA 27(1):61–62.

2. Halleck to Meade, 1 p.m., June 28, 1863, ORA 27(1):62.

3. Halleck to Meade, 3:30 p.m., June 28, 1863, ORA 27(1):63.

4. Meade to Halleck, 11 a.m., June 29, 1863, ORA 27(1):66; Meade to Halleck, 4:30 p.m., June 30, 1863, ORA 27(1):68–69. "Frizellburg" is often spelled "Frizzellburg."

5. "A group of 'contrabands,'" Prints and Photographs Division, Library of Congress. The photograph's caption indicates it was taken at the "Foller" Plantation. However, the location was probably the "Toler" Plantation, which was immediately adjacent to Cumberland Landing. See, e.g., "Map of New Kent, Charles City, James City and York counties," Civil War Maps, Library of Congress; Harris, *Old New Kent County*, 91.

6. Gordon, *A War Diary of Events*, 122–126.

7. John Dix to Catherine Dix, June 25, 1863, John A. Dix Papers, Columbia University.

8. Gordon, *A War Diary of Events*, 122–126.

9. Dix to Halleck, June 27, 1863, John Dix Papers, Columbia University. The day before, Keyes's lead units had arrived after marching along the Peninsula from Yorktown.

10. Diary of Edward Snow Foster, June 27, 1863, American Civil War Collection, Hamilton College.

11. Gordon, *A War Diary of Events*, 122–126. Gordon's division arrived late in the morning on June 27 after a four-hour march from Cumberland, delayed by wagons that had become mired in "villainously muddy roads."

12. James H. Howard Letters, University of Virginia.

13. Diary of Edward Snow Foster, June 27, 1863, American Civil War Collection, Hamilton College.

14. McGrath, *The History of the 127th New York Volunteers*, 57; Hyde, *History of the One Hundred and Twelfth Regiment, N.Y. Volunteers*, 40; *New York Daily Herald*, June 30, 1863.

15. *Chicago Tribune*, July 10, 1863 (reprint of *New York World* account from "Sidney").

16. Claim of Terrill Bradby (6306), Deposition of Bradby, Southern Claims Commission Case Files, RG 217, NARA (Bradby deposition).

17. Unidentified Newspaper Clippings (130th New York), June 27 and 30, 1863, 1st Regiment Of Dragoons New York Volunteers Civil War Newspaper Clippings, New York State Military Museum.

18. Unidentified Newspaper Clipping (130th New York), June 28, 1863, 1st Regiment Of Dragoons New York Volunteers Civil War Newspaper Clippings, New York State Military Museum; Andrew, William G., *The Life of a Union Army Sharpshooter* (blackberries in season at Yorktown); Thompson, *Thirteenth Regiment of New Hampshire Volunteer Infantry*, 172.

19. *New York Daily Herald*, June 30, 1863; Culver to His Brother, June 27, 1863, The Letters of Private Martin Van Buren Culver.

20. Gordon, *A War Diary of Events*, 122–126.

21. Gordon, 122–126.

22. Gordon, 122–126.

23. Diary of Edward Snow Foster (117th N.Y.), June 27, 1863, American Civil War Collection, Hamilton College; McGrath, *The History of the 127th New York Volunteers*, 57; Dix Report, *ORA* 27(2):821; Dix to Corcoran, June 28, 1863, *ORA* 27(3):395; Gordon, 122–126.

24. George W. Pearl Letter, June 25, 1863, American Civil War Collection, Hamilton College.

25. Diary of Edward Snow Foster (117th N.Y.), June 28, 1863, American Civil War Collection, Hamilton College; Oswald Jackson letter, July 1, 1863, William Griffing Collection (Spared and Shared) (recounting reconnaissance conducted toward New Bridge on the Chickahominy on June 29 and 30).

26. Thompson, *Thirteenth Regiment of New Hampshire Volunteer Infantry*, 173.

27. Dix to Halleck, June 29, 1863, 10:45 a.m., *ORA* 27(3):412.

28. Halleck to Dix, June 14, 1863, 12 m., *ORA* 27(3):111.

29. Halleck to Dix, June 14, 1863, 12 m., *ORA* 27(3):111.

30. Dix to Halleck, June 29, 1863, 10:45 a.m., *ORA* 27(3):412.

31. Dix Report, *ORA* 27(2):821–824. Dix informed Halleck of the general plan later that morning, but did not provide any details. Dix to Halleck, June 29, 1863, 10:45 a.m., *ORA* 27(3):412; Dix to Halleck, June 29, *ORA* 27(3):413 (reporting Confederates at Bottom's Bridge).

32. Dix to Halleck, June 29, 1863, *ORA* 27(3):413.

33. Lee to Dix, 4 p.m., June 29, 1863, John A. Dix Papers, Columbia University. Colonel William H. Ludlow, at Fort Monroe, passed along "well founded" rumors that the Confederates had captured Harrisburg and were expected to

capture Baltimore as well. Ludlow to Dix, June 29, 1863, John A. Dix Papers, Columbia University. Generals Prince and Spinola came from Foster's command. Foster to Dix, June 30, 1863, John A. Dix Papers, Columbia University.

34. Dix to Halleck, June 29, 1863, *ORA* 27(3):413.

35. Welles, *Diary of Gideon Welles*, vol. 1, 350.

36. Welles, 348–350.

37. Welles, 348–351.

38. Salmon Chase to Kate Chase, June 29, 1863, *The Salmon P. Chase Papers*, 72.

39. Butterfield to Chase, June 27, 1863, 8 p.m., *Report of the Joint Committee on the Conduct of the War at the Second Session*, Thirty-eighth Congress, 294.

40. Chase to David Dudley field, June 30, 1863, *The Salmon P. Chase Papers*, 73–74.

41. Welles, *Diary of Gideon Welles*, vol. 1, 348–351.

42. Fox to S. P. Lee, June 30, 1863, Confidential Correspondence of Gustavus Vasa Fox, vol. 2, 259.

43. Laas, *Wartime Washington*, 284–286. Elizabeth Blair Lee also wrote the following rough note in her diary: "—& if they would only follow up thing right ere the people at Richmond get over their Consternation strike there & Charleston at once we might feel assured our Nation's future."

44. Fox to S. P. Lee, June 30, 1863, and Lee to Fox, July 2, 1863, *Confidential Correspondence of Gustavus Vasa Fox*, 259–260. In proposing Foster, Fox observed that the general-in-chief "seems averse to bold movements which are always successful."

45. Welles, *Diary of Gideon Welles*, vol. 1, 351–352. Blair to Lincoln, June 30, 1863, Lincoln Papers, Library of Congress.

46. Welles spoke with Blair about Dix's operation and invited the postmaster general to come with him and speak with Stanton about the matter. Blair declined, admitting that had made a habit of avoiding Stanton's department. Welles, *Diary of Gideon Welles*, vol. 1, 352.

47. Welles, 351–352.

48. Foster to Halleck, June 30, 1863, *ORA* 27(3):438–439.

49. Halleck to Kelley, June 25, 1863, 1:29 p.m., *ORA* 27(3):330.

50. Bowen, *Regimental History of the First New York Dragoons*, 81–83.

12. KEYES'S ADVANCE TO BOTTOM'S BRIDGE

1. Dix and Keyes Report, *ORA* 27(2):821 and 855 (Keyes said he had a "trifle less" than 6,000, though the total appears to have been closer to 7,000); Special Orders No. 152, *ORA* 27(3):439 and Abstract of Return of the Department of Virginia, June 30, 1863, 453. Since this return was dated the day before Dix's operation began, it is assumed the numbers represent a fairly accurate count of the troops at hand.

2. Dix Report, *ORA* 27(2):821; Keyes Report (July 15, 1863), 27(2):855.

3. Erasmus Darwin Keyes, Civil war photographs, 1861–1865 (Library of Congress); *Waterbury American*, December 4, 1863.

4. Keyes, *Fifty Years' Observations of Men and Events, Civil and Military*, 440.

5. Sears, *Lincoln's Lieutenants*, 166 and 205. Keyes discussed his McClellan interactions in his memoir, a book that covered fifty years of professional life but curiously devoted only about sixty of its 500 pages to the Civil War and included no mention whatsoever of operations in Virginia under Dix during the summer of 1863. Keyes, *Fifty Years' Observations of Men and Events, Civil and Military*.

6. Special Order No. 152, *ORA* 27(3):439–440; *New York Daily Herald*, July 8, 1863 (Stephen Hayes dispatch; according to the article, Keyes's staff included a Major Whitehead, Major Oswald Jackson, a Captain Howard, and a Captain Rice); Gordon, *A War Diary of Events*, 127–131.

7. Halleck to Dix, July 1, 1863, 11 a.m., *ORA* 27(2):818.

8. Dix to Halleck, June 14, 1863, 12 p.m., *ORA* 27(3):111.

9. Special Order No. 152, *ORA* 27(3):439–440 ("The invalids and bad marchers to stay behind"); Gordon, *A War Diary of Events*, 127–131.

10. *New York Daily Herald*, July 8, 1863 (Stephen Hayes dispatch).

11. *New York Times*, June 8, 1862. Along the route, General Henry Terry joined Keyes for the ride and discussed "military matters." *New York Daily Herald*, July 8, 1863 (Stephen Hayes dispatch).

12. Keyes Report, *ORA* 27(2):854–857; *New York Daily Herald*, July 8, 1863 (Stephen Hayes dispatch); *New York Times*, June 8, 1862.

13. See, Fields, ed., *Worthy Partner*, 454–455. The location of the Washington–Custis wedding remains an issue of dispute.

14. Many of the Federal accounts, including Stephen Hayes's from the *New York Daily Herald*, confused the place-names along Keyes's line of march. The first major crossroads on the route was known as Talleysville (its modern name) or Baltimore Store, a spot a little over four miles south of White House Landing. Hayes mistakenly called this spot "Baltimore Crossroads" in his reports, and some Federal accounts do the same. The next intersection, farther west of Talleysville, was known as Crump's Crossroads, Baltimore Crossroads, or, in some Confederate accounts, simply the "Crossroads." Today, Crump's Crossroads is known as Quinton and is identified as such on modern maps. To simplify matters, this narrative generally refers to the first location as Talleysville and the second, to the west, as Crump's Crossroads. See, e.g., *New York Daily Herald*, July 8, 1863 (Stephen Hayes dispatch); *New York Times*, June 8, 1862.

15. Keyes Report, *ORA* 27(2):854–857.

16. *Columbia Democrat and Bloomsburg General Advertiser*, September 19, 1863 (account of Charles Knorr, 5th US Artillery); *New York Times*, June 8, 1862; Keyes Report, *ORA* 27(2):854–855.

17. *New York Times*, June 8, 1862.

18. Keyes Report, *ORA* 27(2):854–857; Keyes to Dix, July 6, 1863, *ORA* 27(2):835.

19. *New York Daily Herald*, July 8, 1863 (Stephen Hayes's dispatch); Moore, *The Rebellion Record*, vol. 7, 332–334; *Gettysburg Compiler*, July 27, 1897 (describes Kupp's subsequent escape from Libby Prison).

20. Keyes Report, *ORA* 27(2):854–857; *New York Daily Herald*, July 8, 1863 (Stephen Hayes dispatch); Keyes to Dix, July 1, 1863, 5 p.m. and Van Buren to Keyes, July 1, 1863, 10 p.m., *ORA* 27(2):825.

21. Beverly Dixon, SCC File, Southern Claims Commission Approved Claims,

1871–1880: Virginia, RG 217, NARA. Union troops under Philip Sheridan would do more damage to Dixon's property in 1864.

22. Keyes to Dix, July 1, 1863, 5 p.m. and Van Buren to Keyes, July 1, 1863, 10 p.m., *ORA* 27(2):825.

23. Herbert Augustine Claiborne Diary, Claiborne Family Papers, VMHC.

24. *Richmond Dispatch*, July 1, 1863.

25. Jones, A *Rebel War Clerk's Diary at the Confederate States Capital*, vol. 1, 367; Pegram to Chestney, July 1, 1863, *ORA* 27(3):951; Seddon to Colquitt, July 1, 1863, *ORA* 27(3):952; Hill to Elzey, July 1863, *ORA* 27(3):949.

26. Although available documents do not specify the location of D. H. Hill's headquarters (the "Williams House"), period maps identify a "Williams" house southeast of Richmond between the York River Railroad and the Williamsburg Road. That location would have given Hill a spot between his brigades to the east and officials downtown (to the northwest). See, e.g., Gilmer and Campbell, "Map of vicinity of Richmond," Control Number: 2005625083, Geography and Map Division, Library of Congress.

27. Sulivane to Chestney, July 1, 1863, *ORA* 27(3):950 (the companies included Brown's, Downer's, Henley's, Minor's (Navy), and Waller's).

28. Hill to Elzey, July 1863, *ORA* 27(3):949 (Hill also suggested C. Lee move his headquarters to Stewart Farm on the Brook Turnpike north of Richmond).

29. Hill to Seddon, July 1, 1863, *ORA* 27(3):949–950; Burgwyn Diary, Henry Brantingham and W. H. S. Burgwyn Diary. Private Collections, State Archives of North Carolina.

30. Shingler to Wise, July 1, 1863, *ORA* 27(3):950–951; Charges of Henry Wise, April 23, 1863, and Shingler Report, July 1, 1863, W. P. Shingler Compiled Service Record, RG 109, NARA.

31. *Charleston Daily Courier*, October 29, 1863; *Columbia Democrat and Bloomsburg General Advertiser*, September 19, 1863 ("the battery . . . on the right into a little field").

32. *New York Daily Herald*, July 8, 1863 (Stephen Hayes dispatch).

33. *New York Daily Herald*, July 8, 1863 (Stephen Hayes dispatch); Keyes to Dix, July 1, 1863, 7 p.m., *ORA* 27(2):825; *Green-Mountain Freeman*, July 14, 1863. The article in the *Freeman* identified the man killed as "Sergeant Burnet." However, a roster for Company C of the 5th Pennsylvania indicates that a Private Archibald Bennett was killed in the engagement. Bates, *History of the Pennsylvania Volunteers, 1861–65*.

34. *Charleston Daily Courier*, October 29, 1863.

35. *New York Daily Herald*, July 8, 1863 (Stephen Hayes dispatch); Van Buren to Keyes, July 1, 1863, 9:30 p.m., *ORA* 27(2):826.

36. Keyes to Dix, July 2, 1863, 2:30 a.m., *ORA* 27(2):826.

37. Oswald Jackson Letter, July 6, 1863, S. Trout, Private Collection.

38. Keyes to Dix, July 2, 1863, 6:30 a.m., *ORA* 27(2):827.

39. *New York Daily Herald*, July 8, 1863 (Stephen Hayes dispatch); Keyes to Dix, July 2, 1863, 2:30 a.m., *ORA* 27(2):826.

40. Francis Trowbridge to Phebe Trowbridge, July 4, 1863, Spared and Shared.

41. *New York Daily Herald*, July 8, 1863 (Stephen Hayes dispatch).

42. Moore, *The Rebellion Record*, vol. 7, 332–334.

43. Keyes to Dix, July 2, 1863, 6:30 a.m., *ORA* 27(2):827.
44. Van Buren to Keyes to Dix, July 2, 1863, 4:30 a.m., *ORA* 27(2):826.
45. Dix to Gordon, July 2, 1863, 6:00 a.m., *ORA* 27(2):826–827; Dix to Keyes, July 2, 1863, *ORA* 27(2):828.
46. Shingler to Wise, July 1, 1863, *ORA* 27(3):950.

13. THE FIGHT AT CRUMP'S CROSSROADS

1. Keyes to Dix, July 2, 1863, 7 a.m., *ORA* 27(2):854.
2. Moore, *The Rebellion Record*, vol. 7, 332–334.
3. Keyes to Lewis, July 2, 1863, RG 393, Fourth Corps Records, NARA.
4. *Washington Register*, March 11, 1887.
5. Dix to Keyes, July 2, 1863, 3 p.m., *ORA* 27(2):828.
6. *Daily Richmond Examiner*, July 2, 1863.
7. Herbert Augustine Claiborne Diary, Claiborne Family Papers, VMHC.
8. Jones, *A Rebel War Clerk's Diary*, vol. 1, 367.
9. Hill to Seddon, July 1, 1863, *ORA* 27(3):949–950; *Greensboro Patriot*, July 2, 1863.
10. Elzey to Hill, July 2, 1863, *ORA* 27(3):955. Muselman, *The Caroline Light, Parker and Stafford Light Artillery*, 11 (Caroline Light artillery posted downstream from New Bridge).
11. Seddon to Hall, July 2, 1863, *ORA* 27(3):953; Seddon to Hall, July 2, 1863, *ORA* 27(3):953; Hall to Seddon, July 2, 1863, *ORA* 27(3):954; Hill to Seddon, July 2, 1863, *ORA* 27(3):954.
12. Hill to Seddon, July 1, 1863, *ORA* 27(3):949–950.
13. Hill to Seddon, 3 p.m., July 2, 1863, *ORA* 27(3):954.
14. Shingler to Elzey, July 2, 1863, *ORA* 27(3):952–953.
15. Hill to Elzey, July 2, 1863, *ORA* 27(3):954. Hill also hoped Elzey could replace John Cooke's pickets at the New and "Federal" bridges along the Chickahominy to protect the sector between Bottom's Bridge and the Mechanicsville Turnpike.
16. Burgwyn Diary, Henry Brantingham and W. H. S. Burgwyn Diary, State Archives of North Carolina.
17. Clark, *Histories of the Several Regiments*, vol. 3, 330.
18. *Camp Life of a Confederate Boy*, 52–53; John A. Graham to William Graham, July 5, 1863, in Williams, *Papers of William Alexander Graham*, vol. 5, 503–505.
19. Hill to Seddon, July 2, 1863, *ORA* 27(3):956; Shingler to Elzey, July 2, 1863, *ORA* 27(3):952–953. Sources are not consistent about the number Confederate guns in the engagement. *Richmond Daily Examiner*, July 4, 1863 (ten guns); Clark, *Histories of the Several Regiments*, vol. 3, 330 (sixteen guns); Burgwyn Diary, Henry Brantingham and W. H. S. Burgwyn Diary, State Archives of North Carolina (two batteries of Branch's artillery). According to Burgwyn's account, Cooke's brigade also crossed Bottom's Bridge in support, but that is unclear.
20. Peyre, *Career and Character of General Micah Jenkins*, 26; Hill to Cooper, August 19, 1863, Jenkins's Personnel Record, Compiled Service Records, RG 109, NARA; Elzey to Cooper, August 19, 1863, Jenkins's Personnel Record, RG

109, NARA; *Richmond Dispatch*, July 4, 1863; Matt W. Ransom File, NARA M331, Compiled Service Records of Confederate Officers and Enlisted Men Who Did Not Belong to Any Particular Regiment, RG 109, NARA.

21. *Fayetteville Weekly Observer*, July 13, 1863 (letter from "Long Grabs," i.e., Murdoch John McSween). See also, Munson, ed., *Confederate Incognito*, 253; *Philadelphia Inquirer*, July 8, 1863 (excerpt from the *Richmond Sentinel*). (Branch's artillery); *OR Supp.*, vol. 49, 135 (Record of Events, 35th North Carolina); *OR Supp.*, vol. 64, 606, 616 (Record of Events, 6th South Carolina, Jenkins Brigade).

22. *Wilmington Journal*, July 9, 1863 (excerpt from *Richmond Inquirer*).

23. Keyes to Dix, July 6, 1863, 2:30 pm, *ORA* 27(2):835; Francis Trowbridge to Phebe Trowbridge, July 4, 1863, Spared and Shared.

24. Francis Trowbridge to Phebe Trowbridge, July 4, 1863, Spared and Shared.

25. *New York Daily Herald*, July 8, 1863 (Stephen Hayes dispatch); Francis Trowbridge to Phebe Trowbridge, July 4, 1863, Spared and Shared.

26. Francis Trowbridge to Phebe Trowbridge, July 4, 1863, Spared and Shared.

27. *National Tribune*, May 2, 1895; Moore, *The Rebellion Record*, vol. 7, 332–334; Francis Trowbridge to Phebe Trowbridge, July 4, 1863, Spared and Shared.

28. *National Tribune*, May 2, 1895.

29. Moore, *The Rebellion Record*, vol. 7, 332–334. According to Hayes, the 139th New York was armed with only smoothbores, which offered no match to the rifle-toting Confederates. *New York Daily Herald*, July 8, 1863 (Stephen Hayes dispatch); Dix to Watson, December 14, 1862, *ORA* 18:482 (Pennsylvanians arrived with flintlocks).

30. Francis Trowbridge to Phebe Trowbridge, July 4, 1863, Spared and Shared. The Union shells did not reach most of Ransom's regiments in reserve. John A. Graham to William Graham, July 5, 1863, in Williams, *Papers of William Alexander Graham*, vol. 5, 503–505.

31. *New York Daily Herald*, July 8, 1863 (Stephen Hayes dispatch). In his July 2 dispatch, Hayes counted the losses as "eight skirmishers—one killed in the woods and six wounded, two seriously, four but slightly." Hayes listed the following wounded, all members of the 139th New York: John Geerer (Co. K), "neck, badly"; Jacob Van Wickley (Co. F), "leg"; S. B. Howell (Co. H) "scalp wound"; Oscar Lockwood (Co. I) "lower jaw and neck, badly"; Corporal Louis A. Le Blanc (Co. D) "leg"; Denis McCabe (Co. I) "mouth." Moore, *The Rebellion Record*, vol. 7, 332–334.

32. Keyes to West, July 2, 1863, 7:10 p.m., *ORA* 51(2):1068.

33. Moore, *The Rebellion Record*, vol. 7, 332–334; Burr Porter, Combined Service Records of Union Soldiers, RG 94, NARA (account refers to a "Dr. O'Reilly" as the person responsible for saving the wounded; at least eight were brought off the field). Burr Porter, Combined Service Records of Union Soldiers, RG 94, NARA. Porter had been charged with lying about his identity at a picket post and being absent without leave from his camp. As a result of the misconduct charges, he would resign three weeks after the fight.

34. *Camp Life of a Confederate Boy*, 52–53.

35. *Wilmington Journal*, July 9, 1863 (excerpt from *Richmond Inquirer*). One account suggested Branch's artillery had made a substantial impact "firing with

accuracy and a telling effect," according to a Richmond paper. *Philadelphia Inquirer*, July 8, 1863 (excerpt from the *Richmond Sentinel*).

36. *Fayetteville Weekly Observer*, July 13, 1863 (letter from "Long Grabs," i.e., Murdoch John McSween). See also, Munson, ed., *Confederate Incognito*, 253; *Philadelphia Inquirer* ("they hardly remained"), July 8, 1863 (excerpt from the *Richmond Sentinel*); Letter of J. W. Calton, 56th North Carolina, Richmond National Battlefield Park (Federals fired only four rounds of artillery); Burgwyn Diary, Henry Brantingham and W. H. S. Burgwyn Diary, State Archives of North Carolina (five or six rounds); John A. Graham to William Graham, July 5, 1863, in Williams, *Papers of William Alexander Graham*, vol. 5, 503–505.

37. Crow and Barden, eds., *Live Your Own Life*, 154; *Fayetteville Weekly Observer*, July 13, 1863 (letter from "Long Grabs" [i.e., Murdoch John McSween]).

38. Moore, Frank, *The Rebellion Record*, vol. 7, 332–334.

39. *Daily Richmond Examiner*, July 4, 1863.

40. *Wilmington Journal*, July 9, 1863 (excerpt from *Richmond Enquirer*).

41. *Philadelphia Inquirer*, July 8, 1863 (excerpt from *Richmond Sentinel*); *Wilmington Journal*, July 9, 1863 (excerpt from *Richmond Inquirer*); *Richmond Dispatch*, July 4, 1863; Burgwyn Diary, Henry Brantingham and W. H. S. Burgwyn Diary, State Archives of North Carolina; Harrill, *Reminiscences, 1861–1865*, 14; John A. Graham to William Graham, July 5, 1863, in Williams, *Papers of William Alexander Graham*, vol. 5, 503–505; Lewis, *Camp Life of a Confederate Boy*, 52–53.

42. Keyes to West, July 2, 1863, Fourth Corps Records, RG 393, NARA (at Baltimore Store); Moore, *The Rebellion Record*, vol. 7, 332–334; Keyes to Dix, July 2, 1863, 11 p.m., *ORA* 27(2):829.

43. *Columbia Democrat and Bloomsburg General Advertiser*, September 19, 1863; Moore, *The Rebellion Record*, vol. 7, 332–334.

44. Moore, *The Rebellion Record*, vol. 7, 332–334.

45. John Dix to Catherine Dix, July 3, 1863, Dix Papers, Columbia University.

46. Keyes to Dix, July 2, 1863, 7:30 p.m., *ORA* 27(2):828–829; Dix to Keyes, July 2, 1863, 9 p.m., *ORA* 27(2):829; Gordon, *A War Diary of Events*, 127–131.

47. Oswald Jackson Letter, July 6, 1863, S. Trout, Private Collection; Keyes to Dix, July 2, 1863, 11 p.m., *ORA* 27(2):829; Van Buren to Keyes, July 2, 1863, 11 p.m., *ORA* 27(2):829.

48. Francis Trowbridge to Phebe Trowbridge, July 4, 1863, Spared and Shared.

49. "General [M.] Jenkins, who made the attack, estimates the loss of the Yankees at 30 or 40. Six dead bodies were left on the field." D. H. Hill Report, *ORA* 27(2):858–859. *Richmond Daily Examiner*, July 4, 1863; *Richmond Dispatch*, July 4, 1863; Burgwyn Diary, Henry Brantingham and W. H. S. Burgwyn Diary, State Archives of North Carolina; *Wilmington Journal, July 9, 1863*, excerpt from the *Richmond Enquirer*; *Fayetteville Weekly Observer*, July 9, 1863 ("We captured some 15 prisoners, killed 6 and wounded a number. The only casualties on our side were: Private Tate, Co. H., 24th N.C., killed, and wounded, each, from the 24th and 49th.").

50. Francis Trowbridge to Phebe Trowbridge, July 4, 1863, Spared and Shared; *Fayetteville Weekly Observer*, July 13, 1863 (letter from "Long Grabs," i.e., Murdoch John McSween). See also, Munson, ed., *Confederate Incognito*,

253; *Philadelphia Inquirer*, July 8, 1863 (excerpt from the *Richmond Sentinel*; Branch's artillery); Letter of J. W. Calton, 56th North Carolina, Richmond National Battlefield Park; Burgwyn Diary, Henry Brantingham and W. H. S. Burgwyn Diary, State Archives of North Carolina.

51. *Daily Richmond Examiner*, July 4, 1863.

52. *Fayetteville Weekly Observer*, July 13, 1863 (letter from "Long Grabs," i.e., Murdoch John McSween). Cooke's brigade had remained in reserve, probably on the west side of the Chickahominy during the engagement.

53. D. H. Hill Report, *ORA* 27(2):858–859.

54. Lewis, *Camp Life of a Confederate Boy*, 52–53 (Dispatch Station sometimes spelled "Despatch" Station in nineteenth-century accounts); Burgwyn Diary, Henry Brantingham and W. H. S. Burgwyn Diary, State Archives of North Carolina.

55. D. H. Hill Report, *ORA* 27(2):858–859; Hill to Seddon, 11 p.m., July 2, 1863, *ORA* 27(3):955.

56. *Daily Richmond Examiner*, July 4, 1863; *Wilmington Journal*, July 9, 1863 (excerpt from the *Richmond Enquirer*).

57. Dix to Keyes, July 3, 1863, 6:30 a.m., *ORA* 27(2):830; Keyes to Dix, July 3, 1863, 8:00 a.m., *ORA* 27(2):830.

58. Moore, *The Rebellion Record*, vol. 7, 332–334; *Chicago Tribune*, July 10, 1863 (reprinting account from the *New York World*); Keyes to Dix, July 3, 1863, 10:40 a.m., *ORA* 27(2):831.

59. *The History of the 127th New York Volunteers*, 59.

60. Oswald Jackson Letter, July 6, 1863, S. Trout Private Collection (expects a new advance toward Richmond).

61. John Dix to Catherine Dix, July 3, 1863, Dix Papers, Columbia University.

62. Dix to Keyes, July 4, 1863, *ORA* 27(2):831–832; Keyes to Dix, July 4, 1863, 12 midnight, *ORA* 27(2):832; Van Buren to Keyes, July 4, 1863, 12:30 a.m., *ORA* 27(2):832.

63. Keyes to Dix, July 5, 1863, 3:00 a.m., *ORA* 27(2):832–833.

64. Van Buren to Keyes, July 5, 1863, 2:30 a.m., *ORA* 27(2):833.

65. Keyes to Dix, July 5, 1863, 5:30 a.m., *ORA* 27(2):833.

66. Dix to Keyes, July 5, 1863, *ORA* 27(2):834.

67. Keyes to Dix, July 6, 1863, 2:30 pm. *ORA* 27(2):835 (scouting party finds works across Long Bridge on Chickahominy).

68. Keyes to Dix, July 6, 1863, 2:30 pm. *ORA* 27(2): 835–836 ("As you forbade us to destroy the bridges, the object of diverting a force diverting from Getty was accomplished by keeping is a long way this side of the river.").

69. Keyes to Dix, July 6, 1863, 2:30 p.m., *ORA* 27(2):835–836 (estimates that casualties since leaving White House are about twenty killed, wounded, and missing). Keyes provided slightly higher estimates in his subsequent report. *ORA* 27(2):857.

14. GETTY'S EXPEDITION TO THE SOUTH ANNA

1. Getty provided effective service as a division commander in the Sixth Corps at the Wilderness, where he was wounded, and at Cedar Creek, where he rallied

his men to push back a Confederate assault, and at Petersburg, where his division landed a decisive blow against the Confederate works.

2. *Evening Star*, October 3, 1901; *National Tribune*, October 10, 1901; Agassiz, *General Meade's Headquarters 1863–1865*, 91.

3. *Burlington Free Press*, October 15, 1901. Getty's granddaughter published a biography of the general in 1961. Getty, *George Washington Getty*, n.p.: 1961.

4. *Waterbury American*, December 4, 1863.

5. The 21st Connecticut, from Donohoe's brigade, stayed at White House as part of the provost guard. During the expedition, Donohoe commanded this brigade in place of Colonel William Steere. Troops in Department of Va., *ORA* 27(3):452. Diary of Edward Snow Foster (117th New York), American Civil War Collection, Hamilton College (the 117th New York collecting two months' pay).

6. Getty Report, *ORA* 27(2):837–842; Department of Virginia Returns, *ORA* 27(3):450–454; Dix Report, *ORA* 27(2):817–837.

7. Dix Report, *ORA* 27(2):817–837.

8. Claims of Terrel (Terrill) Bradby, Deposition of Adelphia Miles, Southern Claims Commission Case Files, RG 217, NARA (depositions of Adelphia Miles and Terrill Bradby); Dix Report, *ORA* 27(2):817–837.

9. Getty Report, *ORA* 27(2):837; Van Buren to Getty, June 30, 1863, *ORA* 27(2):840.

10. Getty Report, *ORA* 27(2):837; Van Buren to Getty, June 30, 1863, *ORA* 27(2):840.

11. Getty Report, *ORA* 27(2):837; Van Buren to Getty, June 30, 1863, *ORA* 27(2):840.

12. Dix to Stanton, September 12, 1862, *ORA* 18:391.

13. Dix to Stanton, December 13, 1862, *ORA* 18:480–481. See also, Dix to Corcoran, November 26, 1862, *ORA* 18:464.

14. Dix to Cameron, *ORA*, ser. 2, 1:763.

15. Dix to Tilden, December 3, 1861, *Letters and Literary Memorials of Samuel J. Tilden*, vol. 1, 164–165 (early war opposition to emancipation and arming slaves).

16. Dix to Stanton, September 12, 1862, *ORA* 18:391.

17. Taylor, *Embattled Freedom*, 87; Dix to Stanton, December 13, 1862, *ORA* 18:480–481; Dix to Stanton, September 12, 1862, *ORA* 18:391.

18. See, e.g., *Chicago Tribune*, November 8, 1862; *Vermont Christian Messenger*, November 6, 1862; *Baltimore Sun*, November 4, 1862. See also, Voegli, "A Rejected Alternative."

19. Dix to Lincoln, January 15, 1863, Lincoln Papers, Library of Congress.

20. Getty Report, *ORA* 27(2):837; Van Buren to Getty, June 30, 1863, *ORA* 27(2):840.

21. *Richmond Dispatch*, July 4, 1863; Howard to "My Dear Sister," April 16, 1863, James H. Howard Letters, Special Collections, University of Virginia.

22. Spear Report, *ORA* 27(2):852; Getty Report, *ORA* 27(2):837–842; Wardrop Report (99th New York), July 11, 1863, *ORA* 27(2):842 (Wardrop's brigade marched in the rear of Simpson's battery); Cruikshank, *Back in the Sixties*, 43–45 (Cruikshank indicates that Spear camped at "Mrs. Blake's Plantation"); Spear to Dix, July 2, 1863, Dix Papers, Columbia University.

23. Cruikshank, *Back in the Sixties*, 43–45; *Richmond Dispatch*, Saturday, July 4, 1863 (reporting the two companies passed near the Hanovertown and Newcastle Ferry roads).

24. Thorpe, *The History of the Fifteenth Connecticut Volunteers*, 216–218; Diary of Gurdon Robins (Lt. AQM, 16th Conn.), University of Connecticut Special Collections.

25. Hazard Stevens letter to his mother Margaret Hazard Stevens, July 13, 1863, Special Collections, Civil War Letters, University of Washington Libraries. Stevens would earn the Medal of Honor for his actions during the Suffolk Campaign.

26. Hyde, *History of the One Hundred and Twelfth Regiment, N.Y. Volunteers*, 40; Diary of Edward Snow Foster (117th N.Y.), American Civil War Collection, Hamilton College; Allen, *Forty-Six Months with the Fourth R.I. Volunteers*, 207.

27. Howard to "My Dear Sister," July 16, 1863, James H. Howard Letters, Special Collections, University of Virginia; Wardrop Report (99th New York), July 11, 1863, *ORA* 27(2):842–843; William Fanning Wickham Diary, Wickham Family Papers, VMHC.

28. Croffut, *The Military and Civil History of Connecticut During the War of 1861–65*, 337–339; Thorpe, *The History of the Fifteenth Connecticut Volunteers*, 216–218.

29. Howard to "My Dear Sister," July 16, 1863, James H. Howard Letters, Special Collections, University of Virginia.

30. Cunningham, *Three Years with the Adirondack Regiment*, 68–74; Allen, *Forty-six Months with the Fourth R.I. Volunteers*, 208.

31. Howard to "My Dear Sister," July 16, 1863, James H. Howard Letters, Special Collections, University of Virginia.

32. Croffut, *The Military and Civil History of Connecticut During the War of 1861–65*, 337 (field of "Mrs. Pemberton").

33. Allen, George, *Forty-six Months with the Fourth R.I. Volunteers*, 208. The *Richmond Dispatch* confirmed the Federals destroyed the crops of Richard Pemberton, whose plantation stood just northwest of King William Courthouse. *Richmond Dispatch*, Saturday, July 4, 1863.

34. Allen, George, 208.

35. William Fanning Wickham Diary, Wickham Family Papers, VMHC; Getty Report, *ORA* 27(2): 837–842; Cruikshank, *Back in the Sixties*, 43–45.

36. Hyde, *History of the One Hundred and Twelfth Regiment, N.Y. Volunteers*, 40.

37. Thompson, *Thirteenth Regiment of New Hampshire Volunteer Infantry*, 184.

38. Allen, George, *Forty-Six Months with the Fourth R.I. Volunteers*, 208.

39. Getty Report, *ORA* 27(2): 837–842; Wardrop Report (99th New York), July 11, 1863, *ORA* 27(2):842–843; Hyde, *History of the One Hundred and Twelfth Regiment, N.Y. Volunteers*, 41 (members of 112th New York and 13th Indiana captured horses and mules from the home guard near Rumford Academy).

40. Seddon to Hall, July 2, 1863, *ORA* 27(3):953; Hall to Seddon, July 2, 1863, *ORA* 27(3):954.

41. Hill to Seddon, July 2, 1863, *ORA* 27(3):954; Hill to Seddon, 3 p.m., July 2, 1863, *ORA* 27(3):954; Seddon to Hall, July 2, 1863; Seddon to Boyle, July 2, 1863, *ORA* 27(3):956.

42. Thompson, *Thirteenth Regiment of New Hampshire Volunteer Infantry*, 184.

43. Allen, George, *Forty-six Months with the Fourth R.I. Volunteers*, 208.

44. Eighth Census of the United States 1860, Series Number: M653, Record Group: Records of the Bureau of the Census, Record Group Number: 29, NARA.

45. Croffut, *The Military and Civil History of Connecticut During the War of 1861–65*, 337–339; see also, *Daily Palladium* (New Haven), July 24, 1863.

46. Account of William Winston Fontaine, *William and Mary College Quarterly*, vol. 19, July 1910, 179–184.

47. According to one soldier, the accused men were "only kept under arrest a day or two and had their guns and cartridge boxes carried for them." George W. Pearl to his Parents, July 14, 1863, American Civil War Collection, Hamilton College.

48. Diary of Gurdon Robins (Lt. AQM, 16th Conn.), University of Connecticut Special Collections; Thompson, *Thirteenth Regiment of New Hampshire Volunteer Infantry*, 184; Thorpe, *The History of the Fifteenth Connecticut Volunteers*, 216–218 and 337–339; Thompson, *Thirteenth Regiment of New Hampshire Volunteer Infantry*, 184; George W. Pearl to his Parents, July 14, 1863, American Civil War Collection, Hamilton College.

49. Getty Report, *ORA* 27(2):837–842; Wardrop Report (99th New York), July 11, 1863, *ORA* 27(2):842–843; Hyde, *History of the One Hundred and Twelfth Regiment, N.Y. Volunteers*, 40–43. The Taylor property was sometimes referred to as "Taylorsville," not to be confused with the hamlet of the same name in Caroline County on the Little River between the North and South Anna Rivers.

50. Jacobs et al., *Field Music*, 58.

51. Hyde, *History of the One Hundred and Twelfth Regiment, N.Y. Volunteers*, 40–43; Getty Report, *ORA* 27(2):837–842.

52. Hyde, *History of the One Hundred and Twelfth Regiment, N.Y. Volunteers*, 40–43. For examples of modern medical studies of blackberries (*rubus fruticosus*), see Yang, "Effects of blackberry juice on growth inhibition of foodborne pathogens and growth promotion of Lactobacillus," 15–20; Zia-Ul-Haq et al., "Rubus Fruticosus L.," 10998–11029.

53. Robert H. Kellogg to Father, July 11, 1863, Kellogg Letters, Connecticut Historical Society.

54. *Vermont Watchman and State Journal*, July 6, 1887. When Major W. E. Kisselburgh of the 169th New York in Foster's brigade rode out to sample some, his horse bolted out of the blackberry patch at the sound of a rattlesnake near its hooves.

55. Blakesee, *History of the Sixteenth Connecticut Volunteers*, 40; Getty Report, *ORA* 27(2): 837–842; Wardrop Report (99th New York), July 11, 1863, *ORA* 27(2):842–843.

56. Allen, *Forty-six Months with the Fourth R.I. Volunteers*, 209–212.

57. Casa et al., "Historical Perspectives on Medical Care for Heat Stroke, Part 2"; Goldman, "Introduction to Heat-Related Problems in Military Operations."

See also, Browning, *An Environmental History of the Civil War*; Noe, *The Howling Storm*.

58. Mowris, *A History of the One Hundred and Seventeenth Regiment, N.Y. Volunteers*, 73.

59. Kellogg to Father, July 11, 1863, Robert Hale Kellogg Letters, Connecticut Historical Society (16th Connecticut).

60. Croffut, *The Military and Civil History of Connecticut During the War of 1861–65*, 337–339; Senate Report 1887, 49th Cong., 2nd Sess. (discusses chronic injuries developed by Sabine Stocking following the Blackberry Raid and recommends compensation).

61. Mowris, *A History of the One Hundred and Seventeenth Regiment, N.Y. Volunteers*, 73.

62. Thorpe, *The History of the Fifteenth Connecticut Volunteers*, 216–218.

63. Cunningham, *Three Years with the Adirondack Regiment*, 68–74. For maps, see "Map of part of Essex, King and Queen, and King William Counties," LOC # 2002627444, Library of Congress Geography and Map Division, LC Civil War maps (2nd ed.), H29.

64. US Surgeon-General's Office, *The Medical and Surgical History of the War of the Rebellion*, vol. 1, pt. 1, 332; Allen, *Forty-six Months with the Fourth R.I. Volunteers*, 209–212; Gordon, *A Broken Regiment*, 93–95; Woodford to "my mother & friends at home," July 11, 1863, Letters of Harrison Woodford during the Civil War.

65. George W. Pearl to his Parents, July 14, 1863, American Civil War Collection, Hamilton College; Mowris, *A History of the One Hundred and Seventeenth Regiment, N.Y. Volunteers*, 73; National Park Service, US Department of Interior, National Historic Register Nomination Form, "Horn Quarter," March 18, 1980; Cunningham, *Three Years with the Adirondack Regiment*, 68–74 ("sleep came soon"). Several accounts estimate Getty's column marched upward of 25 miles on Friday. However, the actual distance from Fountainebleau to Horn Quarter is about 12 miles, and from the far end of Getty's column the previous evening at Rumford Academy, the distance was only about 15 miles. Perhaps the march seemed long given the day's grueling conditions, or maybe some units lost their way.

66. Getty Report, *ORA* 27(2):837–842; Wardrop Report (99th New York), July 11, 1863, *ORA* 27(2):842–843; Hyde, *History of the One Hundred and Twelfth Regiment, N.Y. Volunteers*, 40–43; Hyde, *History of the One Hundred and Twelfth Regiment, N.Y. Volunteers*, 40–43; Diary of Gurdon Robins (Lt. AQM, 16th Conn.), University of Connecticut Special Collections; Cruikshank, *Back in the Sixties*, 43–45.

67. National Park Service, US Department of Interior, National Historic Register Nomination Form, "Horn Quarter," March 18, 1980; Howard to "My Dear Sister," July 16, 1863, James H. Howard Letters, Special Collections, University of Virginia.

68. Allen, *Forty-Six Months with the Fourth R.I. Volunteers*, 209–212.

69. John Dix to Catherine Dix, July 3, 1863, Dix Papers, Columbia University.

70. *Richmond Dispatch*, July 4, 1863; *Richmond Enquirer*, July 3, 1863; Hill to Elzey, July 3, 1863, RG 109, Compiled Service Records of Confederate

Officers, NARA; Herbert Augustine Claiborne Diary, Claiborne Family Papers, VMHC.

71. D. H. Hill to Seddon, July 3, 1863, ORA 27(2):858–859; *Richmond Dispatch*, July 4, 1863. Writing to Secretary Stanton, Hill suggested the events of the previous day proved Colquitt's brigade was no longer needed from North Carolina.

72. Hall to Elzey, July 3, 1863, ORA 27(3):960.

73. Anderson to Elzey, 11:10 a.m., July 3, 1863, ORA 27(3):961; Chestney to Winder, July 3, 1863, ORA 27(3):962–963 ("Colonel [H. H.] Walker sends word that he has sent 484 men up to the Junction, in addition to the 300 sent yesterday"); Elzey to Hill, July 3, 1863, ORA 27(3):961; Seddon to Hill, July 3, 1863, ORA 27(3):963 (to replace the convalescents in the Richmond fortifications, Hill pulled Colonel T. S. Rhett's command into Richmond's inner defenses); Hill to Seddon, July 3, 1863, 4:30 p.m., ORA 27(3):960–961.

74. Hill to Elzey, July 3, 1863, ORA 27(3):962.

75. Seddon to Hill, July 3, 1863, ORA 27(3):963; Burgwyn Diary, Henry Brantingham and W. H. S. Burgwyn Diary, State Archives of North Carolina.

76. Hill to Elzey, July 3, 1863, ORA 27(3):962; Jones, *A Rebel War Clerk's Diary at the Confederate States Capital*, vol. 1, 368; Furgurson, *Ashes of Glory*, 213 (Lange account).

77. Hill to Elzey, July 3, 1863, ORA 27(3):962.

78. See, e.g., Newsome, *The Fight for the Old North State*, 42 (Davis offered to lead troops against New Bern in January 1863).

79. Jones, *A Rebel War Clerk's Diary at the Confederate States Capital*, vol. 1, 368; Furgurson, *Ashes of Glory*, 213 (Lange account).

80. Seddon to Zachry, July 3, 1863, ORA 27(3):963.

81. Whiting to Beauregard, July 3, 1863, ORA 27(3):965–966. Whiting worried a transfer of Colquitt's brigade north to Virginia "completely uncovers the Wilmington and Weldon Railroad, and even exposes Raleigh to a cavalry raid" on the "immense supplies" there.

82. *Daily Richmond Examiner*, July 6, 1863; *Semi-Weekly Richmond Enquirer*, July 3, 1863.

15. TO THE RF&P BRIDGE

1. Burgwyn Diary, Henry Brantingham and W. H. S. Burgwyn Diary, State Archives of North Carolina; *Richmond Daily Dispatch*, July 4, 1863.

2. *Daily Richmond Examiner*, July 4, 1863; *Richmond Daily Dispatch*, July 4, 1863;

3. Colquitt to Seddon, July 4, 1863, ORA 27(3):969.

4. Hill to Seddon, July 4, 1863, ORA 27(3):968.

5. Hill to Seddon, July 4, 1863, ORA 27(3):968.

6. Hill to Seddon, July 4, 1863, ORA 27(3):968. Hill also remained concerned for the capital's safety. "With his force hanging on each flank, it is dangerous to leave Richmond too far." He expected the Union forces would continue to threaten Richmond until the Confederates took the initiative and drove them away.

7. Hill to Seddon, July 4, 1863, *ORA* 27(3):969. (also asking whether he had "mere command of the three outer brigades or of the whole").

8. Elzey to Seddon, July 4, 1863, *ORA* 27(3):967; Seddon to Colquitt, July 5, 1863, *ORA* 27(3):969.

9. Hyde, *History of the One Hundred and Twelfth Regiment, N.Y. Volunteers*, 43–46; Cruikshank, *Back in the Sixties*, 43–45; Cruikshank to Marguerite Cruikshank and Esther Flowers, July 11, 1863, George L. Cruikshank Letters, State Historical Society of Iowa.

10. Hyde, *History of the One Hundred and Twelfth Regiment, N.Y. Volunteers*, 43–46. The batteries left behind were: J. Gillis's 5th US Artillery, Battery A and J. G. Simpson's 1st Pennsylvania, Battery A.

11. Van Buren to Getty, June 30, 1863, *ORA* 27(2):840.

12. Croffut, *The Military and Civil History of Connecticut During the War of 1861–65*, 337–339.

13. Howard to "My Dear Sister," July 16, 1863, James H. Howard Letters, Special Collections, University of Virginia; Croffut, *The Military and Civil History of Connecticut During the War of 1861–65*, 337–339 (John Taylor captured); Hyde, *History of the One Hundred and Twelfth Regiment, N.Y. Volunteers*, 43–46. John P. Taylor's Service Record, Compiled Service Records of Confederate Soldiers Who Served in Organizations from the State of Virginia, RG 109, NARA (Taylor's record indicates that he was exchanged a few weeks later and detailed in 1864 to operate a "fishery" on the Rappahannock).

14. Croffut, *The Military and Civil History of Connecticut During the War of 1861–65*, 337–339.

15. George W. Pearl to his Parents, July 14, 1863, American Civil War Collection, Hamilton College.

16. Kellogg to Father, July 11, 1863, Robert Hale Kellogg Letters, Connecticut Historical Society.

17. Hyde, *History of the One Hundred and Twelfth Regiment, N.Y. Volunteers*, 43–46; Cunningham, *Three Years with the Adirondack Regiment*, 68–74.

18. Thompson, *Thirteenth Regiment of New Hampshire Volunteer Infantry*, 184.

19. Cunningham, *Three Years with the Adirondack Regiment*, 68–74; Getty Report, *ORA* 27(2):837–842; Wardrop Report (99th New York), July 11, 1863, *ORA* 27(2):842–843; Hyde, *History of the One Hundred and Twelfth Regiment, N.Y. Volunteers*, 43–46; Cruikshank to Marguerite Cruikshank and Esther Flowers, July 11, 1863, George L. Cruikshank Letters, State Historical Society of Iowa; *Daily Richmond Examiner*, July 6, 1863. For reasons not explained, Foster's brigade waited at Littlepage's Bridge until 3 p.m., when it finally received orders to move forward to Hanover Court House.

20. Haas and Talley, *A Refugee at Hanover Tavern*, 144; Hyde, *History of the One Hundred and Twelfth Regiment, N.Y. Volunteers*, 43–46; Cruikshank to Marguerite Cruikshank and Esther Flowers, July 11, 1863, George L. Cruikshank Letters, State Historical Society of Iowa; *Daily Richmond Examiner*, July 6, 1863. The Federals also reportedly nabbed several Confederate Commissary Department employees at Hanover.

21. Getty Report, *ORA* 27(2):837–840: Department of Virginia Return, *ORA*

27(3):454; Wardrop Report (99th New York), July 11, 1863, ORA 27(2):842 (verbal orders from Getty to join Foster); Hyde, *History of the One Hundred and Twelfth Regiment, N.Y. Volunteers*, 43–46.

22. Foster Report, *ORA* 27(2):840–842.

23. On Saturday morning, Getty had ordered Spear to advance toward "Hanover Court-House and then proceed to the Richmond and Fredericksburg bridge at the South Anna and "report to Brig. Gen R. S. Foster." Spear Report, *ORA* 27(2):852.

24. Unidentified Newspaper Clipping, 118th New York File, New York State Military Museum; William Fanning Wickham Diary, Wickham Family Papers, VMHC; Hyde, *History of the One Hundred and Twelfth Regiment, N.Y. Volunteers*, 43–46.

25. Nixon Report (99th N.Y.), *ORA* 27(2):843–844; Spear Report, *ORA* 27(2):852; Stuart, "Samuel Ruth and General R.E. Lee." In the early 1900s, the track bed was shifted several hundred feet to the east to straighten the line and a new bridge was added about 120 yards downstream from the bridge extant during the Civil War. A stone abutment or pier still remains on the south bank at the site of the old bridge crossing. *Railroad Gazette*, vol. 36, 252.

26. *Fayetteville Weekly Observer*, July 13, 1863 (letter from "Karux"); *Greensboro Patriot*, July 16, 1863; *Richmond Sentinel*, July 9, 1863; Cooke to Anderson, July 6, 1863, 11 a.m., *ORA* 27(3):975–976.

27. See, e.g., No. 456 (Prince Edward, South Anna Bridge, &c), No. 1262 ("Louisa, South Anna Bridges"), Confederate Slave Payrolls, RG 109, NARA.

28. Hall to Seddon, June 3, 1863, *ORA* 18:1091; Cooke Report, *ORA* 27(2):857–858; *U.S. War Department's Atlas to Accompany the Official Records of the Union and Confederate Armies (1891–1895)*, Plate XCI; "Map of the northern portion of Hanover County, Va., showing fortifications on the South Anna River near Taylorsville," 2002627447, Geography and Map Division, Library of Congress; *Daily Richmond Examiner*, July 7, 1863. Cooke's after-action report makes it clear the works there were by no means complete in early July. Remains of these earthworks exist today on both sides of the river.

29. Cooke Report, *ORA* 27(2):857–858; Spear Report, *ORA* 27(2):852; Davis Report (7th Massachusetts Battery), *ORA* 27(2):853–854.

30. Spear Report, *ORA* 27(2):852; Davis Report (7th Massachusetts Battery), *ORA* 27(2):853–854.

31. Unidentified Clipping, Civil War Newspaper Clipping, 118th Infantry, New York State Military Museum.

32. Foster Report, *ORA* 27(2):840–842; Keese Report (118th New York), July 15, 1863, *ORA* 27(2):844–845; Wardrop Report (99th New York), July 11, 1863, *ORA* 27(2):842; Norris Report (Co. A, 118th N.Y.), *ORA* 27(2):845–847.

33. Davis Report (7th Massachusetts Battery), *ORA* 27(2):853–854. According to Cooke, the Federals began their probes at dusk and continued to attack "at intervals during the night along the line of the South Anna, covering a front of some 2 miles." Cooke Report, *ORA* 27(2):857–858; Report of Keese, July 15, 1863, *ORA* 27(2):844–845. See also, *Buffalo Sunday Morning News*, August 3, 1913; Richard Nixon Report (99th N.Y.), July 11, 1863, *ORA* 27(2):843–844; Davis Report, *ORA* 27(2):853–854; Spear Report, *ORA* 27(2):852.

34. Foster Report, *ORA* 27(2):840–842.

35. Foster Report, *ORA* 27(2):840–842; Hyde, *History of the One Hundred and Twelfth Regiment, N.Y. Volunteers*, 43–46.

36. Davis Report (7th Massachusetts Battery), *ORA* 27(2):853–854.

37. Foster Report, *ORA* 27(2):840–842; *Buffalo Sunday Morning News*, Aug 03, 1913; Spear Report, *ORA* 27(2):852.

38. Davis Report, *ORA* 27(2):853–854 (by Foster's order, placed battery on a small hill at the crossing of the railroad and county road).

39. Other sources provided similar estimates about the number of Confederate guns. A letter from a Confederate soldier reported there were "6 pieces of artillery," including "12 pd howitzers and 3 inch rifled guns." Back near the bridge, according to reports and accounts in the newspaper, Colonel John Baker placed two guns (a Napoleon and a Blakely Rifle) commanded by Lieutenant Colonel Charles E. Lightfoot and served by members of Thomas Thornton's Caroline Battery and Henry Rives's Nelson Battery. *Fayetteville Weekly Observer*, July 13, 1863 (letter from "Karux"); *Greensboro Patriot*, July 16, 1863; *Richmond Sentinel*, July 9, 1863; Cooke to Anderson, July 6, 1863, 11 a.m., *ORA* 27(3):975–976; Davis Report (7th Massachusetts Battery), *ORA* 27(2):853–854.

40. *Greensboro Patriot*, July 16, 1863; Cooke to Anderson, July 6, 1863, 11 a.m., *ORA* 27(3): 975–976; Department of Richmond Returns, *ORA* 27(3):909 (2,486 in Cooke's entire four-regiment brigade plus Cooper's Battery); Clark, *Histories of Several Regiments*, vol. 1, 741–742; *ORA* 27(3):927.

41. *Fayetteville Weekly Observer*, July 13, 1863 (letter from "Karux"); *Greensboro Patriot*, July 16, 1863.

42. Cooke Report, *ORA* 27(2):857–858; *Fayetteville Weekly Observer*, July 13, 1863 (letter from "Karux"); *Greensboro Patriot*, July 16, 1863; *Fayetteville Weekly Observer*, July 13, 1863; Munson, *North Carolina Civil War Obituaries*, 213. Fleming Service Record, Compiled Service Records of Confederate Soldiers Who Served in Organizations from the State of North Carolina, RG 109, NARA (a legislator from Rowan County, Fleming was killed at the Wilderness in 1864).

16. THE ATTACK ON THE RF&P BRIDGE

1. Cunningham, *Three Years with the Adirondack Regiment*, 68–74. Pruyn later rose to regimental command and was killed at Petersburg on June 15, 1864.

2. See, Phisterer, ed., *New York in the War of the Rebellion*, 3rd ed.

3. According to records from the New York Adjutant-General's Office, Co. E, 99th New York had 83 men, Co. A, 118th NY had 83; Co. D, 118th NY had 81; and Co. F, 118th NY had 82. *A record of the commissioned officers, non-commissioned officers, and privates, of the regiments which were organized in the state of New York*, vol. 4, 284–295.

4. Wardrop Report (99th New York), *ORA* 27(2):842; Norris Report (Co. A, 118th N.Y.), *ORA* 27(2):845–847; Keese Report (118th New York), *ORA* 27(2):844–845.

5. Norris Report (Co. A, 118th N.Y.), *ORA* 27(2):845–847 (Company A on the right; and Company F on the left); Unidentified Clipping, Civil War Newspaper

Clipping, 118th Infantry, New York State Military Museum; Cunningham Report (Co. F., 118th N.Y.), *ORA* 27(2):850–851.

6. The pond (or "marsh," in Cunningham's words) to the west was likely part of Falling Creek, which bends at one point close to the railroad. See "Map of the counties of Charles City, Goochland, Hanover, Henrico, King William, New Kent, and part of the counties of Caroline and Louisa, Virginia, Chief Engineer's Office, D.N.V., [1863]," Civil War Maps, Library of Congress; Cunningham Report (Co. F., 118th N.Y.), *ORA* 27(2):850–851.

7. Norris Report (Co. A, 118th N.Y.), July 14, 1863, *ORA* 27(2):845–847; Cunningham, *Three Years with the Adirondack Regiment*, 68–74.

8. Cunningham, 68–74; Cunningham Report (Co. F., 118th N.Y.), *ORA* 27(2):850–851.

9. Norris Report (Co. A, 118th N.Y.), July 14, 1863, *ORA* 27(2):845–847.

10. *Greensboro Patriot*, July 16, 1863; Cunningham Report (Co. F., 118th N.Y.), *ORA* 27(2):850–851; Cunningham, *Three Years with the Adirondack Regiment*, 68–74.

11. Cunningham Report (Co. F., 118th N.Y.), *ORA* 27(2):849–851; Cunningham, *Three Years*, 68–74; Unidentified Clipping, Civil War Newspaper Clipping, 118th Infantry, New York State Military Museum; Norris Report (Co. A, 118th N.Y.), July 14, 1863, *ORA* 27(2):845–847.

12. Unidentified Clipping, Civil War Newspaper Clipping, 118th Infantry, New York State Military Museum; Norris Report (Co. A, 118th N.Y.), *ORA* 27(2):845–847; Cunningham Report (Co. F., 118th N.Y.), *ORA* 27(2):849–851.

13. Capt. Edward Riggs Report (Co. D., 118th N.Y.), July 14, 1863, *ORA* 27(2):845–847; Norris Report (Co. A, 118th N.Y.), *ORA* 27(2):845–847; Wardrop Report (99th New York), *ORA* 27(2):842.

14. Unidentified Clipping, Civil War Newspaper Clipping, 118th Infantry, New York State Military Museum; Capt. Edward Riggs Report (Co. D., 118th N.Y.), *ORA* 27(2):845–847.

15. Cunningham Report (Co. F., 118th N.Y.), *ORA* 27(2):850–851; Norris Report (Co. A, 118th N.Y.), *ORA* 27(2):845–847; *Fayetteville Weekly Observer*, July 13, 1863.

16. Capt. Edward Riggs Report (Co. D., 118th N.Y.), *ORA* 27(2):845–847. Norris Report (Co. A, 118th N.Y.), *ORA* 27(2):845–847; Unidentified Clipping, Civil War Newspaper Clipping, 118th Infantry, New York State Military Museum (mentions wounds suffered by Corporal [Samuel] Vantassell, Henry M. Millis, and Hiram Yetto).

17. Capt. Edward Riggs Report (Co. D., 118th N.Y.), *ORA* 27(2):845–847.

18. *Daily Richmond Examiner*, July 7, 1863.

19. Cunningham Report (Co. F., 118th N.Y.), *ORA* 27(2):849–851; Cunningham, *Three Years with the Adirondack Regiment*, 68–74.

20. *Greensboro Patriot*, July 16, 1863.

21. Keese Report (118th New York), *ORA* 27(2):844–845; Cunningham, *Three Years with the Adirondack Regiment*, 68–74.

22. Keese Report (118th New York), *ORA* 27(2):844–845; Cunningham, 68–74.

23. Cunningham Report (Co. F., 118th N.Y.), *ORA* 27(2):850–851. Unidentified Clipping, Civil War Newspaper Clipping, 118th Infantry, New York State Military Museum.

24. Keese Report (118th New York), *ORA* 27(2):844–845; Cunningham, *Three Years with the Adirondack Regiment*, 68–74.

25. Cunningham, 68–74 (Stevenson was killed at Drewry's Bluff in May 1864 while trying to save a wounded comrade); Cunningham Report (Co. F., 118th N.Y.), *ORA* 27(2):850–851; Unidentified Clipping, Civil War Newspaper Clipping, 118th Infantry, New York State Military Museum.

26. *Fayetteville Weekly Observer*, July 13, 1863 (letter from "Karux"); *Greensboro Patriot*, July 16, 1863, Riggs Report (Co. D., 118th N.Y.), *ORA* 27(2):845–847; Unidentified Clipping, Civil War Newspaper Clipping, 118th Infantry, New York State Military Museum; Norris Report (Co. A, 118th N.Y.), *ORA* 27(2):845–847. Company H of the 46th North Carolina under Captain Neill McNeill formed part of the reinforcement supporting Fleming.

27. Cunningham, *Three Years with the Adirondack Regiment*, 68–74.

28. Riggs Report (Co. D., 118th N.Y.), *ORA* 27(2):845–847; Foster Report, *ORA* 27(2): 840–842.

29. Foster Report, *ORA* 27(2): 840–842; Capt. Edward Riggs Report (Co. D., 118th N.Y.), *ORA* 27(2):845–847; Wardrop Report (99th New York), *ORA* 27(2):842 (says Foster's orders called off the advance).

30. Cunningham Report (Co. F., 118th N.Y.), *ORA* 27(2):850–851; Riggs Report (Co. D., 118th N.Y.), *ORA* 27(2):845–847.

31. Cruikshank, *Back in the Sixties*, 43–45.

32. Nixon Report (99th N.Y.), *ORA* 27(2):843–844; Getty Report, *ORA* 27(2): 837–842. Years later Cunningham recalled: "This was our first 'close-up' engagement and although a small affair it had all the features of that sort of thing and we learned the fact that every shot from the enemy does not kill somebody." Cunningham, *Three Years with the Adirondack Regiment*, 68–74.

33. Cunningham, 68–74; Wardrop Report (99th New York), *ORA* 27(2):842; Keese Report (118th New York), *ORA* 27(2):844–845; Unidentified Clipping, Civil War Newspaper Clipping, 118th Infantry, New York State Military Museum.

34. *New York Times*, July 14, 1863; Foster Report, *ORA* 27(2):840–842; Wardrop Report (99th New York), *ORA* 27(2):842; Keese Report (118th New York), *ORA* 27(2):844–845; Unidentified Clipping, Civil War Newspaper Clipping, 118th Infantry, New York State Military Museum.

35. Getty Report, *ORA* 27(2): 837–842; Kimball, *History and Personal Sketches of Company I, 103 N.Y S.V., 1862–1864* (talks of going to "Hanover Station," probably meant "Ashland Station").

36. McGuire, *Diary of a Southern Refugee*, 169–170.

37. Stratton Report, *ORA* 27(2):853.

38. *Greensboro Patriot*, July 16, 1863; Getty Report, *ORA* 27(2): 837–842.

39. Cooke Report, *ORA* 27(2):857–858.

40. Stratton Report, *ORA* 27(2):853; *Daily Richmond Examiner*, July 6, 1863; Getty Report, *ORA* 27(2): 837–842; Kimball, Orville Samuel, *History and Personal Sketches of Company I, 103 N.Y.S.V., 1862–1864*.

41. McGuire, *Diary of a Southern Refugee*, 169–170.

42. *Daily Richmond Examiner*, July 6, 1863; Cooke Report, *ORA* 27(2):857–858.

43. *Greensboro Patriot*, July 16, 1863 (letter from "Eusebious").

44. Cooke Report, *ORA* 27(2):857–858; *New York Daily Herald*, July 10, 1863; *Fayetteville Weekly Observer*, July 13, 1863.

45. *Daily Richmond Examiner*, July 7, 1863. On July 7, Cooke reported that: "[P. S.]—The citizens tell me there are thirty-three graves of Yankees in one place, 2 miles below this, and that they also carried of s number of dead in 2 wagons, besides 50 or 60 wounded in ambulances. I have sent to see if this be true, and will let you know." Cooke to Anderson, July 7, 1863, *ORA* 27(3):979.

46. Wardrop Report (99th New York), *ORA* 27(2):842.

47. Captain Norris (Company A) is an exception, listing two killed and seven wounded. Norris Report (Co. A, 118th N.Y.), *ORA* 27(2):845–847. "We find that in last night's affair Martin Sherman and Henry M. Willis were killed; Corporals C. C. LaPoint and Samuel Van Tassell and private Hiram Yatto [Yetto], and two others, wounded; Edgar Comstock and Arad Mickle, missing (they were prisoners), making our casualties 10. The 99th lost one man, killed, with six missing." Cunningham, *Three Years with the Adirondack Regiment*, 68–74.

48. *New York Daily Herald*, July 10, 1863 (contains a full list of casualties by name, unit, and wound, etc.); Capt. Edward Riggs Report (Co. D., 118th N.Y.), *ORA* 27(2):845–847 (Company D of the 118th, under Captain Riggs, apparently suffered only one wounded); *Fayetteville Weekly Observer*, July 13, 1863 (letter from "Karux") (Baker's cavalry captured twelve Federals and found twelve dead in the woods near railroad).

49. Cunningham Report (Co. F., 118th N.Y.), *ORA* 27(2):850–851; Riggs Report (Co. D., 118th N.Y.), *ORA* 27(2):845–847 (Riggs commended First Lieutenant Kellogg in command of his reserves and Second Lieutenant Sherman on the skirmish line).

50. Cooke Report, *ORA* 27(2):857–858.

51. *Greensboro Patriot*, July 16, 1863; *Fayetteville Weekly Observer*, July 13, 1863 (letter from "Karux"); *Greensboro Patriot*, July 16, 1863; Compiled Service Records of Confederate Soldiers Who Served in Organizations from the State of North Carolina, RG 109, NARA.

52. Clark, *Histories of Several Regiments*, vol. 1, 741–742; *Fayetteville Weekly Observer*, July 13, 1863 (letter from "Karux"); Cooke Report, *ORA* 27(2):857–858.

53. Cruikshank, *Back in the Sixties*, 43–45; Cunningham, *Three Years with the Adirondack Regiment*, 68–74.

54. Diary of Gurdon Robins (Lt. AQM, 16th Conn.), University of Connecticut Special Collections; William Fanning Wickham Diary and Lucy Penn Taylor Wickham to Williams Carter Wickham, July 25, 1863, Wickham Family Papers, VMHC; Haas and Talley, *A Refugee at Hanover Tavern*, 144 (Wight identified her neighbor as "Mrs. Winston").

55. Cruikshank, *Back in the Sixties*, 43–45; Cunningham, *Three Years with the Adirondack Regiment*, 68–74.

56. Wardrop Report (99th New York), *ORA* 27(2):842; Report of Lieutenant Colonel Oliver Keese Jr. (118th New York), *ORA* 27(2):844–845; Unidentified Clipping, Civil War Newspaper Clipping, 118th Infantry, New York State Military Museum.

57. Blakesee, *History of the Sixteenth Connecticut Volunteers*, 40 (recalls the 2 p.m. arrival of a wagon train at Horn Quarter sent from White House with rations, though there is no mention of such resupply in the reports).

58. Hyde, *History of the One Hundred and Twelfth Regiment, N.Y. Volunteers*, 43–46 (soldiers led by a Lieutenant "Zentz").

59. Hyde, 43–46; Blakesee, *History of the Sixteenth Connecticut Volunteers*, 41.

60. Cunningham, *Three Years with the Adirondack Regiment*, 68–74.

61. Getty Report, *ORA* 27(2):837–842; Blakesee, *History of the Sixteenth Connecticut Volunteers*, 40; John Cuzner letter, July 13, 1863, Cuzner Letters and Papers, Connecticut Historical Society.

62. Howard to "My Dear Sister," July 16, 1863, James H. Howard Letters, Special Collections, University of Virginia; Hyde, *History of the One Hundred and Twelfth Regiment, N.Y. Volunteers*, 43–46; Getty Report, *ORA* 27(2): 837–842.

63. Croffut, *The Military and Civil History of Connecticut During the War of 1861–65*, 337–339.

64. Member of the 21st Regiment, *The Story of the Twenty-first Regiment, Connecticut Volunteer Infantry*, 131–132.

65. Diary of Gurdon Robins (Lt. AQM, 16th Conn.), University of Connecticut Special Collections. According to William Morey of the 130th New York, more Black refugees arrived at White House on the morning of July 7. A Union picket fired on the group by mistake, hitting one of the refugees in the shoulder. Morey, William C. Diary (July 7, 1863, entry).

66. Getty Report, *ORA* 27(2):837–842 (Getty also highlighted that his men had captured "1 officer and upward of 20 prisoners, with a loss on our part of but 2 killed and 7 wounded by the enemy"); McGuire, *Diary of a Southern Refugee*, 169–170. Getty also commended his officers who "carried out [orders] promptly and to the letter, and a fine spirit and zeal was manifested by all under mv command."

67. Cunningham Report (Co. F., 118th N.Y.), *ORA* 27(2):850–851.

68. Capt. Edward Riggs Report (Co. D., 118th N.Y.), *ORA* 27(2):845–847. Captain Norris did not mention the conduct of his company.

69. See, Getty, George W., Papers in Gibson–Getty–McClure Families Papers.

70. Getty Report, *ORA* 27(2):837–842.

71. McGuire, *Diary of a Southern Refugee*, 169–170.

17. THE PEACE MISSION

1. A. Stephens to Linton Stephens, July 3, 1863, Stephens Collection, Manhattanville College.

2. *ORA*, ser. 2, 6:94–96, Stephens to Davis, July 8, 1863; S. P. Lee Report

(July 4, 1863), ORN 9:106–7, Wyllie, *Confederate States Navy*, 247 (*Torpedo*); Gaines, *Encyclopedia of Civil War Shipwrecks*, 189.

3. ser. 2, 6:94–96, Stephens to Davis, July 8, 1863; S. P. Lee Report (July 4, 1863), ORN 9:106–107; Wyllie, 247 (*Torpedo*); Gaines, 189.

4. Davis to Lincoln, July 2, 1863, ORA, ser. 2, 6:75–76; Lee Report, ORN 9:106–107; ORA ser. 2, 6:78–79, Lee to Welles, July 4, 1863 (forward Stephens note to Lee on the same date); Ludlow to Stanton, July 4, 1863, ORA ser. 2, 6:80.

5. Lee Report, ORN 9:106–107.

6. Stephens to Davis, July 8, 1863, ORA ser. 2, 6:94–96; Lee Report (July 4, 1863), ORN 9:106–107. The original source for Admiral Lee's oft-quoted statement about his loyalty to the United States is unclear. One account, from 1895, states that he said, "There was no Virginia in my commission, but only the United States." Lee, *Lee of Virginia, 1642–1892*, 403.

7. Stanton to Ludlow, July 4, 1863, ORA ser. 2, 6:80; Lamson to Lee, July 4, 1863, 9 p.m., ORN 9:107.

8. Welles, *Diary of Gideon Welles*, vol. 1, 358–359.

9. Stanton to Ludlow, July 4, 1863, ORA ser. 2, 6:80; Lamson to Lee, July 4, 1863, 9 p.m., ORN 9:107.

10. Welles, *Diary of Gideon Welles*, vol. 1, 358–359. Only an hour before the cabinet meeting, Lincoln had issued an announcement to "the country" with news that covered the Army of the Potomac "with the highest honor." Lincoln, July 4, 1863, 10 a.m., ORA 27(3):515.

11. A note in the Lincoln Papers, perhaps Welles's draft, directs Admiral Lee to block Stephens and states "[Stephens] does not make known the subjects to which the communication in writing from Mr. Davis relates, which he bears, and seeks to deliver in person to the President, and upon which he desires to confer." See Lincoln to S. P. Lee [Draft] 1, July [4] 1863, Abraham Lincoln Papers, Library of Congress.

12. Welles, *Diary of Gideon Welles*, vol. 1., 362.

13. Welles, *Diary of Gideon Welles*, vol. 1., 362.

14. Lee to Welles, July 5, 1863, 3 p.m. and 5:30 p.m., ORN 9:108; Stanton to Ludlow, July 4, 1863, ser. 2, 6:83; Stephens to Lee, July 6, 1863, 12 noon, ORN 9:109.

15. Welles to S. Lee, July 6, 1863, 10:45 a.m., ORN 9:108.

16. Ludlow to Stephens, July 6, 1863, ORA ser. 2, 6:84; Stephens Report, ORA ser. II, 6:94; *Richmond Dispatch*, July 14, 1863.

17. Stephens Report, ORA ser. 2, 6:94.

18. See, e.g., *Richmond Dispatch*, July 6, 1863.

19. See, e.g., *Western Democrat*, July 21, 1863; *Weekly National Intelligencer*, July 23, 1863.

20. Rabun, "A Letter for Posterity," 17.

21. ORA 51(2):807–810 (dispatches between Vance and Davis); Rabun, "A Letter for Posterity," 21; ORA 27(3):74–77 (various captured Confederate dispatches). Lee himself had largely planned his movement north. Likewise, Morgan had operated independently, perhaps even more so than Lee. The captured dispatch contained no mention of Stephens's mission.

22. *Richmond Dispatch*, July 14, 1863 (reprinting excerpt from the *Philadelphia Inquirer*).

23. Laas, *Wartime Washington*, 285. Elizabeth Blair Lee's correspondence also mentions opinions expressed by Admiral Lee, her spouse, about Stephens's mission. However, any such correspondence from Admiral Lee is not extent in his letters to his wife at Princeton University. Blair and Lee Family Papers, 1640–1946, Manuscripts Division, Department of Special Collections, Princeton University.

24. *Times-Picayune*, August 7, 1863; *Owensboro Monitor*, September 16, 1863; *Indiana State Sentinel*, September 21, 1863; Jones, A *Rebel War Clerk's Diary at the Confederate States Capital*, vol. 1, 370.

25. *New-York Tribune*, July 31, 1863.

26. *New-York Tribune*, July 31, 1863.

27. For discussions of the Confederate debate about arming enslaved persons, see, Levine, *Confederate Emancipation*.

28. "Stonewall Jackson's Way" (Richmond, VA: J. W. Randolph, 1863). At the beginning of the Civil War, Palmer worked for the *New York Times* preparing stories in Richmond for Northern readers but did not stay long with the *Times* and soon took a position back home in 1862 with the Baltimore and Ohio Railroad. He penned "Stonewall Jackson's Way" following the Maryland Campaign and privately published it in Baltimore as the work of an anonymous sergeant from the Stonewall Brigade killed at Winchester.

29. Sutherland, "Altamont of the Tribune," 54–66.

30. Palmer to Gay, Letters from July 23, 25, 27, and 31, 1863, Sydney Howard Gay Collection, Columbia University Library. Palmer claimed Blair, Stanton, and Chase had confirmed the account to the president of the B&O Railroad, and Palmer's own family physician had received the same information in a letter from Richmond. However, Palmer did not explain why these men would have access to such details.

31. *New-York Tribune*, July 31, 1863.

32. See, e.g., *Ohio Democrat*, August 13, 1863; *Vermont Watchman and State Journal*, August 7, 1863.

33. *Alexandria Gazette*, August 1, 1863.

34. Stephens to Linton Stephens, June 30 and July 1, 1863, Alexander Stephens Collection, Manhattanville College. Stephens did not figure prominently in the Confederate debates over arming slaves later in the war. See, e.g., Levine, *Confederate Emancipation*.

18. THE END AT RICHMOND

1. Herbert Augustine Claiborne Diary, Claiborne Family Papers, VMHC; Jones, *A Rebel War Clerk's Diary at the Confederate States Capital*, vol. 1, 368. On July 5, Custis Lee detailed the disposition of his units—two battalions from the ordnance workshops at Meadow Bridge and Brook Turnpike; Minor's "Naval" battalion and another battalion containing clerks from various departments at the Brook Turnpike; four companies from the clothing bureau under R. P.

Waller east of Brook Turnpike at the county bridge; 1,500 men under Joseph Selden west of the RF&P; and convalescents under H. H. Walker west of Richmond and south of James. Custis Lee to Chestney, July 5, 1863, *ORA* 27(3):972.

2. Gorgas, *The Journals of Josiah Gorgas, 1857–1878*, 71–72.

3. Stevens to Gilmer, July 4, 1863, *ORA* 51(2):734 (gap near the "Morris" house).

4. Hill to Seddon, July 5, 1863, *ORA* 27(3):971 ("We will have no peace till we whip the marauders"); Seddon to Corse, July 5, 1863, *ORA* 27(3):971. On July 5, Seddon once again clarified the command relationship; after some back and forth, Hill agreed to funnel all orders for the local troops through Elzey. Seddon considered dismissing Custis Lee's local defense troops on Sunday, but Elzey recommended keeping them under arms an additional day. Elzey to Seddon, July 5, 1863, *ORA* 27(3):970 (including various enclosures); Elzey to Archer Andersen, July 5, 1863, *ORA* 27(3):971; Herbert Augustine Claiborne Diary, Claiborne Family Papers, VMHC; Monday, July 6 Herbert Augustine Claiborne Diary, Claiborne Family Papers, VMHC ("marched into Richmond and dismissed").

5. Hill to Seddon, July 5, 1863, 9 p.m., *ORA* 27(3):972–973. Hill did not fail to mention that he had recommended the arsenal's fortification "some time ago," though he also commented that capture of the North Carolina legislature would "do the State an infinite service."

6. Robin to Elzey, July 5, 1863, *ORA* 27(3):973 (railroad employee was a "Mr. Williams"); *Daily Richmond Examiner*, July 7, 1863; *Daily Richmond Examiner*, July 7, 1863; *Richmond Dispatch*, July 6, 1863; *Daily Richmond Examiner*, July 7, 1863.

7. *Richmond Sentinel*, July 9, 1863.

8. *Richmond Dispatch*, July 8, 1863; *Richmond Dispatch*, July 9, 1863.

9. *Richmond Dispatch*, July 9, 1863.

10. Hill to Elzey, July 5, 11 p.m., 1863, *ORA* 27(3):973; Chestney to Lee, July 6, 1863, *ORA* 27(3):977.

11. Jones, *A Rebel War Clerk's Diary at the Confederate States Capital*, vol. 1, 370.

12. Seddon wanted the Federals on the Peninsula "dispersed, chastised, or captured" and to end "harassing depredations around the city" and "menace from the capital." He hoped Hill was strong enough to "dispose of them, or at least drive them permanently off" through "early and decisive action." Seddon to Hill, *ORA* 27(3):974.

13. Wise to Elzey, July 6, 1863, *ORA* 27(3):975–979. On the morning of July 6, about 250 Confederates under Colonel John G. Jones from the 35th North Carolina Infantry and fifty cavalrymen from the Holcombe Legion drove past Crump's Crossroads and fought Federal cavalry west of Talleysville. The Federals nearly trapped the rebels in a deep cut in the road there, but the Confederates escaped. Burgwyn Diary, Henry Brantingham and W. H. S. Burgwyn Diary, State Archives of North Carolina; Keyes to Dix, July 6, 1863—4 p.m., *ORA* 27(2):836; Keyes to Dix, July 7, 1863, Fourth Corps Letters Sent, RG 393, Pt 2, NARA.

14. *Daily Richmond Examiner*, July 6, 1863; Burgwyn Diary, Henry Brantingham and W. H. S. Burgwyn Diary, State Archives of North Carolina.

15. Jones, *A Rebel War Clerk's Diary at the Confederate States Capital*, vol.

1, 370–373; *Daily Richmond Examiner*, July 9, 1863; *Daily Dispatch*, July 9, 1863; Cooper to Corse, July 7, 1863. *ORA* 27(3):979; Gilmer to Stevens, July 7, 1863, *ORA* 27(3):980–981. In his too-typical, off-putting style, Hill did not hesitate to lecture Seddon on the obvious: "As the city may have to be defended by local troops, the importance of infantry cover cannot be overestimated." Hill to Seddon, July 7, 1863, *ORA* 27(3):980.

16. Stanton to Dix, July 4, 1863, 8 a.m. and 5 p.m., *ORA* 27(3):529; Dix to Stanton, July 5, 1863, 5:30 p.m., *ORA* 27(3):553; Stanton to Dix, July 5, 1863, 8:00 p.m., *ORA* 27(3):553; Dix Report (Halleck to Dix, July 3, 1863, 1:15 p.m.), *ORA* 27(2):818; Stanton to Dix, July 8, 1863, Telegrams, Department of Virginia, RG 393, NARA.

17. Dix to Halleck, July 7, 1863, 1:15 p.m., *ORA* 27(2):818.

18. Stanton to Dix, July 7, 1863, *ORA* 27(2):818.

19. On June 20, Cooke's entire brigade had 2,486 total effectives present, suggesting he probably had no more than 1,500 from his brigade at the bridge. Coupled with the 500 convalescents as Baker's cavalry, the total force with Cooke at the RF&P bridge probably did not exceed 3,000. *ORA* 27(3):909 and 927; Clark, *Histories of Several Regiments*, vol. 1, 741–742.

20. Dix to Halleck, July 8, 1863, *ORA* 27(2):819; Dix to Halleck, July 8, 1863, John Dix Papers, Columbia University.

21. Dix to Halleck, July 8, 1863, 4 p.m., *ORA* 27(2):819; Dix to Halleck, July 8, 1863, John Dix Papers, Columbia University (places quotes around "no change in orders"—not extant in version published in *ORA*); Halleck to Dix, July 9, 1863, 4:20 p.m., *ORA* 27(3):625; Halleck to Dix, July 9, 1863, Telegrams for Department of Virginia and North Carolina, RG 393, NARA; Dix to Stanton, July 8, 1863, 4 p.m., *ORA* 27(2):819; *Dix Memoirs*, vol. 2, 68 (Dix also wrote Admiral Lee on July 7 about his disappointment in having to leave and his inability to conduct further operations on the Peninsula).

22. Hill to Seddon, July 8, 1863, *ORA* 27(3):984–985; Krick, *Civil War Weather*, 81–114 (July 1863 data); Croffut, *The Military and Civil History of Connecticut During the War of 1861–65*, 337–340.

19. HALLECK'S BOOTLESS PLANS

1. Halleck to Kelley, June 25, 1863, 1:29 p.m., *ORA* 27(3):330; Foster to Halleck, June 30, 1863, *ORA* 27(3):438–439; Halleck to Kelley, July 4, 1863, 11 a.m., *ORA* 27(3):528; Kelley to Townsend, July 4, 1863, 1:30 p.m., *ORA* 27(3):528.

2. Foster to Halleck, June 21, 1863, 9 p.m., *ORA* 27(3):242; Halleck to Foster, July 5, 1863, *ORA* 27(3):553.

3. Foster to Stanton, July 6, 1863, *ORA* 27(3):583.

4. Lewis Report, *ORA* 27(2):860–863; *Daily Journal* (Wilmington), July 8, 1863 (assistance from freedmen); *Western Democrat*, July 14, 1863 ("guided by negroes who had run away from this section"); Foster to Stanton, July 6, 1863, *ORA* 27(3):583.

5. *Biblical Recorder* (Raleigh, NC), July 15, 1863.

6. Lewis Report, *ORA* 27(2):860–863; Foster Report, *ORA* 27(2):859–860; *Western Democrat*, July 14, 1863 (account by "Duplin").

7. *Biblical Recorder* (Raleigh, NC), July 15, 1863; *Daily Journal* (Wilmington), July 8, 1863 (stating there were no Black troops but that African American guides assisted the raid).

8. Lewis Report, *ORA* 27(3):860–863; *Biblical Recorder* (Raleigh, NC), July 15, 1863 (accounts says Federals burned the flour despite handing out the bacon).

9. *Biblical Recorder* (Raleigh, NC), July 15, 1863; 3rd New York Cavalry, Newspaper Clipping, New York State Military Museum; *Western Democrat*, July 14, 1863 (breaking open stores).

10. Lewis Report, *ORA* 27(2):861–863; Foster Report, *ORA* 27(2):859–860. Claiborne's unit was sometimes referred to as the "7th Confederate Cavalry." See, Organization of Troops in the North Carolina Department, *ORA* 27(3):947.

11. Lewis Report, *ORA* 27(2):861–863; Foster Report, *ORA* 27(2):859–860 (Foster says there were 100 men and 300 women and children who "followed the cavalry into our lines").

12. *Fayetteville Semi-Weekly Observer*, July 9, 1863; *Charlotte Democrat*, July 14, 1863. For additional accounts of the raid, see *Weekly Standard*, July 15, 1863, *Wilmington Journal*, July 9, 1863, *Charlotte Democrat*, July 14, 1863; *Weekly State Journal*, July 15, 1863; *Daily Progress*, July 8, 1863; *Daily True Delta* (New Orleans), July 29, 1863.

13. Lehmann Report, *ORA* 27(2):868–869; Morris Report, *ORA* 27(2):869–870. Federal colonel Theodore Lehmann, leading a mixed force of about 500 infantry, cavalry, and artillery, traveled up the Roanoke River on a towed scow for a short distance and marched toward Gardner's Bridge west of Jamesville. Impeded by dense swamp and woods, Lehmann eventually found a stout redoubt opposite the bridge manned by enemy artillery. He was unable to capture the position and waited for the second prong of the expedition to approach the rebel position from the rear. But that second force failed to arrive at the expected time due to an unusually strong current that delayed the boats carrying the force up the Roanoke River and ruined any coordination with Lehmann's force at Gardner's Bridge.

14. Wilson Report, *ORA* 27(2):863. Wilson's report, which Wilson failed to show to Lewis, stated that the "cavalry gangs were not properly organized" despite multiple pleas to Lieutenant Colonel Lewis and that, as a result, the raiders burned no ties, twisted fewer than fifty rails, and destroyed less than a quarter-mile of the track. Lewis to Foster, July 13, 1863, *ORA* 27(2):864.

15. *Biblical Recorder* (Raleigh, NC), July 15, 1863; *Western Democrat*, July 14, 1863 (account by "Duplin"—"infernal hot"); *Fayetteville Semi-Weekly*, July 9, 1863; *Richmond Sentinel*, July 10, 1863.

16. Lee to Jones, June 20, 1863, *ORA* 27(3):906. Various reports on the Confederate expedition to Beverly include: *ORA* 27(2):805–816; *Wheeling Daily Intelligencer*, July 17, 1863 (detailed account of the Beverly engagement by a member of the 10th West Virginia, including list of casualties); *Wheeling Daily Intelligencer*, July 7, 1863.

17. Hoffman Report, *ORA* 27(2):943; Johnson, *Lead, Salt, and the Railroad*.

18. See Wytheville Raid reports at *ORA* 27(2) 941–963; Franklin Report, *ORA* 27(2):1000; Jones Report, *ORA* 27(2):945; Johnson, *Lead, Salt, and the Railroad*. For various newspaper accounts, see *Philadelphia Inquirer*, August 5,

1863; *Staunton Spectator*, July 28, 1863; *Weekly Raleigh Register*, July 29, 1863; *New York Daily Herald*, July 26, 1863.

19. See Potter Report, *ORA* 27(2):964; Norris, *Potter's Raid*.

20. THE FORGOTTEN CAMPAIGN

1. Stanton to Dix, July 7, 1863, *ORA* 27(2):818–819.

2. Dix Report, *ORA* 27(2):824; Dix to Halleck, Dec. 19, 1863, *ORA* 27(1):18–19.

3. General Orders No. 46, *ORA* 27(3):713.

4. See Lichterman, *John Adams Dix, 1798–1879*; Dyer, *A Compendium of the War of the Rebellion*, vol. 3, 254.

5. Halleck to Stanton, November 15, 1863, *ORA* 27(1):14–18.

6. *New-York Tribune*, December 14, 1863. See also, *Manchester Journal*, December 22, 1863 (critical of Halleck); *Chicago Tribune*, December 22, 1863 (critical of Halleck).

7. *New-York Tribune*, December 15, 1863; *Detroit Free Press*, December 19, 1863 (printing column from *New York World*).

8. *New York Times*, December 17, 1863.

9. Dix to Halleck, December 15, 1863, *ORA* 27(1):18–19.

10. Halleck to Dix, December 20, 1863, *ORA* 27(1):19.

11. Dix, *Memoirs of John Adams Dix*, vol. 2, 64–67.

12. *Boston Post*, July 11, 1863; *Burlington Free Press*, July 1, 1863.

13. *Delaware Gazette*, July 15, 1863 (quoting *New York Commercial*).

14. *The Cavalier* (Yorktown), July 14, 1863 (clipping at Civil War Newspaper Clipping Collection, NYSMM).

15. *New Albany Daily Ledger*, July 18, 1863 (reprinting *New York World* column).

16. *New York Daily Herald*, July 10, 1863.

17. *Semi-Weekly Wisconsin*, July 8, 1863.

18. *New-York Tribune*, July 15, 1863. The *Tribune* also argued that, even if Lee's army had survived the fighting in Pennsylvania, reinforcements from Dix would have allowed Meade to renew attacks on the Army of Northern Virginia before it crossed south over the Potomac.

19. *Report of the Joint Committee on the Conduct of the War at the Second Session*, Thirty-eighth Congress, 176–177.

20. Dix's Richmond campaign has received little attention in modern military studies. The two most detailed looks at the operation are: Trudeau, "The Blackberry Raid," and Longacre, "Inspired Blundering." In his survey of the war in the east, historian Brooks Simpson concluded that "at best Dix succeeded in pinning Confederate forces that otherwise might have been dispatched to reinforce Lee, although there remains a sense of missed opportunity in this often-forgotten campaign." Simpson, *The Civil War in the East*, 90.

21. *National Tribune*, December 10, 1908. McElroy also described Fort Monroe, the Department headquarters, as an "honorable shelf" for "high officers who had failed to meet requirements in the early part of the war."

22. *National Tribune*, December 10, 1908.

23. *Buffalo Sunday Morning News* August 3, 1913; *Pittsburgh Post-Gazette,* August 3, 1913; *Lexington Leader,* August 3, 1913.

24. General Orders No. 262, *ORA* 27(3):827.

25. "We have been within seven miles of Richmond and expected to have the pleasure of marching into that city." Samuel Jones Corbett Diary, Samuel James Corbett Papers, 1858–1890, Bancroft Library, University of California—Berkeley.

26. Croffut, *The Military and Civil History of Connecticut During the War of 1861–65,* 337–339.

27. Hyde, *History of the One Hundred and Twelfth Regiment, N.Y. Volunteers,* 43–46.

28. Mowris, *A History of the One Hundred and Seventeenth Regiment, N.Y. Volunteers,* 73.

29. Bowen, *Regimental History of the First New York Dragoons,* 81–83; Headley, *The Great Rebellion,* vol. 2, 191 ("It was a feint . . . which many thought have been a real one.").

30. Thorpe, *The History of the Fifteenth Connecticut Volunteer,* 53–54.

21. QUESTIONS OF SUPPLY

1. Newsome, Horn, and Selby, eds., *Civil War Talks,* 143.

2. See, French Report, *ORA* 27(1):488; Hunt, *Meade and Lee After Gettysburg.* During the fighting at Wapping Heights, the Union advance was led by Brigadier General Francis Spinola, an officer sent by Foster from North Carolina to Fort Monroe to help rebel Lee's incursion into Pennsylvania.

3. Stanton to Kelley, July 5, 1863, and Halleck to Kelly, July 5, 1863, 10 p.m., *ORA* 27(3):550; Halleck to Kelley, July 14, 1863, 2:40 p.m., *ORA* 27(3):699.

4. Kelley to Meade, July 22, 1863, 12:30 p.m., *ORA* 27(3):748–749. For a detailed study of Lee and Meade's operation in mid-July, see Hunt, *Meade and Lee After Gettysburg.*

5. *Richmond Sentinel,* July 9, 1863.

6. *Staunton Spectator,* July 7, 1863.

7. *Daily Richmond Examiner,* July 28, 1863.

8. *Annual Report of the Virginia Central Railroad Company, 1863,* Albert and Sydney Small Special Collections, UVA. Unfortunately, the comprehensive records of railroad operations in July 1863 do not appear to be extant in the files at National Archives.

9. *Staunton Spectator,* July 7, 1863; Bright, "Richmond Grain Receipts and Shipments," n.p. (various reports of Major John C. Maynard, Secretary of War's Incoming Letters, RG 109, NARA compiled by David Bright). These reports suggest no grain arrived at Beaverdam or Gordonsville stations between June 26 and July 17. See also Virginia Central Railroad correspondence, Confederate Papers Relating to Citizens or Business Firms, M346, RG 109, NARA.

10. *The Cavalier* (Yorktown, Va.), July 14, 1863 (clipping at Civil War Newspaper Clipping Collection, NYSMM).

11. Various reports of Major John C. Maynard, Secretary of War's Incoming Letters, RG 109, NARA (compiled by David Bright); Myers to Branch, July 24,

1863, Records of the Quartermaster Department, RG 109, NARA (located and transcribed by David Bright).

12. *Semi-Weekly Richmond Enquirer*, June 30 and July 3, 1863.

13. Pendleton Report, 27(2):351. See also, Alexander, "Letter From General E. P. Alexander, Late Chief Of Artillery, First Corps."

14. Marshall, Charles, *An Aide-de-Camp of Lee*, 218–220.

15. Wilson, *Confederate Industry*, 84 (discusses Confederate supplies sent from Richmond via Staunton, including an urgent request for "twenty thousand pairs of shoes").

16. Allan, "Reminiscences of Field Ordnance Service" (typed copies of excerpts from volumes and correspondence), William Allan Papers, Southern Historical Collection, UNC. Lee's lines of communications were further complicated by the fact that a heavy storm had washed out the Orange and Alexandria Railroad bridge over the Rapidan north of Orange around July 7, cutting off Culpeper from Richmond. Lee to Longstreet, July 19, 1863, *ORA* 27(3):979; Corse to Cooper, July 7, 1863, *ORA* 27(3):979.

17. Murchison Report (54th North Carolina), *ORA* 27(2):487–488; Wingfield, "Diary of H.W. Wingfield," 27–28. Colonel Isaac Avery led Hoke's brigade for most of the campaign.

18. Hoffman Report (31st Virginia), *ORA* 27(2):488–490 ("Reaching Williamsport, Md., on the 5th, I was ordered by General Imboden to take position, and repel any attack that might be made on the wagon train of the army, which had arrived there, but could not cross, owing to the high stage of the river.").

19. Imboden, "The Confederate Retreat from Gettysburg," 426.

20. Waddell, *Annals of Augusta County, Virginia, from 1726 to 1871*, 482.

21. *Weekly Advertiser* (Montgomery, Alabama), July 15, 1863 ("Dispatch from Martinsburg dated July 9 . . . an ordnance train has just passed to Lee who is waiting for it."); *Weekly Raleigh Register*, July 15, 1863 (" . . . an ordnance train had just passed Martinsburg on its way to our army"). See also, Wise, *The Long Arm of Lee*, 400.

22. Lee to Davis, July 10, 1863, *ORA* 27(2):300–301.

22. THE BROADER SCOPE

1. Fox to S. P. Lee, June 30, 1863, *Confidential Correspondence of Gustavus Vasa Fox*, vol. 2, 259.

2. See, e.g., Dix to Lockwood, November 11, 1861, *ORA* 5:424–425.

3. Stanton to Halleck, July 7, 1863, 27(2):818–9 (citing to information about Richmond's defenders in captured letters).

4. *Washington Register*, March 11, 1887.

5. General Order No. 262, *ORA* 27(3):827.

6. *San Francisco Examiner*, October 15, 1863.

7. *Appletons' Cyclopaedia of American Biography*, vol. 3, 530.

8. *Public Opinion Weekly* (Chambersburg, Penn.), May 4, 1875; *Daily Commonwealth* (Topeka) May 13, 1875 (buried at Cypress Hills Cemetery); *Morristown Gazette*, July 7, 1875; *The Times* (Phil.), April 26, 1875.

9. Consistent with some Northern observers, John Beauchamp Jones, at the Confederate War Department, viewed Dix's effort as a "fool's errand" given the strength of Richmond's defenses and mused that the Federal troops could have been better used to "save[] Washington or Baltimore" or protect Pennsylvania. Jones, *A Rebel War Clerk's Diary at the Confederate States Capital*, vol. 1, 368. A 1919 letter from Paul Brandon Barringer, son of a Confederate general and a prominent figure in the study of racial eugenics in the early 1920s, to D. H. Hill Jr. describes a visit to the South Anna crossing where the fighting occurred in 1863. At the time, he noted a redoubt south of the river and east of the railroad, "a quadrilateral some hundred yards square, ramparts still eight to ten feet high, over grown with trees." The redoubt still stands today on private property. Barringer to Hill, March 27, 1919, Richmond National Battlefield Park, National Park Service.

10. Several accounts of the South Anna Bridge fight appeared after the war, including in the widely distributed multivolume history of North Carolina units in the war prepared by Walter Clark. See, Stedman, "Forty-Fourth Regiment," in Clark, *Histories of Several Regiment)*, vol. 3, 24–25; *Asheville Citizen Times*, June 24, 1923 (Bingham account); *Oxford Public Ledger*, September 24, 1903; *The Land We Love*, March 1867, 375 (letter from Robert Bingham); Peace, "Fighting at Great Odds," 370–371; Pearce, "Defenders of the South Anna Bridge," 76–78.

11. Younger, *Inside the Confederate Government-*, 84; *Daily Richmond Examiner*, July 18, 1863; Special Orders No. 165, July 13, 1863, ORA 27(3):1003; Bridges, *Lee's Maverick General*, 192–194.

12. Bridges, *Lee's Maverick General*, 193–194, 271; Special Orders No. 165, July 12, 1863, D. H. Hill Papers, Library of Virginia; Vance to Davis, October 25, 1864, ORA 42(3):1162.

13. *Wilmington Messenger*, August 23, 1889; Winston, "A Rebel Colonel," 84–92.

14. *Semi-Weekly Wisconsin*, July 8, 1863.

15. See Speer, *War of Vengeance*, 88–92; Halleck to Ludlow, July 15, 1863, *Army and Navy Gazette*, vol. 1, 317. In December, Lee's wife, Charlotte Wickham, died following an illness that had begun after her husband's capture.

16. Pollard, *The Lost Cause*, 414.

17. See, e.g., Brasher, *The Peninsula Campaign and the Necessity of Emancipation*; Miller, *Vicksburg: Grant's Campaign That Broke the Confederacy*.

18. Interview of Robert Ellett by Claude W. Anderson, December 25, 1937, Work Projects Administration of Virginia records, 1939–1943, Library of Virginia.

19. Wise to Councill, December 12, 1862, ORA 18:798–799.

20. See Brasher, *The Peninsula Campaign and the Necessity of Emancipation*.

21. Ruffin, *The Diary of Edmund Ruffin*, vol. 3, 50.

22. See Reidy, *Illusions of Emancipation*; Taylor, *Embattled Freedom*; Manning, *Troubled Refuge*.

23. US Colored Troops Military Service Records, 1863–1865, RG 94, NARA (accessed through Ancestry.com database); Allen and Tramuel, *Military Records of United States Colored Troops BORN in New Kent County, Virginia*; Allen and

Tramuel, *Military Records of United States Colored Troops BORN in West Point & King William County, Virginia*, n.d.

24. See, e.g., Allen, "Roses in December"; Lowe, *Republicans and Reconstruction in Virginia, 1856–1870*; Dailey, Jane, *Before Jim Crow*.

25. Michel, "From Slavery to Freedom," 120–121. At Hickory Hill, by 1866, only forty-one Black laborers worked at the farm, and by 1888 the number had dropped to twenty-six. Confederate veteran Williams Carter Wickham, son of William Fanning Wickham, continued to run the farm but spent much of his time as a railroad executive and political figure who supported Republican candidates and served as an elector for President Ulysses Grant in the 1872 election.

26. Fox to S. P. Lee, June 30, 1863, Fox, *Confidential Correspondence of Gustavus Vasa Fox*, vol. 2, 259.

27. Diary of Gurdon Robins (Lt. AQM, 16th Conn.), University of Connecticut Special Collections.

28. Cunningham, *Three Years with the Adirondack Regiment*, 68–74.

BIBLIOGRAPHY

NEWSPAPERS

Alexandria Gazette
Argus and Patriot (Montpelier, VT)
Asheville Citizen-Times
Baltimore Sun
The Bee (Danville, VA)
Biblical Recorder (Raleigh, NC)
Boston Post
Bradford Star (Towanda, PA)
Buffalo Sunday Morning
Burlington Times
Carolina Standard
The Cavalier (Yorktown, VA)
Charleston Mercury
Charlotte Democrat
Chatham Record
Chicago Tribune
Columbia Democrat and Bloomsburg General Advertiser (Bloomsburg, PA)
Daily Alta California
Daily Commonwealth (Topeka, KS)
Daily Dispatch (Richmond, VA)
Daily Independent
Daily Journal (Wilmington, NC)
Daily Palladium (New Haven, CT)
Daily Progress (Raleigh, NC)
Daily Richmond Enquirer
Daily Richmond Examiner
Daily True Delta (New Orleans, LA)
Delaware Gazette
Evening Star (Washington, DC)
Fayetteville Observer
Fayetteville Weekly Observer
Gettysburg Compiler
Greensboro Patriot
Henderson Daily Dispatch
Indiana State Sentinel
The Land We Love (Charlotte, NC)
Leicester Chronicle
Lexington Leader
Lincoln Courier (Lincolnton, NC)
Milwaukee Daily News

Morristown Gazette
National Tribune (Washington, D.C.)
New Albany Daily Ledger
New York Daily Herald
New York Times
New York World
Ohio Democrat
Orangeburg News
Owensboro Monitor
Oxford Public Ledger
Philadelphia Inquirer
Public Opinion Weekly (Chambersburg, PA)
Railroad Gazette
Record-Union (Sacramento, CA)
Richmond Daily Examiner
Richmond Sentinel
Republican & Sentinel
San Francisco Examiner
Semi-Weekly Richmond Enquirer
Semi-Weekly Wisconsin
Spirit of the Age (Raleigh, NC)
The State (Raleigh, N.C.)
Staunton Spectator
The Tennessean
The Times (Philadelphia)
Times-Picayune (New Orleans, LA)
Vermont Christian Messenger
Vermont Watchman and State Journal
Washington Register (Washington, KA)
Waterbury American
Weekly Advertiser (Montgomery, AL)
Weekly Era (Raleigh, NC)
Weekly Raleigh Register
Western Sentinel (Winston, NC)
Wheeling Daily Intelligencer
Wilmington Messenger
Wilmington Morning Star

ARCHIVAL SOURCES

Allan, William. Papers. Southern Historical Collection. University of North Carolina at Chapel Hill.

Annual Report of the Virginia Central Railroad Company. 1863. Small Special Collections. University of Virginia.

Barringer, Paul. Letter, March 27, 2019. Richmond National Battlefield Park Library. National Park Service.

Blair and Lee Family Papers, 1640–1946. Manuscripts Division. Department of Special Collections. Princeton University.

Bratton, John. Papers. Southern Historical Collection. University of North Carolina at Chapel Hill.

Burgwyn, Henry Brantingham, and W. H. S. Burgwyn. Diary. Private Collections. State Archives of North Carolina.

Calton, J. W. (Typescript) letter in Bound Volume #252, June 8, 1863. Richmond National Battlefield Park Library.

Civil War Newspaper Clipping Collection (various units). New York State Military Museum.

Claiborne, Herbert Augustine. Diary. Claiborne Family Papers. VMHC.

Cleary, William Walter. Diary. VMHC.

Confederate States of America. Army. Department of Northern Virginia. Chief Engineer's Office and Edward Porter Alexander. *Map of the Counties of Charles City, Goochland, Hanover, Henrico, King William, New Kent, and Part of the Counties of Caroline and Louisa, Virginia.* [S.l.: Chief Engineer's Office, D.N.V, 1864] Map. Library of Congress.

Corbett, Samuel Jones. Diary. Samuel James Corbett Papers, 1858–1890. Bancroft Library. University of California, Berkeley.

Corse, Montgomery B. Papers. Lloyd House. Alexandria (VA) Library.

Crowninshield to Mammy, July 2, 1863. Caspar Crowninshield Papers. Massachusetts Historical Society.

Cruikshank, George. Letter, June 30, 1863. George L. Cruikshank Civil War Letters. State Historical Society of Iowa.

Culver, Martin Van Buren. Letters. Fredericksburg and Spotsylvania National Military Park.

Dix, John A. John A. Dix Collection. Syracuse University.

Dix, John A. John A. Dix Papers. Columbia University.

Ellett, Robert. Interview of Robert Ellett by Claude W. Anderson, December 25, 1937. Works Projects Administration of Virginia Records, 1939–1943. Library of Virginia.

Foster, E. S. F. Diary of Edward Snow Foster. American Civil War Collection. Hamilton College.

Gay, Sydney Howard. Sydney Howard Gay Collection. Columbia University Library.

Getty, George W. Correspondence. Gibson–Getty–McClure Families Papers. Library of Congress.

Gordon, George H. Papers. Civil War Correspondence, Diaries, and Journals. Massachusetts Historical Society.

Hagood, James. *Memoirs of the First South Carolina Regiment of Volunteer Infantry in the Confederate War for Independence from April 12, 1861 to April 10, 1865.* South Caroliniana Library, University of South Carolina.

Hill, Daniel Harvey. D. H. Hill Papers. Library of Virginia.

Hill, Daniel Harvey. D. H. Hill Papers. North Carolina State Archives.

Howard, James H. Letters. Small Special Collections. University of Virginia.

Jackson, Oswald Jackson. Letter, July 6, 1863. S. Trout Private Collection.

Jenkins, Micah. Jenkins to Caroline Jenkins, June 22, 1863. Micah Jenkins Papers. South Caroliniana Library. University of South Carolina.

Kellogg, Robert. Kellogg Letters. Connecticut Historical Society.

Kimball, Orville Samuel. *History and Personal Sketches of Company I, 103 N. Y. S. V., 1862–1864.* Elmira, NY: Facto, 1900.

Library of Congress. Civil War Photographs, 1861–1865.

Lincoln, Abraham. Papers. Library of Congress.

"[Map of Hanover County, Va.], G3883.H3 186-.M2." Geography and Map Division. Library of Congress.

"Map of Part of Essex, King and Queen, and King William Counties." Geography and Map Division. Library of Congress. Civil War Maps (2nd ed.), H29.

"Map of the Northern Portion of Hanover County, Va., Showing Fortifications on the South Anna River near Taylorsville." 2002627447. Geography and Map Division. Library of Congress.

"Map of the Vicinity of Richmond Made under the Direction of Capt. A. H. Campbell, Chief of Topographical Dept.; Ch'f Engineer's Office D.N.V., Col. J. F. Gilmer, Ch'f. Eng'r, March 21, 1863." Small Special Collections, University of Virginia.

"Map of W. F. Wickham's Plantation Known as 'Hickory Hill.'" February 1878. Hickory Hill. Private Collection.

Mordecai, George W. Papers. Southern Historical Collection. University of North Carolina at Chapel Hill.

Morey, William C. Papers. Department of Rare Books and Special Collections. University of Rochester.

Peace, Alexander. "The Battle of South Anna Bridge." Richmond National Battlefield Park. National Park Service.

Record Group 15. Records of the Veterans Administration. M1279. NARA.

Record Group 24. Records of the Bureau of Naval Personnel (United States Navy). NARA.

Record Group 45. Naval Records Collection of the Office of Naval Records and Library. NARA.

Record Group 94. Records of the Office of the Adjutant General, 1780s–1917. NARA.
> Combined Service Records of Union Soldiers.
> US Colored Troops Military Service Records, 1863–1865.

Record Group 109. War Department Collection of Confederate Records. NARA.
> Confederate Papers Relating to Citizens or Business Firms.
> Compiled Service Records of Confederate Soldiers.
> Confederate Slave Payrolls.

Record Group 217. Southern Claims Commission Case Files. NARA.
> Claim of Terrill Bradby (#6306). Deposition of Bradby.
> Claim of Terrill Bradby (#51404). Deposition of Adelphia Miles.
> Claim of Beverly Dixon (#42979).

Record Group 270. Records of the War Assets Administration. NARA.

Record Group 393. Consolidated Department of Virginia and North Carolina. NARA.
> Fourth Corps Records. Department of Virginia.
> Bureau of Military Information.

Robins Diary. Diary of Gurdon Robins (Lt. AQM, 16th Conn.). Special Collections. University of Connecticut.

Roosevelt Civil War Envelopes Collection. Manuscripts Collection. Booth Family Center for Special Collections. Georgetown University Library.

Rosenheim, Phillip. Letter. The Jacob Rader Marcus Center of the American Jewish Archives.
Skelly ("Skelley"), John A. Skelly to Molly Brady, June 30, 1863. Typescript in Bound Volume #252. Richmond National Battlefield Park. National Park Service.
Smith, Howard M. Diary and Letters (130th New York Infantry, 1st New York Dragoons). Library of Congress.
Southern Claims Commission Case Files. RG 217. NARA.
 Claim of Terrill Bradby (#6306). Deposition of Bradby.
 Claim of Terrill Bradby (#51404). Deposition of Adelphia Miles.
 Claim of Beverly Dixon (#42979).
Stephens, Alexander. Alexander Stephens Papers. Manhattanville College.
Stephenson, William. Letters. Oysterponds Historical Society.
Stevens, Hazard Jr. Special Collections. Civil War Letters. University of Washington Libraries.
Thompson, Millett. Letters, 1863–1864. Millett Thompson Papers. Southern Historical Collection. University of North Carolina at Chapel Hill.
Towner, John Edwin. Typescript of Diary and Letters (15th Connecticut). Fredericksburg and Spotsylvania National Military Park.
Trowbridge, Francis. Letter, Trowbridge to Phebe Trowbridge, July 4, 1863. Transcript at Spared and Shared Website. https://sparedandshared.wordpress.com.
Wickham, Williams Carter. Correspondence. Wickham Family Papers. VMHC.
Wickham, William Fanning. Diary. Wickham Family Papers. VMHC.
Wickham, William F. Letter from William F. Wickham to Robert E. Lee, June 28, 1863. The Papers of Robert E. Lee, 1830–1870. Albert and Shirley Small Special Collections Library. University of Virginia.
Woodson, Harrison. "Letters of Harrison Woodford During the Civil War." Fredericksburg and Spotsylvania National Military Park. National Park Service.

PUBLISHED PRIMARY SOURCES: REGIMENTAL HISTORIES, DIARIES, MEMOIRS, LETTERS, ETC.

Agassiz, George R., ed.. *General Meade's Headquarters 1863–1865: Letters of Colonel Theodore Lyman from the Wilderness to Appomattox*. Boston: Atlantic Monthly Press, 1922. Rpt, Lincoln: University of Nebraska Press, 1994.
Alexander, Porter Edward. *Military Memoirs of a Confederate*. New York: C. Scribner's Sons, 1907.
———. (As Porter Alexander.) "Letter from General E. P. Alexander, Late Chief of Artillery, First Corps." *Southern Historical Society Papers*. Vol. 4, no 3. Richmond, VA: Southern Historical Society, September 1877.
Allan, William. "Reminiscences of Field Ordnance Service." *Southern Historical Society Papers*. Vol. 14. Richmond, VA: Southern Historical Society, 1886. 137.
Allen, George H. *Forty-Six Months with the Fourth R.I. Volunteers, in the War of 1861 to 1865. Comprising a History of Its Marches, Battles, and Camp Life*. Providence, RI: J. A. & R. A. Reid, 1887.

Allen, LaVonne Patterson, and Camilla Lewis Tramuel. *Military Records of United States Colored Troops Born in New Kent County, Virginia.* Lanexa, VA: LaVonne Patterson Allen & Camilla Lewis Tramuel, 2011.
———. *Military Records of United States Colored Troops Born in West Point & King William County, Virginia.* Lanexa, VA: LaVonne Patterson Allen & Camilla Lewis Tramuel, n.d.
Andrew, William G. *The Life of a Union Army Sharpshooter Annual report of the Adjutant-General of the Commonwealth of Massachusetts.* Boston: William White, printer to the State, 1863.
Annual Reunion. United States Military Academy at West Point, New York, June 12th, 1911. Saginaw, MI: Seeman and Peters. Association of Graduates.
A. P. M. "The Capture of the Maple Leaf." *The Southern* 9 (July–December 1871).
Avary, Myrta Lockett. *Recollections of Alexander H. Stephens: His Diary Kept When a Prisoner at Fort Warren, Boston Harbour, 1865.* New York: Doubleday, 1910.
Bagby, Alfred. *King and Queen County, Virginia.* New York: Neale Publishing, 1908.
Bates, Samuel P. *History of the Pennsylvania Volunteers, 1861–65.* Harrisburg, PA: 1868–1871.
Beale, George William. *A Lieutenant of Cavalry in Lee's Army.* Boston: Gorham Press, 1918.
Bigelow, John. *Letters and Literary Memorials of Samuel J. Tilden.* 2 vols. New York: Harper, 1908.
Bingham, Robert. "We Saved General Lee's Communications with Richmond." *Civil War Times Illustrated* 5, no. 8 (September 1966): 22–25.
Blakesee, Bernard F. *History of the Sixteenth Connecticut Volunteers.* Hartford, CT: Case, Lockwood, and Brainard, 1875.
Bowen, J. R. *Regimental History of the First New York Dragoons (originally the 130th N.Y. Vol. Infantry) During Three Years of Active Service in the Great Civil War.* N.p.; J. R. Bowen, 1900.
Burgwyn, William H.S. *A Captain's War: The Letters and Diaries of William H. S. Burgwyn, 1861–1865.* Shippensburg, PA: White Mane Publishing, 1993.
Burnett, Edmund Cody. "Letters of a Confederate Surgeon: Dr. Abner Embry McGarity, 1862–1865, Part 2." *Georgia Historical Quarterly* 29, no. 3 (September 1945): 159–190.
Chase, Salmon P. *The Salmon P. Chase Papers: Correspondence, April 1863–1864.* Vol. 4. Kent, OH: Kent State University Press, 1997.
Clark, Walter, ed. *Histories of the Several Regiments and Battalions from North Carolina in the Great War 1861–'65.* 5 vols. Goldsboro, NC: Nash Brothers, 1901.
Croffut, W. A., and Morris, J. M. *Military and Civil History of Connecticut during the War of 1861–65.* New York: Ledyard Bill, 1868.
Crow, Terrell Armistead, and Mary Moulton Barden, eds. *Live Your Own Life: The Family Papers of Mary Bayard Clarke, 1854–1886.* Columbia: University of South Carolina Press, 2003.
Cruikshank, George L. *Back in the Sixties: Reminiscences of the Service of Company A, 11th Pennsylvania Regiment.* Fort Dodge, IA: Times Job Printing House, 1893.
Cunningham, John L. *Three Years with the Adirondack Regiment: 118th New York Volunteers Infantry.* Norwood, MA: Plimpton Press, 1920.

Davis, Jefferson. *The Papers of Jefferson Davis: October 1863–August 1864.* Baton Rouge: Louisiana State University Press, 1999.

DeLeon, T. C. *Four Years in Rebel Capitals: An Inside View of Life in the Southern Confederacy, From Birth To Death.* Mobile, AL: Gossip Print Co., 1890.

Devine, W. A. "Defense of the South Anna Bridge." *Confederate Veteran* 40. (May 1932): 178–182.

Dix, John A. *Memoirs of John Adams Dix.* 2 vols. New York: Harper and Brothers, 1883.

Fields, Joseph E., ed. *"Worthy Partner": The Papers of Martha Washington.* Westport, CT: Greenwood Press, 1994.

Fontaine, William Winston. "Account of William Winston Fontaine." *William and Mary College Quarterly* 19 (July 1910): 179–184.

Fox, Gustavus Vasa. *Confidential Correspondence of Gustavus Vasa Fox: Assistant Secretary of the Navy, 1861–1865.* 2 vols. New York: Naval History Society, 1918–1919.

Fremantle, Arthur James. *Three Months in the Southern States: April, June, 1863.* Mobile, AL: S. H. Goetzel, 1864.

Gallagher, Gary, ed. *Fighting for the Confederacy, The Personal Recollections of General Edward Alexander.* Chapel Hill: University of North Carolina Press, 1987.

Garfield, James Garfield. *The Wild Life of the Army: Civil War Letters of James A. Garfield.* Ed. Frederick D. Williams. East Lansing: Michigan State University Press, 1964.

Gorgas, Josiah. *The Journals of Josiah Gorgas, 1857–1878.* Tuscaloosa: University of Alabama Press, 1995.

Gordon, George H. *A War Diary of Events in the War of the Great Rebellion, 1863–1865.* Boston: James R. Osgood, 1882.

Haas, Shirley A., and Dale Paige Talley. *A Refugee at Hanover Tavern: The Civil War Diary of Margaret Wight.* Charleston, SC: History Press, 2013.

Harrill, Lawson. *Reminiscences, 1861–1865: General M. W. Ransom's Brigade.* Statesville, NC: Brady, 1910.

Hattaway, Herman, and Archer Jones. *How the North Won: A Military History of the Civil War.* Champaign: University of Illinois Press, 1991.

Haupt, Herman. *Reminiscences of General Herman Haupt.* Milwaukee: Wright and Joys, 1901.

Hayes, Rutherford. *Diary and Letters of Rutherford B. Hayes: Nineteenth President of the United States.* Vol. 2. Ed. Charles Richard William. Columbus: Ohio State Archeological and Historical Society, 1922.

Hewett, Janet B., et al. *Supplement to the Official Records of the Union and Confederate Armies.* 100 vols. Wilmington, NC: Broadfoot, 1994–1997.

History of Battle-flag Day, September 17, 1879. Hartford, CT: Lockwood & Merritt, 1880.

Hyde, William Lyman. *History of the One Hundred and Twelfth Regiment, N.Y. Volunteers.* Fredonia, NY: McKinstry, 1866.

Imboden, John. "The Confederate Retreat from Gettysburg." In Clarence Clough Buell, ed., *Battles and Leaders of the Civil War.* Vol. 3 (of 4 vols.) (New York: The Century Co., 1887–1888), 426.

"Instructions for the Government of Armies of the United States in the Field" (prepared by Francis Lieber), Adjutant General's Office, April 24, 1863. Washington, DC: US Government Printing Office, 1898.

Jacobs, Lisa, Sarah M. Caliandri, and Nancy A. Moran. *Field Music: From Antietam to Andersonville—The Civil War Letters of Lyman B. Wilcox*. Berlin, CT: Berlin Historical Society, 2012. 58.

Joint Committee on the Conduct of the War at the Second Session Thirty-Eighth Congress. Washington, DC: US Government Printing Office, 1865.

Keyes, Erasmus. *Fifty Years' Observations of Men and Events, Civil and Military*. New York: Scribner's, 1884.

Krick, Robert K. *Civil War Weather*. Tuscaloosa: University of Alabama Press, 2016.

Laas, Virginia Jeans. *Wartime Washington: The Civil War Letters of Elizabeth Blair Lee*. Champagne–Urbana: University of Illinois Press, 1991.

Lewis, Richard. *Camp Life of a Confederate Boy, of Bratton's Brigade, Longstreet's Corps, C.S.A.: Letters Written by Lieut. Richard Lewis, of Walker's Regiment, to His Mother, During the War, Facts and Inspirations of Camp Life, Marches, &c*. Charleston, SC: News and Courier, 1883.

Mann, Albert. *History of the Forty-fifth Regiment, Massachusetts Volunteer Militia*. Boston: Spooner, 1908.

Marshall, Charles. *An Aide-de-Camp of Lee: Being the Papers of Colonel Charles Marshall Sometime Aide-de-Camp, Military Secretary, an Assistant*. New York: Little, Brown, 1927.

———. "Events Leading up to the Battle of Gettysburg." *Southern Historical Society Papers*. Vols. 22–24. Richmond, VA: Southern Historical Society, 1894. 226.

McGrath, Franklin, comp. *The History of the 127th New York Volunteers, 1862–65, "Monitors," in the War/or the Preservation of the Union—September 8, 1862, June 30, 1865*. N.p.: n.d.

McGuire, Judith Brockenbrough. *Diary of a Southern Refugee During the War*. Lexington: University Press of Kentucky, 2014.

Member of the 21st Regiment. *The Story of the Twenty-first Regiment, Connecticut Volunteer Infantry, During the Civil War, 1861–1865*. Middleton, CT: Stewart Printing, 1900.

Memorial Addresses on the Life and Character of William H. F. Lee. United States Congress, 52nd Con., 1st Sess., Mis. Doc. No. 320. Washington, DC: US Government Printing Office, 1892.

Moore, Frank, ed. *The Rebellion Record, a Diary of American Events: With Documents, Narratives, Illustrative Incidents, Poetry, Etc*. 7. New York: D. Van Nostrand, 1865.

Mowris, James A. *A History of the One Hundred and Seventeenth Regiment, N. Y. Volunteers*. Hartford, CT: Case, Lockwood, and Co., 1866.

Muselman, Homer D. *The Caroline Light, Parker and Stafford Light Artillery*. Lynchburg, VA: H. E. Howard, 1992.

Newsome, Hampton, et al., eds. *Civil War Talks: Further Reminiscences of George S. Bernard and His Fellow Veterans*. Charlottesville: University Press of Virginia, 2012.

Peace, Alexander. "Fighting at Great Odds." *Confederate Veteran*. Vol. 34 (July 1926): 370.

Peace, Laura P. *To Tranquillity: 1861–1865 Civil War Letters of Six North Carolina Brothers*. CreateSpace Independent Publishing Platform, 2018. 149.

Pollard, Edward A. *The Lost Cause, A New Southern History of the War of the Confederates*. New York: Treat & Company, 1867.

Proceedings of the Massachusetts Historical Society. Vol. 50. Boston: Massachusetts Historical Society, 1917.

Quincy, Samuel Miller. *History of the Second Massachusetts Regiment of Infantry: A Prisoner's Diary*. Boston: George H. Ellis, 1882.

Raburn, James Z. "A Letter for Posterity: Alex Stephens to His Brother Linton, June 3, 1864." Atlanta: The Library, Emory University, 1954.

Reagan, John Henninger. *Memoirs, with Special Reference to Secession and the Civil War*. New York: Neale Publishing, 1906.

A Record of the Commissioned Officers, Non-Commissioned Officers, and Privates, of the Regiments Which Were Organized in the State of New York. 8 vols. Albany, NY: Comstock and Cassidy, 1864.

Report of the Joint Committee on the Conduct of the War at the Second Session. Thirty-eighth Congress. Washington, DC: US Government Printing Office, 1865.

The Reports of the Committees of the Senate of the United States for the Second Session Thirty-eighth Congress, 1864–'65. Washington: US Government Printing Office, 1865.

Roper, John L., et al. *History of the Eleventh Pennsylvania Volunteer Cavalry: Together with a Complete Roster of the Regiment and Regimental Officers*. Philadelphia: Franklin, 1902.

Scarborough, William Kauffman, ed. *Diary of Edmund Ruffin*. 3 vols. Baton Rouge: Louisiana State University Press, 1972.

Shirley, William. "A Raid of the 11th Pa. Cav." *Grand Army Scout & Soldiers Mail*, January 19, 1884.

Stephens, Alexander. *A Constitutional View of the Late War Between the States*. Vol. 2. Philadelphia: National Publishing Company, 1868.

Stevenson, R. Randolph. *The Southern Side; Or, Andersonville Prison*. Baltimore: Turnbull Brothers, 1876.

Stiles, Robert. *Four Years Under Marse Robert*. New York: Neale, 1910.

"Stonewall Jackson's Way." Richmond, VA: J. W. Randolph, 1863.

Strong, George Templeton. *Diary of George Templeton Strong*. New York: Macmillan, 1952.

Thompson, S. Millett. *Thirteenth Regiment of New Hampshire Volunteer Infantry in the War of the Rebellion, 1861–1865: A Diary Covering Three Years and a Day*. Boston: Houghton Mifflin, 1888.

Thorpe, Sheldon R. *The History of the Fifteenth Connecticut Volunteers in the War for the Defense of the Union, 1861–1865*. New Haven, CT: Price, Lee, and Adkins, 1893.

Trimble, Isaac R. "The Battle and Campaign of Gettysburg." *Southern Historical Society Papers*. Vol. 26. Richmond, VA: Southern Historical Society, 1898.

United States Surgeon-Generals Office. *The Medical and Surgical History of the War of the Rebellion*. Vol. 1, pt. 1. Washington, DC: US Government Printing Office, 1870–1888.

US Navy Department. *Official Records of the Union and Confederate Navies in*

the War of the Rebellion. 30 vols. Washington, DC: US Government Printing
 Office, 1894–1922.
US War Department. *Atlas to Accompany the Official Records of the Union
 and Confederate Armies*. Washington, DC: US Government Printing Office,
 1891–1895.
————. *War of the Rebellion: A Compilation of the Official Records of the Union
 and Confederate Armies*. 129 vols. Washington, DC: US Government Printing
 Office, 1881–1901.
*Virginia & Tennessee Railroad Eighteenth Annual Report of the President and
 Directors to the Stockholders of the Virginia & Tennessee Railroad Co*. Lynch-
 burg: Virginia Book and Job Office, 1865.
Von Borcke, Heros. *Memoirs of the Confederate War for Independence*. Vol. 2.
 Philadelphia: Lippincott, 1867.
Welles, Gideon. *Diary of Gideon Welles: Secretary of the Navy Under Lincoln
 and Johnson*. 2 vols. Boston: Houghton Mifflin, 1911.
Wickham, Henry T. *Address Delivered Before the Joint Session of The General
 Assembly of Virginia (Richmond, VA February 23, 1940)*. Senate Document
 No. 10. Richmond VA: Division of Purchase and Printing, 1940.
Williams, Max R. *Papers of William Alexander Graham*. Vol. 5. Raleigh: North
 Carolina Department of Cultural Resources, 1973.
Wingfield, H. W. "Diary of H.W. Wingfield." *Bulletin of the Virginia State Li-
 brary* 16. July 1927.
Winston, Robert. "A Rebel Colonel: His Strange Career." *South Atlantic Quar-
 terly* 30 (1931). 84.
Younger, Edward, ed. *Inside the Confederate Government, The Diary of Robert
 Hill Garlick Kean*. New York: Oxford University Press, 1957.

SECONDARY SOURCES: BOOKS, ARTICLES, AND THESES

Allen, Jody Lynn. "Roses in December: Black life in Hanover County, Virginia
 during the Era of Disfranchisement." Dissertations, Theses, and Masters Proj-
 ects. College of William and Mary, 2007.
Ambrose, Stephen A. *Halleck: Lincoln's Chief of Staff*. Baton Rouge: Louisiana
 State University Press, 1962.
Appletons' Cyclopaedia of American Biography. Vol. 3. New York: Appleton,
 1898.
Baldwin, James. *The Struck Eagle: A Biography of Brigadier General Micah Jen-
 kins, and a History of the Fifth South Carolina Volunteers and the Palmetto
 Sharpshooters*. Shippensburg, PA: Burd St. Press, 1996.
Barrett, John. *The Civil War in North Carolina*. Chapel Hill: University of North
 Carolina Press, 1963.
Bauer, K. Jack, and Stephen S. Roberts. *Register of Ships of the U.S. Navy, 1775–
 1990: Major Combatants*. Westport, CT: Greenwood, 1991.
Bennett, John. *No Word of Them: First Battalion New York Sharpshooters,
 1862–1865*. Raleigh, NC: Lulu.com, 2007.
Bill, Alfred. *The Beleaguered City: Richmond, 1861–1865*. New York: Alfred A.
 Knopf, 1946.

Black, Robert. *The Railroads of the Confederacy*. Chapel Hill: University of North Carolina Press, 1998.

Blakeslee, Bernard F. *History of the Sixteenth Connecticut Volunteers*. Hartford, CT: Case, Lockwood & Brainard, 1875.

Brasher, Glenn David. *The Peninsula Campaign and the Necessity of Emancipation: African Americans and the Fight for Freedom*. Chapel Hill: University of North Carolina Press, 2011.

Brown, Kent Masterson. *Retreat from Gettysburg: Lee, Logistics, and the Pennsylvania Campaign*. Chapel Hill: University of North Carolina Press, 2005.

Browning, Judkin. *An Environmental History of the Civil War*. Chapel Hill: University of North Carolina Press, 2020.

———. *Shifting Loyalties: The Union Occupation of Eastern North Carolina*. Chapel Hill: University of North Carolina Press, 2011.

Bridges, Hal. *Lee's Maverick General: Daniel Harvey Hill*. New York,: McGraw Hill, 1961.

Bright, David. "Richmond Grain Receipts and Shipments." N.p., n.d.

Brock, Sallie A. *Richmond During the War: Four Years of Personal Observation*. New York: Carleton & Co., 1867.

Brumgardt, John R. "Alexander Stephens and the Peace Issue in the Confederacy, 1863–1865." PhD diss., University of California, Riverside, 1974.

Burke, James C. *Wilmington & Weldon Railroad in the Civil War*. Jefferson, NC: McFarland, 2012.

Casa, D. J., et al. "Historical Perspectives on Medical Care for Heat Stroke, Part 2: 1850 Through the Present." *Athletic Training & Sports Health Care* 2, no. 4 (2010): 178–190.

Chesson, Michael B. "Harlots or Heroines? A New Look at the Richmond Bread Riot." *Virginia Magazine of History and Biography* 92, no. 2 (April 1984): 131–175.

Cleveland, Henry. *Alexander H. Stephens in Public and Private with Letters and Speeches, Before, During, and Since the War*. Philadelphia: National Publishing Company, 1866.

Coddington, Edwin Coddington. *The Gettysburg Campaign*. Dayton, OH: Morningside Bookshop, 1979.

Collins, Darrell L. *The Jones-Imboden Raid: The Confederate Attempt to Destroy the Baltimore & Ohio Railroad and Retake West Virginia*. Jefferson, NC: McFarland, 2007.

Cormier, Steven A. *The Siege of Suffolk: The Forgotten Campaign April 11–May 4, 1863*. 2nd ed. Lynchburg, VA: H. E. Howard, 1989.

Cornish, Dudley Taylor, and Virginia Jeans Laas. *Lincoln's Lee: The Life of Samuel Phillips Lee, United States Navy, 1812–1897*. Lawrence: University Press of Kansas, 1986.

Dailey, Jane. *Before Jim Crow: The Politics of Race in Postemancipation Virginia*. Chapel Hill: University of North Carolina Press, 2000.

Daughtry, Mary Bandry. *Gray Cavalier: The Life and Wars of General W. H. F. "Rooney" Lee*. Cambridge, MA: Da Capo Press, 2002.

Dew, Charles B. *Apostles of Disunion: Southern Secession Commissioners and the Causes of the Civil War*. Charlottesville: University Press of Virginia, 2002.

Dowdey, Clifford. *Death of a Nation*. New York: Alfred A. Knopf, 1958.
Dowdey, Clifford, and Louis H. Manarin, eds. *The Wartime Papers of R. E. Lee*. Boston: Little, Brown, 1961.
Driver, Robert J. *Richmond Local Defense Troops, C.S.A.* Wilmington, NC: Broadfoot Publishing, 2011.
Dyer, Frederick. *A Compendium of the War of the Rebellion*. Vol. 2. Dayton, OH: Morningside, 1979.
Erslev, Brit. *Taming the Tar Heel Department: D. H. Hill and the Challenges of Operational Level Command*. Fort Leavenworth, KS: US Army Command and General Staff College, 2011.
Freeman, Douglas Southall, ed. *Lee's Dispatches: Unpublished Letters of General Robert E. Lee*. New York: G. P. Putnam & Sons, 1957.
———. *Lee's Lieutenants*. 3 vols. New York: Charles Scribner's Sons, 1945.
———. *R. E. Lee: A Biography*. 4 vols. New York: Charles Scribner's Sons, 1934.
Fremantle, Arthur. *Three Months in the Southern States: April, June, 1863*. Mobile, AL: S. H. Goetzel, 1864.
French, Samuel Livingston. *The Army of the Potomac from 1861 to 1863: An Inside View of the History of the Army of the Potomac and Its Leaders as Told in the Official Dispatches, Reports and Secret Correspondence*. New York: Publishing Society of New York, 1906.
Frye, Dennis. *12th Virginia Cavalry*. Lynchburg, VA: H. E. Howard, 1988.
Furgurson, Ernest B. *Ashes of Glory: Richmond at War*. New York: Knopf, 1997.
Futrell, Robert Frank Futrell. "Federal Trade with the Confederate States, 1861–1865: A Study of Governmental Policy." PhD diss., Vanderbilt University, 1950.
Gaines, W. Craig. *Encyclopedia of Civil War Shipwrecks*. Baton Rouge: Louisiana State University Press, 2008.
Getty, Mildred Newbold. *George Washington Getty*. N.p.: 1961.
Glasgow, William M. *Northern Virginia's Own: The 17th Virginia Regiment, Confederate States Army*. Alexandria, VA: Gobill Press, 1989.
Goff, Richard D. *Confederate Supply*. Durham, NC: Duke University Press, 1969.
Goldman, Ralph. "Introduction to Heat-Related Problems in Military Operations." *Medical Aspects of Harsh Environments*. Vol. 1. Office of the Surgeon General, US Army. 1st ed. (May 15, 2002).
Gordon, Lesley. *A Broken Regiment: The 16th Connecticut's Civil War*. Baton Rouge: Louisiana State University Press, 2014.
———. *General George E. Pickett in Life and Legend*. Chapel Hill: University of North Carolina Press, 2001.
Grimsley, Mark. *The Hard Hand of War: Union Military Policy Toward Southern Civilians, 1861–1865*. Cambridge: Cambridge University Press, 1995.
Guelzo, Allen C. *Gettysburg: The Last Invasion*. New York: Knopf, 2013.
Halleck, Henry. *Elements of Military Art and Science, Or, Course of Instruction in Strategy, Fortification, Tactics of Battles, &c*. New York: D. Appleton, 1860.
Hanover County Historical Society. *Old Homes of Hanover County, Virginia*. Salem, WV: Walsworth Publishing, 1983.
Harrington, Fred Harvey. "A Peace Mission of 1863." *American Historical Review*. Vol. 46, no. 1 (October 1940): 76–86.

Harris, Malcom Hart. *Old New Kent County [Virginia]: Some Account of the Planters, Plantations, and Places.* Vol. 1. Baltimore: Genealogical Publishing 2006 [reprint].

Hartley, Chris. *Stuart's Tarheels: James B. Gordon and His North Carolina Cavalry in the Civil War.* Jefferson, NC: McFarland, 2011.

Hartwig, D. Scott. "The Army of Northern Virginia and the Gettysburg Campaign." In *Gettysburg: The End of the Campaign and Battle's Aftermath* Gettysburg, PA: National Park Service, 2012.

Hasegawa, Guy R. *Villainous Compounds: Chemical Weapons and the American Civil War.* Carbondale: Southern Illinois University Press, 2015.

Hattaway, Herman, and Archer Jones. *How the North Won: A Military History of the Civil War.* Champaign: University of Illinois Press, 1991.

Hattaway, Herman, and Ethan Sepp Rafuse. *The Ongoing Civil War: New Versions of Old Stories.* Columbia: University of Missouri Press, 2004.

Hattaway, Herman, and Richard E. Beringer. *Jefferson Davis, Confederate President.* Lawrence: University Press of Kansas, 2002.

Headley, J. T. *The Great Rebellion: A History of the Civil War in the United States.* Vol. 2. Chicago: American Publishing, 1866.

Hess, Earl. *Civil War Logistics: A Study of Military Transportation.* Baton Rouge: Louisiana State University Press, 2017.

———. *Civil War Supply and Strategy: Feeding Men and Moving Armies.* Baton Rouge: Louisiana State University Press, 2017.

———. *Field Armies and Fortifications in the Civil War: The Eastern Campaigns, 1863–1864.* Chapel Hill: University of North Carolina Press, 2005.

———. *Lee's Tar Heels: The Pettigrew-Kirkland-MacRae Brigade.* Chapel Hill: University of North Carolina Press, 2002.

"Hickory Hill." National Register of Historic Places. Inventory-Nomination Form, September 17, 1974.

"Hickory Hill Slave and African American Cemetery." DHR No. 042-5792. National Register of Historic Places Registration Form.

Hunt, Jeffrey. *Meade and Lee After Gettysburg: The Forgotten Final Stage of the Gettysburg Campaign from Falling Waters to Culpeper Court House, July 14–31, 1863.* El Dorado Hills, CA: Savas Beattie, 2017.

Hutto, Richard Jay. *A Poisoned Life: Florence Chandler Maybrick, the First American Woman Sentenced to Death in England.* Jefferson, NC: McFarland, 2018.

Johnson, John M. *Lead, Salt, and the Railroad: Toland's Raid on Wytheville, July 18, 1863.* Wytheville, VA: Wythe County Historical Society, 2003.

Johnson, Ludwell H. "Blockade or Trade Monopoly? John A. Dix and the Union Occupation of Norfolk." *Virginia Magazine of History and Biography* 93, no. 1 (January 1985): 54–78.

Johnson, Rossiter, and John Howard Brown, eds. *Twentieth Century Biographical Dictionary of Notable Americans.* Boston: Biographical Society, 1904.

Johnston, Angus J. II. "Disloyalty on Confederate Railroads in Virginia." *Virginia Magazine of History and Biography* 63, no. 4 (October 1955): 410–426.

———. *Virginia Railroads in the Civil War.* Chapel Hill: University of North Carolina Press, 1961.

Jones, John B. *A Rebel War Clerk's Diary at the Confederate States Capital.* 2 vols. Philadelphia: J. B. Lippincott, 1866.

Jordan, Weymouth T. *North Carolina Troops: 1861–1865.* Vol. 10. Raleigh: North Carolina Office of Archives and History, 1985.

Kegel, James A. *North with Lee and Jackson: The Lost Story of Gettysburg.* Mechanicsburg, PA: Stackpole Books, 1996.

Klement, Frank L. *The Limits of Dissent: Clement L. Vallandigham and the Civil War.* Lexington: University Press of Kentucky, 1970.

Kurtz, William. "An American Condottiere: The Civil War Career of General Charles Carroll Tevis." http://www.wkurtz.com/blog/an-american-condottiere -the-antebellum-career-of-general-charles-carroll-tevis-part-1.

Lee, Edmund Jennings. *Lee of Virginia, 1642–1892: Biographical and Genea-logical Sketches of the Descendants of Colonel Richard Lee.* Philadelphia: Franklin Printing, 1895.

Lee, Robert E. *Recollections and Letters of General Robert E. Lee.* New York: Doubleday, 1904.

LeGear, Clara. "The Hotchkiss Collection of Confederate Maps." *Library of Congress Quarterly Journal of Current Acquisitions* 6 (November 1948): 16–20.

Levine, Bruce. *Confederate Emancipation: Southern Plans to Free and Arm Slaves During the Civil War.* Oxford: Oxford University Press, 2006.

Lichterman, Martin. *John Adams Dix, 1798–1879.* PhD diss., Columbia University, 1952.

Lippincott, George E. "Lee-Sawyer Exchange." *Civil War Times Illustrated* 1, no. 3 (June 1962): 39–41.

Longacre, Edward G. "Inspired Blundering: Union Operations Against Richmond During the Gettysburg Campaign." *Civil War History* 32 (March 1986): 23–43.

———. (As Edward Longacre.) *Mounted Raids of the Civil War.* Lincoln: University of Nebraska Press, 1994.

Lowe, Richard. *Republicans and Reconstruction in Virginia, 1856–1870.* Charlottesville: University Press of Virginia, 1991.

Manning, Chandra. *Troubled Refuge: Struggling for Freedom in the Civil War.* New York: Alfred A. Knopf, 2016.

Marlow, Clayton Charles. *Matt W. Ransom: Confederate General from North Carolina.* Jefferson, NC: McFarland, 1996.

Marszalek, John F. *Commander of All Lincoln's Armies: A Life of General Henry W. Halleck.* Cambridge, MA: Belknap, 2004.

Marvel, William. *Burnside.* Chapel Hill: University of North Carolina Press, 1991.

———. *Lincoln's Autocrat: The Life of Edwin Stanton.* Chapel Hill: University of North Carolina Press, 2015.

Michel, Gregg L. "From Slavery to Freedom: Hickory Hill, 1850–1880." In Edward L. Ayers and John C. Willis, eds. *The Edge of the South: Life in Nineteenth-Century Virginia.* Charlottesville: University Press of Virginia, 1991.

Mordecai, John B. *A Brief History of the Richmond, Fredericksburg and Potomac Railroad.* Richmond, VA: Old Dominion Press, 1941.

Munson, E. B. *North Carolina Civil War Obituaries, Regiments 1 through 46: A Collection of Tributes to the War Dead and Veterans.* Jefferson, NC: McFarland, 2015.

National Park Service, US Department of Interior. National Historic Register Nomination Form. "Hickory Hill." September 1974.

———. National Historic Register Nomination Form. "Hickory Hill Slave and African American Cemetery." DHR No. 042-5792. 2020.

———. National Historic Register Nomination Form. "Horn Quarter." March 18, 1980.

Neely, Mark E. Jr. *The Civil War and the Limits of Destruction.* Cambridge, MA: Harvard University Press, 2007.

Nevins, Allan. *The War for Union: The Organized War, 1863–1864.* New York: Scribner, 1971.

Newsome, Hampton. *The Fight for the Old North State: The Civil War in North Carolina, January–May 1864.* Lawrence: University Press of Kansas, 2019.

Noe, Kenneth W. *The Howling Storm: Weather, Climate, and the American Civil War.* Baton Rouge: Louisiana State University Press, 2020.

———. *Southwest Virginia's Railroads: Modernization and the Sectional Crisis.* Chicago: University of Illinois Press, 1994.

Norris, David A. *Potter's Raid: The Union Cavalry's Boldest Expedition in Eastern North Carolina.* Wilmington, NC: Dram Tree Books, 2008.

Nowland, Nicholas. *A Unique Hell in Southwestern Virginia: Confederate Guerrillas and the Defense of the Virginia & Tennessee Railroad.* Master's thesis, Virginia Polytechnic Institute, 2016.

Nye, Wilbur S. *Here Come the Rebels.* Baton Rouge: Louisiana State University Press, 1965.

Parson, Thomas E. *Bear Flag and Bear State in the Civil War.* Jefferson, NC: McFarland, 2007.

Pearce, T. H. "Defenders of the South Anna Bridge." *The State* 51, no. B (January 1984): 76–78.

Phisterer, Frederick. *New York in the War of the Rebellion.* 3rd ed. Albany, NY: J. B. Lyon Company, 1912.

Pierce, Donald. *The Effects of the Cessation of Exchange of Prisoners During the Civil War.* West Point, NY: United States Military Academy, 1980.

Pollard, Henry Robinson. *Memoirs and Sketches of the Life of Henry Robinson Pollard: An Autobiography.* Richmond, VA: Lewis Printing Company, 1923.

Pryor, Elizabeth Brown. "Conflict, Chaos, and Confidence Abraham Lincoln's Struggle as Commander in Chief." *Virginia Magazine of History and Biography* 129, no. 1 (2021): 2–79.

———. *Reading the Man: A Portrait of Robert E. Lee Through His Private Letters.* New York: Viking, 2007.

Rafuse, Ethan. *McClellan's War: The Failure of Moderation in the Struggle for the Union.* Bloomington: Indiana University Press, 2005.

————. *Robert E. Lee and the Fall of the Confederacy, 1863–1865*. Lanham, MD: Rowman & Littlefield, 2009.

Reardon, Carol. *With a Sword in One Hand & Jomini in the Other*. Chapel Hill: University of North Carolina Press, 2012.

Reid, Richard M. *Freedom for Themselves: North Carolina's Black Soldiers in the Civil War Era*. Chapel Hill: University of North Carolina Press, 2008.

Reidy, Joseph R. *Illusions of Emancipation: The Pursuit of Freedom and Equality in the Twilight of Slavery*. Chapel Hill: University of North Carolina Press, 2019.

Richardson, Charles B. *Southern Generals: Who They Are, and What They Have Done*. London: Sampson, 1865.

Roback, Henry. *The Veteran Volunteers of Herkimer and Otsego Counties in the War of the Rebellion*. Utica, NY: L. C. Childs, 1888.

Roulhac, Thomas R. "The Forty-Ninth N.C. Infantry, C.S.A." *Southern Historical Society Papers*. Vol. 13. Richmond, VA: Southern Historical Society, 1895. 53.

Sauers, Richard. *The Burnside Expedition in North Carolina: A Succession of Honorable Victories*. Dayton, OH: Morningside Press, 1996.

Schott, Thomas E. *Alexander H. Stephens of Georgia: A Biography*. Baton Rouge: Louisiana State University Press, 1996.

Scott, Kim Allen. *Yellowstone Denied: The Life of Gustavus Cheyney Doane*. Norman: University of Oklahoma Press, 2005.

Sears, Stephen. *Chancellorsville*. Boston: Houghton Mifflin, 1996.

————. *Gettysburg*. Boston: Houghton Mifflin, 2003.

————. *Lincoln's Lieutenants: The High Command of the Army of the Potomac*. Boston: Houghton Mifflin, 2017.

Shaffer, Duane. *Men of Granite: New Hampshire's Soldiers in the Civil War*. Columbia: University of South Carolina Press, 2008.

Sheehan-Dean, Aaron. *The Calculus of Violence: How Americans Fought the Civil War*. Cambridge, MA: Harvard University Press, 2018.

Shutes, Milton. "Henry Wager Halleck: Lincoln's Chief-of-Staff." *California Historical Society Quarterly* 16, no. 3 (September 1937): 195–208.

Simpson, Brooks. *The Civil War in the East: Struggle, Stalemate, and Victory*. Santa Barbara, CA: Praeger, 2011.

Speer, Lonnie B. *War of Vengeance: Acts of Retaliation Against Civil War POWs*. Mechanicsville, PA: Stackpole Books, 2002.

Steplyk, Jonathan. *Fighting Means Killing: Civil War Soldiers and the Nature of Combat*. Lawrence: University Press of Kansas, 2018.

Stoker, Donald. *Stoker: The Grand Design*. Oxford: Oxford University Press, 2010.

Stovall, Pleasant A. *Robert Toombs: Statesman, Speaker, Soldier, Sage*. New York: Cassel Publishing, 1892.

Stuart, Meriwether. "Samuel Ruth and General R. E. Lee: Disloyalty and the Line of Supply to Fredericksburg, 1862–1863." *Virginia Magazine of History and Biography* 71, no. 1 (January 1963): 35–109.

Survey of Historic Resources, Hanover County Virginia, 1990. Prepared for Hanover County Planning Department by Land and Community Associates. Charlottesville, VA, 1983.

Sutherland, Daniel L. "Altamont of the Tribune: John Williamson Palmer in the Civil War." *Maryland Historical Magazine* 78 (Spring 1983): 54–66.

Symonds, Craig. *American Heritage History of the Battle of Gettysburg.* New York: Harper Collins, 2001.

Takagi, Midori. *"Rearing Wolves to Our Own Destruction": Slavery in Richmond, Virginia, 1782–1865.* Charlottesville: University Press of Virginia, 1999.

Taylor, Amy Murrell. *Embattled Freedom: Journeys Through the Civil War's Slave Refugee Camps.* Chapel Hill: University of North Carolina Press, 2018.

Thomas, Emory M. *The Confederate State of Richmond: Biography of the Capital.* Austin: University of Texas Press, 1971.

Thomas, John Peyre. *Career and Character of General Micah Jenkins.* Columbia, SC: The State Company, 1903.

Titus, Katherine R. "The Richmond Bread Riot of 1863: Class, Race, and Gender in the Urban Confederacy." *Gettysburg College Journal of the Civil War Era* 2, article 6 (2011): 86–146.

Tomblin, Barbara Brooks. *Bluejackets and Contrabands: African Americans and the Union Navy.* Lexington: University Press of Kentucky, 2009.

Trudeau, Noah Andre. "The 'Blackberry Raid.'" *Gettysburg Magazine*, no. 11 (July 1994): 7–18.

———. *Gettysburg: A Testing of Courage.* New York: HarperCollins, 2002.

Tucker, Glenn. *High Tide at Gettysburg.* Dayton, OH: Morningside Bookshop, 1973.

Turner, Charles W. "The Virginia Central Railroad at War, 1861–1865." *Journal of Southern History* 12, no. 4 (November 1946): 510–533.

Varon, Elizabeth. *Southern Lady, Yankee Spy: The True Story of Elizabeth Van Lew, a Union Agent in the Heart of the Confederacy.* Oxford: Oxford University Press, 2005.

Virginia Division of Mineral Resources. *Bulletin, Issue 4.* By the Virginia Division of Mineral Resources, Charlottesville: University of Virginia, 1912.

Voegeli, V. Jacque. "A Rejected Alternative: Union Policy and the Relocation of Southern 'Contrabands' at the Dawn of Emancipation." *Journal of Southern History* 69, no. 4 (November 2003): 765–790.

Waddell, Joseph. *Annals of Augusta County, Virginia, from 1726 to 1871.* Staunton, VA: Russel Caldwell, 1902.

Wallace, Frederic. *Framingham's Civil War Hero: The Life of General George H. Gordon.* Charleston, SC: History Press, 2011.

Warner, Ezra J. *Generals in Blue: Lives of the Union Commanders.* Baton Rouge: Louisiana State University Press, 1964.

Weathers, Willie T. "Judith W. McGuire: A Lady of Virginia." *Virginia Magazine of History and Biography* 82, no. 1 (January 1974): 100–113.

Wilson, Harold. *Confederate Industry: Manufacturers and Quartermasters in the Civil War.* Jackson: University Press of Mississippi, 2002.

Wise, George. *Campaigns and Battles of the Army of Northern Virginia.* New York: Neale Publishing, 1916.

Wise, Jennings Cropper. *The Long Arm of Lee: The History of the Artillery of the Army of Northern Virginia.* Lynchburg, VA: J. P. Bell, 1915.

Witt, Jeffrey. *Escape from the Maple Leaf, Including a Roster of Confederate Officers on the Maple Leaf and a Discussion of the System.* Berwyn Heights, MD: Heritage Books, 1993.

Woodward, C. Vann, ed. *Mary Chesnut's Civil War.* New Haven, CT: Yale University Press, 1981.

Work, David. *Lincoln's Political Generals.* Urbana: University of Illinois Press, 2009.

Wyllie, Arthur. *Confederate States Navy.* N.p., 2007.

Wynalda, Stephen A. *366 Days in Abraham Lincoln's Presidency: The Private, Political, and Military Decisions of America's Greatest President.* New York: Skyhorse, 2014.

Wynstra, Robert. *At the Forefront of Lee's Invasion: Retribution, Plunder, and Clashing Cultures on Richard S. Ewell's Road to Gettysburg.* Kent, OH: Kent State University Press, 2018.

Yang, Hongshun, et al. "Effects of Blackberry Juice on Growth Inhibition of Foodborne Pathogens and Growth Promotion of Lactobacillus." *Food Control* 37, no. 1 (March 2014): 15–20.

Younger, Edward, ed. *Inside the Confederate Government: The Diary of Robert Hill Garlick Kean.* New York: Oxford University Press, 1957.

Zia-Ul-Haq, Muhammad, et al. "Rubus Fruticosus L.: Constituents, Biological Activities and Health Related Uses." *Molecules* 19, no. 8 (August 2014): 10998–11029.

INDEX